WORK MOTIVATION

Theory, Issues, and Applications

THE SCOTT, FORESMAN SERIES IN ORGANIZATIONAL BEHAVIOR AND HUMAN RESOURCES

Lyman W. Porter, Editor

Published:

Baskin/Aronoff	*Interpersonal Communication in Organizations*
Carroll/Schneier	*Performance Appraisal and Review Systems*
Griffin	*Task Design: An Integrative Approach*
Pinder	*Work Motivation: Theory, Issues, and Applications*
Schneider	*Staffing Organizations*
Stone	*Research Methods in Organizational Behavior*
Taylor	*Behavioral Decision Making*
Wexley/Latham	*Developing and Training Human Resources in Organizations*

WORK MOTIVATION
Theory, Issues, and Applications

Craig C. Pinder
University of British Columbia

Scott, Foresman and Company
Glenview, Illinois London

Acknowledgments

From WORK AND MOTIVATION by Victor H. Vroom. Copyright © 1964 by John Wiley & Sons, Inc. Reprinted by permission.

From INTRINSIC AND EXTRINSIC MOTIVATION by Barry M. Staw. Copyright © 1976 by Silver Burdett Company. Reprinted by permission.

From "Some Boundary Conditions in the Application of Motivation Models" by Bronston T. Mayes in ACADEMY OF MANAGEMENT REVIEW, January 1978. Reprinted by permission of the Academy of Management and the author.

From MANAGERIAL ATTITUDES AND PERFORMANCE by Lyman W. Porter and Edward E. Lawler. Copyright © 1968 by Richard D. Irwin, Inc. Reprinted by permission.

"Women Lazy, Expect Sympathy" from the VANCOUVER PROVINCE, March 4, 1982. Reprinted by permission of The Canadian Press.

From "Motivation through the design of Work: Test of a Theory" by J. Richard Hackman and Greg R. Oldham in ORGANIZATIONAL BEHAVIOR AND HUMAN PERFORMANCE, Vol. 16, no. 2, 1976. Reprinted by permission of Academic Press, Inc. and J. Richard Hackman.

"Tendency to Achieve Success" formula from AN INTRODUCTION TO MOTIVATION by John W. Atkinson. Reprinted by permission of the author.

Library of Congress Cataloging in Publication Data

Pinder, Craig C.
  Work motivation.

  Bibliography: p.
  Includes indexes.
    1. Psychology, Industrial.   2. Work—Psychological
aspects.   3. Employee motivation.   I. Title.
HF5548.8.P48   1984   158.7   84-1452
ISBN 0-673-15799-7

6789—EBI—94 93 92 91 90

This book is dedicated with love to my parents—
Charles and Gertrude Pinder: two people for whom
the motivation to work has never been a problem.

CONTENTS

FOREWORD

The Scott, Foresman Series in Organizational Behavior and Human Resources embodies concise and lively treatments of specific topics within the broad area indicated by the Series title. These books are for supplemental reading in basic management, organizational behavior, or personnel courses in which the instructor highlights particular topics in the larger course. However, the books, either alone or in combination, can also form the nucleus for specialized courses that follow introductory courses.

Each book stresses the *key issues* relevant to the given topic. Thus, each author, or set of authors, has made a particular effort to "highlight figure from ground"—that is, to keep the major issues in the foreground and the small explanatory details in the background. These books are, by design, relatively brief treatments of their topic areas, so the authors have had to be carefully *selective* in what they have chosen to retain and to omit. Because the authors were chosen for their expertise and their judgment, the Series provides valuable summary treatments of the subject areas.

In focusing on the major issues, the Series' authors present a balanced content coverage. They have also aimed at breadth by the unified presentation of different types of material: major conceptual or theoretical approaches, interesting and critical empirical findings, and applications to "real life" management and organizational problems. Each author deals with this body of material, but the combination varies according to the subject matter. Thus, each book is distinctive in the particular way in which a topic is addressed.

A final word is in order about the audience for this Series. Although the primary audience is the student, each book in the series concerns a topic of importance to the practicing manager. Managers and supervisors can rely on these books as authoritative summaries of the basic knowledge in each area covered by the Series.

The topics included in the Series to date have been chosen on the basis of their importance and relevance for those interested in management and organizations. As new appropriate topics emerge on the scene, additional books will be added. This is a dynamic Series both in content and direction.

Lyman W. Porter
Series Editor

PREFACE

The mediocre performance of the world's major economies in recent years has heightened the concern of politicians, managers, academics, and social critics over the issue of productivity. Yet control of many of the most potent determinants of productivity (such as capital investment and technological innovation, for example) is beyond the grasp of most managers and administrators. Nevertheless, managers of human resources *do* have some influence over two key factors in the productivity of the workforce: the level of work-related ability and the motivation of the people who work for them.

Accordingly, this book is about the origins, nature, and consequences of one of these human factors—the motivation to work. The most popular theoretic approaches to work motivation and behavior are presented, along with assessments of the quantity and quality of the research evidence attesting to their scientific validity and applied value. A number of the most important controversies associated with the various theories are also presented and discussed.

In addition to the text, seven case examples are provided, with exercises that ask students to apply what they've learned.

In certain respects, this book is intended to be more balanced and scientifically conservative than most other treatments of the topic. For example, the book is not intended to be a manual outlining ways to "motivate" employees, although both the informal applied implications of each theoretic perspective and/or whatever formal managerial techniques that derive from them are examined. Moreover, no attempt is made to reconcile all other approaches with the terms and concepts of any single approach. Finally, no particular theory is advocated above the others, although, at times, it is argued that certain theories and techniques do seem to enjoy superior empirical support or more apparent applied utility.

Work Motivation was written primarily with senior undergraduate and/or graduate students in management, organizational behavior, and organizational psychology courses in mind. It should also be of value in more specialized college and university courses concerned with employee motivation and organizational reward systems. Institutional policy makers and practicing managers who desire a realistic understanding of the role of human motivation and behavior in productivity will also benefit from this book.

I could not have written this book without the financial, intellectual, clerical, and emotional support provided by a number of institutions, friends, colleagues, and mentors. The Social Sciences and Humanities Research Council of Canada and the University of British Columbia sponsored the sabbatical leave that gave me the time to work on the project. Accordingly, I am grateful to SSHRCC and to Dean Peter Lusztig of the Faculty of Commerce at U.B.C., as well as to Lyman Porter, whose scholarship attracted me to the University of California at Irvine for the first half of the sabbatical, and whose support—both as Dean of the Graduate School of Management and as my editor— was invaluable.

In addition, I am grateful to Christopher R. P. Fraser (of U.B.C.), Gary P. Latham (the University of Washington), David C. McPhillips, Vance F. Mitchell, and Larry F. Moore (of U.B.C.), Steven C. Ross (Marquette University), William E. Scott (Indiana University), and William T. Stanbury (of U.B.C.) for their helpful comments and guidance on various chapters and segments of the book. My U.B.C. colleague Gordon A. ("Skip") Walter helped a variety of ways: in addition to benefitting from his comments on a number of chapters after I drafted them, I also made extensive use of one of the main conceptual frameworks presented in *Experiential Learning and Change,* his own recent book (coauthored with Stephen E. Marks). Further, the support Skip provided me during his term as Chairman of the Industrial Relations Management Division at U.B.C. made writing the book a continuous and undisturbed project. Similarly, the cheerful and competent assistance of the staff of the Word Processing Centre at the Faculty of Commerce at U.B.C. (under the supervision of Nancy Schell and Lori Thomas) helped make the writing easier than it otherwise would have been.

I also acknowledge the intellectual debt I owe to my three mentors: George T. Milkovich, Karl E. Weick, and Lawrence K. Williams. Although these men might not entirely agree with either the content or the tone of the book, I thank them for the roles they have played in my career.

Finally, I thank my wife Pat for the constant love that has kindled and reinforced my own work motivation for so many years.

Craig Pinder

WORK MOTIVATION
Theory, Issues, and Applications

MOTIVATION, PRODUCTIVITY AND THE ECONOMY 1

The principal object of management should be to secure the maximum prosperity for the employer, coupled with the maximum prosperity for each employé.

—*F. W. Taylor*

One Saturday in mid January 1978, sixty-two employees of a northern British Columbia sawmill worked a voluntary six-hour shift, producing almost fifty-seven thousand board feet of lumber, worth an estimated value of $2,333. The reason? They were unable to think of anything else to give the mill's owner as a belated Christmas present.

Productivity. There are countless ways to define it and measure it (cf. Norman & Bahari, 1972), but in its simplest terms, it is the value of the economic output achieved in an industry or economy per unit of human labor and fixed capital required to attain it. It is a measure of how much work people accomplish at their jobs, divided by the amount of time they spend doing those jobs—time spent collecting salaries (or wages) and benefits. When the level of economic output per unit of input increases, more people can enjoy more goods and services without causing others to consume less (Rees, 1980). Accordingly, the competitive economic edge and subsequent well-being of countries such as Canada, the United States, Sweden, and Switzerland has, in large measure, been a result of the high comparative levels of productivity in the economies of those countries. High productivity permits high wages, inexpensive goods and services, abundant public amenities and social services, and a generally high standard of living for all (Thurow, 1980). High productivity is both a measure of, and a contributing factor to, the quality of life we can en-   **1** joy. We cannot live well without it, nor can the citizens of the communist bloc: Soviet leader Yuri Andropov declared war on "shoddy work, inactivity, and irresponsibility" in his first major address to the Soviet people upon taking power in 1983. Quite clearly, he was fully aware of the importance of productivity in the health of a nation's economy.

Nevertheless, it is often the case that the wages, salaries, and benefits paid to a nation's workforce rise faster than does its productivity. Hence, when we speak of declining productivity, we mean that it is taking comparatively more and more human labor to accomplish the same amount of economic output as before—fewer goods and services for the same investment as in the past. The consequence, in part, is that the benefits an economy can deliver cost everyone more than in the past—a phenomenon referred to as cost-push inflation (Blair, 1975).

Some economists (e.g., Malkiel, 1979) see declining productivity as the most serious threat to the health of the economies of the Western world. And the fact is that increases in productivity levels have been declining in recent years in many of the countries that have traditionally been the most productive, such as the United States and Japan. The productivity problem is found in both industrial and service sectors (cf. *Business Week,* 1981; Rose, 1977), as well as in government (Main, 1981), affecting the quality of life enjoyed by all of us.

Great Britain is a major example of the problem, one that we often hear and read about in the popular press. Wage rates rose 68.3 percent in Britain in the short period between 1968 and 1971, while the level of productivity in that economy, during that same period, increased at a rate of only 20.1 percent (Florence, 1975). As a consequence of this disparity, the British people suffered inflation at rates ranging in the neighborhood of 20 percent per year for several consecutive years in the late 1970s.

Likewise, although the United States leads the industrial world in overall *level* of labor productivity (Freund, 1981), the rate of increase in productivity in the U.S. has fallen far behind the average annual rate of increase in wages and salaries (O'Toole, 1981). The situation is the same in Canada. In fact, the New York Stock Exchange has reported that, of the major industrial nations, only Italy has increased productivity between 1973 and 1979 at a lower rate than Canada and the United States (Freund, 1981). The point is that North American business and industry is rapidly losing its economic lead on the rest of the world, and with it, the comparatively affluent standard of living to which we have grown accustomed. A major cause of this trend—perhaps *the* major cause—is that productivity in North America is not increasing at a rate that is commensurate with the rate at which wages and other costs of production are increasing (O'Toole 1981).

DETERMINANTS OF PRODUCTIVITY

What determines the level of productivity in an industrial economy? There are a number of contributing factors (Bowen, 1979; Malkiel, 1979), although it is difficult to determine the relative importance of each. For the sake of discussion, it is possible to categorize the factors associated with productivity into two major groups. The first group consists of large-scale factors which are generally beyond the control of individual managers or executives; in fact, many of them seem, at times, to be beyond the control of the world's governments.

The second group of productivity determinants, however, are potentially much more amenable to control by individual managers in an economy. The primary purpose of this book will be to explore the nature of at least one of these more manipulable factors—the level of motivation of the workforce. But before beginning a treatment of the nature and causes of work motivation, let's take a brief look at some of the larger-scale determinants of productivity.

Large-Scale Factors

One key determinant of productivity in an economy is the level of investment made in fixed capital, such as new plants, refineries, office buildings and other operating sites—places which help to make the way the work gets done more efficient (Freund, 1981). The amazing levels of productivity in postwar Germany and Japan can be partially explained by the new industrial facilities constructed in those nations following 1945, although other factors have seen low productivity and inflation infest those countries more recently (Bowen, 1979).

Another factor that contributes to productivity (one that is obviously related to the first) is successful innovation and the development of new technology (Gold, 1979; Reilly and Fuhr, 1983). For example, the U.S. hosiery industry has enjoyed high rates of productivity and profitability in recent years while keeping the cost of a pair of pantyhose almost constant for some time. The reason? New technologies have been developed by the industry for producing, spinning, and dying yarn, as well as for sewing, folding, packaging, and marketing the finished product (Kinkead, 1980). Likewise, the introduction of electronic price scanners has made many retail grocery chains more productive through the new and more efficient price marking, price reading (at the checkout), and inventory procedures the scanners make possible (Coyle, 1978). But innovation takes investment in research and development activities, and it is notable that some critics of the poor performance of Canada's economy in recent times (e.g., Britton & Gilmour, 1978; McFetridge, **3**

1981) cite its comparatively low levels of *R&D* activities as a contributing cause of its productivity problem.

Another cause of low productivity in North America is a gradual shift of the workforce away from productive industries toward service industries. We have, for example, fewer farmers than before, but greater numbers of lawyers, government employees, and travel agents—people in sectors of the economy where major increases in productivity are difficult to achieve.

Increased scarcity of many raw materials contributes heavily to the cost of production of goods and services. The quintupling of energy costs in recent years is a major example with which all of us are too familiar.

Legislation that restricts the natural workings of the marketplace also limits productivity, according to some economic critics who desire a return to a laissez-faire framework for conducting business. Guidelines and regulations pertaining to equal employment opportunity, health and safety, minimum wages, antitrust, and rates that may be charged for service (as was the case in the airline industry until recently) are examples cited by these critics. But, while regulations of this type do contribute to the cost of production, it is also important to consider the economic (and social) benefits they contribute in return. For example, if the aggregate cost of a regulation is greater than the net value it generates, clearly that regulation might be judged dysfunctional from a strict social and economic perspective.

In short, there are a number of large-scale economic and political factors that can interact to restrict productivity and thereby fuel price inflation and compromise the quality of life that is possible for us to achieve in Western society. But all of these factors are beyond the control of the vast majority of managers and executives in industry. For example, not many chief executives can immediately cause a rollback in government regulations (although a few have tried). Likewise, not many first-line supervisors can initiate major changes in the basic physical design of work plants, so as to make their employees significantly more productive. The point is that executives and managers who wish to influence the productivity of the workforce must find alternatives to the means described above. The question becomes: what sources of productivity are there which fall within the grasp of individual employees and employers?

Human Factors in Productivity

There are at least two other major factors that determine the level of productivity in any given organization, industry, or economy which *can* be influenced (within limits) by executives, managers, and first-line supervisors: the level of ability of people who are assigned to work and the amount of effort these people expend doing that work.*

Employee ability. It has been suggested by some critics (who are often advanced in age) that the postwar workforce is less skillful and less devoted to hard work than were the workforces of previous times. It is a simple fact of demographics that *today's worker* is, on average, younger and less experienced than the workers of previous generations. But today's average employee is generally better trained and/or educated as well, so it is difficult to make summary statements concerning the comparative net levels of skill of the employees of various eras. (The reader may wish to hash out this subject with his or her parents, children, or other family members who have views on the matter.) The point is that individual supervisors can sometimes have considerable influence on the level of job-related ability of the people they assign to particular tasks on a day-by-day basis. Training programs, job redesign, and merely making careful person-job matches are means that, within limits, permit supervisors in many work settings to gain some leverage on the problem of productivity in their organizations.

Employee motivation. The second factor over which effective supervisors can often have some control is the level of motivated effort expended by those below them in organizational hierarchies—not always, but often.

Motivation—it is a popular topic that relates directly to all of us, particularly to those of us whose job it is to accomplish organizational goals through the effort of other people. Moreover, it is a topic about which many people claim to have some degree of knowledge, even expertise. *Motivation* is a buzzword in virtually all work settings and educational institutions. Folklore on the topic dates back at least as far as the literature on any other managerial topic, and our current newspapers and magazines regularly feature stories and essays on it. Countless *self-help* books have been published to provide man-

---

*Economists often argue that the large-scale factors such as those discussed here are much more important in their impact on productivity than are the human factors to be discussed throughout the rest of this book. For example, Freund (1981) believes that capital investment is the most important determinant of productivity, and that human factors are far less influential. It is hard to separate the contributions made to productivity by these various factors, but it is important to note that, even when they are working side by side in the same factory, plant, or office, different employees produce widely differing amounts of work output. Lawler (1973) has noted, for example, that the ratio of output produced by the best worker to that produced by the poorest worker in many work settings can be three-to-one or greater. Likewise, the average auto maker in Japan produces twice as many cars per year as his American counterpart, using essentially the same production techniques (Weil, 1979). Therefore, it would seem that human factors are, in fact, important determinants of productivity that must be taken into consideration (O'Toole, 1981).

agers and executives with quick insights into what makes them-selves and their subordinates work (or not work).

But there is also a vast *scientific* literature dealing with work moti-vation, the contents of which only sometimes relates to the wisdom imparted to managers through the popular materials they read. Nev-ertheless, work motivation is one of the most important topics in or-ganizational science: no other issue in the discipline has more signifi-cance for our general economic well-being, and no other topic commands more attention in the journals and textbooks of the field (Staw, 1977). Moreover, in view of the intractability of the other key determinants of productivity, we can expect work motivation to be at least as important an issue in organizational science and manage-ment in the future as it has been in the past.

PURPOSE OF THIS BOOK

The purpose of this book, therefore, is to examine the current state of knowledge pertaining to work motivation, with a view to esti-mating just how much is known about this important phenomenon. This is not a book about how to motivate a workforce, although the applied implications of the various theories and approaches to moti-vation will be identified as we come to them. Rather, the purpose here is to explore a number of the most viable current approaches to work motivation, attempting to evaluate each of them from the per-spectives of both the organizational scientist and the practicing man-ager.

It is important to state at the outset that virtually all of the ideas to be presented in this book are either theory or derived from theory. There are virtually no laws or solid facts pertaining to human behav-ior. The complexity of human behavior is something most of us are quick to acknowledge in some settings, but that we are equally quick to forget when we seek solutions to behavioral problems in other set-tings. Many of the theories to be presented contradict one another, either in concept or in application. But that is the state of the science, and something that the reader will have to accept in order to under-stand and appreciate it.

In the remaining sections of this chapter, we will define and ex-amine the meaning of work motivation and other key concepts that are related to it. It will be argued that individual managers are gener-ally less able to observe their employees' work motivation, per se, than they are to observe their levels of job performance. More specif-ically, we will begin the discussion by providing a definition of work motivation and delineating a number of features and implications of that definition. We will then focus on the meaning of *job perfor-mance,* and show why the difference between the two concepts is so important. As we will see, factors other than motivation determine an employee's level of job performance. One of these other factors is ability; accordingly we will discuss the nature and significance of work-related ability in a later section of the chapter.

To begin, then, what is work motivation?

WHAT IS *WORK MOTIVATION?*

It is only a slight exaggeration to say that there have been almost as many definitions of motivation offered over the years as there have been thinkers who have considered the nature of human behavior. In fact, one classic textbook (Atkinson, 1964) deliberately sidesteps the definitional problem until almost 300 pages of material on the topic are presented. Another major textbook (Cofer & Appley, 1964) presents the definitions of a number of scholars without offering a simple definition of its own. Still another book (Korman, 1974) discusses the issues that motivation is seen as dealing with, but does not tell what the concept is, per se.

There are a number of reasons for the apparent difficulty in defining motivation, although a full treatment of the reasons for that difficulty is far beyond our present purposes. Suffice it to say that there are, paradoxically, no singular definitions of motivation because there are so many definitions of different aspects of motivation, and so many philosophical orientations toward the nature of human beings and about what can be known about them. Moreover, some theorists deny the usefulness of the concept altogether, and concentrate primarily on the consequences of behavior as its causes. Some writers view motivation from a strictly physiological perspective, while others view human beings as primarily hedonistic, and explain most of human behavior as goal-oriented, seeking to gain pleasure and avoid pain. Others stress the rationality of humans, and consider human behavior to be the result of conscious choice processes. Some thinkers stress unconscious or subconscious factors.

The very multiplicity of the views on the nature of motivation and human behavior is reflected in the diversity of chapters found in a recent anthology compiled by Levine (1975). The interested reader is referred to that anthology, as well as to the works of Atkinson (1964) and Cofer and Appley (1964) for thorough treatments of the historical and philosophical perspectives which have been offered over the years. There have been quite a variety.

A Definition of Work Motivation

Where does this leave the student who wants to learn about motivation and job performance in the workplace? Since the topic of this   **7** book is focused upon *work* behavior (as opposed to all of human behavior), a definition that is accordingly focused will be offered and used throughout. The definition draws heavily upon those of a number of previous writers, and attempts to provide some balance in the philosophical assumptions that underly those definitions. The work of Jones (1955), Vroom (1964), Steers and Porter (1975), and Locke, Shaw, Saari, and Latham (1981) are of particular importance in giving rise to the following definition of work motivation:

> Work motivation is a set of energetic forces that originate both within as well as beyond an individual's being, to initiate work-related behavior, and to determine its form, direction, intensity, and duration.

Implications of the definition. A number of features of this definition deserve highlighting. First, it attempts to be both specific enough to relate primarily to work-related behaviors, but general and eclectic enough to avoid many of the basic issues that have divided previous writers who have concerned themselves with the origins of human behavior, particularly work behavior. Thus, for example, it is intended to apply to behaviors such as joining or not joining an organization for employment purposes; being late or on time for work on a given day; obeying or rejecting a supervisor's orders to work harder; accepting or rejecting a directive to relocate to another city; and even retiring or resigning from an organization.

Secondly, the concept of *force* is central to the definition. This makes it consistent with Vroom's (1964) definition of motivation, without necessarily adopting the cognitive orientation or the elements of decision making which are so important to his theory (see chapter seven of this book). The notion of force also makes our definition consistent with the hydraulic metaphors found in Freud's work in psychoanalysis. The definition allows for motivation levels to be either weak or strong, varying both between individuals at any particular time, as well as within a given individual at different times, and under different circumstances.

The definition states that there are a *set* of energetic forces, implying the multiplicity of needs, drives, instincts, and external factors that have been considered over the years with regard to human behavior, without necessarily accepting the primary importance of any of these sources. The idea of force suggests that motivation will manifest itself through effort. In fact, the concepts of effort and motivation are frequently treated as identical. In other places, effort is used as an operationalization of motivation. In this book, effort will be treated as a consequence and primary indicator of motivation, but it is not seen as identical with it.

The definition *implies* the notion of movement, in recognition of
8   the Latin root of the word motivation (*movere,* to move). Moreover,

recognition of both internal and external origins acknowledges the merits of the philosophical positions of both those who believe in free will and those who believe in determinism (cf. Joad, 1957). This feature of the definition permits recognition of the importance of characteristics of the work environment that can arouse behavior (such as the nature of the work being performed or the style of leadership being applied), without ruling out certain work behaviors that originate primarily from within the employee (such as staying home when ill).

The definition does not stress hedonism as a primary force in work motivation, but it does not rule it out, either. Nor does it preclude consideration of a number of other human traits, such as fear, lust, greed, or jealousy in the context of work behavior.

The *direction* toward which motivated force is focused also appears in the definition. Inclusion of this feature recognizes that it is not sufficient merely to consider the intensity and duration of work motivation; rather, one must also take into account the specific goals toward which motivated energy is directed in order to fully understand it (Katerberg and Blau, 1983).

The notion of *duration,* found in the definition, implies that goal attainment may be a possible (but not a necessary) outcome of behavior at the job, keeping the definition not inconsistent with goal-oriented theories such as those of Murray (1938), and Dunnette and Kirchner (1965), among others.

But the most important feature of the definition is that it views motivation as an invisible, internal concept, or what may be called a *hypothetical construct* (MacCorquodale and Meehl, 1948)—a concept representing an assumed physical process that is, as yet, unobservable directly. We cannot actually see motivation, per se, or measure it directly. Instead, we assume that it exists and rely on the theories we have to guide us in measuring what they suggest are its manifestations. Hypothetical constructs of this sort abound in psychology (e.g., personality, perceptions, beliefs, attitudes, and so on), as well as in virtually all other sciences at one time or another during their development. For example, adrenaline was originally an inferred variable: these days it is administered regularly in medical and clinical settings. Nevertheless, while there are countless examples of hypothetical constructs in the sciences, the reliance on invisible internal processes such as motivation constitutes an important point of controversy. In chapters nine and ten, for example, we will discuss a school of thought that rejects the use of such hypothetical constructs in favor of focusing only upon observable behavior.

In short, the definition offered above is intended to apply to work behaviors of all sorts, while at the same time avoiding many of the ontological and epistemological issues that have led to most of the debates and confusion mentioned earlier. Motivation is an important **9** factor in job performance and human productivity: it is the central concept of interest in this book, and when the term is used in subsequent chapters, it will denote the definition provided above.

Work Motivation and Performance are NOT the Same Thing

One of the most important distinctions that needs to be made early in this book is that between job performance and motivation. The difference is much more than a matter of semantics—it is one that has powerful implications for both the understanding and the application of the theories and ideas which will constitute the rest of this book. It is a distinction noted by Vroom (1964) in his early book on work motivation, and one that has been acknowledged frequently since (cf. Cummings and Schwab, 1973; Porter and Lawler, 1968; Lawler, 1973; Terborg, 1977). What *is* the difference between the two concepts?

Managers are primarily concerned with the accomplishment of work through other people. They are responsible for seeing to it that others accomplish the work that is assigned to them. Therefore, a manager is effective when her staff of subordinates accomplishes their respective work goals. But the successful accomplishment of one's work goals is normally the result of an interaction among a number of factors, only some of which can be controlled by the employee himself (such as the amount of effort he invests in the task). Another critical factor, for example, is the level of ability the employee possesses to do the particular job assigned to her. Still other factors which are external to the employee, such as the amount of support she receives from her supervisor and from her own staff (if she has one), or the availability of materials needed to perform the job, will limit the degree to which she can convert all of her well-intended effort into what her organization would call effective job performance. (We will address many of these factors at length in chapter twelve.) In short, we can define job performance as the accomplishment of work-related goals, regardless of the means of their accomplishment.

The importance of the distinction. A common mistake made by managers who notice poor job performance by their subordinates is automatically to attempt to remedy the problem as if it were the result of low motivation. Thus, for example, a sales manager may notice a slump in the average monthly sales figures (low job performance) for a key sales person, and react by increasing the rate of commission that will be paid to that sales rep for future sales. The manager's reaction is an explicit attempt to increase the sales rep's motivation level—as might be reflected in the degree of effort the rep will spend selling the firm's products. The manager assumes that the

10

rep is not trying hard enough for some reason—that the rep has lost interest, or has simply turned lazy.

But in many cases the problem might better be attributed to any (or all) of a number of the types of external factors which were mentioned above. For instance, it may be that the sales rep is now facing stiffer competition in his sales region from representatives of other companies with superior products to sell. It may be that the rep has lost a few traditionally held accounts, and that he is struggling to recapture them. Or, it may be that he is not fully aware of new company policies which are reflected in the firm's marketing strategies. In short, the performance problem might be one of motivation, but it may also be one that can be better understood from an examination of outside factors—factors which are, in part at least, beyond the rep's control. To apply strategies that are implicitly (or explicitly) designed to increase motivation levels when motivation is not the problem, can result in a self-fulfilling prophesy—the employee responds to the new threats or incentives, but still cannot perform up to standard (for the same reasons as before), becomes frustrated, and withdraws. He may ultimately quit trying altogether. (We will take a more complete look at the problem of frustration in chapter four of this book.)

Diagnostic mistakes of the sort made by our fictitious sales manager are common and easy to make. Parents often make a similar mistake when they notice a decline in the performance of their children in high school or college. Many students find they can achieve acceptable standards in high school with a certain level of effort, their natural level of mental ability, and a minimum amount of charm. However, once in college, these same students often find that greater ability is required (sometimes they don't have it) and/or higher levels of effort are necessary. (Charm is *always* important.) Parents who attempt to apply motivational strategies to children who simply do not have the native ability, or a sufficient level of acquired skills, are not usually able to help their children perform more effectively. In fact, the sort of pressure that parents can apply in these cases can result in resentment, fear, and withdrawal by the now-frustrated student. The author has known of cases of student suicide which have resulted from this sort of pressure. Success in college, like success on most jobs, requires a blend of ingredients, only one of which is motivation. Ability is another. And there are usually a host of other factors which function to either magnify or attenuate the effects of motivation and ability on successful performance.

In short, the point here is this: it can be a serious mistake to *automatically* assume that poor performance is the result of low motivation. Other factors in addition to motivation, interact with it to determine job performance. One of these is the level of the individual's **11** ability for the task in question. Therefore, let's take a look at what is meant by the term *ability*.

Ability in the Workplace

As the preceding examples have suggested, employee ability is an important factor in effective job performance. Some psychologists, in fact, have argued that ability is more important an ingredient in job performance than is motivation (e.g., Dunnette, 1972). A person might be highly motivated to lift a heavy weight from the floor up onto a table (after being offered a hundred dollars for doing so), but may not have the physical strength (a type of ability) to do it. The result: high motivation, no ability, no performance.

Defining ability.   But what *is* ability? We run into almost as much difficulty finding a simple definition for ability as we had earlier, when we sought to define motivation. The reason for the difficulty this time seems to be that *ability* is a word which includes and represents a number of other concepts, such as skill and aptitude, for instance. In its simplest form, we might define ability as the capacity of an individual to accomplish tasks, controlling for her level of motivation to attempt those tasks. But this merely begs the question by substituting *capacity* for ability. One author defines ability in terms of the performance people can achieve on tests designed to assess ability (Cronbach, 1970). In other words, ability is what ability tests measure: the circularity is not very helpful.

One way to approach the problem is to define ability by looking at definitions of those things that collectively constitute it. One of these is *aptitude,* which is defined by the Oxford English Dictionary (1961, vol. 1) as, "Natural capacity, endowment, or ability; talent for any pursuit." We can dodge the circularity in this definition, by focusing on two of its key terms—*natural* and *talent.* This suggests that aptitude consists of that part of ability that is innate in people, or which seems to develop naturally in them, without explicit training. An example would be spatial intelligence.

Another element of aptitude is *skill* (Dunnette, 1976). Again, the Oxford Dictionary (1961, vol. 9): "Capability of accomplishing something with precision and certainty; practical knowledge in combination with ability; cleverness, expertness." (The reader should be developing a sense of appreciation for the difficulty in defining these terms independently of one another!) The essence of skill seems to be capacity or capability which results in part from raw, natural aptitude (as we defined it above), as well as from the capability that people gain through both explicit training and development of their aptitudes, as well as through the more passive experiences of life.

12   In sum, we are left with a definition that is similar to, but not identi-

cal with, that reached by Lawler (1973): ability is an aggregation of natural aptitude plus the capacity to behave which results from the application of training and experience to one's aptitude. That is:

Ability = Aptitude + Aptitude (Training & Experience)

Defined as such, ability subsumes common concepts such as wisdom, sagacity, and competence—words we often hear attributed to people in work settings.

The point is: natural talent and the skill which one develops over time are major determinants of effective job performance. Highly motivated people working at jobs for which they lack the necessary ability are not generally capable of job performance.

Types of ability. There are many forms of human ability. Guilford (1967), for example, claims that there may be as many as 120 distinct varieties of basic *mental* ability alone! When combined in various proportions with the many sensory and psychomotor abilities that people can have (cf. Guion, 1965, chap. 10), we are left with virtually an infinite number of possible combinations, or sets of abilities any employee might possess.

This seems like an obvious point, in principle, but it requires explication because of the tendency of so many of us to make remarks such as "Jones has no skill," or "Smith is incompetent." It is true that some people are more richly endowed with skill sets than others— but in organizational settings we must ask: "Competent for what?" Highly competent people who are assigned to jobs for which their ability sets are not appropriate are generally no more effective in organizations than are people with less impressive ability sets who are assigned to jobs for which they have some of the basic requisite abilities (Lofquist and Dawis, 1969). Hence, the importance of careful personnel selection, placement, and job design.

Motivation, Ability, and Job Performance

Empirical studies which have explicitly examined the role of ability in task performance have generally tended to affirm and reaffirm its importance; although the exact ways by which it combines with motivation are still not exactly clear. Some early studies suggested the relationship is interactive, such that high levels of one factor can compensate for low levels of the other (Fleishman, 1958; French 1957). This view, for example, would predict that a person with twice as much ability but only half as much motivation as another individual, would be approximately of equal effectiveness on the job. Moreover, if either factor were essentially absent (i.e., the person has no ability for the job and/or has no motivation to engage in it), performance would not be possible. Later studies by Locke (1965) and **13**

Terborg (1977) support the importance of ability as a determinant of performance, but challenge its interactive relationship with motivation: that is, they would conclude that it is not necessary for both factors to be at least somewhat operative for performance to result.

Before leaving our discussion of employee ability and its role in job performance, it is worth noting one type of ability which is an especially important factor in job performance in many organizations. We might refer to this sort of ability as *savoir faire,* or simply *savvy.* For college students, savvy is knowing which classes they can afford to skip in order to go skiing. It is having a *feel* for which professor's assignments can be turned in late, and which ones stand tough by the deadlines they require. For the junior employees in an organization, savoir faire involves a host of things, such as knowing the clique structure of the workgroup, and knowing the people with whom they should or should not exchange rumors. It is knowing how to read their supervisor's facial expression and the mood of the boss's secretary. It is being acquainted with the *ropes.* A delightful and highly instructive treatment of these matters—one that can be very useful to the new college graduate—is Ritti and Funkhouser's (1977) book.

In brief, both ability and motivation are required by employees in order to perform most jobs, although the exact form of the relationship between motivation, ability, and performance is not clear. Regardless of the precise nature of this relationship, however, the important point is that not all performance problems in the workplace are a consequence of low levels of motivation to work, so the supervisor or manager in charge must be careful in diagnosing the causes of whatever performance problems are observed. As we will see in chapter twelve of this book, there are a host of other factors in most work settings that can either magnify or attenuate the effects of both motivation and job-related ability on task performance. Tactics to increase motivation, when it is not the problem, may make matters worse, both for the individual employee and for the organization.

SUMMARY

In this chapter, it has been argued that productivity is an issue of major economic concern in Western civilization. Our ability to live in comparative economic affluence depends, in large measure, upon the productivity of the workforce in all sectors of the economy. But many of the most powerful determinants of productivity in any economy are well beyond the influence of individual managers and executives. However, the levels of motivation and ability of the workforce are two factors that can, within limits, be influenced by enlightened managerial practices. The importance of human productivity in economic well-being is not a new topic; it has been written about and studied before (e.g., McClelland and Winter, 1969; O'Toole, 1981; Thurow 1980). The purpose of this book is to provide a scientifically-based treatment of our knowledge of work motivation and its role in job performance, and ultimately, the overall level of productivity in Western economies and the quality of life we can expect to enjoy.

OUTLINE OF THE BOOK

Now that we have dealt with a few basic concepts and definitions, we can begin the major task of this book—to examine current knowledge pertaining to work motivation. A major theme of the book is that what we know about work motivation consists of theory. *Theory* is an aversive word in some quarters, but a failure to recognize the fact that most social and behavioral science knowledge is merely that can lead to a number of disappointments for the student or manager who wishes to utilize this knowledge and finds it limited in what it can provide. Therefore, chapter two will present a framework that illustrates how theories of work motivation are developed. Understanding the framework will be important for comprehending much of the analysis that follows in subsequent chapters, where specific details about current theories of work motivation are presented.

When we speak of human motivation, we necessarily speak about human nature; to understand why people behave the way they do, we must have some understanding of the essential nature of human beings. Therefore, a number of alternative models of human functioning will be presented at the beginning of chapter three, laying a groundwork for the presentation of formal theories of work motivation in subsequent chapters. It will become clear as the book develops that different theories of work motivation do in fact rest upon entirely different assumptions concerning human nature. The second half of chapter three will then begin the analysis of work motivation by looking at theories that assume human beings are wanting animals, driven by sets of basic needs.

Chapter four will focus on the so-called higher order needs, explaining current thought on what is called *intrinsic motivation,* and describing what happens when people's behavior is prevented from fulfilling their needs.

There is a group of three important theories of work motivation which assume that people's beliefs, attitudes, and intentions are the ultimate determinants of their behavior. Accordingly, chapter five will discuss the nature of human beliefs, attitudes, and intentions, and provide the basic concepts needed to understand the cognitive theories which follow in chapters six, seven, and eight.

Chapter six will deal with the so-called *equity* theories of motivation; chapter seven will discuss the popular *Valence-Instrumentality-* **15**

Expectancy (or simply *expectancy*) theories; and chapter eight will look at *Goal Setting Theory*. In each of these chapters, we will present the rudiments of the respective theories, examine the research evidence that has been gathered to attest to their validity, and evaluate the quality of that evidence. Finally, important applied implications of the theories presented in each of these chapters will be discussed.

Chapters nine and ten will present an approach to work behavior that rests on a different model of human functioning: it assumes neither the existence of needs (as in chapters three and four), nor the operation of invisible internal cognitive factors (as is the case in the theories presented in chapters five through eight). In fact, adherents to this school reject the usefulness of the concept of motivation altogether. Instead, this approach merely assumes that behavior is determined by its consequences, and that people learn from their experiences. This so-called *behaviorist* approach will be explained in its more or less pure form in chapter nine. Then, in chapter ten, we will look at how its fundamental principles have been adapted to the modification of work behavior.

In chapter eleven we will deal with current thinking on the generation of intrinsic work motivation through the creative design of jobs.

Chapter twelve will present a succinct summary of the most important principles of work motivation having potential for application by managers in organizations. Following the summary, we will address a host of practical constraints found in most work organizations—constraints that can make it difficult, in practice, for enlightened managers to implement even the most powerful applied principles of work motivation.

Finally, chapter thirteen will provide a brief assessment of the "state of the science" dealing with work motivation, and propose a new framework to guide future research and theory toward new advances on the topic.

To begin then, because of the fact that most of what is to follow in this book is theory, chapter two will explain the meaning of theory, and show how the theoretic nature of our knowledge of work motivation is an important feature of that knowledge, for both the student and the practicing manager.

THE DEVELOPMENT OF WORK MOTIVATION THEORY 2

No way of thinking or doing, however ancient, can be trusted without proof.

—H. D. Thoreau

In chapter one it was argued that managers might benefit from an understanding of human work motivation because such knowledge may help them contribute to the productivity of the workforces in their respective organizations, and, indirectly, to the aggregate level of economic prosperity of the nation. Most managers are quite aware of the need for some knowledge of employee motivation, and as will be argued in chapter three, most managers hold implicit models in their minds about what makes employees *tick*. In response to the widespread desire for solutions to the problem of employee motivation, many consultants, academics, and business people have developed and promulgated theories of work motivation. Some of these theories have merit, others do not.

The purpose of this chapter is to provide the reader with an understanding of the means by which theories of work motivation are developed and made available to practitioners for application in organizational settings. A model will be developed that represents the cyclical process through which research and theory development often proceed as new ideas about work motivation are generated and refined for application. It is important for the reader to understand the nature of this process in order to appreciate and (if so desired) apply the theoretic notions that are presented throughout the rest of this book, as well as in other books having to do with human behavior in organizations. This cyclical process will be illustrated **17** through a detailed summary of the development and promulgation of one of the most influential and controversial theories of work motivation yet to have appeared—*Herzberg's Motivator-Hygiene Theory.*

Finally, this chapter will discuss the general problem of the ways by which a practitioner can determine the readiness for application of any theoretical framework that has its roots in behavioral and social science. The issues and concepts introduced in this part of the chapter will have relevance for the discussion in most of the remaining chapters, where various theories and techniques of employee motivation will be presented in greater detail.

To begin, let's look at the cycle of events that is typical during the development of most new theories in behavioral science—a cycle that is particularly common in the development of theories of work motivation.

WHENCE DO THEORIES COME?

The knowledge base of most social and behavioral sciences results from a cycle of activities—a cycle that many practitioners are either not aware of, or that they tend to ignore. Our base of knowledge about work motivation is no exception to this cycle, so it is important for the student or manager who wishes to apply these theories to understand the nature of their origins. For the sake of discussion, the cycle is illustrated graphically in Figure 2-1.

FIGURE 2-1:   The Cycle of Events Leading to a Theory of Work Motivation

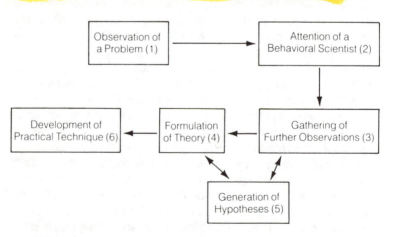

Although the sequence of events varies to some degree from one case to another, it is common for the cycle to begin with the observation of a problem, or a phenomenon of concern to someone

(such as a manager or administrator) who is responsible for dealing with it (See Box 1 in Figure 2-1). Low job performance, absenteeism, tardiness, insubordination, or the occurrence of wildcat strikes are a number of examples that are of particular relevance to us here. At some time or other, the problem may come to the attention of a behavioral scientist, at which stage any of a number of things may occur (see Box 2). In some cases, the scientist may set about to explore the phenomenon of interest, gathering more preliminary observations related to it (Box 3). In other cases, the scientist may already have a number of hypotheses or hunches that can be tested with the data already in hand. Regardless, once a phenomenon comes to the attention of a social or behavioral scientist, the cycle of scientific activity gets underway, leading sooner or later to a formal *theory* to explain it.

The term *theory* is often viewed with suspicion, or as a dirty word by practical people (such as managers and students), so many academics and consultants avoid using it when dealing with them. Nevertheless, the fact is that virtually all of our knowledge about business, organizations, and the behavior of people in organizations consists entirely of theory. There are few irrefutable *facts* pertaining to human behavior. This point has a number of important implications for anyone who wishes to permit behavioral science to influence his policies and practices as a manager of human resources. Later sections of this chapter will deal with some of these implications, but since the bulk of the ideas to be presented in this book consist of or derive from theory, it is important that we define the term and begin to understand it.

What is a Theory?

As usual, definitions abound, but in this case they tend to converge. One definition that seems to represent most others holds that, "Theories are nets cast to catch what we call 'the world': to rationalize, to explain, and to master it" (Popper, 1968, p.59). They are like templates that are fashioned as representations of reality: sometimes they are accurate reflections of that reality; sometimes they are not. When a theory truly represents that part of reality it purports to represent, it is said to be *valid*. Proposing a theory can be easy; proposing a valid theory can be much more difficult. But validity is not an all or nothing phenomenon. It is possible for some aspects of a theory to be more valid than other aspects. Moreover, as the phenomenon of interest changes, the theory that purports to represent it may become less valid unless it is changed accordingly (cf. Cronbach, 1975). **19**

The Formation of Theory

The point is that theories result from observations, and are intended to make sense of those observations. There is usually a prolonged sequence in which the scientist gathers observations through the conduct of formal research, formulates propositions based on those observations, and then gathers more data to confirm, modify, or reject the propositions. Often there are many scientists involved, such that some gather and report data, others criticize those data or the inferences that are derived from them, while still others may be responsible for integrating the ideas of several other researchers into the formulation of a theory. The iterative relationship between the collection of observations, the casting of propositions, and the refinement of theory is represented by Boxes 4, 5, and 6 in Figure 2-1.

The Potential for Error

Because theories ultimately rest on the more or less structured observations of scientists (gathered during their research activities), it stands to reason that mistakes made in the data collection can result in theories that are less valid than they might otherwise be. While a full treatment of research methodology is not our purpose here, the reader should recognize that erroneous observational techniques can lead to inaccurate theories, and/or make it difficult to assess the level of validity of extant theories. In fact, there are countless mistakes possible in the research process, some of which are more common than others. Nevertheless, the reader is reminded that virtually all of the ideas concerning work motivation presented in this book consist of or are derived from theory, and the true level of validity of these theories is often open to dispute.

In the following section, we will illustrate the cycle described above and represented in Figure 2-1 by relating the story of the development of one of the most widely-known theories of work motivation—that which was proposed nearly a quarter century ago by Frederick Herzberg and his colleagues. In addition to illustrating the cycle of activities that commonly occurs in the development of a science, the following section will also serve to introduce the student to the first of the major theories of work motivation to be described in this book.

THE MOTIVATOR-HYGIENE THEORY

Based on an exhaustive review of hundreds of early studies of the causes, correlates, and consequences of job attitudes, Herzberg and his colleagues (Herzberg, Mausner, Peterson, and Capwell, 1957) developed the preliminary hypothesis that the factors which cause positive attitudes toward one's job are different from the factors that generate negative job-related attitudes. This hypothesis was revolutionary at the time, because it implies that job satisfaction is not simply the opposite of job dissatisfaction, as had commonly been assumed. Instead, the new hypothesis held that feelings of job satisfaction and job dissatisfaction are independent of one another, such that an employee can simultaneously be happy about some aspects of his job while being unhappy about other aspects. Using the terms shown in Figure 2-1, the *problem* of interest was employee work attitudes, and the *observations* that led to the preliminary hypothesis were, in this case, actually the observations of hundreds of other researchers and behavioral scientists—a much wider and more justifiable base for offering an hypothesis than is usually the case in behavioral science.

Herzberg's Own Research

To test the two-factor concept, Herzberg and his colleagues (Herzberg, Mausner, and Snyderman, 1959) gathered their own original data (observations) from a sample of 203 engineers and accountants who worked for a variety of organizations in the Pittsburgh area. Using a semistructured interview technique (meaning that both the researcher and the interviewee influenced the direction taken during the interview), the researchers asked the employees, one at a time, to think of an occasion when they felt "exceptionally good" or "exceptionally bad" about their jobs. Interviewees were permitted to recall such *critical incidents* from either their current or any previously held jobs. They gathered two or three incidents of this sort, on average, from each employee. For each incident, detail was requested concerning three things: (1) a description of the objective conditions surrounding and causing the incident; (2) a description of the reasons why the employee felt the way he did at the time of the incident; and (3) a summary of the consequences of the incident for the employee and his job.

Analysis of the incidents. Once the data are gathered in a research project, they must be analyzed. (We will see later in this chapter that both the collection and the analysis phases of such a project are potentially problematic.) Herzberg and his colleagues broke each interview down into almost five hundred separate *thought items,* and then classified these items into categories based on the degree of similarity that appeared among them. Notice that the researchers allowed the nature of the items to determine the categories to emerge from this analysis, rather than sorting them into predefined categories. Care was taken to assure that independent researchers could agree on the classification of particular items into **21**

the various clusters that resulted. The items were also categorized as being either long-term or short-term in the effects they had on the employees at the time. Sixteen separate groups of items, or factors, emerged from this exercise—sixteen sets of items that were related in one way or another with instances of extremely satisfying or dissatisfying job experiences.

The next step was to see whether any of these groups of factors seemed to be more closely associated with instances of positive job attitudes than with instances of negative job attitudes, and likewise, whether certain of the factors appeared more frequently in stories of negative incidents than in stories of positive job attitudes.

Further detail of the data analysis techniques employed is well beyond the scope of this book; the interested reader is referred to the original report (Herzberg et al., 1959). What is important to the present discussion is a summary of the results, and—even more important—the way the results have been interpreted, misinterpreted, and fought over by pro- and anti-Herzberg factions ever since.

The *motivators*.   In fact, certain patterns did seem to emerge from the data. As had been the researchers' hunch before the data were collected, there was a set of factors that appeared more frequently in stories of positive job attitudes than in stories of negative job attitudes. For example, reports of *achievement* appeared in 41 percent of the instances of positive job attitudes, making it the single feature most frequently related to job satisfaction experiences. (An example from the study is the case of a marine engineer who described an instance when he succeeded in designing a propellor for a new boat design.) Similarly, *recognition* appeared in 33 percent of the positive stories; challenging, varied, or *interesting work* appeared in 26 percent; *responsibility* appeared in 23 percent, and *advancement* was an element of fully 20 percent of the stories of high job satisfaction.

On the other hand, ten of the sixteen factors that were previously identified appeared in fewer than 7 percent of the job satisfaction episodes, suggesting, as had been expected, that they were not usually related to job satisfaction experiences. Because the interviewees indicated that the occurrences of these highly favorable periods of job attitudes tended to result in greater job performance, Herzberg labeled these sources of satisfaction *motivators*.

A number of special features emerged from a close look at the five most frequently mentioned satisfiers/motivators. First, positive stories that featured one of these factors tended to include elements related to one or more of the other four—they seemed to go hand in hand in producing job satisfaction. Further, the researchers noted

22

that the positive feelings tended, by comparison to the negative feelings, to be relatively long-lasting rather than short-term in effect. They also tended to be related to aspects of the *content* of the job, and to the personal relationship between the worker and the job. Finally, it was discovered that the reason these five factors were associated with job satisfaction was that they tended to cause feelings of *growth* and *personal development.*

The *hygiene factors.* The researchers then looked at the stories that referred to instances of job dissatisfaction, and found that the eleven remaining factors revealed in their earlier analysis seemed to appear most frequently in them. Thus, *company policy and administration* was at least partly blamed for 31 percent of the reported cases of job dissatisfaction. Likewise, unhappy relationships with the *employee's supervisor* appeared in 20 percent of these stories, while poor interpersonal relations with one's *peers* was the critical factor in 15 percent of the instances of poor job attitudes.

Similarly, unhappiness with *technical aspects of the employee's supervisor* was a critical factor in 20 percent of the stories of low job attitudes, while *bad relations with the supervisor on a personal level* appeared important in 15 percent of these stories. Two other factors that figured predominantly in the episodes of low job attitudes were *poor working conditions* and *unfriendly relationships with one's peers,* which appeared in 11 percent and 8 percent of the stories of dissatisfaction, respectively. Compared to the frequency with which this second set of factors appeared in stories of job dissatisfaction, they were not frequently related to instances of high job attitudes.

Herzberg and his colleagues (1959) named this second set of factors *hygienes* because, analogous to the concept of mental hygiene in psychiatry, these items were seen as necessary, but not sufficient, for healthy adjustment. (Or, in this case, they are necessary for preventing job dissatisfaction, but they are not capable of generating either job satisfaction or motivated behavior.)

The researchers noted a number of features shared among the hygiene factors. First, they all tend to be related to the *context* of the work—the circumstances within which the individual performs his job. (Recall that the motivators were more closely linked to the *content* of the work.)

Secondly, the hygiene factors tended to be associated with shorter-lasting job experiences than were the motivators. Herzberg (1981) argues that providing decent working conditions and cordial interactions on the job, for example, may serve to *move* people in the short run, but that their *zero point* escalates, so that people quickly take these things for granted, and become likely to ask, ''What have you done for me lately?'' On the other hand, the provision of motiva- **23** tor factors in the employee's work is seen as having a much longer-lasting effect on the individual, resulting in motivation rather than simple movement.

The predominant reason given by the respondents in the original study (Herzberg et al., 1959) to explain why the lack of hygiene factors was associated with dissatisfaction was that their absence tended to cause feelings of being unfairly treated. So, whereas the provision of motivators led to feelings of growth and development, a sense of injustice seemed to explain the link between the absence of hygienes and job dissatisfaction.

Overlap in the factors. There was at least one other important aspect of the hygiene factors noted by Herzberg and his colleagues—a feature that is highly relevant to the controversy sparked by the theory. There were a number of stories of job dissatisfaction that featured elements of some of the so-called motivator factors, especially recognition, work itself, and advancement. For example, failure to receive recognition was attributed as the principal cause in 18 percent of the stories of job dissatisfaction. It is important to acknowledge that the researchers recognize these deviations from the basic split in their original book:

> All the basic satisfiers, recognition, achievement, advancement, responsibility, and work itself appeared with significantly greater frequencies in the highs [stories of job satisfaction] than they did in the low sequences of events [stories of job satisfaction]. However, some of these factors also appeared with some frequency in the low stories: recognition, 18 percent; work itself, 14 percent; and advancement, 11 percent. Evidently these three satisfiers are not so unidirectional in their effect on job attitudes as the factors that cause job dissatisfaction. From these results it would appear that a better statement of the hypothesis would be that the satisfier factors are much more likely to increase job satisfaction than they would be to decrease job satisfaction but that the factors that relate to job dissatisfaction very infrequently act to increase job satisfaction (1959, p. 80).

Anyone who has ever worked at a dull or dirty job knows from experience that the nature of the work, by itself, can be a very powerful cause of job dissatisfaction, as can instances in which either recognition for accomplishment is hard to come by, or in which employees are not advanced at a rate that is deemed fair. Quite clearly, these motivators can be, if absent from an employee's job, great sources of frustration and dissatisfaction.

There are two issues that require highlighting here. The first is a technical point, but one with significance for the argument being presented in this chapter: notice that in their well-intended acknowledgement of the lack of perfect symmetry between the causes of job **24** satisfaction and dissatisfaction, Herzberg and his colleagues indicated the possibility that the three motivators in question could also decrease job satisfaction. The problem lies in the fact that their data, as well as their own theoretical interpretation of those data, imply that satisfaction and dissatisfaction are not opposite sides of the same emotion. Instead, they are held to be entirely independent and different from one another—but not opposites.* What the caveat should have said about the three common crossovers, in order to be consistent with the rest of the theory, is that like the major hygiene factors, these motivators are also capable of causing job dissatisfaction (as opposed to decreasing job satisfaction) among people. The difference is important, because it illustrates the ways by which misinterpretations and misunderstandings can arise as a theory is developed and then passed from one researcher to another in the cycle of testing and modification shown in Figure 2-1.

The second point is that, although they drew attention to the fact that their data featured these (as well as other) crossovers, both Herzberg and others who followed him seemed to lose sight of this acknowledgement in the original statement of the theory. In popularized interpretations of his own theory, for example, Herzberg himself (1968, 1981) lists his basic motivators as associated with motivation and satisfaction, and his hygienes as causative only of dissatisfaction, failing to mention the reversals in the data that originally gave rise to the theory.

In short, these two points illustrate how the refinement of a theory can encounter snags and delays, making the process shown in Figure 2-1 less precise than one might wish it to be.

The role of salary. The most ambivalent of the sixteen factors found in the stories of satisfaction and dissatisfaction was salary. It appeared in almost as many stories (proportionately) of job satisfaction as it did in stories of dissatisfaction. However, because it was related to more stories of long-term negative attitude shifts than to long-term positive shifts, Herzberg and his team classified salary in the hygiene category.

The Two-Factor Theory in a Nutshell

Briefly, the two factor theory proposes that human beings have two basic sets of needs, and that different elements of the work experience can serve to meet these two sets (Herzberg, 1966). The first set of needs are for basic survival, or maintenance. They are characterized as being concerned with avoiding pain and discomfort, and as

---

*In a later book, Herzberg (1966) describes how the motivators are responsible for meeting growth needs, while the hygienes are needed to provide for basic survival only.

providing for *primary* drives such as sex, thirst, and hunger. The second set of needs are called *growth needs*. They express themselves in attempts by people to become all that they are capable of becoming, by exploring and conquering challenges posed by their environments. (See chapter four of this book where the notion of growth needs is discussed in greater detail.) Minimum levels of the hygiene factors (such as salary, for example) are necessary for the fulfillment of the survival needs, but when they are present, they do not cause feelings of job satisfaction: they merely prevent feelings of job dissatisfaction. Hygienes can be useful motivators, according to the theory, only until the survival needs are somewhat provided for. Then they lose effect.

In order to produce positive job attitudes, and in order to motivate an employee, the theory claims that those things originally identified as motivators must be built into an employee's job. The content of the work, rather than the setting in which it is conducted, is the important thing. The work must allow the individual opportunities to feel achievement, and the person must receive recognition for that achievement. The work should be interesting, provide for advancement, and require responsibility. When jobs are designed according to these principles (or *enriched*), motivation and positive attitudes will be forthcoming. When these factors are missing, however, no dissatisfaction results, simply an absence of satisfaction.

The original study revealed a number of other findings, but those mentioned above are the most important as well as the most controversial and the most relevant for the present discussion.

The Ensuing Controversy

The cycle shown in Figure 2-1 indicates that newly developed theories are often, if not always, put to the test of reality, either by their original proponents or by other people who are interested in confirming, refining, or refuting them. Accordingly, the Motivator-Hygiene Theory quickly drew a lot of attention. Within a few years, dozens of attempts were made to interpret the theory, develop means of measuring the various factors included in it, and ultimately to gather data, and compare the results found in the data with predictions that followed from the theory.

As is often the case, the results were highly mixed. Some studies seemed to support the two-factor concept, others did not. As evidence accumulated on both sides of the ledger, a dispute between pro- and anti-Herzberg factions developed, generated in part by a number of allegations that Herzberg's results (and therefore the theory itself) could be explained primarily by the methods he and his colleagues used to both gather and analyze the data! This point is crucial. A theory of work motivation is supposed to reflect the true underlying nature of just that—work motivation. Such a theory should not, in fact, be merely an artifact of the methodology used to generate it.

The argument was that the storytelling technique (described above) naturally tended to cause the interviewees to link instances of satisfaction to their own accomplishments, and—not wanting to look bad—cause them to associate instances of negative feelings with factors that were somewhat beyond their control or responsibility. So, for example, it was alleged that the engineers and accountants quite understandably blamed company policies, their supervisors and peers, and other contextual factors for the negative events reported in their stories. This criticism was a serious challenge to the validity of the theory because it cast fundamental doubt on the very meaning of the data. Moreover, the criticism grew in seriousness when it was noted that studies using the Herzberg methodology tended to support the theory, whereas those which used other methods to gather and analyze the data tended not to support it (Behling, Labovitz, and Kosmo, 1968).

A complete history of the Herzberg debate is beyond the scope of this book. Interested readers are referred to papers by Bockman (1971), Grigaliunas and Weiner (1974), House and Wigdor (1967), and Whitsett and Winslow (1967) for summaries of the controversy and insight into the many fine points that are involved. Briefly however, by 1970 enough data had been gathered that cast doubt on the theory for Korman (1971) to conclude that research had ". . . effectively laid the Herzberg theory to rest. . . (p.149)." Subsequent pronouncements of the demise of the theory have been plentiful.

But more than a decade after the two-factor theory was formally proposed, some of its proponents claimed that it was seldom tested fairly, so that the conclusion that it is invalid is itself not well-founded (Grigaliunas and Weiner 1974). For example, these writers argued that virtually none of the studies that were conducted to test the theory used measures of job satisfaction and job dissatisfaction that represented two separate and independent continua, as the theory would demand. Moreover, data are presented that imply that the social desirability explanation for the original data (as discussed above) is not tenable. Grigaliunas and Weiner also point out that critics of Herzberg's theory have tended to ignore the substantial evidence that has accumulated to support the theory's prescriptions for job design. In short, these authors believe that it may not be possible to test the theory fairly, and that attempts to do so before 1974 failed to provide sufficient grounds to conclude that it is not valid. (One study that employed a methodology that Grigalinas and Weiner propose— Ondrack [1974]—failed to support the theory.) **27**

Herzberg himself has alleged at times that he has been misinterpreted (e.g., Herzberg, 1976). The problem is that in order for the self-correcting cycle of scientific activity shown in Figure 2-1 to occur, the first necessary step is for the theory in question to be interpreted accurately, and without biases or nuances that are not founded on the basis of the observations that gave rise to it in the first place. To the extent that Herzberg and his codefendants are correct in their position that the theory has been misinterpreted and tested with instruments that are inappropriate, there is no way anyone— including academics, students, or practitioners—can be sure that the theory has anything to offer to help them understand and/or influence work motivation.

Aside from the allegation that inappropriate instruments have been used to examine the Motivator-Hygiene Theory, it has been demonstrated by King (1970) that there have been as many as five different interpretations of the two factor notion, and that none of these five interpretations enjoys much empirical support that cannot be attributed to methodological artifact, as was alleged of the original study. To illustrate, one interpretation suggests that all of the motivator factors combined contribute more to job satisfaction than to job dissatisfaction, and that all hygienes combined contribute more to dissatisfaction than to satisfaction. A different interpretation holds that all motivators combined contribute more to satisfaction than do all hygiene factors combined, and that all hygiene factors combined contribute more to dissatisfaction than do all motivators combined. Remarks made in Herzberg's 1966 book suggest that this is what the theory implies. Regardless, King (1970) shows that only those studies which used the Herzberg method have been successful at replicating and supporting the theory, and that the various interpretations fail, as tested, to provide unequivocal support to the two-factor feature of the theory.

In balance, when we combine all of the evidence with all of the allegations that the theory has been misinterpreted, and that its major concepts have not been assessed properly, one is left, more than twenty years later, not really knowing whether to take the theory seriously, let alone whether it should be put into practice in organizational settings. As we will see in chapter eleven, there is support for many of the implications the theory has for enriching jobs to make them more motivating. But the two-factor aspect of the theory—the feature that makes it unique—is not really a necessary element in the use of the theory for designing jobs, per se. One need only believe that building jobs to provide responsibility, achievement, recognition for achievement, and advancement will make them satisfying and motivating. There is no need to assume that failure to provide these

28   factors will not lead to job dissatisfaction, or that the provision of certain hygiene factors in the work place cannot also be motivating, in the true sense of the word.

Implications of the Herzberg Controversy

Why have we devoted so much attention to the details surrounding the development of the Two-Factor Theory and to the controversy that it generated? One obvious purpose was to explain the theory, because it remains one of the best known approaches to work motivation among practitioners today. But there are several other reasons for examining it so closely.

First, the Herzberg story permits us to illustrate a number of important problems and issues that relate to the development of new theories in behavioral science. (These problems and issues are certainly not unique to the case of the Motivator-Hygiene Theory.)

Consider, for example, the difficulty of developing tools or instruments for assessing hypothetical concepts such as motivation. As was noted in chapter one, we must *infer* the existence of motivated force from the observation of effort, or by asking people about what is going on inside them. We cannot directly weigh or measure concepts such as attitudes and motivation as we would physical objects. This means we must worry about whether our crude proxy measures (such as Herzberg's interview technique) really allow us to measure those things we think we are measuring. This is referred to as the problem of *construct validity* (Schwab, 1980). It is a constant issue in assessing nonphysical entities.

To make matters worse, we must also worry about the possibility that the measurements we make may vary from one time to the next (when in fact we know that the entity being measured has not changed). That is, do the measures we take fluctuate from one instance to the next, or are they relatively stable? This is referred to as the problem of *reliability* of measurement. Clearly, we cannot develop or test a theory with instruments that give us inconsistent assessments of the concepts that must be calibrated, yet the stability of measurement in behavioral science when interviews and/or questionnaires are used is usually a problem (Nunnally, 1967).

Further, consider the possibility that the very process of asking a person how he feels toward his job may, in itself, influence the type of response the employee makes. Some critics (e.g., Salancik and Pfeffer, 1977, 1978) claim that it is virtually impossible to assess job attitudes without changing those attitudes merely by asking about them. This is referred to as the problem of *reactivity* of measurement (Webb, Campbell, Schwartz, and Sechrest, 1966). It too is endemic in behavioral research and figures heavily into the problem of measurement reliability. In the case of Herzberg's research, the allega- **29** tion that his results could be accounted for by the ego-defense (or social desirability) motives of the interviewees provides an example of how difficult it is to assess attitudes and motives in a social vacuum without influencing them through asking about them.

The Herzberg example also illustrates that there are many ways to make observations, and that once a theory has been proposed, there are many ways to test its validity (i.e., to determine whether it actually reflects reality). The story shows that it is often the case that theories are not tested appropriately, and, as a result, they may be either confirmed or rejected for the wrong reasons. Hypotheses that are supported by poorly conducted research (when, in fact, they should be rejected) can accumulate, resulting in theories that misrepresent the nature of things. Alternatively, valid hypotheses that do not pass the scientist's test (as a result of poor research) may be ignored and forgotten. The result—potentially useful knowledge is discredited.

The Herzberg case also illustrates what can happen when a theory, once developed, is oversimplified, misinterpreted, or misrepresented. In chapter three we will see that Maslow's famous theory of needs has suffered a similar treatment, as has the currently popular expectancy theory of motivation, which will be discussed in chapter seven. If a new theory is not accurately interpreted, how can its true level of validity be determined, and how can either the scientist or the practitioner decide whether it has any value for understanding and/ or influencing the world?

In short, the story of the development of Herzberg's theory helps illustrate many of the difficulties involved in the advancement of new theories of work motivation. It helps us understand the potential for error on the part of any new theory that purports to reflect the nature of work motivation. It also suggests that certain theories, because of difficulties inherent in operationalizing them for testing, may be more valid than scientists are able to demonstrate—a proposition that will be advanced repeatedly in later chapters. On the other hand, the story shows that progress in organizational science, as in the case of other sciences, is a nonlinear affair, such that new theoretical developments can earn widespread attention and influence, in spite of— rather than because of—the quality of the research upon which they are based (see Bourgeois and Pinder, 1984 for further examples). Hopefully, the Herzberg story will help the reader understand the necessity for caution on the part of behavioral scientists as they generate new theories. But more importantly, it is hoped that the reader with applied interests will learn to be somewhat discriminating and cautious in the adoption of new theoretical ideas for application in real organizational settings.

APPLYING MOTIVATION THEORY

The preceding analysis raises a number of questions. First, if it is accepted that caution is required in the application of new theories of motivation, how can an enlightened manager know when it is safe or advisable to adopt and begin applying new theories to her human resource problems? What criteria or standards are available to suggest that such applications are appropriate? Further, just how valid are our best theories of work motivation?

Simple answers to these questions are not possible, but the following sections are intended to shed some light on the issues involved.

Field Testing vs. Commercial Application

When we consider the issue of the application of new theories of motivation in real organizational settings, it is important to keep in mind a distinction between two different types of application. The first type is that which is done by behavioral scientists, whose purpose is to examine the validity of the new theory in *real* settings. The second type of application is that which is conducted by practitioners who (more or less) assume that the theory being adopted holds some probable value for them in dealing with actual organizational problems.

The first type of application is a necessary step in the appropriate refinement and ultimate confirmation of a theory of motivation. Scientists simply cannot determine whether a theory represents reality without comparing it to samples of that reality (Garner, 1972)! As we will see in later chapters, some theories (such as Equity Theory) have shown promising levels of accuracy when tested in contrived artificial settings, but have failed to hold up to the scrutiny provided by testing in the field. On the other hand, Goal Setting Theory (see chapter eight) has benefitted considerably by research conducted to examine it in real settings (Latham and Yukl, 1975). In short, application of the first type is advisable and necessary in the development of new theoretic ideas.

But when is application of the second type warranted? In other words, when is it safe and reasonable for a new theoretic idea to be distilled into formalized, commercial packages and programs for use by *practitioners* in their respective organizations? Too frequently it has been the case that new, applied motivation-oriented programs, based on behavioral science, have been widely disseminated among practitioners with unrealistic expectations for what they could accomplish (Pinder, 1977; Walter and Pinder, 1980).

Two important examples are job enrichment and Management-By-Objectives (MBO) programs. As we will see in later chapters, MBO (which has its theoretic underpinnings in the very successful **31**

Goal Setting Theory mentioned above) has failed in most organizations in which it has been installed. Years after so many failures, more complete understanding of the organizational circumstances necessary for it to succeed became understood (Jamieson, 1973). Similarly, only after several years of experienced difficulties with formal job enrichment programs has it been learned what organizational preconditions are necessary for these programs to succeed (cf. Oldham and Hackman, 1980; Yorks, 1979). The point here is not that motivation theories have no applied utility, nor is it that they should not be implemented in real organizational settings. Rather, the point is that too often the urgency of applied managerial problems (such as employee motivation) has occasioned the premature widespread commercial application of new behavioral science technology in situations where it has not been appropriate, and, consequently, where it has failed. Why does this happen?

Managers tend to be practical people who seek practical tools to deal with urgent organizational problems. They tend to process information very quickly, looking for the essential elements of the problems they face, as well as of the solutions they consider in their decision making (Mintzberg, 1973). Often, however, managers' preferences for practicality translate into demands for simplicity—managers often seek and expect relatively simple solutions to problems that they, themselves, openly recognize as complex. They often prefer nuts and bolts solutions, stripped of most cautions, caveats, and reservations that might appropriately accompany the advice they seek from others. In response, people with managerial programs (such as motivation-oriented techniques) frequently cater to the managerial preference for simplicity by offering or advocating scientifically based procedures stripped of all the "ifs, ands, and buts" that are justified by the research findings which underly those procedures. In short, complex phenomena such as human work motivation are often oversimplified so as to make them palatable to practical people. Techniques that require unrealistic and oversimplifying assumptions are doomed to be ineffective when installed in complex, real settings.

Costs of premature application.   Repeated instances of failure of hastily applied behavioral science are costly and unfortunate. Changes implemented on the basis of such techniques can have a profound influence on both the job satisfaction and life satisfaction of people in organizations—usually the lower participants whose jobs are changed in accordance with the theory being applied. Organizational change is necessary for effectiveness and survival, but changes that are ill-advised and inappropriate are disruptive and unfair to those affected (e.g., Pringle and Longenecker, 1982).

32

But premature and ill-advised applications are costly in other ways as well (Pinder, 1977, 1982; Walter and Pinder, 1980). Organizations that adopt programs such as MBO, job enrichment, or flextime (to cite three examples) must invest considerable amounts of money and managerial effort in the installation and operation of these programs. When the programs fail, management groups are justified in investigating the soundness of the advice in which they have invested. In cases where it becomes clear that the technique in question was really not appropriate, disappointment and/or hostility *toward behavioral science and behavioral scientists* is understandable.

To illustrate, Nord and Durand (1975) provide a case example of a medium-sized manufacturing company that attempted to install a set of behavioral science programs, all aimed at increasing motivation and performance through a participatory managerial style. The changes actually brought about were far below those expected, in large part because the programs installed were not appropriate for the organization involved. The disappointment and frustration that resulted for the managers in the firm were understandable, and would doubtlessly influence their willingness to adopt other innovations that have their roots in behavioral science. Alienation of this sort is unfortunate in view of the absolute necessity for science to interact with practice (Garner, 1972) and because of the fact that behavioral science *can* help the practitioner (Dunnette and Bass, 1963; Pinder, 1982).

If managers and behavioral scientists are mutually dependent upon one another in the ways described above, how can a progressive management group decide in favor of formal attempts to install behavioral science based programs and engage in application of the second type described above? One obvious basis for deciding that a theory is ready and safe for application is the level of scientific validity the theory has demonstrated in research-oriented applications of the first type described above. On the other hand, there may be a case against reliance on validity alone, as we shall see in the following section.

Application: Validity or Utility?

In response to a paper written by this author (Pinder, 1977), Bobko (1978) has suggested that the absolute level of validity of a theory of motivation is an inappropriate basis for determining whether formal application of that theory is warranted or justified. He argues that managers must make decisions on a day-to-day basis, using implicit theories of human nature and motivation to guide them (see chapter three of this volume). The decisions reached on the basis of these **33** implicit, informal theories result in more or less value (or *utility*) for their respective organizations. Bobko (1978) argues that whether a manager should employ a formal theory or motivation to guide his human resource related decisions should depend upon the *marginal utility* (or extra value) added by the application of the theory. (Cronbach and Gleser, 1965, make the same argument with regard to the use of psychological tests for the selection of personnel into organizations.)

Bobko's argument is compelling, but, as argued elsewhere, the application of his *marginal utility* criterion for determining whether or not to apply a formal theory of motivation is impractical (Pinder, 1978). In order to follow Bobko's advice, a manager would be required to estimate the *base rate* of effective motivation-related decisions (or influence attempts) between himself and each of his employees prior to the application of a particular theory. He would then have to estimate the value of decisions (or influence attempts) that are made with the assistance of the particular theory in question, and determine whether the value added as a consequence of the advice provided by the theory is sufficient to justify its use. This would be quite impractical, if not impossible, in view of the many difficulties associated with assessing individual job performance (Cummings and Schwab, 1973; Latham and Wexley, 1981) and the fact that a particular supervisor's *success* would vary from one subordinate to another, as well as across time and across circumstances for all employees. Moreover, in view of the complexity of organizational events, it would be very difficult to rule out explanations other than the application of theoretical principles if changes in decision making effectiveness did seem to occur. In balance, utility may be a reasonable criterion, in principle, for deciding when a theory is ready for application, but the practical difficulties it poses make it hard to employ. The enlightened manager is left, therefore, with the validity of a new theory as the only basis for deciding on its formal adoption in practice.

Validity of Theories of Work Motivation

How valid are the currently popular theories of work motivation? In other words, to what extent do they accurately reflect the part of reality they purport to reflect?

Recent reviews by Locke (1975), Campbell and Pritchard (1976), Staw (1977), and this author (Pinder, 1977, 1982) suggest that we have somewhat limited grounds for optimism at present. As subsequent chapters in this book will show, however, the degree of validity of a number of the most popular current theories has yet to be determined because of limitations in the research efforts that have been made to examine their validity. As indicated earlier in this chapter, even the often criticized Motivator-Hygiene Theory still has a following of believers who argue that the theory has been unjustly and prematurely discarded (Grigaliunas and Weiner, 1974). When we focus on other major work motivation theories in later chapters, we will see that many of the studies that have attempted to estimate the validity of these theories have themselves suffered from limitations in research design similar, in many cases, to those discussed earlier. Consequently, in spite of a tremendous increase in the amount of research activity into work motivation in recent years, *it is hard to estimate the actual validity of many of the theories that are available.* When one considers the myriad practical, measurement, statistical, and research design difficulties that must be overcome to conduct a fair test of the validity of any work motivation theory, it may be that many of the current theories are, in fact, better representations of reality (i.e., they may be more valid) than mortal researchers are capable of demonstrating (Pinder, 1977). *In other words, the coefficients that scientific efforts have produced to reflect the validity of many of our theories may be gross underestimates of the actual validity of many theories of motivation!*

Finally, most of our current theories of work motivation are multifaceted: most of them make several assertions concerning the nature of work effort, job performance, and/or employee attitudes. It is often the case that research evidence supports some facets of a particular theory, but fails to find sufficient evidence for other aspects. Herzberg's two-factor theory provides an excellent example. The bulk of the evidence indicates that the asymmetrical two-factor feature of the Motivator-Hygiene Theory is not valid, the defense of Grigaliunas and Weiner (1974) notwithstanding. But does that mean that we should ignore the theory altogether? Of course not! There seems to be substantial evidence that Herzberg's ideas concerning the design of jobs (building in plenty of responsibility, achievement potential, and chances for recognition) have considerable validity and applied utility (Ford, 1973; Paul, Robertson, and Herzberg, 1969). As was mentioned earlier, it is not necessary to assume that Herzberg's motivators cannot be dissatisfying, or that his hygiene factors cannot be sources of satisfaction in order to profitably follow the prescriptions the theory makes for designing and/or assigning people to jobs.

In short, it may be that the tools and techniques of behavioral science are simply too crude at present to permit either the unequivocal development of valid work motivation theories or the fair testing of such theories once they have been developed. **35**

SUMMARY AND A LOOK AHEAD

It has been argued in this chapter that our knowledge of work motivation consists largely of theory, and that much or most of that theory is of either limited or unknown validity. Moreover, it has been argued that there are risks to the premature application of work motivation theory—risks that can result in costs for the organizations that engage in such premature application, as well as for the future prospect for organizational scientists to contribute to the economic well-being of our economy. In short, work motivation is an important issue, about which our current knowledge is still limited. But that knowledge base is growing, and the purpose of this book is to examine and evaluate it.

In the next chapter, we will explore a variety of basic assumptions that underpin current approaches to work motivation and behavior, and begin a presentation of the most important current theories available today.

HUMAN NATURE AND NEEDS 3

It is a characteristic of man that the more he becomes involved in complexity, the more he longs for simplicity; the simpler his life becomes, the more he longs for complexity; the busier he becomes, the stronger is his desire for leisure; the more leisure he has, the more boredom he feels; the more his concerns, the more he feels the allure of unconcern; the more his unconcern, the more he suffers from vacuousness; the more tumultuous his life, the more he seeks quietude; the more placid his life, the lonelier he becomes and the more he quests for liveliness.
—*Hisamatsu, Shin'Ichi "The Zen Understanding of Man"*
The Eastern Buddhist (new series), Vol. 1, No. 1, 1965.

To some extent, almost all of us harbor beliefs about the nature of human beings, about "what makes people tick." To some extent, we all tend to be amateur philosophers and "naive psychologists" (Heider, 1958). In fact, the pursuit and discovery of the basic "essence of man" has occupied thinkers since the days of early philosophy (cf. Fromm and Xirau, 1968; Mitchell, 1972), and continues even today. For example, the current *sociobiology debate* (Gregory, Silvers, and Sutch, 1978) can be seen as one of the most recent efforts to understand the true nature of human beings.

It should come as no surprise that philosophers and psychologists have failed to reach unanimity on the issue of human nature. On the other hand, an analysis of many of the attempts that have been made to grapple with the problem reveals that there has been some convergence concerning a number of essential attributes of human **37** beings (where essential attributes are seen as elements common to all humans, but that do not, by themselves, comprise the *essence* of humanity, per se). The most common of these attributes is rationality—humans are commonly thought of as more or less rational beings. Secondly, there is wide agreement that we are gregarious creatures—we tend, more or less, to exist in the presence of others.

A third essential attribute of human beings is that we tend to be producers. Although many lower animals are also producers, only human beings produce according to plans developed in their own minds, and only humans are effective producers of tools, which in turn are used for further production. A final commonly agreed upon attribute is that human beings are symbol-making creatures. We generate, acknowledge, and make use of countless symbols, the most important of which are words (Fromm and Xirau, 1968).

The point is that people tend to assess other individuals and behave in their presence according to beliefs they have about their essential characteristics, whether or not the specific set of beliefs they hold matches the set identified above. Nowhere is this more the case than in work and organizational settings (Knowles and Saxberg, 1967; McGregor, 1960; Tead, 1929; Urwick, 1967). To quote McGregor (1960, p. 33): "Behind every managerial decision or action are assumptions about human nature and human behavior."

The purpose of this chapter is to examine a number of widely held sets of assumptions about human begins—assumptions that are particularly relevant when we consider work motivation and how it might be influenced. As theories of motivation and techniques based upon them are presented in later chapters of this book, the reader should bear in mind that each of them is predicated upon certain sets of assumptions regarding human nature. Often, the nature of these assumptions is not explicitly recognized by those who advance theories of work motivation, or who develop managerial techniques based on their theories. The careful consumers of behavioral theories and techniques will allow themselves to be influenced by them only to the extent that the assumptions they make seem appropriate.

THEORY X AND THEORY Y

One of the most insightful observations ever made by behavioral science concerning work is that of Douglas McGregor (1957, 1960), who was acutely aware of the pervasiveness of a set of assumptions concerning human beings at work—assumptions held by managers and administrators in particular. He referred to this set of assumptions as *Theory X,* the key elements of which are the following:

38

1. The average human adult is *by nature* (italics added) indolent—he works as little as possible.
2. He lacks ambition, dislikes responsibility, and prefers to be led by other people.
3. He is inherently selfish and indifferent to organizational needs and goals.
4. He is resistant to change, by his very nature.
5. Finally, he is gullible, not very intelligent, and is easily duped by manipulators.

The importance of this implicit theory of human nature, McGregor claimed, is that it lies behind much of what we observe in the practice of management. If managers believe that human nature is inherently as described by Theory X, they will formulate policies and utilize motivational and control strategies designed to tame the human brute and coerce work effort from him. The direct result of policies, practices, and procedures of this sort is that they often *cause* the very behaviors that reinforce managers' beliefs that people are, in fact, like the Theory X model—a self-fulfilling prophecy of the sort diagrammed in Figure 3-1.

FIGURE 3-1: The Self-Fulfilling Prophesy of Theory X Assumptions.

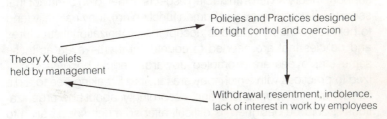

Policies and Practices designed for tight control and coercion

Theory X beliefs held by management

Withdrawal, resentment, indolence, lack of interest in work by employees

Managers caught in this cycle believe that the problem lies in the basic nature of human beings. McGregor recognized that low interest, resentment, embezzling, sabotage, tardiness, and absenteeism are, in fact, commonly observed in organizations. The wisdom in his analysis lies in his recognition that these behaviors are frequently caused by managerial practices which, in turn, are based on Theory X beliefs about human nature: a case of chicken and egg, with powerful implications for the design of motivation and reward systems. In practice, who can blame any particular manager for holding views of the Theory X variety—he regularly observes the sorts of behaviors that reinforce those beliefs, and, after all, the policies that give birth to Theory X behavior are usually designed and enforced by senior management, or by some committee.

An alternative view of human nature in work organizations is proposed by McGregor. He calls it, simply, *Theory* Y. The main tenets of Theory Y are:

1. People are *not* passive by nature. They have become so as a consequence of the way they are usually treated in organizations.
2. People possess, by nature, the potential to develop, assume responsibility, and behave in accordance with organizational goals. Management's re-

39

sponsibility is to recognize these potentials, and to make it possible for employees to develop them, themselves.

3. To do this, management should structure organizational policies so that human beings can achieve their own goals, while in the act of pursuing the goals of the organization.

When McGregor first forwarded his observations a quarter of a century ago, he noted how difficult it would be to see Theory X supplanted by Theory Y as the basic model of human nature underlying organizational policies and procedures. The reason is that belief systems are very hard to change, especially when the person holding a set of beliefs (such as those of Theory X) constantly observes behaviors that reinforce them.

McGregor's pessimism seemed well-founded at the time. If he were alive today, one wonders whether he would be any more optimistic: we still see an abundance of time clocks, highly differentiated and boring jobs, close supervisory practices, and "carrot-and-stick" reward systems. Clearly, as employees enter the lower ranks of organizational hierarchies, and observe behaviors around them that support Theory X views (including aspects of their own behavior that seem to reflect this model of human functioning), they naturally tend to believe in Theory X, and to accept the organizational structures and policies that are needed to counteract them—even as these same employees are promoted upward. People become socialized to practices with which they are familiar. Breaking free to a different view of human nature, and, accordingly, about how organizations should be designed, is difficult after so much socialization to Theory X beliefs and methods. So the negative view of human nature continues to characterize managerial behavior and organizational policy.

A TYPOLOGY OF HUMAN FUNCTIONING

More recently, Walter and Marks (1981) have developed a theory of how human beings change and develop. As they note, if you wish to understand something, try changing it! (Or, in order to gain an understanding of human beings, try changing them.) Drawing from the works of Maddi (1976), Levy (1970), and others, they have compiled a typology (or classificatory scheme) that summarizes the models of human nature that have been developed and studied by more than sixty behavioral and social scientists. Their typology is especially useful as a means of setting the stage for a presentation of the most popular theories of work motivation (later in this book), because the assumptions about human nature underlying most of these theories correspond with various categories in Walter and

Marks' typology. Let's look briefly at the major categories Walter and Marks (1981) have identified, emphasizing the ones most frequently found behind current theories of work motivation.

First, there are the *fulfillment models* (Maddi, 1976, 1980). Representing these views are the theories of Rogers (1959) and Maslow (1943, 1954). These theories share the notion of human beings as unfolding—as developing their innate potentialities. They see people as experiencing pressure ". . . that leads to the direction of their becoming whatever it is in their inherited nature to be" (Maddi 1980, p. 90). Different people hold different *types* of potential, based on their unique sets of abilities, interests, and genetic characteristics. In the case of Maslow (1955, 1962), fulfillment motivation is less urgent in the short run as a motivating force behind behavior than are the forces that are directed at assuring the continued existence of the person—first survival, then fulfillment. More will be said about Maslow's theory of motivation later in this chapter.

Consistency models of human nature (Maddi, 1980; Walter and Marks, 1981) emphasize

> . . . that there is a particular kind of information or emotional experience that is best for persons, and hence, that they will develop personalities which increase the likelihood of interaction with the world such as to get this kind of information or emotional experience (Maddi, 1980, p. 156).

The critical aspect of this set of models is that human nature is the result of interactions of the people with their environments, rather than the result of inherited attributes of the people themselves (a position similar to that of the philosopher John Locke). These theories are more concerned with consistency among the acts, beliefs, and predispositions that reflect human nature than with understanding the precise nature of the content of those acts, beliefs, and predispositions. They see people as driven to be consistent and to seek circumstances that are compatible with their previous experiences. Korman's (1970, 1976) theory of work motivation (which will be discussed briefly in chapter twelve) is predicated largely on this model of human nature.

The *cognitive/perceptual* models (Levy, 1970; Walter and Marks, 1981) see human beings as information processing systems. On this view, human behavior results from the *interpretation* of events in the environment, rather than from the strict, objective nature of those events, per se. This model does not deny the existence of an external reality, but views human action as caused by the way that reality is perceived and understood by people. Work motivation theories predicated on this assumption of human nature will be presented in chapters five through eight of this book.

The *learning* models of human functioning are composed pri-   **41** marily of the various brands of behaviorism that were first promulgated in the 1940s (cf. Hull 1943), and that have since evolved in the work of Skinner (1953, 1969, 1971). This view avoids recourse to internal states and processes such as those used in the cognitive/perceptual models (such as beliefs and expectations). Rather, they tend to see behavior as determined solely by the consequences in which it results. Thorndike's (1911) *Law of Effect* underlies this perspective. In short, it states that people will be more likely to do those things which their experience has shown them to be rewarding; they will be less likely to do those things which they have found aversive. Behavior is a function of its consequences. Period. The application of this model in the form of motivation-oriented programs in organizations will be presented in chapters nine and ten.

The *contextual* models of human nature (Levy, 1970; Walter and Marks, 1981) focus primarily on the social/gregarious aspects of individuals. There are no current theories of work motivation that derive exclusively from this perspective, as such. However, many of the theories to be treated in this book include social needs and/or social comparison processes as part of more general need-oriented perspectives to work motivation. Finally, while it has not yet been articulated into a theory of work motivation, per se, the *Social Information Processing Approach* to job attitudes recently developed by Salancik and Pfeffer (1978) is entirely consistent with the contextual models of human nature described by Levy (1970), and Walter and Marks (1981), although it also places heavy reliance on the cognitive/perceptual assumptions described above.

Walter and Marks' typology of models of human nature includes two other categories of theory—the so-called *conflict* and *life sciences* models. The former views share an orientation toward intrapsychic and social conflict, in which life is seen as a compromise and balancing process. The latter approaches—the life science models—are biological in nature, drawing most heavily on ethology, sociobiology, and neuroscience. Whereas these three disciplines are active in their own right, they have yet to enter any formal theories of work motivation. Likewise, the author is not aware of any theories of work motivation that have their philosophical roots in the conflict models of human functioning.

Recapitulation

In short, five of the seven major categories in Walter and Marks' (1981) typology of models of human nature lie behind the many theories of work motivation that have appeared during the past half century. Three of these—the fulfillment model, the cognitive/perceptual model, and the learning model—are the three most important.

Whereas evidence will be presented throughout this book concerning the validity of the various motivation theories discussed, it will not be possible to conclude which of the five sets of assumptions concerning human nature is "correct," or most valid. For, as Walter and Marks (1981, p. 57) conclude: "Each of the models of human functioning has [its own] implications . . . when used in combination their explanatory power is increased—the whole is greater than the sum of its parts."

In later sections of this chapter, we will examine two major work motivation theories that rest primarily upon the fulfillment model of human functioning. Before we do, however, more detail is required about the basic view that humans are wanting, self-fulfilling creatures, and, in particular, we need to gain an understanding of the exact nature of human needs. Accordingly, let's take a closer look at the fundamental elements underlying this perspective.

"MAN IS A WANTING ANIMAL. . . ."

The model of human nature implied by this statement (Maslow, 1954, p. 24) is one that has underpinned a great deal of the scientific work by psychologists into the nature of human motivation. It reflects a set of assumptions that we humans, whatever else we might be, are always in *need* of something. This raises a question concerning the nature of the *energetic force* (see chapter one) that actually constitutes motivation—what *is* it?

Over the years, psychologists have studied a number of concepts that have represented the essential energetic force which constitutes human motivation. Among the earliest of these concepts was instinct—it was thought that people, like most animals, are born with certain behavioral capacities inherent in their very constitution. McDougall (1923) defined an instinct as:

> . . . an innate disposition which determines the organism to perceive (or pay attention to) any object of a certain class, and to experience in its presence a certain emotional excitement and an impulse to action which find expression in a specific mode of behavior in relation to that object (p. 110).

Instincts were invoked to explain acts of all varieties. But, by explaining everything, as it were, the concept really does not explain anything. Before long, there were lengthy lists of instincts attributed to human nature. They were cumbersome, ascientific, and somewhat ludicrous. For example, an early book by Tead (1918) discussed the role of ten instincts (such as parental, sex, workmanship, and pugnacity) in employee behavior in industry.

After the publication of the book *Dynamic Psychology* (Woodworth, 1918), the notion of instinct gave way to the concept of **43** *drive* as the root explanation for why people do things. According to drive theorists, people have primary and secondary drives. *Primary drives* arise from deficiencies of substances necessary for survival, or from excesses in substances that are harmful to survival. For example, Hull (1943) listed the following primary drives: hunger, thirst, air, temperature regulation, defecation, urination, rest, sleep, activity, sexual intercourse, nest building, care of the young, and avoidance of, or relief from, pain. *Secondary drives* are seen as being learned, through association with primary drives. For instance, fear is associated with the pain of bodily injury, and itself comes to be learned as a source of energy that can arouse behavior.

A detailed treatment of the historical and scientific development of instinct theory and drive theory is beyond the scope of this book. The interested reader is referred to Atkinson (1964), and Cofer and Appley (1964). Instead, our focus in this chapter is on the meaning and nature of human *needs,* since needs have been the most commonly invoked concept in theories of work behavior.

What are Needs?

Again, a problem of definition, and again, the reader is referred to Atkinson (1964), or Cofer and Appley (1964) to gain an appreciation of the multitude of uses and interpretations the concept of need has assumed over the years. For the purposes of this book, however, Henry Murray's (1938, pp. 123–124) definition will be adopted, because it is most compatible with the need-oriented theories that have been developed to explain work motivation. For Murray, a need is:

> . . . a construct (a convenient fiction or hypothetical concept) which stands for a force . . . in the brain region, a force which organizes perception, aperception, intellection, conation and action in such a way as to transform in a certain direction an existing unsatisfying situation. A need is sometimes provoked directly by internal processes of a certain kind . . . but, more frequently (when in a state of readiness) by the occurrence of one of a few commonly effective press (or features of the environment). . . . Thus, it manifests itself by leading the organism to search for or to avoid encountering, or when encountered, to attend to and respond to certain kinds of press. . . . Each need is characteristically accompanied by a particular feeling or emotion and tends to use certain modes . . . to further its trend. It may be weak or intense, momentary or enduring. But usually it persists and gives rise to a certain course of overt behavior (or fantasy) which . . . changes the initiating circumstance in such a way as to bring about an end situation which stills (appeases or satisfies) the organism (1938, pp. 123–124).

There are a number of elements of this definition that deserve highlighting. First, notice that a need, like the concepts of instinct, drive, personality, interest, or ambition, is a hypothetical entity (recall chapter one). We cannot assess it directly or determine its color. It **44** has no physical mass, density, or specific gravity. We must infer its existence by indirect means, such as observing the behavior of the person who is said to have a particular need.

Second, notice the use of the force metaphor, making it consistent with the definition of work motivation given in the previous chapter. The *organizing* function of needs is something with which most of us are familiar—it underlies the concepts of perceptual vigilance and perceptual defense in psychology (see Zalkind and Costello, 1962). Thus, for example, an employee's need state may make him more likely to notice a job opportunity at another organization—an opening that may have existed long before the employee reached the particular need state he was in when he read the advertisement. The emergence of a need makes the individual more likely to notice things that may satisfy it.

Third, notice the possibility for needs to be induced by characteristics of the environment. In much the same way as seeing an attractive member of the opposite sex may arouse one's sexual needs, for example, being promoted into a job with supervisory responsibilities can arouse an erstwhile dormant need for power in an upwardly-mobile employee.

Fourthly, Murray's definition of need also helps us understand approach behaviors as well as avoidance behaviors. An example from the work setting would be the preferences employees develop for particular types of jobs, and the aversion they have to other types of jobs.

One very important feature of the definition is that *needs are seen as either strong or weak, and as either momentary or enduring*. Thus, some employees are constantly gregarious and seeking social interaction on the job, while for others, working in groups may be less important. People differ among themselves, and the same person can experience increases and decreases in the strength of various needs. For example, consider the avoidance of further fatigue that motivates certain employee behaviors toward the end of a tedious day in an office setting.

Finally, the definition states that needs give rise to behavior (or fantasy) aimed at reducing the force behind the needs. A number of points need elaboration here. First, not all need-driven, goal-oriented behavior is successful in reaching whatever goals are sought. The result is defined as frustration, a topic discussed later in the next chapter. Notice the possible role fantasy can play, especially when behavior itself is not feasible. At one time or another, most people fantasize about what they would do with the windfall that comes from winning a lottery. Likewise, many frustrated workers fantasize about the regimes they would administer if, magically, they were promoted to powerful managerial positions.

Throughout the rest of this book, the term *need* will imply all that **45** is involved in Murray's definition. A solid grasp of that definition, and the implications that arise from it, will be essential to understanding the rest of the material to be presented, particularly in the remainder of this chapter and in chapters four, eleven, and twelve.

The Relationship Between Needs and Behavior

Consider the difficulty involved in making inferences about the need(s) that determine an individual's behavior. First, most behavior is said to be *overdetermined,* meaning that most behavior, either deliberately or inadvertently, is driven by the force to satisfy more than one need (Maslow, 1954). For example, an employee may seek a promotion for the sake of meeting several of his needs (although he may be more conscious of the importance of some of them as he seeks to be promoted). Second, the same particular need may be satisfied by any of a variety of acts. So our upwardly aspiring employee may be seeking, in part, greater satisfaction of his esteem needs. Notice that gaining a promotion would be one way, but only one way, to have his esteem needs met. Volunteer service after hours or becoming president of his union are alternative behaviors he might employ. In short, there is no one-to-one relationship between the force of particular needs and the type of behavior one will observe.

To complicate matters, there is a common tendency for people to *project* their own need-behavior styles into their interpretations of the behavior of others (Zalkind and Costello, 1962). So, for example, in attempting to infer why their subordinates frequently exaggerate the stress levels of their jobs, supervisors are apt to come to reasonably sound understandings of why they, themselves, would make such exaggerations.

The importance of all this lies in the difficulties and risks it implies for the application of need theories to understand employee behavior. Remember, we cannot observe needs directly, so we must make inferences about their role in behavior by observing that behavior. But the lack of one-to-one correspondence between needs and behavior, and the natural tendency to impute our own behavior-motivation styles onto others, makes the inference process very hard (cf. Bandura, 1977). Yet, managers do it all the time, especially those who consciously attempt to *motivate* their employees.

Need Satisfaction

Most people tend to view need satisfaction as the state a person feels after the tension associated with a need has been removed (such as the pleasurable feeling of a full stomach, for example). In the case of **46** certain needs, however, satisfaction may consist more of the experience one has while in the process of *reducing* the tension (Murray and Kluckhohn, 1953). Using the example of eating again, this principle would suggest that satisfaction consists more of the joy of eating than of the joy of having eaten. Moreover, greater satisfaction seems to occur when more tension is reduced, implying that people may be motivated to deprive themselves of gratification (within safe limits) so as to be able to subsequently experience greater satisfaction from the process of need fulfillment. Sexual foreplay illustrates this principle, as does the notion of skipping lunch to assure that one has a sharp appetite before a special dinner meal.

In work settings, this principle would imply that employee satisfaction results from the process of interacting with one's peers, for example, rather than from having done so. As we will see in chapter five, job satisfaction has typically been equated with the satisfaction of one's needs on the job, particularly with the experience of *having met* one's needs. It may be that researchers have overlooked the importance of the fulfillment process, per se, in their understanding of job satisfaction.

Now that we have examined the general concept of need, and have a brief understanding of the emergence of that concept in the recent history of psychology, we turn our attention to a discussion of some of the most important theories of work motivation—theories that have invoked needs as the concept representing the force behind employee behavior. In the terms of Campbell, Dunnette, Lawler, and Weick (1970), we will be dealing with the question of *what* determines work motivation—a question of content (hence these theories are labelled *content* theories). In later chapters we will deal with *how* and *why* motivation occurs when we look at a number of so-called *process* theories (see chapters six through ten, in particular).

Maslow's Hierarchical Theory of Needs

The hierarchical theory of human motivation developed by Abraham Maslow (1943, 1954, 1968) is the most paradoxical of all the current approaches to work motivation. On the one hand, it is by far the most familiar theory among academics and practitioners. On the other hand, it is also probably the most misunderstood, and the most frequently oversimplified and misrepresented. Further, in spite of its widespread popularity, it is a theory which, to date, enjoys very little scientific support.

Rudiments of the theory. Maslow's theory holds that there are basically five categories of human needs, and that these needs account for much or most of human behavior—but not all of it. The needs vary in their relative *prepotency,* or urgency for the survival of **47**

the individual, arranging themselves in a sort of hierarchical order. As the most prepotent needs become reasonably satisfied, the less prepotent ones (referred to as the *higher order* needs) become increasingly more important for causing behavior.

The most prepotent category of needs in the theory are physiological in nature. They function in a homeostatic fashion, such that imbalances or deficiencies in certain physiological substances instigate behavior aimed at restoring the balance by filling the deficiencies. Hunger, sex, and thirst are three examples. The physiological needs correspond closely to the so-called primary drives in the drive theories mentioned earlier. When an individual lacks satisfaction of his physiological needs, according to Maslow, he is obsessed with acquiring those things that are necessary to satisfy them and restore equilibrium. In short, deficiency causes domination of the person's behavior, and no other need set is more dominating of behavior when it is unfulfilled than are the physiological needs. According to Maslow (1954, p. 39):

> If the physiological needs are relatively-well gratified, there then emerges a new set of needs, which we may categorize roughly as the safety needs (security; stability; dependency; protection; freedom from fear, from anxiety and chaos; need for structure, order, law, limits; strength in the protector, and so on).

Next to the physiological needs, these safety needs are the most prepotent determinants of behavior. When unfulfilled, they possess the same sort of potential for dominating a person's behavior as the physiological needs do when they are not being met.

A problem of interpretation. It is worth stopping at this point to consider one of the ways that Maslow's hierarchical theory has been oversimplified and misrepresented. The theory is often interpreted as if all of the force motivating a person's behavior at a given time originates in one and only one need state, and that this total domination continues until satisfaction is experienced, at which time that need state somehow *shuts off*, or goes away, while the next set of needs immediately *clicks on* to take its place. (This discrete, shutting off/clicking on image is fostered by the staircase-like pictures that are often used in management textbooks to represent the hierarchy.)

Instead, Maslow saw most behavior as multimotivated or *overdetermined* (1954, p. 55)—any particular behavior will tend to be the consequence of the simultaneous functioning of more than one need, perhaps several. It is a matter of *relative* deprivation or satisfaction (as stated in the passage quoted above), and *relative* influence of the various needs in determining behavior. Clearly, when a person faces an emergency such as extreme hunger, desperate thirst, or an onrushing assailant, one need set does dominate until gratification occurs. But once gratification is achieved, that need does not disappear as a factor in behavior. It does, however, account for less of the total force working on the individual, because other needs then take on relatively more importance than before. Maslow wrote (1954, pp. 53–54):

> In actual fact, most members of our society . . . are partially satisfied in all their basic needs and partially unsatisfied . . . at the same time. A . . . realistic description of the hierarchy would be in terms of decreasing percentages of satisfaction as we go up the hierarchy of prepotency. . . .
>
> As for the concept of emergence of a new need after satisfaction of the prepotent need, this emergence is not a sudden, salutory phenomenon, but rather a gradual emergence by slow degrees from nothingness.

The author has chosen to quote Maslow directly to emphasize the point: Maslow never intended to portray the emergence of new need states in the crisp, all or nothing, lockstep fashion implied by so many of his interpretors. Human behavior is clearly not that simple, and Maslow never portrayed it as such.

Now, let's return to the hierarchy.

Love, esteem, and self-actualization. The next most prepotent set of human needs, according to Maslow, are the love needs. They take on comparatively more influence in behavior as the physiological and safety needs are reasonably gratified. The individual desires relations with other people, and he will feel more compelled than before to achieve such relations. Feelings of loneliness, ostracism, rejection, and friendlessness will be experienced much more than before. Maslow (1954, p. 44) claims that the thwarting of the love needs ". . . is the most commonly found core in cases of maladjustment." A person who suffers frustration of these needs becomes ill, although the illness is mental rather than physical. It is important to note that the theory claims that people need both to give and receive love, and that social interactions need not be cordial to satisfy these needs.

The *esteem* needs are the next most prepotent category in Maslow's hierarchy. He groups them into two sets. One set includes desires for strength, achievement, adequacy, mastery and competence, independence, freedom, and a fundamental confidence in facing the world. Gratification of these needs for self-esteem leads to feelings of self-confidence, capability, and worth, whereas frustration of them results in neurotic feelings of weakness, inferiority, and even helplessness.

The second subset of esteem needs refers to needs for prestige and reputation—the esteem of others. It motivates people to seek recognition, praise, dominance, glory, and the attention of other **49** people. When people fail to achieve these outcomes in sufficient quantity, they suffer the same sort of feelings as result when the need for self-esteem is thwarted.

The esteem needs are seen as less prepotent than the highest set of needs on the hierarchy—the so-called need for self-actualization. Maslow himself seems to give differing interpretations of the meaning of this need (cf. Maslow, 1943, 1954 with Maslow, 1968), but the clearest and most widely accepted view is that it consists of a requirement for individuals to fulfill their potentialities, to become that which they are capable of becoming. Hence, amateur athletes who are already well established economically, and who have many friends, and all the prestige that being world champions have earned for them, will still be motivated to continue to improve their performance. Why? Because they feel that they are still capable of running faster or jumping higher than they have in the past. The force behind this urge to become even more of what they are capable of becoming, is referred to as the need to self-actualize. (Note that some of the lower needs could help explain the athletes' continued striving for further excellence, such as a fear of losing their championship status, the esteem of their admirers, or their contracts for the commercial endorsement of athletic equipment. Remember that most behavior is multiply determined.) At the time of this writing, the U.S. Army is employing a recruitment campaign that includes a catchy jingle: ''Be all that you can be—in the Army,'' an appeal to the self-development and actualizing needs of prospective soldiers.

An important feature of self-actualization needs is that they express themselves in different behaviors in different people. So, for example, one person may seek fulfillment through the refinement of his musical skills, while another may seek to develop his talents as a father. Moreover, the satisfaction of self-actualization needs tends to *increase* their importance rather than reduce it (Maslow, 1962). They become somewhat addictive. This is an important difference between self-actualization and the other needs in the hierarchy, all of which are seen as losing their capacity to motivate behavior once they are relatively fulfilled.

Fine points of the theory. These are the primary elements of Maslow's theory. Now let's look at some of the less frequently recognized features of the theory, features that, when dropped, lead to many of the misrepresentations mentioned earlier.

First, Maslow recognized that there are many differences among people in the relative prepotency of their needs (although the order described above is held as the most common). He referred to variations from the basic ordering as *reversals,* and he acknowledged several common varieties. For instance, many people seem to place self-esteem ahead of love, seeking respect rather than affection from others. As another example, some people are innately creative, and seem to pursue self-actualization in spite of (rather than because of) the fact that their lower level needs are not met (as in the starving artist syndrome). Still other individuals, who have been deprived of social interaction for extended periods of time, seem to lose the capacity to respond to the affection of others. Maslow notes other reversals (1954, pp. 51–52), but the point is that the basic hierarchy was never intended to be totally universal and invariant.

Another important point in the theory is that not all behavior is seen as resulting from the force provided by the basic needs. Much of human behavior can be determined by forces outside an individual (recall Murray's notion of environmental press, discussed earlier). In addition, some behavior is obsessive-compulsive, and some behavior is simply *expressive* of an individual's personality (for instance, the random movements of a child, or smiles made by a happy person when he is alone).

A third fine point of the theory is that the needs are seen as neither necessarily conscious or unconscious, but that, on the whole, most people are not consciously aware of their needs at the time they behave. This point will be important in subsequent chapters of this book, where we will discuss the issues of designing jobs and reward systems to match employee needs.

The key point here is that Maslow's theory, as seemingly well-known as it is, is much more complex and much less mechanistic than is implied in many management and human relations textbooks. The importance of acknowledging the details lies in the implications they have for both understanding human behavior and for attempts to influence it. For example, supervisors who assume that their subordinates are constantly conscious of their needs, and are therefore under total control of their acts, will likely attribute far too much blame and/or credit for these acts. (See Mitchell, Green, and Wood, 1981, for a formal theory of the means by which supervisors attribute credit and blame to their personnel.) Likewise, reward and punishment systems which implicitly assume that employees are motivated by single needs, one at a time ("George is into security needs"), will be misguided and quite ineffective. Finally, automatically assuming that everyone seeks to satisfy their needs according to the same strict order will foster the development of managerial policies that will frustrate as many employees as they satisfy.

How valid is the theory?   It was stated earlier that Maslow's theory is paradoxical—most people in organizations think they know about it, while many tend to oversimplify it. An additional aspect of the paradox centers on the fact that, until quite recently, there has **51**

been very little evidence to attest to its scientific validity. In other words, the theory has been popular, in spite of a lack of evidence that it is valid. To make things worse, most of the research conducted to test the theory has not been conducted appropriately (Mitchell and Moudgill, 1976), although most studies that have been done have resulted in negative conclusions (Wahba and Bridwell, 1976).

In balance, Maslow's theory remains very popular among managers and students of organizational behavior, although there are still very few studies that can legitimately confirm (or refute) it. One recent attempt used techniques that were more appropriate than most that have been employed (Rauschenberger, Schmitt, and Hunter, 1980), but failed to support the theory. It may be that the dynamics implied by Maslow's theory of needs are too complex to be operationalized and confirmed by scientific research. If this is the case, we may never be able to determine how valid the theory is, or—more precisely—which aspects of the theory are valid and which are not.

Modifications of the hierarchy. Since Maslow's last writings on the subject of his hierarchical theory of needs, there have been at least two modifications of the theory as it relates to work motivation. Both modifications propose a reduction in the number of levels in the hierarchy and converge, accordingly, with the suggestion by Maslow in some of his later work that we might fruitfully consider two basic levels of human needs (Maslow, 1968). One of these modifications (Lawler and Suttle, 1972) resulted from an unsuccessful attempt to empirically support the original five-level theory. Another modification (Alderfer, 1972) resulted from a deliberate attempt to develop and test a model with fewer need levels. Let's examine this second theory, since it is the most comprehensive alternative generated to date.

Existence, Relatedness, and Growth

For the most part, Maslow's theory of human needs was based on induction from his own clinical observations rather than from any empirical research conducted in organizational settings, as such. Nevertheless, as suggested above, it provided an attractive and intuitively acceptable perspective to writers in the human relations movement of the time (e.g., Argyris, 1957; McGregor, 1957, 1960).

One of the earliest attempts to empirically generate and test an alternative to Maslow's theory was that of Alderfer (1969, 1972) who proposed an *Existence, Relatedness, and Growth* model of his own. Alderfer's theory has its roots in Maslow's work, as well as in the theory and research of a number of other psychologists before Maslow who had been concerned with human motivation.

52

The theory posits three general categories of human needs. These categories are similar to, and partly derived from, those in Maslow's model, but they are not identical to Maslow's. Each of the needs is seen as *primary,* meaning they are innate to human nature, rather than learned, although learning can increase their strength.

The theory concerns itself with the subjective states of need satisfaction and desire, and how satisfaction of certain needs influences the strength of the desires of other needs. *Satisfaction* refers to the internal state of a person who has obtained what he is seeking to quell his desires. It is synonymous with getting or fulfilling (Alderfer, 1972, p. 7). *Desire* refers to an internal state that is synonymous with concepts such as want, need strength or intensity, or motive. Let's take a look at the three categories of needs.

Existence needs. The first set in the model is referred to as the *existence* needs. They correspond closely to Maslow's physiological needs, as well as to those aspects of Maslow's category of security needs that have to do with physical (as opposed to interpersonal) security. Typically, the substances required to satisfy existence needs are concrete in nature. Moreover, these substances are often scarce, such that more satisfaction for one person will tend to result in lower potential satisfaction for others. In work settings, pay and fringe benefits are examples—the more money that is paid to the office staff, the less is available to pay the shop workers. The types of outcomes (such as money) instrumental for gratifying Maslow's physiological needs are basically the same as those required to provide for physical safety; and according to Alderfer, Maslow's physiological and physical safety needs are approximately equal in importance to the existence of the individual. For example, people who are threatened with physical violence quickly abandon all behaviors that are not intended to provide for their safety. There are logical grounds, at least, for joining them into a single class.

Relatedness needs. Similarly, the goals typically sought by people to satisfy what Maslow calls love needs are basically the same as those that are necessary to provide for the need for the prestige or esteem of others, as well as for the interpersonal security needs included in the second level of Maslow's hierarchy. Successful satisfaction of each of these Maslow needs requires interaction with other human beings, and the development of meaningful relationships with others. Moreover, each of these three varieties of social needs, on a logical level at least, seem equally important, or prepotent.

The interaction among people needed to satisfy this category of needs, referred to as *relatedness* needs by Alderfer, does not neces- **53** sarily have to be positive or cordial. In fact, the expression of hostile feelings toward others is seen as an important aspect of developing meaningful interpersonal relationships.

Finally, unlike the zero-sum aspects of the satisfaction of existence needs, relatedness need satisfaction by one person tends to be positively associated with the same sort of satisfaction for others, by virtue of the very nature of social interaction. Therefore, Alderfer's theory combines all of Maslow's need categories pertaining to social interaction into a single class called *relatedness needs*.

Growth needs. The third category of needs in Alderfer's model is referred to as the *growth* needs. They are similar to the needs for self-esteem and self-actualization in Maslow's theory, but not identical. Whereas Maslow saw self-actualization as consisting of the fulfillment of innate potential (a potential that may have a unique form for a given individual), Alderfer's growth needs consist of desires to interact successfully with one's environment—to investigate it, explore it, and to master it. As the person's environment changes, so too will the expression of growth needs, according to Alderfer. Nevertheless, the highest level needs on Maslow's hierarchy are similar enough to the needs classed as growth needs by Alderfer (if for no reason other than the fact that self-actualization activities tend to enhance one's self concept) to justify combining them into a single class.

In short, whereas Maslow posited five major groups of human needs, Alderfer's model is more parsimonious, suggesting only three discrete categories.

Differences between Maslow and Alderfer. Aside from these similarities, however, there are a few key differences between the two theories. For instance, ERG Theory holds that all three sets of need are active in all human beings, although the notion of hierarchy and general prepotency found in Maslow (his *reversals* notwithstanding), is absent in ERG Theory. Thus, Alderfer's model does not require that a person be satisfied at the level of existence in order to witness a shift *upwards* in importance from relatedness to growth needs. Hence, it would be possible for employees who work under short-term contracts with their employers to derive sufficient satisfaction of their relatedness needs, that they could experience an increase in the importance of gaining growth experiences through their work.

Another important feature in ERG Theory that does not appear in Maslow's work, is what Alderfer refers to as the *Frustration-Regression Hypothesis*. As we will see in chapters four and five, frustration is defined as the situation where individuals' behavioral attempts to satisfy their needs are blocked or thwarted (by forces that

54

lie either inside the individuals themselves, or beyond their control). ERG Theory posits that failure of a person to satisfy his growth needs can result in an increase in the importance of that person's relatedness needs; likewise, a failure to satisfy one's relatedness needs can result in an increase in the importance of his existence needs. In hierarchical terms, these two propositions imply a movement downward in the face of frustration. To repeat, more will be said about the causes and consequences of frustration in later chapters of this book.

Initially, Alderfer proposed seven basic propositions that summarized how the satisfaction or frustration of needs at a particular level influence the satisfaction and the strength of desires at that same level, as well as at other levels. He subjected his theory to a four-year study, involving hundreds of research subjects and several different types of organizations. By most standards, the research was reasonably well conducted. Some of his original propositions received empirical support, while others did not. Some were revised based on the evidence gathered. The reader is referred to Alderfer (1969, 1972), for more complete detail concerning the total set of propositions, both before and after the research was conducted.

NEED HIERARCHIES: SOME CONCLUSIONS

Is there such a thing as a hierarchy of needs? There is evidence that different needs do exist, and that they can be measured (Alderfer, 1972; Mitchell and Moudgill, 1976); but there is much less empirical support that these needs vary in their relative importance so consistently across individuals that we can safely speak of a generalizable hierarchy, as such. To do so seems grossly to ignore substantial differences among people at various stages in their lives and careers (cf. Katz, 1980).

But before we abandon the concept of hierarchy altogether, a word of caution is in order. While it is unwise to unabashedly advocate a theory in the absence of any proof that the theory has empirical validity (recall chapter two), it is equally irresponsible to abandon a theory that has yielded primarily negative results when those results come from empirical tests that are largely inappropriate, or unfair. As stated earlier, it may be that many of the theories presented in this book are, in fact, better representations of the nature of work motivation than organizational researchers are capable of demonstrating. For example, there are countless complex problems associated with developing instruments that are truly appropriate for operationalizing and measuring the various dimensions associated with motivation theories, as well as many more problems involved in appropriately gathering and analyzing data yielded by these instru-   **55** ments, once they are developed (cf. Campbell and Pritchard, 1976). In the case of the concept of a hierarchy of human needs, there is some agreement that biologically-based needs (such as Alderfer's existence needs, for example) are probably more prepotent than other needs (Lawler and Suttle, 1972), but the nature of any clear-cut hierarchical ordering beyond that has not yet been demonstrated. On the other hand, work by Schein (1978) and Katz (1978, 1980), among others, continues to remind us that there are some predictable patterns among people at various life and career stages in the desires they express on their jobs. It may be that we will eventually be forced to abandon the search for a universal hierarchy of needs, and settle instead, for a number of middle-range theories (Pinder and Moore, 1980) that take individual and organizational circumstances more fully into account. More will be said on this in chapter thirteen.

Looking Ahead

One purpose of the present chapter has been to provide a grounding in the various perspectives that might be adopted about the essential nature of human beings. As we will see throughout the rest of this book, all approaches to understanding human behavior rely, either implicitly or explicitly, on one or more of the fundamental sets of assumptions described above. Approaches to understanding human *work* behavior are no exception—each of them rests on a more or less well articulated set of basic assumptions concerning the nature of the human being. Some of these theories see humans as need-fulfilling organisms, so they explicitly discuss the role of internal, hypothetical constructs, such as needs. Others combine this assumption with a second one, which posits the importance of human information processing, and accordingly, make use of other internal, unobservable concepts such as beliefs, attitudes, perceptions, and the like. Still other theories reject internal factors as useful causal explainers of behavior, in favor of relying on the external contexts in which behavior takes place. We will address all of these theories in this book.

In the following chapter, however, we will finish our discussion of human needs by focusing more closely on two specific topics—the nature and importance of growth needs in work motivation, and the causes and consequences of need frustration.

GROWTH NEEDS AND INTRINSIC WORK MOTIVATION 4

It matters not how strait the gate
How charged with punishments the scroll
I am the master of my fate
I am the captain of my soul
                    —W. E. Henley

Imagine you are walking with a friend through your neighborhood on a warm summer evening. As you walk, you notice a 9-year-old boy pushing a lawn mower in erratic circles and strips around the grass on his parents' front yard. The boy has his head lowered between his straight, extended arms, and he is bent over at the waist as he runs and pushes the mower. Upon getting closer, you hear him making sounds like an engine—an airplane engine. You stop and ask the young man what he is doing, and learn that he is pretending to be a pilot flying an airplane. The sounds he was emitting, of course, were those made by the plane's motor. The young pilot seems friendly enough, so you stop to chat for a while. The conversation reveals that the boy is having fun with his fantasy Beechcraft and that he did not consider his activity to be work. Further probing on your part informs you that the boy receives no pay or other form of direct compensation from his parents for cutting the grass (or flying his airplane). You part company, wishing him a safe flight.

Is the boy in this example working (cutting the lawn), or playing (flying his aircraft)? Or, does it matter at all what you call or how you classify his behavior? For the boy, the behavior clearly was playing. On the other hand, the boy's father would view it as work—a chore that he would now not have to perform himself. It may simply be a **57** matter of one's perspective, as seemed to be the case when Tom Sawyer managed to lure his friends into whitewashing his Aunt Polly's fence.

Using some of the concepts and tools of chapter three, we can look a bit deeper behind the reasons for our young pilot's behavior, asking, for example, what motivated him to behave the way he did. We can probably rule out existence and relatedness needs as explanations for the boy's action, because it did not seem that he was deriving any monetary rewards for his play, nor did he seem to be seeking any social interaction from it. If we assume that the boy's behavior was, in fact, motivated (as opposed to being simply random or compulsive), we are left with the conclusion that the boy must have been motivated largely by growth needs. What, you may ask, has *growth* got to do with the erratic flight of a low altitude lawn mower?

The purpose of this chapter is further to examine a set of needs that we classified in the last chapter as growth needs. Specifically, we will look at the role of growth needs in explaining what has come to be called intrinsic motivation, or intrinsically motivated behavior. Chapter eleven of this book will introduce a set of managerial techniques that are designed, in large measure, to appeal to these needs and to permit for their satisfaction through employee work activities.

WHAT IS INTRINSIC MOTIVATION?

Current thinking in work motivation would view the boy's behavior as being *intrinsically* motivated. Or, we might say the boy was intrinsically motivated to do what he was doing. Intrinsically motivated behavior can be defined, loosely, as behavior that is performed for its own sake, rather than for the purpose of acquiring any material or social rewards. One scholar who has extensively investigated intrinsically motivated behaviors defines them as those ". . . which a person engages in to feel competent and self determining" (Deci, 1975, p. 61). Consistent with this view, Wexley and Yukl (1977, p. 89) define intrinsic motivation in work settings as ". . . a term used to describe effort that is expended in an employee's job to fulfill growth needs such as achievement, competence, and self actualization." In short, these various definitions imply a motivational force that originates in what Maslow (1954) would call the higher order needs, or what Alderfer (1972) would classify as growth needs—a force directed toward behavior that is its own incentive.

The distinction between internal and external work motivation originated with Herzberg, Mausner, and Snyderman's (1959) study of the determinants of job satisfaction (see chapter two). And although the concepts of intrinsic and extrinsic motives, rewards, and outcomes have not always been consistently understood and used in recent years (Dyer and Parker, 1975), the distinction is important, and intrinsic motivation is a major factor in explaining much of the work behavior of many employees. In fact, it may be that intrinsic motivation (and hence the intrinsic rewards required to satisfy it) will become increasingly more important as the workforce becomes more highly educated and less threatened by challenging jobs (Cooper, Morgan, Foley, and Kaplan, 1979).

Intrinsic and Extrinsic Outcomes

Insofar as we can distinguish between intrinsic and extrinsic motivation, we can also distinguish between intrinsic and extrinsic job outcomes (Lawler, 1969). Intrinsic outcomes relate to either the satisfaction or frustration of the higher level, or growth needs. Examples of intrinsic outcomes would include positive feelings of accomplishment or a sense of diminished self-esteem. Intrinsic outcomes occur, when they occur, immediately upon the performance of the acts that produce them. They are, in a sense, self-administered by the individual, rather than distributed by others.

Extrinsic outcomes tend to relate more to the gratification and frustration of the existence and relatedness needs. They include things such as pay, promotions, and social interaction with one's colleagues. Moreover, they tend to be mediated by outsiders, such as one's supervisor or peers.

There is some dispute about the precise dividing line between intrinsic and extrinsic outcomes (Dyer and Parker, 1975), so some writers discourage continued use of the distinction (e.g., Guzzo 1979). This author's view is that some job outcomes can often appeal to both higher and lower level needs (e.g., pay increases can enhance one's feelings of self-esteem), and although there may be some disagreement concerning where one draws the boundary, it is useful to refer to intrinsic outcomes as those job-related consequences that, at least in part, function either to gratify or frustrate a person's growth needs.

The Origins and Nature of Intrinsic Motivation

According to Deci (1975), there have been at least three general approaches taken by psychologists to understand intrinsically-motivated behavior. One of these, represented by the work of Hebb (1955), posits that human beings seek preferred or *optimum* levels of arousal (where arousal is seen as the stimulation of the brain and central nervous system). Arousal levels result primarily from the stimulation that is found in the individual's environment. If the arousal level is too low in comparison with a person's desired level, the per- **59** son will be motivated to behave in such a way as to increase it. For example, an employee who is used to a fairly hectic work pace, but who finds things slower than usual on a particular day, will be motivated to seek out other people for conversation, set new tasks to be accomplished, or do something, simply to "stir things up." On the other hand, if the person's level of arousal is sufficiently greater than the preferred level, the individual will attempt either to withdraw from the highly arousing circumstances, or take steps to slow things down toward the desired level (for example, by turning off a noisy radio or moving into a job that is less demanding). In this view then, intrinsically motivated behavior is behavior intended to increase or decrease the physiological stimulation a person experiences, in order to bring it into line with desired levels.

A second approach (which is similar to the first), posits that people desire and behave to achieve an optimum level of uncertainty or *incongruity*, where incongruities consist of psychological inconsistencies in a person's beliefs, thoughts, perceptions, values, or behaviors (Zajonc, 1960). Unlike Festinger (1957) who posited that people find *cognitive dissonance* aversive, and that they are motivated to minimize the number of inconsistent cognitions they hold, this approach claims that individuals vary in the number and intensity of disparate beliefs, acts, and perceptions they prefer in their lives. When a person is experiencing either too little consistency ("Things just don't add up!") or too much consistency ("The world is in total harmony with itself"), behavior is instigated either to reduce or increase the level of congruity in the person's mind. Whereas the optimum arousal approach described above is physiological in orientation, the optimal congruity approach stresses the level of psychic comfort or discomfort a person experiences as a consequence of his or her acts and perceptions. The work of Hunt (1965) and Berlyne (1973) represents this second approach to explaining the origins of intrinsically motivated behavior.

The third approach to intrinsic motivation identified by Deci (1975) is best represented by White's (1959) concept of competence (or *effectance*) motivation, and deCharm's (1968) notion of personal causation.

According to White (1959), competence refers to a person's capacity to master and deal effectively with the surroundings—to be in charge of them. The exploratory behavior of children characterizes a desire to be competent, as do adult behaviors that are intended to enquire, to manipulate, and to learn about things. Competence motivation represents a need that is always available to instigate and direct behavior, although this need is less urgent (or prepotent to use Maslow's term) than are the types of existence needs we have examined in the previous chapter. When it is aroused, however, compe-

60

tence motivation causes people to seek out challenging situations in their environments, and then to conquer those situations, leading to feelings of competence and efficacy.

Likewise, according to deCharms (1968), people desire to be the *origin* of their own behavior, rather than the *pawns* of circumstances beyond their control. People strive for personal causation, to be in charge of their own lives, and for the outcomes that accrue to them.

In short then, Deci (1975) sees intrinsically motivated behaviors as those behaviors a person engages in to feel competent and self-determining. These behaviors consist of two general types—those intended to find or create challenge and those intended to conquer it. Hence, the adult who deliberately takes a clock apart merely to see how it works, or who learns a foreign language simply for the sake of learning it, are two other examples of intrinsically motivated behavior from this third perspective.

In summary then, there have been at least three conceptual interpretations of intrinsic motivation, each of them predicated on a different fundamental assumption regarding human nature: the first one is primarily biological/physiological; the second is cognitive/perceptual; and the third is based on a need fulfillment model of human functioning. Does this mean that there is no similarity or overlap among the three approaches?

Similarities among the three approaches. Notice that the *challenge* associated with any of the exploratory behaviors mentioned in connection with the third approach (above) might serve to increase or decrease a person's level of arousal, and/or the level of consistency he experiences, suggesting that the three general approaches to understanding intrinsic motivation are somewhat compatible with one another.

For example, the man who disassembles a machine that does not need repair opens (literally) a great deal of new arousal as he perceives and manipulates the delicate internal mechanisms. Further, there is a strong chance that he may either confirm or disconfirm his prior beliefs about what he would find inside the machine, thereby either reducing or increasing the net level of congruity he holds in his mind about the way things operate. Finally, if he were successful at reassembling the machine, he is likely to experience feelings of mastery and competence. The point is that the three concepts of intrinsic motivation cited by Deci (1975) are compatible (or at least reconcilable) with one another, so one might conclude that, in a sense, a process of increasing incongruity, arousal, and challenge followed by attempts to reduce this incongruity, arousal, and challenge constitute the psychological mechanisms behind behav- **61** iors we refer to as intrinsically motivated behavior. Thus, Deci (1975, pp. 61–62) states:

> Only when a person is able to reduce incongruity . . . and only when a person is able to conquer the challenges which he encounters or creates will he feel competent and self-determining. He will feel satisfied when he is able to seek out pleasurable stimulation and deal effectively with overstimulation. In short, people seem to be engaged in the general process of seeking and conquering challenges which are optimal.

According to Deci (1975), the need to be competent and self-determining is innate among humans, although the specific types of behaviors required of an individual to satisfy it varies from one person to the next. Deci considers self-actualization to be one common manifestation of the need for competence and self-determination; he sees achievement motivation as another. In fact, achievement motivation has been one of the most thoroughly researched needs in psychology and is one that has special relevance to work behavior. Therefore, let's take a close look at this particular human need.

Achievement Motivation

Henry Murray (who provided us with the general definition of need we adopted in the previous chapter) generated numerous lists of human needs. One of these needs is referred to as the *need for achievement,* which he defined as a need to:

> . . . accomplish something difficult. To master, manipulate, or organize physical objects, human beings, or ideas. To do this as rapidly and as independently as possible. To overcome obstacles and attain a high standard. To excel oneself. To rival and surpass others. To increase self regard by the successful exercise of talent (Murray, 1938, p. 164).

The overlap between this need and the notion of self-actualization from Maslow is apparent, although not complete. The essence of achievement motivation might be seen as a struggle against one's *own* standards of excellence, which clearly is consistent with the idea of becoming all that one is capable of becoming. But the element of achievement motivation having to do with mastering objects and overcoming obstacles and challenges is not necessarily part of self-actualization, although the two can, in practice, go hand in hand. Further, the aspects of the need for achievement pertaining to mastering and organizing the environment are clearly consistent with White's (1959) concept of competence motivation, and de Charm's (1968) notion that people prefer to be responsible for their outcomes rather than merely being pawns.

In short, these various growth needs are not identical, in large measure because they have been identified and studied by scholars working more or less independently of one another. But they do converge considerably in terms of the types of behaviors they instigate.

David McClelland, a student of Henry Murray, has devoted much of his career to developing our understanding of achievement motivation and to the role it plays in entrepreneurial behavior and the economic prosperity of nations (Stewart, 1982). His work is far too extensive to be summarized completely here, so the reader is referred to some of the original sources (e.g., McClelland, 1961, 1962, 1965; McClelland and Winter, 1969). But a number of features of this work of particular relevance to our understanding of employee work motivation, will be discussed here.

The origins of achievement motivation. First, McClelland believes that all motives are learned from experiences in which certain cues in the environment are paired with positive or negative consequences. Accordingly, the need for achievement is learned when opportunities for competing with standards of excellence become associated with positive outcomes. Hence, childhood rearing practices that encourage youngsters to independently tackle challenges and to do well against them, are critical. In fact, McClelland holds that child rearing practices are the most important determinants of the level of a person's achievement motivation (McClelland, 1961, pp. 340–350). However, McClelland has also shown that deliberate programs of training that involve the development of an achievement-oriented mentality can induce entrepreneurial behavior among adults where it did not previously exist (McClelland, 1965; McClelland and Winter, 1969). In other words, adults can be trained, it seems, to create and respond to opportunities to strive against challenges, and to behave in the ways described in the definition above. It is important to recognize that most of McClelland's research evidence pertains to boys and men, so his theory is limited to males. Attempts to generalize it to females have not yet been successful (Stein and Bailey, 1973).

Characteristics of achievement-motivated behavior. It was stated in the last chapter that we can sometimes detect the existence of many particular needs in an individual by observing the person's behavior and drawing inferences from it. Accordingly, the behavior of achievement-motivated individuals is commonly characterized by three features. First, achievement-motivated people prefer tasks of *moderate* levels of difficulty. Secondly, achievement-motivated people prefer tasks for which successful performance depends upon their own efforts, rather than upon luck. Finally, achievement-motivated people demand feedback and knowledge about their successes and failures to a far greater degree than do people who are low in achievement motivation.

The preference for tasks of moderate levels of difficulty deserves **63** special attention. According to Atkinson (1964), the total *achievement-oriented force* impacting a person who confronts a task is determined by three variables. Further, the three combine multiplicatively, so that if one of them is inactive, or "zero," there is no psychological force to engage in the task.

The first factor is the strength of the person's underlying need for achievement. This remains constant from one day to the next, although, as suggested above, it can be developed among male adults using focused training procedures.

The second factor is the level of difficulty of the task, as the person perceives it. Whether a particular task will be viewed as easy or difficult depends on a host of variables, such as the individual's perception of his ability to perform the task, for example.

The third factor which determines the strength of achievement-oriented motivation is the degree of intrinsic reward (or feelings of accomplishment) the individual expects he will experience if he manages to accomplish the task. Naturally, achieving a difficult challenge will bring the person greater feelings of accomplishment than will achieving a task that is perceived as simple. Therefore, the value of this third factor is inversely related to the second factor—the perceived level of difficulty of the task. Symbolically:

$$T.A.F. = nAch \times P.S. \times I.S.$$
$$I.S. = (1 - P.S.)$$

Where:

T.A.F. = Total achievement-motivated force
nAch = Strength of the person's underlying need for achievement
P.S. = The perceived probability of task success
I.S. = Intrinsic feeling of accomplishment

To illustrate how this formula works, consider the net force operating on an employee if (a) he has a very low level of the need for achievement, or (b) if he perceives the task to be too difficult for him to succeed, or (c) he perceives the task as very easy. In all three cases, we would not expect much achievement motivation in the person contemplating the task. His level of effort toward performing the task would be determined by the strength of other needs and incentives he believed would result from task success (such as the recognition of a female he might be trying to impress).

The importance of perceived task difficulty. Notice that insofar as a person's level of underlying need strength is constant in **64** the short run, the net level of achievement-related force acting on him to engage in a particular task will be determined by his perception of the level of difficulty of that task. The implication of this for the design of jobs and for the assignment of people to jobs is clear: in order to arouse motivational force associated with achievement needs, a supervisor must structure jobs and assign people to them so that employees see their chances of job performance as "50/50": not too low, but not too high. There must be a moderate level of challenge perceived. In practice, application of this principle can be difficult, because it requires that a supervisor be capable of accurately perceiving the difficulty level of a task as the employee sees it. So, a supervisor who overestimates or underestimates an employee's ability vis-à-vis a task will probably fail to arouse and take advantage of a certain amount of the natural achievement motivation of that worker. In theory, the principle is relatively simple; effectively applying it can be another matter.

COMBINING INTRINSIC AND EXTRINSIC MOTIVATION

Return for a moment to the hypothetical case of the boy and the lawn mower that opened this chapter. Consider what would happen if the boy's father elected to compensate him for cutting the lawn, using pay or some other form of extrinsic reward. Further, assume his father agreed to pay the boy some amount of money for cutting the grass each time he did it, thereby making the receipt of the money contingent upon his cutting the lawn. What would happen to the boy's net level of motivation to cut the lawn, and what would happen to the amount of fun the boy would have in cutting the grass/flying his imaginary airplane?

Both common sense and considerable research evidence (Lawler, 1971) support the proposition that compensation systems that tie pay and other rewards to the performance of an activity increase the level and rate of performance of that task. It would stand to reason, therefore, that paying the boy to fly his lawn mower would add considerable extrinsic motivation to the level of intrinsic motivation the boy already had for that task. In other words, the net level of motivation in the lad to cut the lawn should now be greater than before, because the extrinsic motivation provided by the money will somehow combine with his prior level of intrinsic motivation, resulting in a greater overall level of motivation than the boy had before he started to receive the pay. Again, common sense would support this reasoning, as do some formal theories of work motivation (e.g., Galbraith and Cummings, 1967; Porter and Lawler, 1968).

A series of experiments by Deci (e.g., 1971, 1972) and others (e.g., Condry, 1975; Greene and Lepper, 1974; Pritchard, Campbell and Campbell, 1977) has generated sufficient cause to believe, **65** however, that intrinsic and extrinsic motivation may not always "add up" (in a psychological sense) the way common sense suggests. Instead, it may be that in some circumstances, the addition of an extrinsic, contingently paid incentive (such as money) to a work context in which the employee is intrinsically motivated to do the work, may result in a loss of some (or all) of the employee's prior level of intrinsic motivation toward that task, and maybe toward other tasks perceived as similar.

The possibility that intrinsic and extrinsic incentives may not be additive has generated considerable research (see Notz, 1975; and Guzzo, 1979 for two reviews), although the evidence on the issue is mixed (e.g., Arnold, 1976; Hamner and Foster, 1975; Pinder, 1976). Sometimes extrinsic rewards have been shown to reduce intrinsic motivation; other times the opposite effect occurs—the contingent reward enhances intrinsic motivation. How can we explain the inconsistent results of studies into the matter?

Among others, Staw (1976) has reviewed the evidence on this so-called *overjustification hypothesis,* and has suggested that whether extrinsic rewards enhance or reduce intrinsic motivation depends on at least five factors:

1. The degree of saliency of the reward.
2. The prevailing norm regarding the appropriateness of payment for the activity in question.
3. The prior level of commitment of the person to the task.
4. The degree of choice the individual has to perform, or not to perform, the task.
5. The existence of potential adverse consequences.

So, according to Staw, extrinsic rewards are more likely to reduce subsequent levels of intrinsic motivation if the reward is highly salient, meaning that it is obvious to those who are to receive it, and that it is understood that the reward will be received upon the performance of the act. The more salient the reward, the more likely it is to have an adverse impact on intrinsic motivation (Ross, 1975).

Second, Staw suggests that rewards that are normally provided for a behavior in our culture are less likely to reduce a person's intrinsic motivation to engage in that behavior. He notes that in many of the studies in which rewards have been observed to reduce intrinsic motivation, those rewards were provided for the performance of acts that are not usually followed by reward (such as participating in games and puzzles in a laboratory setting). On the other hand, behaviors that are normally compensated in our culture (and that we might be inclined to classify as work) are less likely to be influenced by the provision of extrinsic outcomes. Hence, rewards may be more damaging to play behavior and learning behaviors than they are to work behavior.

66

Salient = prominent

Third, if the person is initially *very* committed to the task being rewarded, according to Staw, extrinsic rewards are less likely to dampen intrinsic motivation. Those studies that have demonstrated an adverse impact of extrinsic rewards have tended to involve tasks of only moderate prior levels of intrinsic motivation (cf. Arnold, 1976 with Pinder, 1976).

A fourth factor is the level of choice or compulsion a person feels with regard to performing the task. If the individual feels a high level of external pressure to engage in a task, she is more likely to believe that she is extrinsically motivated to behave in that manner, so little intrinsic rationale is available, and little damage can be done by the provision of extrinsic rewards. Finally, the perception that failure to perform the task might result in adverse consequences also contributes to the chances that the person will not attribute her own behavior to internal causes.

The point here is this: it is believed that people observe and rationalize their own behavior in a manner similar to that by which they observe the behavior of others and make attributions about the causes of that behavior. When an act is conducted in the context of a highly salient, highly compelling set of extrinsic circumstances (such as the fear of threats or the inducement of rewards), individuals are more likely to attribute their own behavior to these external causes. Otherwise, when there are few apparent external forces to which their behavior can be attributed, the individuals are more likely to assume that they are behaving in a certain manner because they want to—they like doing so. It seems that the presence or absence of such external factors largely determines whether people make intrinsic or extrinsic attributions about their own acts, as well as the cultural appropriateness of those external factors (such as money). While research on this issue is far from conclusive, one thing is clear: money is an interesting incentive and reward for a number of reasons, and it may not have the simple psychological effects on human motivation that appear at first glance.

Cognitive Evaluation Theory

Deci (1975; Deci and Porac, 1978) has developed a *Cognitive Evaluation Theory* in an attempt to reconcile the contradictory evidence pertaining to the relationship between intrinsic and extrinsic motivation. According to the theory, rewards can bear at least two fundamental features for the individual receiving them. The first of these is referred to as feedback, meaning that rewards given for performance of a task can convey information to the individual concerning how well she is doing at the task. A second feature of rewards can be the messages, if any, they have for the individual about why she is **67** performing the task. Deci refers to these as *control* perceptions (i.e., "Why am I doing this job? For the reward, of course!").

Depending upon which of these two features of a reward system is more salient for an individual, it can serve either to enhance or reduce the person's intrinsic motivation toward it. If control perceptions are more salient, they may cause a shift in the person's perceived *locus of causality,* such that she attributes her reasons for engaging in the task to the external inducements surrounding it, rather than to any internal satisfaction provided by the task itself.

This notion draws on self-perception theory (Bem, 1967), which states that people examine their own behavior, much as they do the behavior of other people, and make attributions about their own motives for behaving as they do. In Deci's theory, control perceptions arising from a reward are said to shift from self-perceptions of intrinsic motivation ("I am cutting the lawn because it is fun") to extrinsic self-attributions ("I am doing it for the money"). As the perceived locus of causality shifts, the person's intrinsic motivation to do the task diminishes. Highly contingent rewards (such as in a piece rate or commission payment system) seem more likely to imply control perceptions, and thereby reduce intrinsic motivation, than less contingent pay systems (such as monthly salaries or hourly wages), largely because they are salient and undeniably connected with the behavior.

According to Deci, feedback perceptions may either enhance or reduce intrinsic motivation. If the feedback indicates to the person that he is doing well at a task, his feelings of competence are enhanced, and his intrinsic motivation for the task is increased (because, for Deci, competence and self-determination are the essence of intrinsic motivation). But if the person perceives that he is doing poorly as a result of the feedback implied by the rewards (or lack of rewards), his feelings of competence will be diminished, as will his intrinsic motivation, and the person will be less likely to engage in the task in the future without some form of extrinsic incentive.

A major shortcoming of Cognitive Evaluation Theory is that it fails to specify the conditions under which either of the two facets of reward (feedback or control) will be more salient for a particular individual in a given situation (Guzzo, 1979). In a recent statement of the theory, Deci and Porac (1978) state only that " '. . . individual differences and situational factors' are related to the way people interpret the meaning of the rewards they receive" (pp. 163–164). Arnold's (1976) work suggests that when an individual's prior level of intrinsic motivation for a task is very high, feedback perceptions may be more salient, although one experiment failed to confirm this hypothesis (Pinder, Nord, and Ramirez, 1984).

In sum, the relationship between intrinsic and extrinsic motivation is not as simple as originally assumed (Lepper and Green, 1978), and further study is needed before final conclusions are warranted. At present, however, there is some cause to believe that paying people, especially children, for performing voluntary activities is probably detrimental to their continued intrinsic motivation to engage in these activities.

A major implication of the "Deci effect" for industrial work settings (if and when it occurs) is that contingent payment systems may offset or undermine the intrinsic motivation generated by managerial programs, such as job enrichment (Deci, 1975). At present, however, there seems to be little empirical evidence that this occurs in practice (Staw, 1977), in spite of our common, everyday encounters with surly employees who refuse to perform duties that are not strictly within the formal definitions of their jobs ("I'm not paid to do that!"). More research is needed to determine whether this phenomenon bears the same applied importance in work settings as it does in educational settings.

Summary and Conclusion

In brief, human needs for growth can exhibit themselves through a variety of behaviors for different individuals. It would seem that as our society continues to enjoy relative economic abundance and high levels of education, growth needs will continue to account for a significant proportion of our overall motivation to work, and to behave on the job as we do. Members of the older generation are often critical of younger employees, whom they perceive as irresponsible, or as lacking in the *work ethic,* when they observe them leaving jobs for no apparent reason, or complaining about not receiving enough challenge from their work. The point is that older employees in today's workforce had their views about work and the value of holding a job formed during tougher economic times than have been experienced by most employees who are less than forty years of age today. This generation gap in work values is understandable, although at times it contributes to considerable inter-generation conflict and intolerance.

The principles of intrinsic motivation discussed above will have particular relevance in chapter eleven, when we focus directly on topics related to job design, employee participation, and the like. Before we address those, and other topics that make use of our knowledge of human needs however, a number of other issues must be discussed. The first of these concerns frustration—what happens when, for whatever reason, behavior that has been learned for the sake of satisfying needs is blocked, so that motivated people are un- **69** able to use that behavior (or those behaviors) to meet their needs? The causes and consequences of frustration at work are the topic of the remaining sections of this chapter.

NEED FRUSTRATION AT WORK

The discussion of needs and need satisfaction throughout the last two chapters has largely ignored the point that people are not always able to achieve those goals in their lives that are necessary for them to fulfill their needs. In fact, if one takes an approach such as those offered by either Maslow or Alderfer, it becomes clear that human beings exist almost constantly in a state of only partial need fulfillment. The situation where one's behavior is not successful in achieving need-fulfilling goals is defined as frustration. In this section, we will examine some common causes of need frustration in work settings as well as a number of predictable consequences of this frustration. The concepts discussed come primarily from the work of Norman Maier (1973) and his associates.

Needs and Goals

Before we begin, it is essential to sort out the meanings of two terms—needs and goals. Successful understanding and application of our knowledge about frustration depends largely upon keeping the distinction between the two concepts in mind.

Needs, as we have discussed at length, are hypothetical concepts that represent the basic internal forces posited to explain motivated behavior (see chapter three). They are characteristics of individuals, and are relatively fixed, at least in the short run. On the other hand, *goals* are things people seek and try to attain for the sake of fulfilling their needs. Goals such as food and sleep are necessary, respectively, for satisfying the human physiological needs referred to as hunger and fatigue. Likewise, in work settings, pay, promotions, recognition from one's superior, and a chance to show one's skill are examples of goals that people may seek to satisfy their existence, relatedness, and growth needs on the job, and through their work.

But as we noted in chapter three, different people often pursue different goals to satisfy the same need. For example, relatedness needs may be expressed by a gregarious employee through constant chitchat during work hours, while another employee may attempt to satisfy that same need by seeking election to the organization's social committee. Further, a given goal, if achieved, may simultaneously serve the satisfaction of several needs. A promotion, for instance, may be instrumental for the fulfillment of a person's ex-

70

istence, relatedness, and growth needs. In short, there is no one-to-one correspondence between needs and goals, and it is essential to keep the two concepts separate from one another when we consider the causes and consequences of frustration.

Causes of Frustration

In the day-to-day process of living, people tend to associate certain goals with satisfactions of their particular needs (although there is no one-to-one correspondence, as just stated). Each of us tends to find certain things satisfying, and other things less so. A simple example is the act of going to the refrigerator for a cold drink (the goal) for the sake of quenching one's thirst (the need). The more frequently a particular goal object proves successful in meeting a need, the more likely the person is to seek that same goal in the future to meet his needs. To some extent, we form habits.

What happens when the traditionally successful behavior fails to reach the goal being sought? What happens when, for whatever reason, the behavior itself is not possible? Or, what happens when a person's behavior, itself, tends to make goal accomplishment more difficult, rather than more easy? Situations of this sort are common in virtually all job settings. They are often difficult to identify, as well as difficult to ameliorate. Nevertheless, the behavior that tends to occur in response to frustration is common in organizational settings, and is usually (although not always) dysfunctional. Managing frustrated behavior is a major challenge for supervisors, and it is not always done effectively.

What types of things block a person's learned behavior from reaching work goals? In other words, what causes frustration in work settings? We can classify causes of frustration, for the sake of discussion, into two categories. The first of these categories includes factors that are, for the most part, external to the person, although they may or may not be beyond her control. Examples abound in organizations. The structure of the organization is a common cause of need frustration, because hierarchies that tend to be pyramid shaped prevent most of us from "reaching the top." Policies that prevent people from interacting with one another on the job, policies that stipulate when a person may take a rest, and policies that prevent people from taking a vacation when they want, are other examples. A job which is boring and repetitive is another example, one faced by a vast number of us. A supervisor who won't cooperate and assist an employee can frustrate that employee; likewise, low-performing employees constitute barriers that prevent supervisors from achieving their job goals. Co-workers who exclude a newcomer and ignore his attempts to be friendly constitute another example. In short, there **71** are myriad behaviors people may attempt for the purpose of meeting their various needs, and there are countless potential barriers external to a person that can interfere with those behaviors, preventing him from meeting his basic needs at work.

A second category of potential frustrators consists of characteristics of the person being frustrated. A lack of ability to do the work (where work accomplishment is the goal) can block a person's attempts and leave his needs unfulfilled. Likewise, characteristics such as one's sex (Bartol, 1978; Larwood and Wood, 1977), age (Rosen and Jerdee, 1976), or departmental affiliation (Dalton, 1959) are other factors that can pose barriers and prevent a person from acquiring jobs, promotions into new jobs, or even access to information that they need to be effective on their jobs. Handicapped employees provide a powerful example of how a personal characteristic, or set of personal characteristics, can prevent a person from reaching his work-related goals.

It tends to be easier to identify causes of frustration external to the person being frustrated than it is to identify internal causes; although it is often the case that frustrated individuals blame factors other than themselves for their frustrations at work (Harvey and Albertson, 1971; Mitchell, Green, and Wood, 1981; Vroom, 1964). Often, however, diagnosing the real causes of an employee's frustration can be difficult for a number of reasons. First, frustrated individuals are not always aware, themselves, of the barriers to their goal achievement, especially when these barriers are internal to themselves, or when they are rooted in organizational factors that are beyond their cognizance. An employee with unusual religious beliefs is an example of the former; a company's advertising campaign that projects an unfavorable image of the product he is attempting to sell illustrates the latter.

Secondly, the behavior which results from need frustration will vary from one person to another, and there is no one-to-one universal correspondence between the force of particular needs and the behavior that results (recall chapter three). Also recall the human tendency to *project* our own need-behavior linkages to others, even when they are not appropriate. Hence, a supervisor who observes frustrated behavior on the part of one of her subordinates may have difficulty both in diagnosing the need(s) that are seeking satisfaction, and in determining the nature of the barrier(s) that are responsible for the frustration of the behavior aimed at those needs—a complex problem indeed!

To summarize, frustration is defined as the situation in which habitual and learned behaviors are thwarted from the effective attainment of goals that are sought for meeting human needs. The barriers that thwart the behavior are often difficult to identify; moreover, because of the complicated linkages between needs and the behaviors aimed at satisfying those needs, outsiders face a tough task when they try to assist someone else who is frustrated. Moreover, it is easier to talk about and understand the frustration of existence and relatedness needs than it is to understand and identify the frustration of growth needs, in large part because the goals typically sought for the satisfaction of existence and relatedness needs are usually relatively concrete and tangible. But, as noted in the first half of this chapter, growth needs are responsible for a considerable amount of the behavior we observe at work, and they may become even more important in the future. The goals people seek to satisfy their growth needs are more often amorphous and idiosyncratic, making their attainment difficult at times. In fact, most of the jobs we perform in our economy do not readily satisfy human growth needs. As a result, the frustration of growth needs is a major problem in organizations, one that manifests itself in job-related boredom and dissatisfaction (as we will see in chapter five). There are limits to the degree to which jobs can be structured to permit the ongoing satisfaction of human needs for competence, self-esteem, and self-actualization, although, as we will see in chapters eight and eleven, a number of formal managerial programs have been advanced to try to ease the situation and to make it more possible for people to satisfy their growth needs through their work.

Consequences of Frustration

Need frustration tends to result in any of a number of typical classes of behavior, although, as suggested earlier, specific individuals manifest these classes of behavior in different ways.

The most constructive reaction to frustration is exploration and *problem solving:* the individual sets about (with or without the help of others) to diagnose the cause, or barrier, and remove it (Wong, 1979). This sort of behavior occurs regularly in the lives of all of us, so much so that we usually take it for granted. In fact, successful problem solving in response to frustration can, in itself, contribute to the satisfaction of growth needs.

A second reasonably constructive adaptation to frustration is the adoption and pursuit of *alternative goals.* Hence, rather than seeking to increase her income through a promotion or a raise in pay, a single working mother might take on a part-time job. Likewise, an employee who works in physical isolation from his co-workers may seek fulfillment of his social needs through the pursuit of friendships off the job. The need(s) remain the same, but the goal(s) sought change.

Aggression is a common and highly predictable reaction to need frustration. Defined as some form of attack that is accompa- **73** nied by anger (Maier, 1973, p. 73), aggression can be open and aboveboard, or more covert and less obvious. Obvious examples of aggression would include bawling out a subordinate or hitting a co-worker. Less obvious examples include gossiping about an individual behind his back or voting against a colleague's project proposal in an executive committee meeting. Overt or covert, aggression is intended to somehow damage, hurt, or frustrate its target.

Often, however, the targets of aggressive acts are not the actual causes of the frustration. This phenomenon is referred to as displaced aggression or *scapegoating*. In organizational settings, a middle manager who is disciplined or frustrated by a superior may in turn vent his frustration on his own subordinates. Similarly, employees whose education levels are blocking them from receiving further promotions, may turn their aggression against their supervisors or co-workers, none of whom are responsible for causing their frustration. Finally, assembly-line employees who deliberately sabotage the products they build (e.g., Dubois, 1979) can be seen as taking out the aggression caused by the monotonous nature of their jobs on a handy, convenient scapegoat.

The principle of availability is a potent predictor of the targets a person may select to aggress against. People or objects that are readily at hand and unable to strike back are frequently the object of a frustrated person's aggression. Wife beatings and child abuse by chronically unemployed workers are examples.

One reason that aggression so commonly results from frustration is that it often works to remove the frustrating barriers. A bully who usually wins through intimidating others soon learns that intimidation and the threat of force is quite effective in helping him achieve his goals. People do those things they find to be rewarding (see chapter nine). Moreover, aggressive styles may evolve as a person ages and advances from the simple use of brute force to the use of less physical, but equally forceful tactics, such as verbal attack with a sarcastic flavor. Employee behavior ranging from theft and pilfering through to the formation of a union may be seen as aggressive responses against organizational realities that perpetually frustrate human needs (Hamner and Smith, 1978; Stagner, 1956). Employees who feel locked into their jobs have limited constructive means for dealing with their frustration and, accordingly, are more likely to resort either to aggression or displaced aggression on their jobs as a result.

In our discussion of Alderfer's ERG Theory, the concept of frustration-regression was introduced. *Regression* consists of the use of behaviors that are less sophisticated and less mature than those befitting a particular individual. They are childlike, or at least

74

characteristic of behaviors learned during one's earlier developmental stages (Maier, 1973). Common manifestations of regression include behaviors such as horseplay and swearing among males, and, among women, crying.

Crying represents a particularly complex example, as does the use of foul language or physical violence. On the one hand, these styles of behavior are representative of adaptive responses a youth or adolescent might employ in reaction to frustration. They may even have been useful during a person's younger years, as a means of removing frustrating barriers. When employed as a response to frustration by adults, however, regressive acts often function to increase the intensity of the frustration. So, for example, a woman who characteristically cries in response to frustration or attack in board meetings, can inadvertently (but quite naturally) increase the tendency of her male colleagues to discount her managerial "cool" and ability. Likewise, a foul-mouthed male may add to his own exclusion from the inner circles of a management group simply by reconfirming that, as an immature lout with a dirty mouth, he deserves to be excluded. The point is that regression works, sometimes, to assist in the removal of the barriers that cause employee need frustration. On the other hand, it can boomerang and make the frustration worse.

Fixation is another common behavioral response to need frustration. It involves the repeated use of the same goal-seeking behaviors, over and over, in spite of their ineffectiveness. For example, a student who approaches a mathematics problem over and over, using only one or two strategies, in spite of evidence that those strategies are not appropriate, is engaging in fixated behavior. Repeated failures breed even greater feelings of futility and make the adoption of more adaptive behaviors less likely. In work settings, fixated behavior can be rather pathetic because, unlike aggression or regression which sometimes result in goal accomplishment, by definition, it cannot lead to success. Resorting to fixated behavior can be damaging to one's self-concept, because of the image of helplessness it entails (see Korman, 1970, 1976; and Hall, 1976 for discussions of the importance of success experiences for one's self-esteem).

It is worth noting at this point that one reason lying behind the oft-noted resistance to change in organizations (Zaltman and Duncan, 1977) is that change can make learned and familiar behaviors by employees obsolete and frustrating. In other words, change (such as a redesigned organization structure or a new work process) can generate very real barriers to the behaviors employees have used in the past, barriers to the behaviors that have been associated with goal accomplishment, and with it, need satisfaction. There are many examples of how the introduction of new computer technology (e.g., **75**

Mann and Williams, 1972) has been seen by workers as a threat and source of frustration, resulting in considerable unhappiness for them, as well as reduced effectiveness of the new technology.

Another response to frustration that has particular relevance to work behavior is referred to as *resignation*. In simple terms, this amounts to "giving up"—becoming docile, uninspired and nonchalant. In many ways it is a non-response, insofar as the frustrated individual merely continues to show up for work, performing to a minimum expected standard, obeying the rules and getting by. This style of adaptation is, in essence, the style which reinforces belief in Theory X, according to McGregor (1962). Argyris (1957) claims it is the natural response one can expect when employee needs for growth collide with organizational structures and procedures that are designed to achieve efficiency and control. It accounts for much of the half-hearted service we observe from workers in service industries, as well as much of the apparent lack of intelligence and creativity exhibited by many people in various industrial settings. People adapt to the frustration caused by their job experiences by simply bringing their bodies to work and leaving their hearts, minds, and souls at home. We will return to resignation and other forms of withdrawal from the job (such as absenteeism and turnover) in chapter five when we examine work-related beliefs and attitudes in detail.

The choice of a response. The particular type of response (or responses) we can expect to see exhibited in reaction to the frustration of a particular employee will depend upon a host of factors, including, for example, the following:

a. The number and relative importance of the needs being blocked from satisfaction.
b. The degree of deprivation and/or its duration.
c. The extensiveness of the blocking and the completeness of the frustration that results (i.e., is it constant or intermittent?).
d. The perceived motives (if any) of the source of the frustration.
e. The person's prior experiences of success and failure in using various reactions to frustration.
f. The probable threats or costs perceived to be associated with the various response alternatives.

So, for example, we would expect to witness the use of aggression in cases where a person's existence needs are blocked (because they are so prepotent), where the frustration is intense and prolonged, and/or where the person attributes malevolent motives to the supervisor (for example) who is perceived as the source of the frustration. More passive responses (such as fixation and/or resignation) are more likely when, for whatever reasons, aggression is impossible, or is seen as too risky. According to Katz (1980), passive resignation and goal displacement are very common responses by many or most working adults who have mastered their jobs so that no real challenge remains.

CONCLUSIONS AND A GLANCE AHEAD

The first sections of this chapter focused on the human needs for growth, achievement, self-actualization, and feelings of competence and self-determination. We examined the nature of the *intrinsic motivation* that consists of the forces originating in these needs and attempted to show their relevance for employee work behavior. Intrinsic motivation and growth needs will be of particular relevance to the discussion of programs such as job enrichment and employee participation, which will be presented in later chapters of this book. Finally, the phenomena associated with frustration were discussed.

The reader is encouraged to use Maier's (1973) frustration framework as an insightful means for viewing, understanding, and dealing with dysfunctional employee behaviors ranging from tardiness and absenteeism to poor quality, and low levels of work effort. Maier's insights are among the most useful that are available at present for understanding work motivation (or the lack of it), and negative job-related attitudes.

Before closing our discussion of human needs and their role in theories of work motivation, it must be repeated that not all approaches to understanding work behavior recognize the importance of these concepts. Specifically, the so-called behavior modification or operant conditioning approach (Luthans and Kreitner, 1975; Skinner, 1953) avoids the use of such "black box" explanations of behavior, relying instead upon the circumstances that surround behavior, and that serve either to encourage or discourage it. The debate between need-oriented theorists and those who focus on other internal concepts on the one hand, and the behaviorists on the other, constitutes one of the most fundamental controversies in psychology in general, and in organizational science in particular.* We will attempt to provide the reader with a fair representation of both schools of thought in subsequent chapters of this book.

In addition to the attack on needs from the behaviorist camp, there has also been radical criticism of the reliance on needs from a number of cognitive theorists. Two of these suggest that a better explanation for employee actions and attitudes toward their jobs is found in their interpretations of the social cues surrounding them at a particular time. The reader who is interested in this perspective is re-

---

*See Hitt (1969) and the debate between Scott (1976) and Deci (1976), as well as the debate between Locke (1977, 1979) and Gray (1979), and the subsequent comment by Parmerlee and Schwenk (1979). Also see Locke (1980) for an interesting lesson on how the adoption of different assumptions concerning human nature lead to entirely different interpretations of work motivation.

ferred to Salancik and Pfeffer (1977, 1978) and to Alderfer (1977) for a rejoinder to it. A second radical attack on need-based approaches to human behavior is forwarded by Bandura (1977).

Nonetheless, in spite of these criticisms, it is clear that the majority of the research and theory on work motivation has come from those who assume that the most effective means of explaining and predicting work related behavior and attitudes must rely on internal states and concepts, such as needs, beliefs, attitudes, and the like. Accordingly, more space will be devoted to these cognitive/perceptual approaches in this book than to the noncognitive approaches. Thus, to set the stage for an examination of the major cognitively based theories, we turn in chapter five to a general discussion of work-related beliefs and attitudes. Theories that rely on these constructs will then be presented in chapters six through eight, while an examination of the behavior modification model will be presented in chapters nine and ten.

To proceed then, let's take a closer look at the nature of beliefs and attitudes in general, and their role in the cognitive/perceptual models of work motivation.

WORK RELATED BELIEFS, ATTITUDES AND INTENTIONS 5

If work was really good, the rich would have found a way to keep it to themselves.

—Haitian proverb

A recent article in *Psychology Today* reports some of the most recent (and fascinating) findings of national surveys dealing with the attitudes North Americans have about work in general and about their own jobs in particular (Yankelovich, 1982). The main conclusion of the article is that the "work ethic" is as strong as it has ever been, in spite of the fact that productivity gains have declined so much in recent years (see chapter one of this book). The reason for this apparent paradox, according to the research reported in the article, is that people don't believe that working hard (or harder) is of benefit to them; rather, they believe that someone else—such as customers, stockholders, or management—are most likely to be the prime beneficiaries of their increased effort and diligence on the job. In short, the feeling seems to be: "Why should I work harder, since there's nothing in it for me?"

The *Psychology Today* article is important for at least a couple of reasons. First, the findings of the studies it reports are inherently interesting, and are suggestive of a number of implications for the design and management of organizational reward systems. Secondly, the article is representative of the interest shown by the public in general toward the issue of work-related attitudes. Similar articles appear regularly in most major newspapers and news magazines throughout North America.

The point is that we tend to be widely interested in how, as a whole, people feel about their jobs. A further manifestation of the **79** common interest in work attitudes is found in the frequency with which people ask one another, "How are things going at work?" hoping that they will receive a positive response. In short, job attitudes seem almost universally important to people, including those who hold jobs as well as those who do not.

WHY AN INTEREST IN WORK ATTITUDES?

Why are people so interested in work-related attitudes? More specifically, why might managers be concerned about work attitudes, and why are we interested in them here, in the midst of a book on employee motivation?

Smith, Kendall, and Hulin (1969) provide four commonly accepted answers to these questions. First, it has long been assumed by many managers, parents, teachers, and people in general that attitudes influence behavior. The importance of this assumption for our present purposes lies in the possibilities it holds for managers and supervisors who wish to influence employee motivation and job performance. That is, it has long been assumed that *work-related attitudes must somehow be related to work behaviors* (cf. Brayfield and Crockett, 1955). Early forms of this belief held that higher levels of job satisfaction are associated with higher levels of job performance; "A more satisfied employee is a more productive employee." Although years of research have shown that the relationship is not so simple, there is still some basis for believing that attitudes and behaviors *can* be related to one another in some circumstances (Ajzen and Fishbein, 1977; Cialdini, Petty, and Cacioppo, 1981). Accordingly, it remains important to develop a precise understanding of what attitudes are, of the factors that influence them, and of whatever connections they may have with behavior.

Secondly, Smith et al. (1969) point out that a great deal of management's activities with regard to personnel selection and placement, training, career counseling, and so on, are based in part on a concern for employee attitudes and, in turn, for employee behavior. Third, Smith and her colleagues note that improving employee job satisfaction is a desirable goal in its own right, for humanitarian reasons. In other words, one need not expect some form of managerial payoff in order to justify attempts to understand employee work attitudes, and then to proceed to do something to improve them through restructuring work and organizations.

Finally, understanding the nature of job attitudes may be beneficial for the greater scientific concern for understanding attitudes in general: work is only one arena in which human attitudes are formed and altered, albeit an important one. In short, we are interested in the study of job attitudes because they are believed to be related to work behavior, because a great deal of managerial activity is concerned with positively influencing them, for humanitarian reasons, and for more general scientific reasons. The purpose for discussing them in this book is influenced, in part, by each of these three sets of concerns.

The purpose of this chapter is to examine the issue and importance of work-related beliefs and attitudes. We will explore the meaning of beliefs and attitudes in general, and then discuss the specific meaning of a number of beliefs and attitudes that are of particular importance in the context of work and work motivation. Finally, we will look at the research that has been conducted into the consequences of holding work-related attitudes of various sorts. The most central reason for focusing on work-related beliefs and attitudes here is that they are assumed to be important causes of work motivation by three important theories to be examined in chapters six, seven, and eight of this book.

Before we begin, however, it is important to note again that not all theories of work motivation recognize the importance of employee attitudes. In fact, whether hypothetical concepts such as attitudes have any bearing on understanding work behavior has been the topic of considerable debate in organizational psychology and its related disciplines for many years (see, for example, Karmel, 1980). There are some camps in the discipline that, following schools of behaviorism in psychology, do not deny that people hold attitudes toward objects and phenomena, but they do dismiss as unnecessary the invocation of concepts such as attitudes for explaining or predicting work behavior. We will examine this perspective in detail in chapters nine and ten.

To begin then, what are attitudes?

THE NATURE OF ATTITUDES IN GENERAL

Before we can begin a discussion of the nature and importance of *work-related* attitudes, it is necessary that the reader become familiar with the nature of human attitudes in general. Once this understanding has been acquired, it will be easier to appreciate the difficulties associated with understanding employee attitudes toward work, and it will be easier to comprehend why so much of the attitude-related research on the topic of employee motivation has been inconclusive to date. The concepts of the nature and structure of human attitudes adopted here draw heavily from the work of Ajzen and Fishbein (1977), Fishbein and Ajzen (1975), Salancik and Pfeffer (1978) and Calder and Schurr (1981).

81

What Are Attitudes?

An *attitude* can be defined as the degree of positive or negative feeling (or affect) a person has toward a particular attitude object, such as a place, thing, or other person (Fishbein and Ajzen, 1975). Thus, when we speak of positive *job* attitudes, we mean that the people involved tend to have pleasant internal feelings when they think about their jobs, although different aspects of one's job are bound to bring about different sorts of feelings. On one level, this concept of attitude makes intuitive sense and fits with our everyday understanding of the meaning of the concept. On the other hand, we must still address the question of the origins and causes of these affective reactions. In other words, what causes us to feel particularly good or bad about specific things or people?

The Nature of Beliefs

Part of the answer to this question lies in the *beliefs* we hold about the objects, persons, or things in question. A belief is a person's ''. . . subjective probability judgement concerning a relation between the object of the belief and some other object, value, concept, or attribute'' (Fishbein and Ajzen, 1975, p. 131). It is a mental linkage tying an entity with a property in a probabilistic manner.

For example, we might hold the belief that a certain occupation is challenging. The attitude object here is the occupation. The attribute is the property of being challenging. The *strength* of a person's belief about an attitude object consists of the magnitude of the probability in her mind that the object is associated with the attribute (Fishbein and Ajzen, 1975, p. 134).

How are beliefs formed? According to Fishbein and Ajzen (1975), we can think of three different types of beliefs, each of them formed by a different means. These are referred to as descriptive beliefs, inferential beliefs, and beliefs formed on the basis of information from outside sources. Let's take a brief look at these, one at a time.

Descriptive beliefs are formed on the basis of a person's own observations. For example, an employee may notice that his supervisor keeps his office neat and form the belief that his supervisor is a tidy individual.

Inferential beliefs result from logical connections people make in their minds between certain thoughts. For example, consider a person who holds anti-union attitudes and who simultaneously believes that promotions should be based on merit, rather than upon seniority. Assume further that this person has never considered the possible link between these two concepts (unions and the various bases for promotion). When asked to indicate whether he believes that unions normally favor seniority or merit as the primary basis for promotion, it is likely that the individual would reply that unions probably favor seniority. The person would reach such a conclusion for either of two reasons. First, because it is inconsistent for a person to hold conflicting or unbalanced perceptions and beliefs about objects and issues (Heider, 1958), it is unlikely that he would associate something he positively evaluates (promotion on the basis of merit) with something else that he evaluates negatively (unions). Therefore, out of a desire to be internally consistent, he would most likely conclude that unions favor promotions on the basis of seniority, rather than merit. A second reason for his likely conclusion has to do with probabilistic reasoning on his part, such as the following: (1) antimanagement groups naturally tend not to favor promotions on the basis of merit; (2) unions are generally antimanagement; therefore (3) unions probably favor promotions on the basis of seniority rather than merit. In short, inferential beliefs result from either the desire to be internally consistent and/or any of a number of logical processes.

A third source of beliefs consists of other people or *outside information sources,* such as newspapers. Once they are accepted, beliefs originating from external sources are similar in nature to beliefs formed on the basis of personal observations (Fishbein and Ajzen, 1975).

A number of important points follow from Fishbein and Ajzen's concept of belief. Notice that beliefs may or may not be valid, depending upon the accuracy of the information upon which they are based. In fact, descriptive beliefs are less prone to the influences of a person's prior beliefs and attitudes than are inferential beliefs (Fishbein and Ajzen, 1975). In other words, people are much less likely to formulate false beliefs based upon their personal observation of events than they are when their beliefs are based on any of the types of inferential processes described above.

Secondly, notice that because of the potential role of personal bias in the formation of inferential beliefs, it is quite possible for any two individuals to hold differing beliefs about the same attitude object, even when they share common experiences. For example, two students may both spend a summer working as interns in the same accounting office, causing one of them to conclude that accounting is a dull occupation, while leaving the other student with quite the opposite belief ("Accountancy is fun!"). Even descriptive beliefs vary between people when they pay attention to different aspects of their experiences with attitude objects.

A third point worth underlining has to do with the important influence outside sources can have in the structuring of beliefs (cf. Salancik and Pfeffer, 1978). This phenomenon is particularly powerful for newcomers to work settings, who must learn new jobs, become acquainted with new colleagues, and assimilate myriad other details **83** about aspects of that work setting (see Graen, 1976; Van Maanen, 1977; Wanous, 1980).

A fourth point concerns the number of beliefs people hold about attitude objects. Because of the natural limits to human cognition, it is likely that most attitudes are formed on the basis of no more than between five and nine different beliefs concerning an attitude object. Of course, many people seem to desire fewer than five pieces of information about another person or object. In fact, beliefs differ in the salience as well as in the importance they hold for people, such that individuals formulate their attitudes about objects on the basis of those characteristics that stand out for them, or seem most crucial. Thus, for example, an employee who is acutely aware of his low rate of pay is likely to mention it early in any conversation he has about his job.

A final important feature of beliefs is that they tend to be internally consistent with one another. For example, there is evidence that people tend to link personal attributes of other people in predictable clusters, such that, for example, a belief that a person is poised will lead to the assumption that the same person is also calm, composed, and non-hypochondriacal (Fishbein and Ajzen, 1975). Clusters about attitude objects other than people also tend to go hand in hand, in large measure because, as mentioned before, human beings tend to prefer consistency among their beliefs, actions, and attitudes (Festinger, 1957; Heider, 1958).*

Beliefs and Attitudes

As suggested earlier:

> An attitude represents a person's general feeling of favorableness or unfavorableness toward some stimulus object . . . as a person forms beliefs about an object, he automatically and simultaneously acquires an attitude toward that object. Each belief links the object to some attribute; the person's attitude toward the object is a function of his evaluations of these attributes (Fishbein and Ajzen, 1975, p. 216).

So, to return to our previous example, one summer intern may have a positive attitude about accountancy because he believes it is interesting and because, in turn, he positively evaluates the property of being interesting. Likewise, an employee may dislike his job because he *believes* he is underpaid for the work he performs at it, and he *negatively evaluates* the condition of underpayment he perceives. In this view then, attitudes are the affective (emotional) reac-

---

*The reader is reminded, however, that people differ in the degree of incongruity and inconsistency they desire in their minds (recall chapter four).

tions people hold about attitude objects based upon the way they evaluate the attributes they associate with those objects.

The *overall attitude* a person has toward an object is seen as an aggregation of all the beliefs she holds about it, each weighted by the positive or negative evaluations she places on these various beliefs. Therefore, two employees may have the same set of beliefs about a job ("It's repetitive") but hold different attitudes toward it, because one of them prefers routine work, while the other desires more uncertainty. Alternatively, the same two employees may have differing beliefs about an object or person (such as their common supervisor), but have similar attitudes toward him. For example, one employee may be aware of the supervisor's prowess at the pub after work and admire him for it, while the second employee may positively evaluate the supervisor for what he believes to be his characteristic fairness.

To summarize, we can say that the connection between beliefs and attitudes is the following: if a person approves of or positively evaluates the attributes that he associates in his belief structure with an object, he will tend to hold a positive overall attitude toward that object. On the other hand, if the attributes he connects in his beliefs with an object are characteristics he evaluates negatively, he will hold a negative overall attitude toward the object. So, to influence a person's attitudes about an object (say a job), we might introduce new information about that job—information that links the job with attributes that the employee positively evaluates (such as its variety and status). Alternatively, we might attempt to change the employee's assessment about the desirability or undesirability about the attributes the employee already associates with the job in question.*

Stability and Change of Beliefs and Attitudes

How stable or susceptible to change are human beliefs about attitude objects? Traditional thought on this matter has held that attitudes (and the beliefs on which they rest) are relatively permanent predispositions of people toward attitude objects (such as other people, jobs, organizations, or whatever). More recent thinking (e.g., Salancik and Pfeffer, 1978) recognizes that attitudes are heavily influenced by the social contexts in which people exist; that is, how people feel about attitude objects is determined largely by the descriptive and evaluative information they acquire through their social interactions with other people. This alternative view, however, fails to

---

*Notice again the potential role of inaccurate beliefs for the formation of attitudes. Propaganda programs designed to change peoples' attitudes toward enemy groups focus heavily on introducing *belief-structuring* information to the populace about the enemy more than upon trying to make the populace evaluate the information they hold differently.

recognize that there is *some* consistency and stability to attitudes over time—they do not swing wildly from one social setting to another. Therefore, a third view has recently been advanced that balances the *attitudes-as-fixed-dispositions* position and the *attitudes-as-socially-constructed-beliefs* position. For the sake of discussion, we will refer to this third position as the *information processing approach* (Calder and Schurr, 1981).

For Calder and Schurr (1981), an attitude is an integration of the evaluative meaning of sets of thoughts an individual holds in memory (p. 287). Thoughts are similar to beliefs, as we have discussed them above. Thus an attitude might be reflected in statements such as the following: "I think the company's transfer policy is quite liberal" or "I think the people I work with are dull and uninteresting." But these thoughts need not be uttered in any way—they can be privately held by an individual. (Notice the role of evaluation in this conception of attitudes. It corresponds with the evaluative nature of attitudes in the Fishbein and Ajzen model, presented earlier.)

The concept of storage in memory is important. This view considers both long-term memory and short-term memory. The former serves two functions: the ongoing storage of information pertaining to an attitude object, as well as the interpretation of new incoming information that is being processed in a particular setting by the person's short-term memory. As a person interacts with his surroundings, information is gathered about attitude objects. This information is processed with the assistance of information that has been stored by the person in long-term memory. The contents of long-term memory help the person make sense out of new information, as it were. So, for example, if an employee hears a manager promise to redistribute work loads so as to make it possible for her staff to get away early on a long weekend, she will process this promise, while remembering other promises made by the supervisor on other occasions in the past. As new information is interpreted through the perceptual apparatus provided by memory, it, in turn, enters long-term memory and modifies or updates the contents of the memory bank.

Thus, attitudes are influenced by the characteristics and nuances of the settings in which attitude objects are considered, but they are also heavily subject to the interpretive assistance provided by past experiences, thereby featuring some degree of stability over time. We might say that the information processing approach sees attitudes as being structured and developed according to a type of dynamic equilibrium process.

A recent study by Griffin (1982) has illustrated that one type of belief which is of particular interest to this book is in fact relatively slow changing—the nature of the perceptions people have about the capacity of their jobs to bring about intrinsic motivation and satisfaction. In chapter eleven, we will examine four approaches to job redesign, the most popular of which relies heavily on employee beliefs that their jobs possess motivating qualities. Griffin's research suggests that these beliefs are relatively stable over time, although people's affective reactions to these beliefs (their attitudes) may be less stable.

Attitudes, Intentions, and Behavior

There has been considerable debate over the years concerning the nature of the relationship between attitudes and behavior. As mentioned earlier, it seems to make intuitive sense to many people that attitudes are major causes of our behavior: we behave in certain ways toward various people and objects as a consequence of the way we feel about them. But years of research in social psychology have been frustrated in confirming this apparently obvious connection (Ajzen and Fishbein, 1977). In fact, some have concluded that the opposite relationship may be a more accurate reflection of the relationship—peoples' behaviors toward objects and other people may help shape their attitudes toward them (Bem, 1967, 1972). Nevertheless, there is still cause to believe that attitudes and behavior are, in fact, related to one another, but the nature of the connection between them is far more complicated than one might expect (Cialdini et al., 1981). Having stated these caveats, what exactly is the connection between attitudes and behavior?

Attitudes affect behavior only to the extent that they influence a person's *intentions* to act. That is, *attitudes can create a set of possible intentions to behave in certain ways toward the object in question,* although a particular attitude usually does not relate to any single intention on a one-to-one basis.

For example, an employee may have a generally positive attitude toward his new supervisor following a transfer, and that generally positive attitude may predispose him to act in a variety of positive ways toward the supervisor, although, in itself, it will not be useful as a predictor of any specific behavior (such as volunteering to help the supervisor on a special project without pay during off-hours). Nevertheless, it is possible that the generally favorable attitude will, in fact, create an intention to do such free overtime work, should the occasion arise. The point is that attitudes foster sets of intentions that are consistent with one another, as well as consistent with the tone of the attitude itself. But single attitude-intention connections can seldom be predicted in advance.

On the other hand, every intention, once formed, is associated with specific behaviors. To the extent that behavior is volitional (as opposed to being strictly reflexive or coerced by the environment), people will attempt to do those things they *intend* to do (Ryan, 1970). **87**

Therefore, while the employee likes his new supervisor (because he positively evaluates the beliefs he holds about her), that general attitude may foster a number of positive intentions. When a specific behavioral opportunity presents itself, the positive attitude may (or may not) translate into an intention to act in a positive or helpful way toward the supervisor. And once an intention is formed to act in a way that is in keeping with the positive attitude, the employee will strive to behave in the way intended. To summarize:

> Thus attitude is viewed as a *general* predisposition that does not predispose the person to perform any specific behavior. Rather, it leads to a set of intentions that indicate a certain amount of affect toward the object in question. Each of these intentions is related to a specific behavior, and thus the overall affect expressed by the pattern of a person's action with respect to the object also corresponds to his attitude toward the object (Fishbein and Ajzen, 1975, p. 15).

The specificity of intentions. In order to fully understand the connection between attitudes and intentions, however, it is first necessary to understand more about intentions themselves—particularly about the importance of the specificity of the intentions involved.

According to Fishbein and Ajzen (1975), intentions consist of four elements: the *particular behavior* being considered; the *target object* toward which the behavior might be directed; the *situational context* in which the behavior may be performed; and finally, the *time* at which the behavior is to occur. Each of these elements can vary in terms of how specifically it is considered. The most specific situation involves an intention to perform a clearly defined act toward a specific target in a highly specified place and time. For example, "I intend to walk off the job tomorrow morning after nine o'clock, as soon as I have convinced the rest of the gang to join me!"

Intentions are more closely connected to behavior when they are specific (Ajzen and Fishbein, 1977; Jaccard, King, and Pomazal, 1977). In other words, the more any of the four elements of an intention is left general (as opposed to specific), the weaker is the connection between the intention and subsequent behavior (Ajzen and Fishbein, 1977). For example, an employee might indicate that she intends to be more punctual in reporting to work. Left at this low level of specificity, we might expect this intention not to result in real punctuality as much as an intention of the form, "I intend never to come to work later than nine o'clock again this year." In the second case, the particular *behavior* was more specifically articulated than it was in the first case (as was the time involved). Likewise, if the target object of an intention is left general, rather than specific, behavior is less probable. Statements such as, "I would never vote for a union" may prove to be poorer predictors of actual behavior than statements such as, "I will never vote for the Sheepherder's Union, Local 123." The more specific the target of the intention, the more likely it will be associated with behavior that is consistent with the intention.

What about the specificity of the time element? Ajzen and Fishbein (1977) would suggest that statements such as, "I plan to go on a diet" will not be as likely to lead to a loss of weight as a statement such as, "I plan to start a diet in the New Year!" (although we are all familiar with the fate of most New Year's resolutions).

Finally, we can consider the specificity of the situation. If an employee says he intends to stop smoking on the job, we can expect to see less smoking on his part than if he were simply to say, "I will stop smoking."

The point, in brief, is that increases in specificity with regard to the behavior, the target, the time, or the situation involved, will be associated with a higher likelihood that an intention will result in actual behavior that is consistent with it (Ajzen and Fishbein, 1977).

Intentions and behavior. The final step in understanding why and how attitudes result in behavior requires that we examine how intentions, once formed (at whatever level of specificity), lead to behavior.

According to Fishbein (1967), there are two important factors that determine intentions, once attitudes have been formed toward objects. The first of these is itself an attitudinal factor, while the second is referred to as a *normative* factor. The attitudinal factor has to do with the person's feelings concerning the act being considered. In other words, it consists of the individual's attitude toward performing the behavior in question, under a particular set of circumstances. Moreover, this attitude (toward the behavior) is determined by the person's perceived consequences of the behavior, and his evaluations of those consequences.

It is important not to confuse the attitude a person has toward an object with the attitude he holds toward behaving a certain way toward that object. The first of these attitudes, as we have said, consists of the individual's evaluations of the beliefs he holds about the object itself. Whether he develops an intention to act in a way consistent with that attitude depends on his attitude toward the action implied by the intention. This second attitude, in turn, is determined by the person's beliefs about the probable consequences of his action and his evaluation of those consequences.

To return to our earlier example, the new employee may hold a positive general attitude toward his supervisor and may, therefore, be generally predisposed to act toward her in a positive fashion. Suppose the employee learns that the boss requires help at the office after-hours on a particular night, but that he would have to work **89** without pay and therefore in violation of the union contract if he were to volunteer. Will the employee's positive attitude translate into the specific act of offering assistance? Fishbein (1967) would suggest that the employee will form an attitude *about the act of volunteering to help.* That attitude will be determined by the consequences the person expects will follow from working after-hours, as well as from the individual's evaluation of those consequences. In balance, whether our friend decides to volunteer for the job will depend, in this view, upon whatever consequences he expects might result from volunteering, and how favorably or disfavorably he evaluates these consequences.

Again, we have an evaluation of a set of beliefs, although, to repeat, these beliefs pertain to the likely consequences of behavior, not to the supervisor, per se. The theory predicts that if the employee believes that consequences he positively evaluates will outweigh consequences that he negatively evaluates, he will volunteer. But if the employee believes that most of the consequences of volunteering will be negative (such as being reprimanded by the shop steward), he will not intend to volunteer, and, accordingly, will not do so.

The second determinant of whether an attitude results in an intention—the so-called normative component—concerns the influence of the social environment. In other words, it has to do with the person's beliefs about what significant others around him expect him to do. Different people will be sensitive to the expectations placed on them by various people, such as one's spouse, one's co-workers, and so on. An individual in a particular situation may consider the expectations of a variety of reference groups in the context of considering a particular behavior. So it may be that helping the supervisor at night without pay is something that is expected by members of the work group of their youngest member, regardless of who it is, and regardless of the fact that such work violates the union agreement. On the other hand, the employee's new spouse may have a different view of the situation, leaving the employee with some ambivalence, and causing the generally positive attitude toward the boss not to result in an offer to work at night.

To summarize, whether an attitude toward an object results in a specific intention to behave in a certain way toward that object depends upon the person's attitude about the behavior itself and upon his beliefs about the expectations of relevant others with regard to the behavior.

Notice two or three things about this theory. First, consider the important role played by the individual's beliefs, both about the attitude object as well as about the probable consequences of specific acts toward that object. Clearly, beliefs are not always accurate or valid, and they are certainly subject to change. Moreover, beliefs about either an attitude object or about the consequences of certain acts toward it can be heavily influenced by other people, as well as by one's own personal experiences. Notice too that a generally positive (or negative) attitude toward an object may not result in certain specific behaviors related to that object (such as helping one's supervisor at night), but may result in other behaviors that seem to outsiders to be quite similar (such as volunteering to assist the supervisor with a special project during regular working hours).

Recapitulation

Let's stop for a minute and review where we have been. So far we have seen that beliefs are the core of attitudes. They consist of perceived linkages between attitude objects and attributes. Strong beliefs consist of high subjective probabilities that particular objects are characterized by particular attributes. People tend to emphasize the most salient and the most important beliefs they hold about objects as they form attitudes toward them. Attitudes are evaluative reactions people have with regard to the beliefs they hold about objects. The connection between attitudes and behavior, however, is unpredictable, for a number of reasons.

First, for an attitude to result in behavior that is consistent with it, that attitude must result in an intention to act. But in order for an intention to be developed, the person must hold a positive attitude toward the act itself, and she must believe that significant others around her would see her act as appropriate. But even then, the holding of a particular intention will result in a specific behavior only if the intention is somewhat specific with regard to a variety of factors, including the exact nature of the behavior itself, the precise target toward which the behavior will be directed, the circumstances within which the act is contemplated, and, finally, the time at which the act is to take place.

In short, there is never a simple connection between the holding of a particular attitude toward a person, a job, or some object, and specific behaviors toward that person, job, or object. Using attitudes to predict specific behaviors is a risky business. So, for example, an employee may like his job because he positively evaluates those things he *believes* about it (that it pays better than other comparable jobs, that he can trust his co-workers, and that it may provide him with long-term security). But, based on this attitude, we cannot predict whether he will work hard, seek promotions, take training courses, or help to organize a union. In order to make such behavioral predictions, we would need a great deal more information about the employee's beliefs about the consequences of these particular acts, as well as about his evaluative attitudes toward those be- **91** liefs and his understanding of what is expected of him by significant others. On the other hand, we *are* able to make predictions, in advance, that because an employee holds a generally positive attitude toward his job, positive job behaviors are more likely to result from him than are negative job behaviors, although the specific acts cannot be foreseen.

Theory X and Theory Y Revisited

Before leaving our discussion of the relationship between beliefs, attitudes, and behavior, it is worth recalling from chapter three two particular sets of beliefs commonly held by many managers concerning the nature of human beings. These beliefs, referred to as Theory X and Theory Y, are seen as resulting in managerial behaviors that are consistent with either the view that people like to work, can be trusted with responsibility, and so on (Theory Y), or that they are lazy, dislike work, and cannot be trusted with responsibility (Theory X). According to McGregor (1957, 1960), Theory X beliefs are the cause as well as the result of apathetic and withdrawn employee behavior—a self-fulfilling prophecy. And, while there is no claim that either Theory X or Theory Y beliefs are connected in a one-to-one basis with any specific managerial behaviors, McGregor believed that these basic underlying beliefs are associated with managerial acts and policies that tend to be self-reinforcing. This association between a *set* of beliefs and a *set* of behaviors is entirely consistent with the model of beliefs, attitudes, and behaviors presented above (Ajzen and Fishbein, 1977; Fishbein and Ajzen, 1975).

Now that we have examined the general nature of human attitudes, we can turn our attention to the more specific issue of people's attitudes toward their jobs.

JOB-RELATED ATTITUDES

Organizational scientists have spent considerable time researching the nature, causes, and correlates of a variety of work-related attitudes (cf. Locke, 1975). Without doubt, the most commonly studied of these is job satisfaction, which is often defined as the degree to which one's work is useful for satisfying one's needs. (A more rigorous treatment of job satisfaction will be presented shortly.) A second construct that has been investigated in more recent years is variously referred to under the general rubric *organizational commitment* (or sometimes *attachment*). It has to do with the strength of the ties one feels toward one's employer or organization. A third concept of interest has been referred to as *job involvement.* It generally has to do with the attachment of the individual to her work,

92

per se (as opposed to her organization, her career, or other work-related referents). Different authors use these terms to denote different things, so it is often easy to become confused by reading the literature on these topics.

The purpose of the following sections is to examine the theory and research related to each of these constructs. As the discussion proceeds, the reader may form the opinion that job involvement and job/company commitment might be more reasonably categorized as *beliefs,* or values, rather than as attitudes, given the distinctions that were made in the previous sections. Nevertheless, we will treat involvement and commitment in this chapter, both for the sake of simplicity and because, appropriately or not, they are usually included under the general rubric, work-related attitudes.

Job Satisfaction

As was mentioned earlier, job satisfaction is, without doubt, the job-related attitudinal construct that has attracted the most attention in modern times. Scientists, managers, and the "man on the street" are all familiar with the term, and share a concern for understanding it. (In fact, it is not unfair to state that most people believe themselves to be experts on the issue!) A literature review by Locke (1976) has estimated that over thirty-three hundred research projects have been conducted and reported on job satisfaction during the past twenty-five years. Considering that only a fraction of the studies that are conducted by academics ever find their way into print, Locke's estimate is clearly conservative. In brief, job satisfaction is a popular issue. But what is it, exactly?

The nature of job satisfaction. There have been myriad implicit and explicit definitions of job satisfaction offered over the years, but the most thoughtful one (and the one to be adopted here) comes from Edwin Locke (1969, 1976). For Locke, job satisfaction is an emotional reaction that

> . . . results from the perception that one's job fulfills or allows the fulfillment of one's important job values, providing and to the degree that those values are congruent with one's needs (1976, p. 1307).

Unless otherwise indicated, this definition will be the one intended whenever the term job satisfaction is used in the present volume, and its obverse will be intended whenever the term job dissatisfaction is used.

Locke notes that job satisfaction is not the same thing as *morale.* While satisfaction has to do with a retrospective assessment of one's job, morale is seen more as concerned with a positive desire to continue to work at one's job. Further, the term morale is often used to **93** describe the overall attitudes of a work group, rather than of a single individual.

Locke's definition of job satisfaction is a conceptual one. In practice, researchers and managers often operationalize job satisfaction as having to do with the gratification of one's *needs* on the job or through the work setting. (Recall the discussion in chapters three and four of the multitude of needs that might be considered in such a context.) Moreover, interest is often directed at the satisfaction one has with a variety of specific aspects of one's job, and the circumstances surrounding it. For example, the Theory of Work Adjustment (Lofquist and Dawis, 1969) concerns itself with employee satisfaction and dissatisfaction for twenty-one different aspects of work and organizations, ranging from creativity and recognition to social status and working conditions. Thus, as noted by Locke (1976) and confirmed by Ben-Porat (1981), the list of potential causes of job satisfaction and dissatisfaction that has been investigated includes both *agents* (such as pay levels or one's supervisor) and *events* (such as the level of responsibility one is usually permitted to assume on the job). Moreover, different writers over the years have tended to contrive their own measures of satisfaction, making what is learned from one study difficult to compare with the results of other studies. Compounded by the common problems of reliability and validity of measurement that we discussed in chapter two, we are left with a vast volume of research on job satisfaction/dissatisfaction but, sadly enough, only a limited understanding of what it is, how it is actually influenced in work organizations, and what its consequences are for understanding and managing work organizations. (By this point in the book, the reader must have noted that this state of affairs is common in the research on organizational behavior!)

The causes of job satisfaction. All of the aforementioned problems notwithstanding, there has been some degree of convergence on the issue of the general nature of the causes of job satisfaction (or dissatisfaction). As mentioned above, some authors see job satisfaction as resulting from the fulfillment of *needs* through the activities one performs at one's job, and from the context in which the work is performed. In other words, job satisfaction is a function of need satisfaction, or at least the degree of correspondence or complementarity between the individual's needs on the one hand and the need-gratifying capacity of the work setting on the other. Characteristic of this work is that of Lofquist and Dawis (1969); Pervin (1968); Porter (1962, 1963); Betz (1969); Tuckman (1968); Seybolt (1976); and Fredericksen, Jensen, Beaton, and Bloxom (1972).

Other authors, such as Ilgen (1971) conceive of job satisfaction as resulting from the size of the *discrepancy* one perceives, if any, between what he expects to receive from his work and what he perceives he is receiving. Thus, large differences between the amount of pay an employee receives and the amount he expects to receive would result in dissatisfaction with pay, no reference being made to needs, per se.

A third approach considers employee *values,* which are defined as those things one sees as conducive to his or her welfare. It is important to distinguish between needs and values. Needs, as defined in chapters three and four, are basic forces that initiate and guide behavior for the sake of the preservation and health of the individual. Values are those things that a person *believes* are conducive to his welfare. Thus, while the author might place high value on a new foreign sports car, he has trouble convincing his wife that he really *needs* one! The point is that some approaches to satisfaction, such as that of Locke (1976), emphasize the role of values being met as the key determinant of job satisfaction, at least to the degree that these values are congruent with one's needs.

Still another view sees satisfaction or dissatisfaction resulting from comparisons a person makes between herself and other individuals around her. In this view (generally referred to as *Equity Theory*), a person is most likely to be dissatisfied when she perceives that the relationship between the contributions she makes to the organization and the benefits she derives in return, is less satisfactory than the relationship she perceives between the inputs and outcomes derived by some other person or group of persons. Feelings of inequitable treatment have been shown to be predictive of intentions to quit organizations. A more thorough treatment of Equity Theory will be presented in the next chapter.

To summarize, there have been a variety of approaches to the definition and conceptualization of job satisfaction. A comprehensive treatment of this literature is not possible in this chapter, but the interested reader is referred to a thorough review by Locke (1976).

The nature and causes of job dissatisfaction. Traditional thought on the matter has always held that job dissatisfaction is simply the opposite of job satisfaction, such that if an employee becomes more satisfied with her job, she necessarily becomes less dissatisfied, and vice versa. In chapter two, Herzberg's challenge to this assumption was presented and discussed at length. Briefly to review it, Herzberg and his colleagues argued that the concepts of job satisfaction and dissatisfaction are not the opposite of one another; rather, they are independent of one another. The reader will recall from that discussion that this asymmetrical aspect of the Motivator-Hygiene Theory is the one responsible for much of the so-called "Herzberg controversy." Because of the lack of clear and consistent **95**

support for the two-factor approach that has not been based on research of questionable quality,* the perspective adopted here is the traditional one—that satisfaction and dissatisfaction represent opposite ends of the same continuum. Nevertheless, it is clear that jobs have multiple facets, so *it is recognized that people can simultaneously be satisfied and/or dissatisfied with different aspects of their jobs.* (See Mahoney [1979] for an approach that reconciles the two-factor approach with the more traditional one.)

It is important to note as well the connection between what was presented in chapter four as need frustration and what is commonly viewed as job dissatisfaction: when dissatisfaction is conceived of as an emotional reaction to the blockage of attempts on the job to satisfy one's needs, then job dissatisfaction amounts to the same psychological state of frustration as we discussed in chapter four; and we can expect any of the usual human responses to it (cf. Spector, 1978).

What causes the blockage? Organizational policies that prevent individuals from being effective, in spite of their best efforts. Fellow employees who don't cooperate. Too much work to be done in the time permitted, such that none of it can be accomplished effectively. Shoddy machinery or supplies. A supervisor who doesn't listen, or who fails to provide assistance when it is needed. An organizational structure that prohibits rapid advancement or promotion. One's own sex (being the wrong one), or lack of abilities. Inconsistent expectations from one's bosses or members of one's job environment. Being assigned to undesirable working hours, such as the night shift. In short, frustration results from a blockage of one's efforts in pursuit of goals, and the blockage can emanate from any of a countless number of sources in an organization. The emotional reaction to frustration on the job is job dissatisfaction.

To understand job dissatisfaction as a specific form of frustration, we must understand the nature of the needs that can be blocked on the job. Remember that there are a variety of human needs in addition to those for existence and relatedness. The various forms of growth needs have become much more important to members of the modern workforce than they were in previous times, in large measure because of the relatively high levels of education and economic abundance enjoyed by western society over the past generation. The point is that the modern workforce expects greater challenge and stimulation, greater opportunities to self-actualize on the job, more chances to feel competent and efficacious, and more frequent opportunities to achieve and develop (O'Toole, 1981). But

---

*In fairness to Herzberg, and as noted in chapter two, much of the research that purports to refute the Motivator-Hygiene Theory has also been flawed (Grigaliunas and Weiner, 1974).

there are not enough jobs in business and industry that provide sufficient challenge and stimulation to make this sort of universal need satisfaction possible from work. The result is widespread job dissatisfaction, and indications that it may be increasing, although the evidence on this point is not totally conclusive (cf. Hoerr, 1979; Smith, Roberts, and Hulin, 1976; Smith, Scott, and Hulin, 1977 with Organ, 1977).

Consequences of job dissatisfaction. Setting the theory of frustration aside for a moment, it is instructive to consider what job dissatisfaction *feels like* to those who are experiencing it. It often carries feelings of gloom and despair, sometimes anger and resentment, sometimes futility. Jobs that are frustrating tend to make people tired and more mentally fatigued than they would otherwise be. Dissatisfying jobs can fill up lives, such that people feel depressed off the job as much as they do while at work, making the pursuit of leisure activities more critical, yet often less rewarding at the same time. Moreover, job dissatisfaction can be a major contributor to poor mental health, as well as to poor physical health (Herzberg, 1976; Jamal and Mitchell, 1980; Kavanaugh, Hurst, and Rose, 1981; Kornhauser, 1965). Job dissatisfaction hurts.

When a blockage occurs and frustration follows, we can expect the same sorts of reactions as occur in response to frustration in off-the-job settings, such as aggression, regression, fixation, withdrawal, and so on (see chapter four). Which of these general classes of reaction will occur, and the specific manifestation it will take varies from one person to the next, and from one job situation to the next, depending upon a number of factors. But we can anticipate bickering, theft, deliberate tardiness, insubordination, sabotage, espionage, and union activity, for example, to reflect impulses of aggression and anger directed at the job, or the organization. We can also expect a certain amount of displaced aggression, such as child and spouse beating, in cases where the individual cannot (or dares not) focus the aggression toward the job. Regressive responses such as pettiness, gossiping, complaining, crying, or foul-mouthing can also be expected—probably more frequently than aggressive behaviors, but sometimes in conjunction with aggressive acts. (Physical violence, for example, can be classed as both aggression and regression.)

The diversity of conceptual and operational definitions of job satisfaction (and dissatisfaction) used by investigators and managers (e.g., Wanous and Lawler, 1972) makes it somewhat difficult to generalize the findings of research into the organizational consequences of holding favorable or unfavorable job attitudes. Nevertheless, it does seem safe to conclude that job attitudes are more closely **97** related to employee decisions to participate in organizations than they are to employee decisions concerning performance levels (March and Simon, 1958). In other words, job satisfaction and dissatisfaction are much better predictors of attendance (or absenteeism), tardiness (as opposed to punctuality), and turnover, than they are of performance levels. The following section will focus on the evidence behind these conclusions, and discuss the costs *and benefits* of the consequences associated with unfavorable job attitudes.

Job dissatisfaction and withdrawal behaviors. Withdrawal in response to job dissatisfaction takes a number of characteristic forms, sometimes together. Tardiness, absenteeism, and turnover are the three most commonly acknowledged forms of withdrawal, but psychological withdrawal is also a problem. Psychological withdrawal consists of passive compliance and minimal attempts to perform on the job, demonstrating a general lack of desire to excel, to be creative, or to perform "above and beyond the call of duty." It sometimes manifests itself as laziness, sometimes as stupidity. While tardiness, absenteeism, turnover, and psychological withdrawal are separate phenomena, they do tend to be related to one another—to appear hand in hand (Beehr and Gupta, 1978; Edwards, 1979; Stumpf and Dawley, 1981). Research evidence suggests that job satisfaction will be conducive to lower levels of absenteeism (Breaugh, 1981; Dittrich and Carrell, 1979; Ilgen and Hollenback, 1977; Mirvis and Lawler, 1977; Nicholson, Wall, and Lischeron, 1977), higher levels of motivation to attend work on a given day (Smith, 1977; Steers and Rhodes, 1978), lower levels of tardiness (Adler and Golan, 1981), and lower levels of voluntary turnover (Arnold and Feldman, 1982; Dunnette, Arvey, and Banas, 1973; Karp and Nickson, 1973; Nicholson et al., 1977), possibly including early retirement (Schmitt and McCune, 1981). A number of studies have shown that employees' expressed *intentions* to leave an organization are more closely correlated with actual subsequent turnover than are other indicators of job dissatisfaction (Kraut, 1975; Mitchel, 1981). Note that this finding is entirely consistent with the belief-attitude-intention-behavior approach to attitudes (presented earlier in this chapter): intentions, once formed, are more closely connected to behavior than are attitudes (Fishbein and Ajzen, 1975).

The importance of these findings from a management perspective lies in the fact that these various forms of withdrawal can be disruptive to smooth organizational functioning, and very costly. For example, it was found in a study of an American bank that the average cost (during the mid-1970s) of replacing a teller was over $2,500. The attendant cost savings potentially associated with an improvement in job satisfaction of one-half standard deviation among a group of 160 tellers would be approximately $17,600 (Mirvis and Lawler, 1977). When other factors, such as comparable increases in levels of intrinsic motivation (recall chapter four) and job involvement (which will be discussed later in this chapter) were added to the analysis, it was estimated that the employer might have saved as much as $125,000 over a one-year period. Sibson (1975) reports a case in which it cost a company over $47,000 to recruit and hire a $60,000 per year executive.

The point here is to demonstrate that turnover can be very costly to an organization. In addition to the disruption that turnover can cause in the work process, there are costs associated with recruitment, training, and supporting new employees until they are creating enough value to offset the compensation they earn on the job (Pinder and Das, 1979).

Absenteeism (which, as we have argued, is related to unfavorable job attitudes) is also expensive. One source estimates that 400 million person-days are lost in United States business and industry every year, about four times as many days as are lost to strikes (Yolles, Carone, and Krinsky, 1975), and that the annual cost of this absenteeism may be as high as $26.4 billion (Steers and Rhodes, 1978)!

On the other hand, while absenteeism does not appear to have any redeeming qualities, it has been argued that turnover is not without its benefits to the organizations and individuals involved, as well as to society as a whole (Dalton, 1981; Dalton and Todor, 1979, 1982a). For example, it can be shown that an organization can reap real dollar cost savings through turnover, especially in cases where those who leave can easily be replaced by newcomers who are compensated at lower rates of pay and benefits (Dalton and Todor, 1982a). In addition, turnover can help introduce new ideas, new "blood," and the potential for change and adaptation of the organization involved, a necessity for organizations facing even moderate levels of change in their environments (Aldrich, 1980; Gross, 1965). People who leave tend to be the ones who withdraw other ways, so turnover may help reduce absenteeism, tardiness, psychological withdrawal, and their associated costs (Mobley, 1982).

Turnover may also be the only solution in cases of extreme conflict between organizational members, as often occurs following mergers and other forms of reorganization (Mobley, 1982). For the individual, moving to a new organization can serve as an adaptive escape from a job that is stressful or conducive to marital discord, alcohol and drug abuse, or general life maladjustment.

From a societal point of view, turnover helps cross-organizational institution building, as ideas and techniques developed in some organizations are taken into others, often at the cost of **99** certain individual organizations, but often for the benefit of entire industries or networks of organizations. (See McKelvey, 1982, for a discussion of the transmission of "genes" among organizations.)

A few final points concerning the relationship between job attitudes and turnover need brief mention. First, it is important to distinguish between voluntary and involuntary absenteeism, tardiness, and turnover, and to realize that job attitudes can be predictive only of withdrawal behaviors that are voluntary in nature (Steers and Rhodes 1978). Many times employees are late for work, absent from work, or must quit their jobs for reasons that are somewhat or totally beyond their control. For example, many employees find they must quit their jobs in order to accompany their spouses to new job sites in other cities following transfers. It would be unreasonable to include turnover of this sort in any analysis of the connection between job attitudes and turnover. The point is that job dissatisfaction is not the only cause of the various types of withdrawal behaviors we have discussed here, although it does contribute to decisions of voluntary withdrawal. The interested reader is referred to Porter and Steers (1973), Steers and Rhodes (1978), Mobley, Griffeth, Hand, and Meglino (1979), Price (1977), and Michaels and Spector (1982) for more comprehensive theoretical and empirical treatments of voluntary and involuntary withdrawal behaviors.

Secondly, while job dissatisfaction may generate a desire to leave one's organization in favor of employment elsewhere, we cannot assume that low levels of turnover are indicative of generally positive work attitudes in a workforce. There are a number of things that can lock-in disgruntled employees, preventing them from leaving dissatisfying work settings (Flowers and Hughes, 1973; Hershey, 1973). For example, while an employee may be very dissatisfied with some aspects of her job (such as the nature of the work itself), she might be quite unwilling to leave it and lose the high levels of pay it brings her. (Some critics claim that such has been the case in the auto industry, where the production work is terribly boring, but where the United Auto Workers have managed to negotiate handsome hourly wages for its members, to somehow "buy them off" for suffering the tedium of assembly-line work.)

In addition, tight labor markets often prevent dissatisfied employees from turning over, as do a host of familial and economic factors. ("I like it here in Chilliwack, why should I leave?") Sometimes a generalized fear of the unknown, often based on real or imagined self-perceptions of obsolescence, prevent dissatisfied employees from quitting.

Finally (although this list is not exhaustive), many organizations inadvertently prevent their employees from leaving them because of the "golden handcuffs" they manage to lock onto their workforce over the years through pension plans, health insurance plans, and other benefits. The importance of this point is that while there is no necessary connection between job attitudes and performance, disgruntled employees are often those who perform their jobs at the minimum levels required, and who seldom demonstrate any desire to be creative, or to excel "above and beyond the call of duty" when the occasion to do so presents itself. Moreover, there is evidence, as presented earlier, that dissatisfied personnel are more likely to be absent and tardy, disrupting the normal flow of events for their employers, customers, and co-workers. Hence, an organization may benefit from ridding itself of those who are dissatisfied. On the other hand, it is often the case that those who leave are those who are capable of leaving, and the reason they are capable of leaving is that they are competent and quite marketable; they are often people who, when they do leave, represent a loss of talent to the organization losing them, and an equal increase in the stock of talent that works for other employers (such as the competition). Whether turnover occurs among an organization's high performers or low performers may depend upon its reward system; competent personnel seem less likely to leave when pay and other rewards are contingent upon performance, whereas they are more likely to leave when rewards are not distributed in accordance with performance (Dreher, 1982).

In summary, while job dissatisfaction is a contributing factor to voluntary turnover, it is not responsible for most cases of involuntary quitting, and, because of the reasons just listed, we cannot assume that turnover will rid an organization of either its most dissatisfied or its lowest performing employees. Hence, turnover may be beneficial for the employee who leaves and for the organization to which he goes. But turnover may be either beneficial or detrimental to the organization that suffers it, depending on the costs associated with the economic and noneconomic considerations discussed above. An exhaustive analysis of the causes, costs, and benefits of turnover is beyond the scope of this chapter. Mobley (1982) provides a thorough review of the issues for the interested reader.

Job satisfaction and performance. At least since the beginning of the Human Relations movement in the 1940s, it has commonly been assumed that employees who are more satisfied with their work tend to be more productive. Among many managers, politicians, and social critics, it makes intuitive sense to assume that "a satisfied employee is a productive employee." After countless studies into the relationship between these two variables, *it can be concluded that there is no simple relationship between job attitudes and job performance.* (Recall from our discussion earlier in this chapter that it is seldom the case that attitudes lead to specific behaviors in a **101**

predictable fashion.) Sometimes high levels of satisfaction are associated with high levels of performance; other times, the opposite is the case. It may be, for example, that a *dissatisfied* employee will become quite productive if she perceives that high performance levels may help her earn a promotion, a raise in pay, or even a chance to successfully attain a job elsewhere. Alternatively, highly satisfied employees can become complacent, resting on their reputations and assuming that contributions made in the past have earned them the right to ''coast'' on the job, perhaps until retirement.

In short, in spite of the intuitive appeal of the common-sense axiom that satisfaction leads to performance, there is abundant evidence to show that this is simply not reliably true (see Bhagat, 1982; Brayfield and Crockett, 1955; Schwab and Cummings, 1970; and Vroom, 1964, for reviews of the evidence). Some authors have suggested that even in those cases where performance and satisfaction are related, it may be that performance levels cause satisfaction levels, rather than the other way around (e.g. Lawler and Porter, 1967), or that a host of organizational factors simultaneously influence both satisfaction and performance, causing them to *appear* to be causally interrelated. The point is that we can conclude that managerial attempts to improve job satisfaction will not necessarily have any impact on productivity levels in the workforce, although they may help save money through reducing rates of withdrawal. Improved job satisfaction may also be beneficial from a strictly humanitarian/quality-of-life perspective.

Job satisfaction and union activism. One consequence of unfavorable job attitudes among employees that is usually of concern to managers is unionization activity. While job dissatisfaction is certainly not the only cause of unionization, recent studies have shown that unfavorable work attitudes are associated with pro-union activity in certification attempts in 125 units of a large American retailer (Hamner and Smith, 1978). Other research has found connections between job dissatisfaction and pro-union voting among production workers (Schriesheim, 1978) and among faculty members at a private eastern U.S. university (Hammer and Berman, 1981). The implication of these findings is that managers who wish to prevent or reduce the chances of unionization in their workforces are well advised to do what they can to maintain positive employee attitudes, among other things.

Organizational Commitment

Whereas job satisfaction generally has to do with the degree to which one's needs or values are satisfied by one's job, *organizational commitment* is a psychological construct that is somewhat

102

broader in scope, and may be of more value as a predictor of turn-over and other withdrawal behaviors (Porter, Crampon, and Smith 1972). Organizational commitment has been defined in a variety of ways, although there is considerable convergence among the most well-developed perspectives. For example, Porter et al. (1972) see commitment as consisting of three interrelated (although not identi-cal) attitudes and intentions: (1) a strong belief in, and acceptance of, the organization's goals and values; (2) a willingness to exert consid-erable effort on behalf of the organization; and (3) a definite desire to remain a member of the organization (Porter et al., 1974).

A more recent view of organizational commitment defines it as ''. . . the totality of internalized normative pressures to act in a way that meets organizational goals and interests'' (Weiner, 1982). In this view, commitment causes individuals to behave in ways that they be-lieve are morally right, rather than in ways that are going to be instru-mental for their own personal goals. Therefore, people who are com-mitted to their organizations are more likely to make sacrifices for them, to persist in their attempts to serve them, and to be pre-occupied with them, devoting a considerable proportion of their time and energy to the pursuit of the objectives of their organizations.

In short, we can think of organizational commitment as a form of extreme loyalty to one's organization. The important aspect of this construct for our present purpose is that the attitude object here is the organization, per se, not the person's particular job, department, or work group.

Causes of commitment. From the time they enter the em-ployment of organizations, most individuals witness attempts to make them committed and devoted. For example, organizational rules serve to assure that employees behave according to the norms and expectations of the organization. There is often an attempt made to impress the newcomer with the merit of the organization's mission and major goals, as well as to provide a sense of the history and tradi-tions of the organization (Pondy, Frost, Morgan, and Dandridge, 1983).

For example, induction programs and other socialization rituals attempt to inculcate the employee with an understanding of, and an appreciation for, ''our way of doing things'' (Feldman, 1977, 1981). Pensions and other benefit plans sometimes constitute so-called ''golden handcuffs,'' which make it increasingly more difficult for employees to consider leaving (cf. Angle and Perry, 1982). Organi-zational logos and insignia, off-the-job social functions, and pro-grams for employees' spouses are all designed, in part, to build loy-alty. (See Becker, 1960 on the role of social involvement in commitment building.) Company newsletters are common in large **103** organizations, serving more to build a sense of loyalty and commitment than to communicate real news. It has been argued that even certain formal personnel transactions conducted upon employees once they are "on board" facilitate commitment, binding them to the organization as a primary source of emotional and social support. For example, Edstrom and Galbraith (1977) have suggested that the transferring of employees to positions at the various operating sites of geographically-dispersed organizations functions, in part, to make them less likely to build connections outside the organization that may be distracting, or that may serve to compromise their complete and undivided devotion. Finally, there is some evidence that reward systems (including promotions and merit pay) that link performance to rewards will tend to make employees more committed (Dreher, 1982). Many of these commitment builders are more deliberate than others, and some of them can be very subtle. The point is that organized activity requires commitment among organizational members (Katz, 1964), so organizational procedures are necessary to generate and sustain such loyalty.

A number of researchers have shown that in addition to active and deliberate organizational procedures for building commitment, there are other factors that can contribute to it; factors related to the employees themselves, to their jobs, as well as to other elements of the work environment (e.g., Angle and Perry, 1982; Morris and Sherman, 1981; Steers, 1977). For example, in a study of scientists, engineers, and hospital employees, Steers (1977) found that the individual's need for achievement, education, and age were associated with commitment to their organizations. (Education was inversely correlated, meaning that higher levels of education were related to lower levels of commitment. This is a common phenomenon among professional employees, whose loyalty is devoted toward the profession first, and toward the employer second.) Pro-organizational attitudes of the individual's work group were associated with greater commitment. Jobs which permitted the employee greater degrees of voluntary interaction with co-workers, and jobs which permitted employees to understand how their work related to the jobs done by others in the organization, also seemed to be conducive to commitment (probably through the satisfaction these job characteristics fostered). However, Steers' (1977) results showed that certain work-related *experiences* were more powerful as predictors of commitment than were either the personal, job, or other organizational factors considered. Specifically, Steers found that positive group attitudes among one's peers, feelings that the organization had met the individual's prior expectations, feelings that the organization could be relied upon to carry out its commitments to its personnel, and feelings that the individual was of some importance to the organization collectively, seemed to be the most important influences on commitment levels. Similar results were found in separate studies by Angle and Perry (1982), Buchanan (1974), and Morris and Sherman (1981). For the sake of instilling and maintaining commitment, these results are encouraging to the manager, because they suggest that commitment can, in fact, be built, and that it is not going to be determined simply by the inherent characteristics of employees.

Consequences of commitment. There is evidence that people who are less committed to their organizations are more likely to be absent (Steers, 1977), as well as more likely to leave them, thereby generating the same costs and/or benefits for the organizations involved that can result from low satisfaction levels (Angle and Perry, 1981; Hom, Katerberg, and Hulin, 1979; Porter, Crampon, and Smith, 1976; Porter, Steers, Mowday, and Boulian, 1974). Nevertheless, we can still ask whether organizational commitment is a good thing. The answer to this question will doubtlessly vary with the perspective of the individual who addresses it. If turnover is primarily a negative phenomenon for organizations (in spite of the benefits identified by Dalton and Todor 1979, 1982a), then it would seem from a managerial perspective that it is desirable to attempt to develop and foster high levels of employee commitment. Moreover, high levels of commitment are no doubt beneficial from the point of view of long-term employee job performance, in its intensity, its duration, and for the sake of periodic efforts above and beyond the call of duty (Katz, 1964). Certainly the success of Japanese business and industry since World War II rests heavily on the unique Japanese managerial style that relies on unquestioned loyalty to one's employer (Ouchi, 1981). Thus a recent study found that union stewards who were highly committed to their organizations tended to process fewer formal grievances (Dalton and Todor, 1982b).

One interesting consequence of extreme levels of organizational commitment may be reduced levels of commitment to other sources of support (as was mentioned earlier). Sometimes this can be dysfunctional for the organization involved. For example, Rotondi (1975) found that R&D engineers who were more committed to their organization tended to be less creative and innovative, probably because devotion to one's scientific discipline can often clash with devotion to one's employer (cf. Shepard, 1956).

What are the benefits of commitment from the *employees'* point of view? If high levels of commitment are the consequence of consistently fair (even generous) treatment by an employer, then commitment is probably desirable, because an employee who is committed to his employer may suffer less anxiety about the prospect of **105** losing his job, and may generally feel much more secure and content as a result. Commitment is accompanied by feelings of nurturance and mutual trust and fosters a generally positive outlook in life. For those who have it, in short, commitment can be a source of comfort and security.

On the other hand, individuals who become highly committed often tend to anthropomorphize or reify their organizations: while organizations are made up of human beings, they are not, in themselves, human beings!! Organizations are complex social systems that structure themselves and behave so as to survive. They do not have memories, and they do not have hearts. Senior managers and executives may be capable of remembering who deserves support and loyal treatment for jobs done well in the past, but senior executives come and go. Loyalty earned during one era can lose all value as new managerial regimes evolve. The survival of the organization is tantamount; if it is expedient to continue to support the faithful servants of the past, they will be supported. But when economic or other exigencies arise to threaten the survival or effectiveness of an organization, the highly committed individual's loyalty is often unrequited.

The author was personally acquainted with the senior executive, in Canada, of a large foreign airline—an individual who devoted most of his adult life to the profitability and effectiveness of the firm. The executive's hard work led to a stroke at age forty-six, although he eventually recovered. The company kept him on, but organizational policies requiring that he have his health examined by corporate doctors (rather than local doctors) precipitated a second stroke twelve years later. Obeying the firm's orders rather than acting according to his own best interest, the executive undertook to travel halfway around the world for a medical check, in spite of his protestations that his health was poor at that time, and that it would be further threatened by a trip of such demanding proportions. The trip killed the executive, and his wife was granted a small settlement.

Aside from the possibility that commitment may not be reciprocated by one's organization, leaving the person abandoned in hard times, there is the issue, of course, of the nature of the organizational goals to which individuals commit themselves. Clearly, if a person becomes enthralled by the goals of an organization, the legality and the morality of those goals have important implications for the committed employee (Weiner, 1982). Many cases of corporate corruption and crime have been perpetrated by highly committed employees, whose zealous pursuit of their employer's goals required them to engage in illegal and immoral activities, in which they probably would not have otherwise engaged.

106   The point is this: organizations require the commitment of their members in order to survive, so they do what they can to develop and foster it. But economic necessities can force even the most benevolent of employers to lay off, or otherwise abandon, those who have helped make them effective. Even in Japan, where loyalty to one's organization is an inherent part of the culture, managers in many industries have been laid off, North American–style, as the economic advantage previously enjoyed by Japanese industry has suffered in recent years (Rowan, 1981). In short, while commitment is necessary for the organization's survival, it may or may not be best for an individual's best long-term interests, notwithstanding all the things our parents told us.

Job Involvement

A third psychological construct related to work behavior that has received considerable attention in recent years is referred to as *job involvement*. There have been a number of attempts to define it and to differentiate it from other, related constructs, such as job satisfaction and intrinsic motivation; and these efforts tend to converge (Lawler and Hall, 1970; Lodahl and Kejner, 1965; Saleh and Hosek, 1976).

Job involvement, loosely defined, has to do with the strength of the relationship between an individual's work and his self-concept. Specifically, a person is said to be involved in his job if he (1) actively participates in it; (2) holds it as a central life interest; (3) perceives performance at it as central to his self-esteem; and (4) sees performance on it as consistent with his self-concept.

People who are highly job involved tend to be obsessed with their work. When they perform poorly, they feel poorly. They like others to know them for their work, and to know that they do it well. For a highly job involved person, work is one of the most important aspects of life, if not the most important. There is some evidence that job involved people tend to be more satisfied with their work (Gorn and Kanungo, 1980) and more intrinsically motivated (Lawler and Hall, 1970), but it is important to repeat that involvement, satisfaction, and intrinsic motivation are distinct constructs (Lawler and Hall, 1970). Moreover, this construct has to do with one's commitment to her job, not to her employer, per se, and these two forms of commitment are only slightly related to one another (Stevens, Beyer, and Trice, 1978; Weiner and Vardi, 1980).

Causes of job involvement. What determines the level of involvement a person has in his job? A number of studies suggest that, as was the case in the determinants of commitment, characteristics of both the individual and of the organization must be taken into account. For example, Rabinowitz and Hall (1977) found that job involvement was correlated with the strength of the individual's growth **107**

needs (see chapter four) and with the strength of one's belief in the so-called "Protestant Work Ethic." In addition, the length of time the person was on the job, as well as the scope provided by the job, were positively associated with involvement. Another study found that employees whose jobs served to satisfy their most salient needs (regardless of whether these were intrinsic or extrinsic) were higher in both involvement with the particular jobs they held at the time, as well as with work in general (Gorn and Kanungo, 1980). In a third study, it was found that employees who participated more in the decision making related to their jobs were more involved in those jobs (Siegel and Ruh, 1973).

In short, the level of involvement people feel with regard to their jobs is most likely determined by an interaction between their own needs and values on the one hand, and a variety of features of the job and the job setting on the other. Consequently, we might assume that job involvement may be somewhat manipulable through the enactment of appropriate organizational policies and procedures.

Consequences of job involvement. As we did in our discussion of commitment, we can suitably ask whether job involvement is a good thing. And, as before, we must conclude that the answer may depend upon who provides it. There is some evidence that job involved employees tend to be more satisfied with their jobs than employees who are less job involved (Cheloha and Farr, 1980; Gannon and Hendrickson, 1973; Gorn and Kanungo, 1980; Lawler and Hall, 1970). Likewise, there is suggestive evidence that job involved employees are likely to be somewhat happier with their organizations (Schwyhart and Smith, 1972), as well as more committed to them, and less absent from them (Cheloha and Farr, 1980), although, as was mentioned earlier, the relationships are mixed and moderate (Gorn and Kanungo, 1980). This means that it is quite possible for employees to enjoy their jobs, but not feel fully involved in them. Or, it is possible for individuals to be attached to their jobs and to enjoy them, but not be very committed to their employing organization. (Such is often the case with managerial, professional, technical or other highly skilled employees.)

Is there any relationship between job involvement and employee effort and performance? Very little research has been reported on this issue, and so caution is necessary. One study found moderately strong linkages between involvement and self-report measures of effort and performance (as measured by salary) among a group of insurance sales representatives who worked on commission (Gorn and Kanungo, 1980).

It is critical to note that virtually all of the studies reported above were conducted in a cross-sectional manner, making it impossible to determine, when there were relationships observed, which variables were causal and which were the results of the workings of others. For example, are highly involved employees more likely to devote higher levels of effort to their jobs because of the fulfillment it provides them? Or is it the other way around—could more highly involved employees become more satisfied with their jobs because their devotion to them results in mastery and feelings of achievement and competence? What seems most plausible is that certain characteristics of employees, their jobs, and their organizations are likely to be responsible for causing levels of commitment, satisfaction, and involvement; these in turn both influence, and are influenced by, the individual's performance level. Therefore, managers may be able to affect this cluster of events and associations by thoughtful application of enlightened policies and practices but it is probable that the characteristics of their employees will limit (or magnify) the impact that they can have on these various outcome variables.

Involvement and commitment in the extreme. Before we leave our discussion of the benefits of job involvement, we should ask whether extreme levels of job involvement, like extreme levels of commitment, might have any unfortunate consequences for the employee. The person on the street often uses the term *workaholism* to refer to the construct labeled job involvement by students of organizational science. Is workaholism a good thing?

The answer is yes and no. Without workaholics, many organizations could not function as effectively as they do (Oates, 1971). Workaholics are always there to backstop the errors made by others. (Of course they are also often the cause of many of these errors themselves.) They make up for the low commitment of others. They can be counted on to perform the jobs others avoid, and generally, to attack them with passion. They work hard; they provide management more "bang for the buck." Every person reading this volume must be familiar with at least one workaholic, as well as with how others around that person have grown dependent upon him, or her, in the job setting.

It is common to pity workaholics, or sometimes to look upon them with disdain, as if they are afflicted with some form of social or occupational disease. For example, Schwartz (1982) has recently defined involvement as a manifestation of neurotic obsession-compulsion. In fact, a leading authority on workaholism has found that most workaholics are generally healthy and happy people (Machlowitz, 1980). Workaholics are people who live to work. They are *extremely* devoted to their work.

109

Machlowitz (1980) estimates that about 5 percent of the adult population are workaholics, and that the proportion of the *workforce* who are workaholics is probably higher, since, almost by definition, these people tend not to be unemployed.

While not all hard workers are workaholics, all workaholics are hard workers. They plan their lives around their jobs, and love it. Both men and women can be workaholics, although the difficulties faced by female workaholics are different (and sometimes worse) than those faced by male workaholics. Many workaholics contribute to the effectiveness of their organizations at levels that are detrimental to their own health (Caplan and Jones, 1975), but don't mind doing so, and are often not aware that they are doing so.

On the other hand, Machlowitz (1980) claims that while they spend long hours of hard-driving work effort at their jobs, workaholics are often very poor performers, for a variety of reasons. One reason is that they have an inherent aversion to delegating responsibilities to other people. They insist on maintaining control, and would generally rather do everything themselves. As a result, they often spread themselves too thin, and take on so many tasks that they simply cannot be effective at all of them, in spite of the long hours they spend at their work. Workaholics often try to create and foster the impression that they are indispensible (and, due to their reluctance to delegate, this is often the case). But much of the flurry surrounding them is artificial, rather than truly warranted. Moreover, workaholics tend to intimidate and annoy others around them who are not so completely obsessed with work. As supervisors, they push their subordinates with impunity, often causing high levels of stress and low levels of job satisfaction among them, and sometimes driving away talented people. And there is no cause to believe that the high levels of energy they expend *necessarily* result in greater levels of performance efficiency than would be attainable by working at more "normal" speeds. Workaholics often lose sight of work priorities; in their attempts to get everything done, they often get little actually accomplished. Their obsession with their own time and time schedules means they frequently fail to honor the time requirements of others; they are characteristically late for meetings, and are most frequently the ones to leave in the middle of meetings.

Finally, there are a number of other difficulties caused by, and faced by, workaholics and those around them, including their spouses, friends, and families. They tend to be isolated from their friends and strangers to their children. Marriages suffer greater strains when one member of the couple is a workaholic than when neither is (although a marriage between two workaholics sometimes can be very successful).

The point here is this: many of us seem to wish that more members of the workforce would take their work more seriously. A casual consideration of concepts such as company commitment and job involvement might bring the response that we wish more people were more committed and involved. Many members of the older generation point with suspicion at the younger generation, accusing them of not having enough of these attitudes about work. But Machlowitz (1980) reminds us that too much of this view toward work can be unfortunate, for both the organizations and the individuals involved. More job involvement, on a national scale, may be beneficial, but only to a point.

CONCLUSION

In conclusion, we can state that employee attitudes are important, both to the individuals who hold them, and to all organizations that employ people. Although the connections are unpredictable, attitudes can result in behaviors—behaviors that can have either positive or negative consequences for both people and organizations. Managers often assume that the connection between employee attitudes and behaviors is stronger than it in fact is, and sometimes they overreact to what they see as extreme attitudes of either positive or negative tone.

To a certain limit, both organizational commitment and job involvement are necessary, and potentially beneficial, for both employees and employers. In the extreme, however, too much commitment may make employees emotionally and occupationally vulnerable, and too much job involvement may result in the sorts of human consequences associated with workaholism. To date, however, there has been nothing to indicate that too much job satisfaction has any harmful effects, but we seem to be a long way from reaching the stage where, on a macro level, this will ever be the case. In the foreseeable future, there will continue to be a vast number of undesirable jobs to be done (cf. Faltermayer, 1974).

Finally, it is important to note that the three job-related attitudes discussed in this chapter are not the only ones that have been investigated by organizational scientists. Job satisfaction, organizational commitment, and job involvement were singled out for discussion here, both because they have been the subjects of considerable research in recent years, and because they are important. It is critical to note that these three constructs do not exhaust all the possible forms employee attitudes may take. Identified and articulated in the ways they have been presented here, these constructs represent only three of an infinite number of mental and visceral reactions people may have toward their work. In many ways, these concepts are arbitrary—who is to say that they represent the most common or **111** even the most important attitudes that can be found in the minds and hearts of working people? In short, the careful reader will pay attention to these three constructs as important, but will realize that, in many ways, they represent the mental events of the researchers and scholars who have identified (created?) and discussed them (cf. Schwab, 1980).

Now that a few fundamental concepts about the nature of beliefs and attitudes and their relationships with behavior have been discussed, we turn our attention in chapters six, seven, and eight to three popular theories of work motivation, all of which rely upon important assumptions about the role of cognitive processes in motivated work effort. Specifically, the three theories of motivation to be examined in the next three chapters assume a cognitive/perceptual view of human nature, and attribute behavior to the influence of human perceptions, beliefs, attitudes, and intentions.

BELIEFS, ATTITUDES AND MOTIVATION
Equity Theory 6

You remember Thurlow's answer . . . you never expected justice from a company, did you? They have neither a soul to lose, nor a body to kick.

—Rev. Sydney Smith

As noted at the conclusion of chapter five, the primary purpose for our attention to the nature and consequences of work-related beliefs, attitudes, and intentions was to set the stage for an examination of three specific theories of work motivation that assume that behavior results from the operation of these cognitive factors. In the present chapter, we will discuss a theory (or body of theories) referred to as *Equity Theory*. This theory assumes that people's perceptions and beliefs about the fairness of their treatment on the job explains a variety of work-related attitudes and behaviors.

In the following chapter, we will look at a second theory that rests on the cognitive/perceptual model of human functioning—a theory that purports to explain the formation of intentions to behave certain ways on the job. Then, in chapter eight, we will examine a third approach—one that assumes that human behavior is determined by intentions, but that underplays the origins of these intentions, per se.

While reading chapters six, seven, and eight, the reader is advised to keep in mind the meaning of beliefs, attitudes, and intentions, as well as the fact that the model of human nature which utilizes these hypothetical constructs constitutes only one of several models that might be assumed. Chapters nine and ten, for example, adopt an entirely different set of assumptions about the ultimate causes of human behavior.

113

To begin then, let's look at the causes and consequences of employee beliefs about the equity of the treatment they receive on their jobs.

EQUITY THEORY

Professional athletes often make the news by demanding that their contracts be torn up before their terms expire. The reason for this apparent lack of respect for contract law usually has to do with feelings on the part of these athletes that the rates of pay agreed to in their contracts are, by some standard, not fair. In 1982, for example, the Los Angeles Dodgers found that their ace pitcher Fernando Valenzuela was quite unhappy about the $40,000 he was scheduled to earn during the second year of his contract—the year following his spectacular Cy Young–winning performance as a rookie. Likewise, Sparky Lyle, of the New York Yankees, was miffed when that team hired Reggie Jackson and Don Gullett (whose leg was in a cast at the time of the signing), because he felt that compared to the salaries being paid by the Yankees to these star newcomers, his own salary was far too low.

But baseball players are not the only ones who sometimes feel that, compared to what they perceive other people earn, they are being underrewarded. Further, this sort of reaction is not unique to professional athletes. The point is that people tend to hold beliefs about the value of their contributions at work, and about how well these contributions are recognized and rewarded. Moreover, these beliefs are formed in a social context in which people tend to compare how well they are being treated with how well they believe others are being treated. When people believe that, relative to others, they are being undercompensated or somehow underrecognized, they become unhappy and motivated to do something about it. Professional athletes have been known to sit out whole seasons over contract disputes of this sort, and labor unions in many nonsports industries go on strike every year for similar reasons.

This chapter is about a collection of theories generally and collectively referred to as *Equity Theory*. Actually, there are a variety of theories which fit under this general heading, but, due to limitations of space, the discussion provided here will be somewhat general and relevant to all of them, as opposed to being devoted to a precise analysis of the nuances of each of them, and the differences among them. (The interested reader is referred to Adams [1963, 1965], Homans [1961], Jacques [1961], and Patchen [1961] for treatments of many of the specific versions of Equity Theory.) On the other hand, it is acknowledged that the following discussion is most heavily influ-

114

enced by the work of Adams (1963, 1965), because his version seems to have been the most influential in the research and theoretic work among organizational scientists interested in work motivation and behavior (Pritchard, 1969).

THE ELEMENTS OF EQUITY THEORY

Equity Theory rests upon three main assumptions (Carrell and Dittrich, 1978). First, the theory holds that people develop beliefs about what constitutes a fair and equitable return for their contributions to their jobs. Secondly, the theory assumes that people tend to compare what they perceive to be the exchange they have with their employers, vis à vis what they perceive to be the nature of the exchange other individuals have with their employers (although the employers being considered need not be one and the same). Finally, the theory holds that when people believe that their own treatment is not equitable, relative to the exchange they perceive others to be making, they will be motivated to do something about it, as in the aforementioned examples of disgruntled athletes.

More specifically, the theory states that individuals hold perceptions about the number and value of the contributions they make to their work. These contributions are usually referred to as *inputs.* For example, people may consider the education and training they bring to their jobs, the number of hours they work, and how hard they try to perform when they are at their jobs. Different people tend to pay attention to different inputs, and there is a tendency for people to place greater emphasis upon those inputs which they themselves have to offer (e.g., Cummings, 1980). For example, highly educated people often place great importance upon their schooling, even in work contexts where what they have learned in university is not related to the nature of the work they do. The college graduate with a major in German literature, for example, often becomes quite frustrated when she learns that her degree is discounted by prospective employers who are seeking to hire computer operators! Equity Theory assumes that people aggregate their perceived inputs into some sort of psychological total, representing the net value they believe they contribute to their jobs.

In addition, people hold beliefs about the nature and quantity of the consequences or *outcomes* they receive as a result of doing their work. Pay, fringe benefits, job satisfaction, status, opportunities to learn, as well as physical outcomes such as company cars, represent the range of things that people might consider as outcomes. Again, different people tend to recognize different outcomes, depending upon what their own jobs provide them. Thus, for years, **115** members of Canada's prestigious Royal Canadian Mounted Police enjoyed tremendous status and respect from the citizenry, somewhat offsetting what many of them believed to be comparatively low pay levels. Likewise, junior professors at highly prestigious universities (none will be mentioned here by name) are often expected to work for lower starting salaries than they might receive elsewhere, in part because of the status they are expected to derive from being affiliated with these institutions.

Equity Ratios

Equity Theory holds that people evaluate their outcomes relative to their inputs, and form opinions about how well they are being treated. Most (but not all)* versions of the theory stress that this evaluation often takes place in a comparative, social sense, such that people consider their inputs and outcomes relative to the inputs and outcomes they perceive other people contribute and take away from their work.

The crucial aspect of this social comparison process is that it is believed that inputs and outcomes are considered in *ratio* terms, rather than in absolute terms. So, for example, the reader may believe that his sister makes twice as much money as he does, but whether that belief results in annoyance for him will depend upon his beliefs about the value of the contributions his sister makes to her work, compared to the value of the contributions he believes he makes to his own job. People can tolerate seeing others earn more money and other benefits than they do if they believe that the others also contribute more in the way of inputs to their respective jobs. But when we see other people making a lot more money (or other forms of outcome) than we do, while not appearing to be contributing more in the way of relevant inputs, a tension results—a tension that the theory says will motivate behavior to equalize the ratios. In fact, the tension is particularly strong, according to the theory, when the other person's outcomes are perceived as higher than our own, while that person's inputs are simultaneously perceived to be lower (Adams, 1963).

---

*For example, Pritchard (1969) states that

> . . . feelings of inequity arise *first* and foremost from the correspondence between [the] Person's own inputs and outcomes. . . . If his inputs are greater than outcomes, he will experience inequity, which will lead to feelings of dissatisfaction regardless of the input-outcome ratio of anyone else (1969, p. 206).

However, Pritchard is a bit inconsistent, because elsewhere (1969, pp. 205–206; Pritchard et al., 1972) the role of external referents is included in his thinking and empirical research (Törnblom, 1977).

Symbolically, we can represent these two ratios for a hypothetical person (named George) as follows:

$$\frac{\text{George's beliefs about his own outcomes}}{\text{George's beliefs about his own inputs}} \overset{?}{=} \frac{\text{George's beliefs about someone else's outcomes}}{\text{George's beliefs about that person's inputs}}$$

If George perceives that, psychologically, his ratio of outcomes to inputs compares favorably with that of some other person with whom he compares, the theory suggests he will be content. Tension builds, however, when George perceives that the ratio of outcomes to inputs of his comparison person is sufficiently more favorable than the ratio he attributes to his own situation.

The eye of the beholder. A number of points must be made clear here. First, the ratios represented above reflect George's view of the world; they may not be shared by other people, such as George's supervisor, or the person with whom George compares himself. Therefore, the same two people could compare themselves with one another, and each conclude that the other has a better deal—it would depend entirely upon the degree to which their beliefs about each other's (and their own) inputs and outcomes matched.

The choice of a referent. A second point concerns the choice of a referent for comparison. With whom does George compare ratios? Some equity theorists have suggested that people often experience equity or inequity in terms of the degree of balance they perceive, between their own inputs and outcomes, compared to some internalized standard (e.g., Weick and Nesset, 1968). Alternatively, there is cause to believe that many people evaluate their current equity situations with the situations they recall having been in on other jobs, in earlier times. ("Damn! I was better off at my last job!") Finally, some people compare their equity situation with that which they expected when they first started their jobs. Thus, when a person begins a job, she develops a set of expectations about the types and amounts of inputs and outcomes that will be involved. When this psychological contract (Schein, 1970) is violated, inequity perceptions develop, and the individual becomes less satisfied with her job and more likely to withdraw from it (Ilgen and Seely, 1974).

Social comparison theory predicts that people attempt to compare their beliefs and attitudes with other individuals whom they perceive as being similar to themselves (Festinger, 1954). Hence, George may have someone in mind who performs the same job he performs, either at his own organization or elsewhere. Labor unions

117

frequently construct their wage demands using this principle, comparing their own wages (usually unfavorably) to the wages earned by workers in the same industries in other places, or to the wages earned by unions in other, similar industries at the same location (Ross, 1948). Perceived similarity is the key factor.

While there has been very little research into the question of the choice of referents for comparison purposes, there is some basis to believe that the general classes of referents mentioned above constitute common comparison points, and that people may tend to use more than one referent at a time. Moreover, professionals seem to be more inclined to compare their equity situations with people outside of their own organizations, than are nonprofessionals (Goodman, 1974), and people from different cultures may or may not consider equity issues as we do in North America (Weick, Bougon, and Maruyama, 1976).

Beliefs, attitudes, inequity, and behavior. A third point is that we are dealing here with people's beliefs and attitudes: the beliefs consist of thoughts such as "George has a key to the Executive Washroom, and I don't," while the attitudes consist of evaluations of these beliefs ("Who cares about having a key to the Executive Washroom, anyway?"). The point is that beliefs and attitudes about equity are formed and modified in the same way as are all beliefs and attitudes, as was discussed in the previous chapter. Moreover, Equity Theory beliefs and attitudes are as unpredictably related to employee behavior as are all beliefs and attitudes; that is, they must be converted into intentions in order to result in relevant behaviors.

Consequences of Inequity Perceptions

Nevertheless, the theory claims that people find conditions of perceived inequity uncomfortable, or dissonant (Festinger, 1957), and when the tension becomes great enough, it predicts that the person will do something to redress it. *States of perceived inequity are seen as constituting a need of the sort we examined in chapter three, possessing all the characteristics of needs discussed there.*

Notice that it is possible for a person such as George to perceive that he is being overly well-treated in relation to his comparison person. The theory states (and research evidence supports the proposition) that people have a greater tolerance for this sort of inequity situation than they do for cases where they believe that they are being poorly treated, although it still predicts that, eventually, they will be motivated to equalize the ratios as they perceive them (Adams, 1963; Andrews, 1967; Weick and Nesset, 1968).

Theoretically, how is equity restored? First, remember that equity is in the eye of the beholder. The theory states that people will be motivated to change elements of either (or both) of the ratios they perceive. For example, George might demand a raise from his boss if he feels that he is being poorly treated in comparison to his partner. Or, he might demand some other form of increased outcome, something that he values enough to make himself feel that justice has been done. Alternatively, George might attempt to change the nature of the *denominator* of his own equity ratio by, for example, reducing the quantity or quality of his work. ("Fine, if that's all you wish to pay me, you won't be seeing me around here on Sundays anymore.") The author has known colleagues who have proclaimed that their employers ". . . seem able to afford less of my time every year!"

Changing effort to restore equity.   It is important to note that the theory makes different predictions about whether an employee (who believes she is being inequitably treated) will increase or decrease her effort level, depending upon the nature of the payment system under which she is working. If the employee is working for a piece rate, for example, the theory predicts that feelings of underpayment inequity (as a result of a belief that the rate of payment per unit produced is too low) will lead to attempts to increase productivity levels, thereby maximizing the net level of pay earned overall. On the other hand, underpayment inequity is predicted to result in reduced performance levels in situations of hourly pay. Similarly, Equity Theory predicts perceptions of overpayment under a piece rate pay plan to result in a restriction of output and an increase in quality, thereby limiting the net amount of overpayment the individual earns, while at the same time providing greater input to the exchange. Finally, overpayment perceptions under an hourly compensation plan would be expected to result in increased performance levels, because higher productivity is one means of increasing one's inputs and restoring balance. Reference to the equity ratios represented earlier helps explain why different behavioral reactions are predicted in the various underpayment and overpayment conditions.

Notice that George might be able to restore equity in the ratios he perceives by influencing *either the numerator or the denominator (or both)* of the ratio he attributes to his comparison person. If George were brash enough, for example, he might enquire about the inordinately high level of pay being earned by his mate. More likely however, George might attack the numerator of his partner's ratio: he might behave in such a way as to assure that his comparison person actually earns his fancy salary and keys to the Executive Washroom.

The point here is that feelings of inequitable treatment are viewed as motivational forces (using the terminology of chapter five, we would call them beliefs and attitudes with the potential to become **119** intentions) that instigate behavior to reduce the tension, and that there are often a variety of behaviors available to a person to try to correct a situation of perceived inequity.

But we know from chapter four that not all goal-directed behavior is successful—people do not always succeed at what they attempt to do. Moreover, it is not always feasible even to try certain acts. For example, it would be quite risky in most circumstances for George to attempt to have his partner's pay cut, or to try to get the other person to contribute more to the organization. Consequently, people in George's position often find that they have more control over elements of their *own* perceived ratios, particularly over the level and quality of inputs they provide. In other words, the theory predicts that people like George may deliberately reduce the level of effort they put into their jobs. But even this can be difficult or risky at times. Galley slaves in ancient Rome had difficulty withdrawing their services for very long at a time! Likewise, George's job may be one which is machine paced, such that it is not possible for him to reduce the quantity of work he performs. And it may be that reductions in the *quality* of the work he performs will be detected, thereby further increasing the frustration George experiences.

But if behavior to influence the value of any of the four main elements of the two equity ratios in George's mind is impossible, what can George do to reduce the motivational force?

Changing cognitions to restore equity. Remember that the elements of the two ratios are simply George's *perceptions* of the nature and quantity of his own and his partner's inputs and outcomes. When reality cannot be changed, the theory says, the perceptions that give rise to the motivational force will be changed. Hence, George may reevaluate any (or all) of the beliefs he holds about either the numerators or the denominators he has in mind. For example, he may investigate and learn that his apparently overpaid co-worker has a better set of credentials than George initially thought he had. George may notice that the other person actually works harder than he had given him credit for previously. Or George may decide that his own Ph.D. in anthropology really is not a material input to his job as a dishwasher. Finally, George may also reevaluate his beliefs about his outcomes, noticing that the people he works with are very congenial, and that low-paying as it is, at least his job is clean.

The point is that when *behavior* is not possible to restore a perception of equity, the theory predicts that the person will attempt to change his *beliefs* about his equity ratios, and/or his evaluative reactions to those beliefs.

120   But what if it is simply not possible to sufficiently change one's

beliefs about equity matters? The theory predicts that when behavior is not possible, and when it is not possible to change perceptions sufficiently to restore feelings of equity, people will respond with denial, repression, or withdrawal—the way people react in the face of other types of frustrating circumstances (recall chapter four). Hence, perceptions of being inequitably treated contribute to job dissatisfaction (Pritchard, 1969), which, in turn, results in higher rates of absenteeism and turnover (Carrell and Dittrich, 1976; Telly, French, and Scott, 1971) and other forms of withdrawal (see chapter five).

Inequity and job performance: The research evidence. As noted earlier, the theory predicts that one way for individuals to attempt to rectify situations of perceived inequity on their part is to adjust the number and amount of inputs they provide, the direction of the adjustment depending on the type of pay system under which they are working. Since most inputs people provide to a job are somewhat fixed in the short run (such as education and experience), the individuals' levels of effort (and subsequent performance) are the one input over which they have some control. In fact, the empirical results on this matter are somewhat mixed, although there seems to be some support for the following conclusions:

1. Underpayment on a piece rate pay system tends, as predicted, to result in higher levels of quantity and lower levels of quality (Andrews, 1967; Lawler and O'Gara, 1967).
2. Underpayment on an hourly basis may, in fact, result in reduced inputs by an individual, although the evidence on this is sparse (Goodman and Friedman, 1971; Lawler, 1968).
3. Equity Theory predictions concerning perceptions of overpayment have not been tested in a sufficient number of studies by experimental methods that have allowed unequivocal interpretation of the results; in other words, most of the studies that have been conducted to test the overpayment propositions have been flawed by experimental design, making it difficult to draw conclusions (Carrell and Dittrich, 1978; Pritchard, 1969). Nevertheless, it is interesting that many people believe that overpaying others is an effective means of improving their performance, providing another strand of support at least for the hypothesis that people in our culture think in terms of equity and distributive justice (see Garland, 1973; Greenberg and Leventhal, 1976).

In balance, the evidence attesting to the validity of Equity Theory *as a predictor of changes in effort and performance* is not as impressive as the elegance of the predictions made by the theory. However, we will see in the following section that this evidence is itself suspect, leaving conditions about validity hard to draw at present.

Problems with Equity Theory Research

In chapter two, we discussed the necessity for conducting research **121** to evaluate the validity of theories of work motivation. But we also discussed the difficulties associated with performing research that provides fair tests of these theories. Since then, we have seen a number of instances where the research that has been conducted to evaluate certain theories has been flawed, or somehow inappropriately executed. Research into the validity of Equity Theory is no exception to the problem; there have been a number of mistakes made by researchers pursuing this theory, mistakes that leave us with only an uncertain feel for its level of scientific validity.

For example, many of the experiments that have been conducted to test the theory's predictions of behavior under conditions of perceived overpayment have utilized a ploy that probably generated feelings in the minds of experimental subjects that they were unworthy of the pay they were receiving. In other words, the experimental induction used has tended to influence these people's feelings of self-esteem, rather than simply manipulating their equity beliefs, per se. As a result of this confounding, the results yielded by these experiments are equivocal—we cannot be sure whether they reflect the impact of inequity perceptions or the effects of esteem degradation (Schwab, 1980).

Secondly, in spite of the obvious importance of comparison individuals to the dynamics posited by the theory, many studies to date have ignored the issue of which referents experimental subjects use to compare themselves. And in those studies in which referents have been identified, researchers have failed to control or observe the types and amounts of information provided to their subjects concerning the inputs being provided by the referents (Middlemist and Peterson, 1976). So, on the one hand, the theory states that people will pay attention to a variety of inputs provided by themselves and by comparison others. On the other hand, researchers have been lax, on the whole, in manipulating or even monitoring the information available concerning the (real or imagined) levels of qualification or effort being contributed by comparison referents. Without such control, the results obtained in these studies are hard to interpret.

A third problem with much of the research is that *pay* has tended to be the primary outcome provided to experimental subjects in exchange for their work. The reason for such a heavy reliance on money is understandable—it is easy to measure and dispense, and it is generally valued by people. But the theory claims that people may recognize a variety of outcomes as they form their mental images about how equitably they are being treated, and that many of these outcomes are nonpecuniary, as well as nonphysical. A few studies have examined task satisfaction, providing the only major exception to this shortcoming (e.g., Weick, 1967).

But perhaps the major problem with the almost exclusive reliance on pay as the experimental outcome is that money has been found to have a variety of influences on the perceived value of other outcomes, such as intrinsic satisfaction with the task (recall chapter four), and see Lepper and Green, 1978). Related to this problem is the possibility that outcomes of various sorts simply do not aggregate in value psychologically the way the theory has implicitly assumed (see Porac and Salancik, 1981, for an, example). The point is that the ease of measurement and control gained through the use of money by researchers may have added to the other deficiencies of the research on Equity Theory, compromising our ability to assess the merit of the theory.

A fourth problem with this research (albeit one that is not unique to Equity Theory) is that it has been predominantly conducted in contrived laboratory settings, using college students working on tasks of limited degrees of realism, generally over very short periods of time. The author believes that laboratory research is a valuable means for developing and refining hypotheses derived from theory, but that it must be combined with the use of research observations gathered in real-life settings. (The reader is referred to Runkel and McGrath, 1972 for a thorough discussion of the iterative use of different research methodologies and sites.) The reason for the heavy reliance on the lab is, of course, the convenience it offers to researchers, as well as the experimental control that can be exercised over variables which might interfere with the experimental manipulations the researcher wishes to impose. There have been a few valiant attempts to increase the realism of the settings in which Equity Theory has been tested (e.g., Evan and Simmons, 1969; Pritchard, Dunnette, and Jorgenson, 1972), but they have been rare.

A fifth problem has concerned the way perceptions of equity and inequity have been created and assessed by researchers. For example, the tendency has been to manipulate either the numerator or the denominator (or both) of the research subject's equity ratio, and/or those of some comparison person, assuming that the feelings of inequity so created are somewhat similar in terms of the impact they have on people. In fact, there is a range of possible situations of inequity that can influence people's beliefs about the treatment they receive (Törnblom, 1977), so that the nature of the actual feelings of inequity created in the minds of research participants has been poorly understood to date.

The point here is that for a number of very understandable and practical reasons, the research on Equity Theory has generally not been conducted well enough to provide us with a fair sense of its validity. So, while the theoretic propositions advanced by Adams **123** and others seem to make considerable intuitive sense, many specific features of the theory remain unsubstantiated, and its nuances are far from understood.

On a more positive note, and in fairness to Equity Theory researchers, these difficulties have already been noted by other observers and current work tends to take many of them into account. Garland's (1973) work, for example, illustrates a way around the use of self-esteem reduction as a by-product of attempts to create feelings of overpayment. Likewise, other researchers have attempted to avoid the problems caused by the identification and addition of inputs and outcomes by making use of the individual's net perceptions of the *fairness* of exchange relationships (see Carrell and Dittrich, 1978, for examples). Finally, it seems reasonable to predict that the urgency of understanding the nature and consequences of equity and inequity, generated by the ongoing concern for human rights, will continue to support the development of new theories of distributive justice as well as means for testing them. The forces associated with the issue of *comparable worth* provide an important current example, as will be discussed shortly.

Organizational Causes of Perceived (and Actual) Inequity

In practice, what creates feelings of inequity among employees? Most answers to this question involve the sensitivity and responsiveness of organizational reward systems. Feelings of inequitable treatment tend to occur when people believe that they are not receiving fair returns for their efforts and other contributions. Therefore, in order to prevent this sort of perception from developing, the organization must structure its reward system so that it actually distributes rewards in accordance with employee beliefs about their own value to the enterprise. In practice, of course, this is very difficult. One reason for this concerns the difficulty of achieving agreement among people concerning what constitutes value. ("Is your MBA degree really relevant to the work you perform here? I don't think so. . . ." Or, "Who cares if you held several other farm laboring jobs before coming to this one? I can train someone much younger than you are to pick as many berries as you can pick, probably more. . . .")

Another problem concerns the difficulty of noticing good performance, or of recognizing it when it is available to be noticed. As stated in other places in this book, performance appraisal is a very complicated process, one that is fraught with potential for errors and the creation of inequities, either real or imagined. Union contracts often require that seniority be rewarded. For those who are senior, such provisions seem very equitable, because they tend to see their seniority as valuable experience (a type of input) that should be compensated. On the other hand, junior employees often do not agree, especially when they also believe that they contribute more or better job performance to the organization than their older colleagues.

Favoritism, in all of its manifestations, tends to generate feelings of inequitable treatment. Nepotism is a particularly interesting example of this. Members of the boss's family are often in the difficult position of making sure that their co-workers see that they deserve any and all outcomes and benefits they receive, sometimes to the point where the boss's family members feel that rather than being overly well-treated, they are inequitably treated, to their disadvantage.

The point is that there are myriad practical factors in most work settings that can contribute to feelings of inequity among employees, and that many of these factors are difficult for managers to manage. One particularly intractable problem of equity and inequity is discussed in the following section.

Internal and External Equity

Most large organizations (as well as many smaller ones) employ some form of job evaluation system, designed to assure that there is a relationship between the amount of *pay* that is provided to incumbents of its various jobs and the value of those jobs to the organization. A complete treatment of these programs is beyond our present purpose; the interested reader is referred to a comprehensive treatment of formal pay plans by Belcher (1974). But while plans of this sort are often capable of providing reasonable degrees of pay equity within an organization at a particular point in time, they generally do not account for fluctuating labor market conditions, which can heavily influence the compensation levels that must be offered to attract new employees from outside. Sometimes there is a trade-off between internal and external equity considerations, which can make it very difficult to maintain perceptions of equity inside the organization while permitting it effectively to recruit new employees from the labor market.

One solution that is often adopted, in part to deal with the internal versus external equity trade-off, is to keep pay levels secret throughout the organization—people are not told how much money one another earn (Miner, 1974). Such *pay secrecy* policies have a number of interesting features. First of all, people often talk informally about salaries and wages, sometimes about their own and sometimes about the compensation earned by others. Often, the "rumor mill" on the issue of money is not accurate, as people knowingly or inadvertently distort figures they associate with themselves and with oth- **125** ers. Moreover, there is some evidence that managers may tend honestly to underestimate the compensation levels of their superiors, and to overestimate the compensation levels earned by their peers and subordinates. When this occurs, people are likely to feel underpayment inequity vis à vis their subordinates. Furthermore, the belief that higher organizational levels don't fetch that much more compensation may tend to reduce the incentive value that promotions might otherwise have (Lawler, 1965, 1967a; Milkovich and Anderson, 1972).

As a result, it has been suggested on theoretical grounds that compensation levels should not be kept secret (Lawler, 1972), but that they should be opened up to the scrutiny of all concerned, in spite of the initial difficulties the opening-up process may create. On the other hand, at least one study has shown that so-called open pay schemes do not result in more accurate perceptions of other people's pay, in spite of the availability of the necessary information (Milkovich and Anderson, 1972). Moreover, it is not always the case that open pay schemes result in the higher levels of pay satisfaction that Equity Theory would predict (Mahoney and Weitzel, 1978).

In short, the fact that organizations must recruit and retain a labor force from external markets can make the maintenance of equitable internal compensation plans a very complicated problem—one for which no easy solution seems available. Moreover, plans of this sort can deal only with the equitable distribution of pay; they have virtually nothing to do with the equitable distribution of other forms of either formal compensation (such as fringe benefits) or informal rewards (such as recognition, praise, and so forth). It is very difficult, in practice, to administer rewards in a manner that will be perceived as equitable by everyone concerned.

THE ISSUE OF COMPARABLE WORTH

The problems of establishing and maintaining equity in compensation for work has become particularly salient in recent years with the emergence of widespread concern about sex differences in pay and career opportunities. For example, one source estimates that full-time female employees in Canada earn about 60 percent as much money as do full-time male employees. Moreover, this gap doubled in the period 1955–1969, and it is still widening, in spite of the womens' movement. This same source further estimates that, even if it were assumed that women should be paid, on average, only 70 percent as much as men, the total "pay discrimination bill" in Canada in 1977 was over $7 billion!! No figures are provided for the actual amount of the discrimination bill, given that women were earning less than 70 percent of what men earned that year (McDonald,

1977). The situation in the United States is at least as bad as it is in Canada (cf. England and McLaughlin, 1979).

Causes of the Sex Pay Gap

Why does this gap exist? There have been a number of explanations offered (Mahoney, 1983). McDonald (1977) suggests that approximately half of the gap is attributable to the fact that women tend, on average, to occupy lower paying jobs than men, and that the other half can be attributed to simple discrimination against women, meaning that women are simply paid less than men, even when they perform the same jobs. On the other hand, England and McLaughlin (1979) argue against the simple discrimination explanation. Instead, they suggest that the gap exists because women, in addition to occupying lower paying jobs, also tend to be at the lower pay brackets within the jobs they do occupy because so many of them have entered the labor market only recently.

Nevertheless, there is little disagreement in either Canada or the United States that there is a sex-related pay gap, and that the gap is definitely not narrowing. Further, there is also little doubt that cultural norms about what constitutes "woman's work" and "man's work" are still prevalent, even among many women (Mahoney and Blake, 1982; Oppenheimer, 1968), and that the proportion of females working in an occupation is directly related to lower pay levels for that occupation, even after controlling for the level and type of skill it requires (England and McLaughlin, 1979). If it's "woman's work," it earns less.

Why do women occupy lower paying jobs? There are a variety of reasons (Bartol, 1978). First, many women simply do not enter labor pools in search of jobs that are traditionally male-dominated, in part because of the cultural norm just mentioned, and in part because of the socialization of females which fosters this norm (Stein and Bailey, 1973). In addition, the lower starting salaries offered women by many organizations discourage them from seeking employment in male-dominated occupations.

Secondly, there is evidence that when they do compete for jobs, women are disproportionately offered lower paying positions, often of the clerical variety, or of some type that is consistent with the sex-labelling norm (Cash, Gillen, and Burns, 1977; Cohen and Bunker, 1975; Rosen and Jerdee, 1974a, 1974b). Moreover, women who *are* admitted to managerial jobs are often not provided with the early task assignments that permit them the chance to demonstrate their competence, and get off to as fast a start as their male counterparts (Rosen and Jerdee, 1974b; Terborg and Ilgen, 1975). In addition, work that is performed by women often tends not to be as highly **127** evaluated as work done by men, even when the judges themselves are female. Finally, when women do perform well at certain tasks, there is some evidence that people are more likely to attribute their success to luck rather than to ability (Garland and Price, 1977), and that both males and females are likely to attribute failures on the job to the contributions made by female group members (Heilman and Kram, 1978).

Personality traits generally associated with being male are more closely related to those associated with being a manager than are female traits, by both males and females (Schein, 1973, 1975), reinforcing the tendency to exclude women from managerial positions. And, in fact, studies of women who have succeeded in climbing the corporate ladder suggest that females may have to demonstrate those traits that are usually defined as male in our culture (Stein and Bailey, 1973; Van Der Merwe, 1978). Sometimes "token" women are hired into responsible positions for the sake of window dressing, often when they are not really qualified for these positions. The failures that naturally result tend to further reinforce the prior beliefs about the competence of women for male-type (read managerial) positions.

The point here is that there are a variety of reasons why women tend not to occupy managerial and other high paying jobs. Cultural beliefs about the role of females and the nature of what constitutes men's work and women's work perpetuate the gap between male and female earnings.

Legislation and Equity

As a result, there have been a number of laws passed to attempt to deal with the problem (such as the Canadian Human Rights Act and the Civil Rights Act and the Equal Pay Act of 1963 in the United States), although the real impact of these laws is still to be determined, as cases of alleged pay discrimination appear before the supreme courts of the United States and Canada. To date, however, these laws have had little impact on the size of the gap (O'Kelly, 1979).

In the meantime, the fact remains that women tend to be disproportionately concentrated in lower paying jobs, and it is fair to ask why these jobs continue to be paid less than are traditionally male jobs of apparently similar skill level. How can we compare the worth of two or more jobs that require different types of skill and ability? Who is to say, for example, that education, experience, or physical risk should be rewarded higher than other inputs provided to jobs?

The so-called *comparable worth* issue is concerned with this problem—it focuses on the comparison of jobs across occupations, as opposed to within occupations. As it is defined in United States law, at least (under the Equal Pay Act of 1963), the concept of comparable worth implies that jobs that are judged to be of equal intrinsic worth or difficulty must be paid equal rates of compensation. The surface similarity of the jobs in question is of minor importance. Moreover, the jobs need not be from the same organization. Hence, the comparable worth concept ignores (or even counteracts) the effects of the marketplace on wage rates, on the grounds that whole classes of apparently dissimilar jobs have been undervalued by the market forces of supply and demand because they have traditionally been held by women.

Any employer, therefore, who pays the market wage for a job could be seen under this law as perpetuating the sex-based discriminatory pay practices of the past, in spite of the sex of the employees involved in a particular instance (Carmell, 1981). So, for example, is the work performed by a public health nurse worth more than that performed by a tree pruner who works for the same civic administration? This particular example was disputed in a case recently in Denver, Colorado. Likewise, is the job of a historical researcher worth more than that of a federal librarian? The Human Rights Commission of Canada decided recently that it is *not* worth more and ordered the back-payment of $2.3 million dollars to 470 (mostly female) librarians (Thomsen, 1981).

On the other hand, the United States Supreme Court rejected an appeal by Mary Lemmons, the Denver public health nurse mentioned above, to overturn the decision against her case by the U.S. Court of Appeals. The upshot of this case is that tree pruners in Denver earn higher pay than professional nurses.

Similarly, the Canadian Human Rights Act prohibits employers in the federal sphere (including all federal Public Service departments as well as employers in industries that fall under federal jurisdiction, such as banks, airlines and interprovincial truckers, for example) from paying men and women different levels of pay for work of equal value (Campbell, 1983). The Act, which was proclaimed in 1978, states that jobs, even if they are considerably different in nature, may be compared directly to determine whether they are of equal intrinsic value, regardless of whatever values might be suggested for them by the forces of supply and demand in the marketplace. When it is combined with similar legislation in the province of Quebec, this legislation means that approximately one-third of the Canadian workforce is covered by some form of equal pay law.

The full impact of the various laws that are enacted to provide for equal pay of equal value is beyond the scope of this book. The reader is advised to monitor court decisions in the coming years to see how these laws will be interpreted and enforced. In the mean- **129** time, however, the further introduction of comparable worth concepts into the day-to-day practice of wage administration will be slow, for a variety of reasons. First, there is still considerable disagreement at the conceptual and philosophical levels concerning what constitutes equity and comparable value (Mahoney, 1983; Wallace, 1983). Mahoney (1983), for example, has identified four widely disparate schools of thought. Such disagreement will doubtlessly result in conflict and resistance at the practical level, as adherents of different perspectives on the matter attempt to apply their respective conceptual models of equity and comparable worth to specific wage and salary systems. As noted by Mahoney (1983), regardless of one's particular philosophical or conceptual views on the matter, subjective tastes and preferences ultimately characterize everyone's practical definition of what is equitable.

A second practical impediment to the further growth of comparable worth as an influence in pay administration will be the tremendous difficulties associated with the development and maintenance of a universal taxonomy of jobs (Milkovich, 1980). The failure of the organizational sciences to date in developing useful schemes for categorizing phenomena of interest has been a general problem for many years (Pinder and Moore, 1979; Wallace, 1983). Therefore, it is not surprising that little has been accomplished in the development of the sort of job taxonomy that would be required to translate concepts of comparable worth (*anyone's* concepts) into practice throughout business and industry in North America.

Finally, the introduction of comparable worth programs on a widespread basis, especially if they were to include retroactive provisions for dealing with inequities of the past, would have a tremendous impact on the aggregate payroll of the nations' employers. Consequently, there is, and will continue to be, strong and consistent resistance on the part of business to such sweeping change (Thomsen, 1981).

SUMMARY AND CONCLUSION

This chapter has reviewed what is known about the human need for distributive justice and equitable treatment in work settings. It is important to keep in mind that the major theories dealing with the issue posit that equity is a *need,* possessing all of the capacity to arouse and direct human behavior that other needs possess. By itself, however, Equity Theory does not discuss how this need state, once aroused, results in intentions to act. It is also important to keep in mind that people's feelings about whether they (or others) are being equitably treated are based on their own perceptions and beliefs, subject to the same influences as are other types of perceptions and beliefs. Current perspectives assume that equity beliefs are formed and changed in a social context, and held in a sort of psychological ratio format, although research of the future may ignore the ratio concept and begin with the individual's net feelings of fairness of treatment. Finally, the incredible complexity of creating conditions that will be universally perceived as equitable within a given organization should be apparent, as should be the complexity of the legal and economic issues associated with assuring that occupations of equal value receive equal compensation.

While the research on equity theories has been difficult to interpret for methodological reasons, there is little doubt that equity and the conditions that create or subvert it in organizations is an issue of great importance to an understanding of the motivation to work.

BELIEFS, ATTITUDES AND MOTIVATION
7 Valance– Instrumentality– Expectancy Theory

Never is there either work without reward, nor reward without work being expended.

—*Livy (Titus Livius)*

Probably the most popular theory of work motivation among organizational scientists in recent years has been that which is referred to as Valence-Instrumentality-Expectancy Theory or Expectancy Theory (Locke, 1975). Actually, there are a variety of theories included under these general titles, although the similarities among them are more important than are the differences. Each of these theories has its modern roots in Vroom's (1964) book on work motivation, although earlier theory in psychology relating to general human motivation quite clearly predates Vroom's interpretation for organizational science (e.g., Atkinson, 1958; Davidson, Suppes, and Siegel, 1957; Lewin, 1938; Peak, 1955; Rotter, 1955; Tolman, 1959), and an early study by Georgopoulos, Mahoney, and Jones (1957) demonstrated the relevance of the theory for work behavior.

Since Vroom's book was published, there have been a number of variations and revisions of his basic concepts, although most of the theoretical work has been vastly superior to the numerous empirical attempts to test the theory in all of its various forms. In fact, it can be defensibly argued that, in spite of the numerous studies conducted since 1964 that have ostensibly sought to test versions of the theory, very little is known about its validity. This is because, as has been the case with so much research on employee motivation, studies directed at VIE Theory have been fraught with serious flaws—flaws which make it almost impossible to conclude whether the theory, in any of its forms, holds any scientific merit (Arnold, 1981; Campbell and Pritchard, 1976; Locke, 1975; Pinder, 1977). Nevertheless, let's take a look at the theory in its most basic form—that proposed by Vroom (1964) for application to work settings.

VROOM'S ORIGINAL THEORY

Vroom's theory assumes that ". . . the choices made by a person among alternative courses of action are lawfully related to psychological events occurring contemporaneously with the behavior" (1964, pp. 14–15). In other words, people's behavior results from conscious choices among alternatives, and these choices (behaviors) are systematically related to psychological processes, particularly perception and the formation of beliefs and attitudes. The purpose of the choices, generally, is to maximize pleasure and minimize pain. Like Equity Theory then, VIE Theory assumes that people base their acts on perceptions and beliefs, although, as we saw in chapter five, we need not anticipate any one-to-one relationships between particular beliefs and specific behaviors (such as job behaviors).

To understand why Vroom's theory and those which have followed it are referred to as *VIE Theory*, we must examine the three key mental components that are seen as instigating and directing behavior. Referred to as Valence, Instrumentality, and Expectancy, each of these components is, in fact, a *belief* (using the terminology developed in chapter five).

The Concept of Valence

VIE theory assumes that people hold preferences among various outcomes or states of nature. For example, the reader probably prefers, other things equal, a higher rate of pay for a particular job over a lower rate of pay. Here, pay level is the *outcome* in question, and the preference for high pay over low pay reflects the strength of the reader's basic underlying need state. Likewise, some people hold preferences among different types of outcomes (as opposed to greater or lesser amounts of a particular outcome). For example, many employees would seem to prefer an opportunity to work with other people, even if the only jobs featuring high levels of social interaction entail less comfortable surroundings, lower pay, or some other trade-off. The point is that people have more or less well-defined preferences for the outcomes they derive from their actions. (Notice that these outcomes correspond roughly with what we referred to as goals in the discussion of employee frustration in chapter four, as **133** well as to the outcomes we examined in the previous chapter, in the context of Equity Theory.) Preferences, in short, relate to a person's relative desires for, or attraction to, outcomes.

Vroom uses the term *valence* to refer to the affective (emotional) orientations people hold with regard to outcomes. An outcome is said to be positively valent for an individual if she would prefer having it to not having it. For example, we would say that a promotion is positively valent for an employee who would rather be promoted than not be promoted. Likewise, we say that an outcome which a person would prefer to avoid has negative valence for her, or simply that it is negatively valent. For example, fatigue, stress, and layoffs are three outcomes that are usually negatively valent among employees. Finally, it is sometimes the case that an employee is indifferent toward certain outcomes; in such cases, the outcome is said to hold zero valence for that individual.

The most important feature of people's valences concerning work-related outcomes is that they refer to the level of satisfaction the person *expects* to receive from them, *not from the real value the person actually derives from them*. So, for example, the reader may be enrolled in a program of business management because she expects that the outcomes to follow (an education and a diploma, among others) will be of value to her when she is finished. It may be the case, however, that when the student graduates there will be little or no market demand for the services she has to offer the world of business and administration, so the degree may have little real value. The point here is that people attribute either positive or negative preferences (or indifference) to outcomes according to the satisfaction or dissatisfaction they *expect* to receive from them. It is often the case that the true value of an outcome (such as a diploma) is either greater or lesser than the valence (expected value) that outcome once held for the individual who was motivated to either pursue it or avoid it. As a final example, consider the individual who fears being fired, but learns after actually being dismissed from a job that she is healthier, happier, and better off financially in the new job she acquired after having been terminated by her former employer. In this case, being fired was a negatively valent outcome before it occurred, but eventually turned out to be of positive value after it occurred.

Performance as an outcome. Of the many outcomes that follow an employee's work effort, one of the most important, of course, is the level of performance that is accomplished. In fact, for the sake of understanding Vroom's theory, the strength of the connection in the mind of the employee between his effort and the performance level he achieves is very important, as we will see shortly.

Further, the degree to which the employee believes that his perfor-mance will be connected to other outcomes (such as pay, for exam-ple) is also critical. The point here is that work effort results in a variety of outcomes, some of them directly, others indirectly. The level of job performance is the most important outcome for understanding work motivation from a VIE Theory perspective. So, V stands for valence—the expected levels of satisfaction and/or dissatisfaction brought by work-related outcomes.

The Concept of Instrumentality

We have just stated that outcomes carry valences for people. But what determines the valence of a particular outcome for an em-ployee? For example, we noted that performance level is an impor-tant outcome of a person's work effort, but what determines the va-lence associated with a given level of performance? For Vroom, the answer is that a given level of performance is positively valent if the employee believes that it will lead to other outcomes, which are called *second-level outcomes.* In other words, if an employee be-lieves (through all of the belief construction processes we discussed in chapter five) that a high level of performance is *instrumental* for the acquisition of other outcomes that he expects will be gratifying (such as a promotion, for example), and/or if he believes that a high perfor-mance level will be instrumental for avoiding other outcomes that he wishes to avoid (such as being fired), then that employee will place a high valence upon performing the job well.

Consider the meaning of the adjective *instrumental.* The au-thor's typewriter at the present time is instrumental in the preparation of this book. It contributes to the job; it helps. Something is said to be instrumental if it is believed to lead to something else, if it helps achieve or attain something else. Hence, studying is commonly seen by students as instrumental for passing exams. In turn, passing ex-ams is often *believed* instrumental for the acquisition of diplomas, which, in turn, are *believed* to be instrumental for landing jobs in tight labor market conditions.

Vroom (1964) suggests that we consider instrumentality as a probability belief linking one outcome (performance level) to other outcomes, ranging from 1.0 (meaning that the attainment of the sec-ond outcome is certain if the first outcome is achieved), through zero (meaning that there is no likely relationship between the attainment of the first outcome and the attainment of the second), to -1.0 (meaning that the attainment of the second outcome is certain with-out the first and that it is impossible with it). For example, bonus pay that is distributed at random would lead to employee instrumentality perceptions linking bonus pay to performance equal to zero. ("Per- **135** formance and pay have no connection around here!") On the other hand, commission pay schemes which tie pay directly to performance, and only to performance, are designed to make employees perceive that performance is positively instrumental for the acquisition of money. Finally, an employee who has been threatened with dismissal for being drunk on the job may be told by his supervisor, in effect, that lack of sobriety at work is negatively instrumental for continued employment, or, alternatively, that further imbibing will be positively instrumental for termination. (The notion of negative instrumentalities makes Vroom's original formulation of VIE Theory somewhat more difficult and cumbersome than it might otherwise be, so subsequent versions of the theory have avoided using it, choosing instead to speak only of positive instrumentalities.)

Consider the case of an employee who perceives that high performance will *not* lead to things he desires, but that it will be more instrumental for attaining outcomes to which he attributes negative valences. High performance will not be positively valent for such a person, so we would not expect to see him striving to perform well. As a further example, an employee might perceive that taking a job as a traveling salesman will be instrumental for attaining a number of outcomes, some of which he expects will be positive, some of which he believes will be negative. On the positively valent side, meeting new people and seeing the countryside may be appealing to him, because he expects that these outcomes will be instrumental for satisfying his relatedness and growth needs, while the possible threat to his family life may be aversive to him, the popularly acknowledged exploits of traveling salesmen notwithstanding!

In short, the *I* in VIE Theory stands for instrumentality—an outcome is positively valent if the person believes that it holds high instrumentality for the acquisition of positively valent consequences (goals or other outcomes), and the avoidance of negatively valent outcomes. But in order for an outcome to be positively valent, the outcomes to which the person believes it is connected must themselves, in turn, be seen as positively valent. If an employee anticipates that high levels of performance will lead primarily to things he dislikes, then high performance will not be positively valent to him. Likewise, if the individual perceives that high performance is generally rewarded with things he desires, he will place high valence on high performance and—other things being equal—he will strive for high performance. Of course, the valence of such second-level outcomes is determined by the nature of the person's most salient needs and values.

Already, the reader should be able to distill a few implications for the design of reward systems in organizations: if management wants high performance levels, it must tie positively valent outcomes to

136

high performance *and be sure that employees understand the con-nection.* Likewise, low performance must be seen as connected to consequences that are of either zero or negative valence.

The Concept of Expectancy

The third major component of VIE Theory is referred to as *expectancy.* Expectancy is the strength of a person's belief about whether a particular outcome is possible. The author, for example, would place very little expectancy on the prospect of becoming an astronaut. The reasons are, of course, personal, but the point is that he doesn't believe that any amount of trying on his part will see him aboard the space shuttle! If a person believes that he can achieve an outcome, he will be more motivated to try for it, assuming that other things are equal (the other things, of course, consist of the person's beliefs about the valence of the outcome, which, in turn, is determined by the person's beliefs about the odds that the outcome will be instrumental for acquiring and avoiding those things he either wishes to acquire or avoid, respectively).

Vroom (1964) spoke of expectancy beliefs as *action-outcome* associations held in the minds of individuals, and suggested that we think of them in probability terms ranging from zero (in the case where the person's subjective probability of attaining an outcome is psychologically zero—"I can't do it") through to 1.0, indicating that the person has no doubt about his capacity to attain the outcome. In practice, of course, people's estimates tend to range between these two extremes. (The reader will recall from chapter four that achievement-oriented individuals tend to prefer tasks that are neither too difficult nor too easy, such that, for example, we might say they prefer tasks with perceived expectancy values near .5, meaning that there is a 50/50 perceived chance of success.)

There are a variety of factors that contribute to an employee's expectancy perceptions about various levels of job performance. For example, his level of confidence in his skills for the task at hand, the degree of help he expects to receive from his supervisor and subordinates, the quality of the materials and equipment available, the availability of pertinent information and control over sufficient budget, are common examples of factors that can influence a person's expectancy beliefs about being able to achieve a particular level of performance. Previous success experiences at a task and a generally high level of self-esteem also strengthen expectancy beliefs (Lawler, 1973). The point is that an employee's subjective estimate of the odds that he can achieve a given level of performance is determined by a variety of factors, both within his own control and beyond it (see chapter twelve for more detail). **137**

The Concept of Force

Vroom (1964) suggests that a person's beliefs about expectancies, instrumentalities, and valences interact psychologically to create a motivational force to act in those ways that seem most likely to bring pleasure or to avoid pain. "Behavior on the part of a person is assumed to be the result of a field of forces each of which has a direction and magnitude" (p. 18). Vroom likens his concept of force to a variety of other metaphorical concepts, including things such as *performance vectors* and *behavior potential*. In keeping with the terminology developed in chapter five, we can think of the force as representing the strength of a person's *intention* to act in a certain way. For example, if a person elects to strive for a particular level of job performance, we might say that the person's beliefs cause the greatest amount of force to be directed toward that level, or that he intends to strive for that level rather than for other levels.

Symbolically, Vroom (1964, p. 18) summarizes his own theory as follows:

$$F_i = f \sum_{i=1}^{n} (E_{ij}V_j) \quad \text{and} \quad V_j = f[\sum_{j=1}^{n} I_{jk}V_k]$$

Where:

F_i = the psychological force to perform an act (i) (such as strive for a particular level of performance)

E_{ij} = the strength of the expectancy that the act will be followed by the outcome j

V_j = the valence for the individual of outcome j

I_{jk} = instrumentality of outcome j for attaining second-level outcome k

V_k = valence of second-level outcome k

or, in his words:

> The force on a person to perform an act is a monotonically increasing function of the algebraic sum of the products of the valences of all outcomes and the strength of his expectancies that the act will be followed by the attainment of these outcomes.

So people choose from among the alternative acts the one(s) corresponding to the strongest positive (or weakest negative) force. People attempt to maximize their overall best interest, using the information available to them and their evaluations of this information. *In the context of work motivation, this means that people select to pursue that level of performance that they believe will maximize their overall best interest* (or *subjective expected utility*).

Notice from the formula above that there will be little or no motivational force operating on an individual to act in a certain manner if any of three conditions hold: (1) if the person does not believe that she can successfully behave that way (that is, if her expectancy of attaining the outcome is effectively zero); (2) if she believes that there will be no positively valent outcomes associated with behaving in that manner; (3) if she believes the act will result in a sufficient number of outcomes that are negatively valent to her.

The choice of a performance level. When we think of the levels of job performance that an employee might strive for as the outcome of interest, Vroom's theory suggests that the individual will consider the valences, instrumentalities, and expectancies associated with each level of the entire spectrum of performance levels and will elect to pursue the level that generates the greatest positive force (or lowest negative force) for him. If the person sees more good outcomes than bad ones associated with performing at a high level, he will strive to perform at that level. On the other hand, if a lower level of performance results in the greatest degree of psychological force, we can anticipate that he will settle for such a level. The implication is that low motivation levels result from employee choices to perform at low levels, and that these choices, in turn, are the result of beliefs concerning the valences, instrumentalities and expectancies held in the mind of the employee. These beliefs are formed and modified in the ways described in chapter five, and suggest, accordingly, a number of implications for the management of work motivation. We will address these implications later in this chapter.

REFINEMENTS TO THE THEORY

Since the publication of Vroom's book in 1964, there has been a considerable amount of both theoretical and empirical attention paid to expectancy-type models of work motivation. Aside from attempting to test the validity of the theory in its simple form, most of these efforts have sought to study the characteristics of people and organizations that influence valence, instrumentality, and expectancy beliefs, or to examine the types of conditions within which VIE-type predictions of work motivation can be expected to apply. A complete discussion of these refinements could easily constitute an entire book—well beyond our present purposes. The reader who is interested in pursuing major theoretic advances in VIE Theory is referred to the following sources: Campbell, Dunnette, Lawler, and Weick, 1970; Dachler and Mobley, 1973; Feldman, Reitz, and Hiterman, 1976; Graen, 1969; House, Shapiro, and Wahba, 1974; Kopelman, 1977; Kopelman and Thompson, 1976; Lawler, 1971, 1973; Naylor, Pritchard, and Ilgen, 1980; Porter and Lawler, 1968; Reinharth and Wahba, 1976; Staw, 1977; and Zedeck, 1977. Thorough reviews of the *research evidence* pertaining to VIE Theory are provided by **139**

Heneman and Schwab, (1972), Mitchell and Biglan (1971), and Campbell and Pritchard (1976).

For the purpose of the present discussion, only one of the many theoretical advancements of VIE Theory will be presented, followed by a brief summary of the validity of the theory and a number of difficulties that have been encountered in determining its validity. Finally, as mentioned above, the chapter will conclude with a discussion of the major implications of VIE Theory for the practice of management. So, to begin, let's take a look at one of the most important modifications and extensions offered to Vroom's work—the model offered by Porter and Lawler (1968).

The Porter/Lawler Model

Vroom's (1964) statement of VIE Theory left a number of questions unanswered. Perhaps the most important of these concerned the origins of valence, instrumentality, and expectancy beliefs, and the nature of the relationship, if any, between employee attitudes toward work and job performance. Porter and Lawler (1968) developed a theoretic model and then tested it, using a sample of managers, and revised it to explore these issues. The revised statement of their model is provided in schematic form in Figure 7-1.

FIGURE 7-1: The Revised Porter/Lawler Model

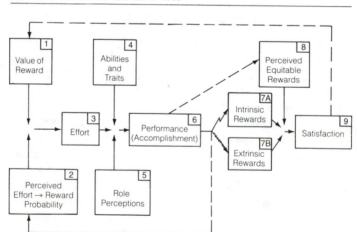

In a nutshell, their theory suggests the following. *Employee effort* is jointly determined by two key factors: the *value* placed on certain outcomes by the individual, and the *degree to which the person be-*

lieves that his effort will lead to the attainment of these rewards. As predicted by Vroom, Porter and Lawler found that these two factors interact to determine effort level; in other words, they found that people must both positively value outcomes and believe that these outcomes result from their effort for any further effort to be forthcoming.

However, effort may or may not result in *job performance,* which they defined as the accomplishment of those tasks that comprise a person's job. The reason? The level of *ability* the person has to do his job, and his *role clarity,* the degree of clarity of the understanding the person has concerning just what his job consists of (see chapter twelve for more detail). Thus, a person may be highly motivated (putting out a lot of effort), but that effort will not necessarily result in what can be considered performance, unless he has both the ability to perform the job as well as a clear understanding of the ways in which it is appropriate to direct that effort. The student reader is probably familiar with at least one colleague who has high motivation to learn and succeed in university, but who lacks either the ability or the *savior faire* needed to direct his energy into what can be considered performance in the academic context: learning and self-development. In short, all three ingredients are needed to some degree, and if any of them is absent, performance cannot result.

Next, what is the relationship between performance (at whatever level is accomplished) and *job satisfaction?* As reflected in Figure 7-1, Porter and Lawler argue that performance and satisfaction may or may not be related to one another, depending upon a number of factors. First, they note that it is not always the case that performance results in rewards in organizations. Further, they recognize that there are at least two types of rewards potentially available from performance: intrinsic and extrinsic. (We have dealt with the distinction between intrinsic and extrinsic outcomes earlier in this book; the reader is referred to chapter four.) Porter and Lawler recognize that intrinsic rewards can be much more closely connected with good performance than extrinsic rewards, because the former result (almost automatically) from performance itself, whereas the latter depend upon outside sources (both to recognize that performance has been attained and to administer rewards accordingly).

Porter and Lawler suggest that the level of performance a person believes she has attained will influence the level of rewards that she believes will be *equitable* (see the discussion of internalized standards of equity in chapter six). So, if an employee believes that her efforts have resulted in a high degree of performance, she will expect a greater level of reward than would be the case if she believes that her performance is not as high. As a result, a particular reward, if any is forthcoming, will be assessed in terms of its level of equity in **141** the mind of the employee, rather than in terms of its absolute level. We sometimes hear statements such as "That pay increase was an insult, considering all I do for this company," reflecting Porter and Lawler's belief that it is not the absolute amount of reward that follows performance which determines whether it is satisfying; rather, the amount, however large or small, must be seen by the employee as equitable in order for it to be satisfying.

Satisfaction was defined in Porter and Lawler's research as ". . . the extent to which rewards actually received meet or exceed the perceived equitable level of rewards" (p. 31). And, as suggested by the feedback loop at the top of Figure 7-1, the level of satisfaction or dissatisfaction experienced by the person as a result of his treatment by the organization helps determine the value he places in the future on the rewards in question. Moreover, notice the feedback loop at the bottom of the diagram. It suggests that the strength of the person's belief that effort will result in rewards is also determined through experience.

Comments and Criticisms of Porter and Lawler

A number of points must be made about this model. First, the primary focus of the research that accompanied its development was upon *pay* and the role of pay in employee motivation. Although the authors limited their consideration of outcomes other than pay, they argued that the general model should be relevant for consequences other than pay. In addition, since pay was the focus, the emphasis was upon positive consequences only rather than upon both positive and negative consequences (such as fatigue, demotions, or various forms of punishment).

Secondly, Porter and Lawler tested the propositions they derived from their model *cross-sectionally* (rather than over time), and using only managers from the extreme ends of the distributions on the important variables in that model, excluding those individuals who fell near the middle in each case. This is a common practice in research, but one that causes overestimates of the validity of the model being tested (Taylor and Griess, 1976). Additionally, they measured job satisfaction using a technique that is also commonly used, but one which has subsequently been shown to be inappropriate, probably reducing the apparent validity of the model (Johns, 1981).

A third point is that although their model posits the importance of ability as an interactive factor with motivation as a determinant of job performance, Porter and Lawler's *own research* did not pay much attention to examining the specific role of ability. As was noted in chapter one of the present volume, however, other researchers have addressed this issue, and the results seem to suggest that while ability has an important influence on performance, it may not *interact* with motivation in the manner believed by Vroom (1964) and Porter and Lawler (cf. Terborg, 1977).

Fourthly, while Porter and Lawler use the term *value* rather than *valence,* it seems clear that they had the same concept in mind as Vroom. The reader is reminded again of the importance of distinguishing between valence and value when considering motivation from a VIE Theory perspective: it is the anticipated value (valence) of an outcome that is crucial in determining effort, not actual value, per se.

Another point has to do with the way the connection between effort and rewards was conceptualized and measured. Current theories recognize that employee beliefs about the strength of the connection between effort and reward distribution can usefully be broken down into two components: (1) the strength of the belief that a person's effort will result in job performance; and (2) the strength of the person's belief that performance, if achieved, will eventuate into rewards. Porter and Lawler acknowledge the prospect for breaking this overall cognition down into its component parts, and subsequent work by Lawler (1973) and others maintains this distinction.

Performance and satisfaction (again). A major contribution of the Porter-Lawler model consists of the implications it holds for the issue concerning the relationship between performance and satisfaction. Consider the diagram in Figure 7-1. According to the theory, will satisfaction and performance be related to one another? If so, when? The figure suggests that these two factors may or may not be related to one another, but that when they are, the order of causality is far from simple.

First, how might satisfaction be a contributing determinant of performance levels? A number of conditions must hold:

1. That satisfaction must leave the person desirous of attaining more of the same outcome(s). Recall from chapter three that satisfied needs tend to lose their capacity to motivate behavior, although growth need satisfaction seems to increase the strength of these needs.
2. Even if the reward maintains its valence, effort will result only if the person believes that effort results in the attainment of the reward (which, as we have discussed, is not always the case).
3. In order for the individual's effort to result in performance, the person must have the ability to perform, as well as have a clear idea concerning how to try to perform—where to direct his effort.
4. The performance must result in rewards, and these rewards must be perceived as equitable, for the reasons discussed earlier.

In short, in order for satisfaction to be a contributing cause of performance, as was believed during the days of the human rela- **143** tions movement (and as is still commonly believed by managers and people on the street), all of the foregoing individual and organizational conditions must apply. Rather complicated, to say the least.

Can performance be a cause of satisfaction? The model implies that it can. First, as already noted, high performance can be an immediate cause of intrinsic satisfaction, assuming that the job provides sufficient challenge to appeal to growth needs. Secondly, however, performance can contribute to extrinsic satisfaction if at least three conditions hold:

1. Desired rewards must be tied to that performance (as opposed to being tied to chance or other factors).
2. The person must perceive the connection between his performance and the rewards he receives.
3. The person must believe that the rewards he receives for his performance are equitable.

Again, not a very simple relationship, but Porter and Lawler's model helps explain why the relationships observed between performance and satisfaction have traditionally been so low, although, in their research, the two factors were found to be more strongly connected than is usually the case.

In conclusion, Porter and Lawler have provided a useful elaboration of the fundamental concepts of VIE Theory as presented only a few years earlier by Vroom. The dynamic features of their model (as reflected in the feedback loops) indicate the ongoing nature of the motivation process, and sheds some light on why some employees are more productive than others, why some employees are more satisfied with their work than others, and when we can expect to find a relationship between employee attitudes and performance.

THE VALIDITY OF VIE THEORY

In spite of the fact that there have been innumerable tests of the scientific validity of VIE Theory, only recently have researchers begun to perform studies that can be considered fair or appropriate, given the claims made by the theory itself (recall the discussion of this issue in chapter two, where we saw how it related to Herzberg's two-factor theory). In fact, Campbell and Pritchard (1976) have identified at least twelve common problems in the many studies conducted to that time.

The Between/Within Issue

Probably the most important of these problems has had to do with testing the theory as if it were intended to make behavioral and attitudinal predictions *across* individuals, as opposed to *within* individuals

(Arnold, 1981; Kopelman, 1977; Mitchell, 1974). In other words, the theory is intended to make predictions about which behavioral alternatives an individual will choose from among those that confront him. The theory states that the alternative which is perceived to maximize the individual's overall expected utility and satisfaction will be the one selected. On the other hand, a major proportion of the investigations reported to date have ignored or violated this assumption by computing expected levels of motivational force (or effort) for a number of people using those peoples' scores on VIE factors, and then correlating these predicted scores, across individuals, with ratings on some other form of score representing actual behavior or attitudes.

To illustrate more completely, suppose we were to compute expected effort scores for a sample of twenty people, using the information these people provide us through interviews or questionnaires. We would calculate these scores using some form of $E(\Sigma VI)$ formula. Then suppose we rank ordered these people on the basis of the magnitude of this overall predicted effort level. Next, we gather supervisory ratings of the actual typical effort levels of these same people and rank order them again, this time on the basis of their supervisory ratings. Finally, assume we correlate these *actual* effort scores with our predicted effort scores, attempting to determine whether the people with the highest predicted scores tended to have the highest supervisory ratings, and whether those with the lowest predicted scores also had the lowest ratings.

The approach just described is referred to as a between-individual one, for apparent reasons. This has been the methodology which has been erroneously used so many times, and the results generated from this type of research design have appeared not to support the theory, because, in fact, there has tended not to be very strong relationships between predicted effort and rated effort, when the data were compiled in this fashion. Accordingly, researchers have concluded that, by and large, the theory is only moderately valid.

Consider the mistake being made in studies conducted this way. The theory merely purports to make predictions concerning *single* individuals, one at a time, about the decision alternatives each of them will select. So, for example, Parker and Dyer (1976) were able to make better than chance predictions about the decisions reached by naval officers as to whether or not to retire voluntarily. Likewise, Arnold (1981) made predictions supportive of the theory concerning the choices of jobs made by undergraduate students; Matsui, Kagawa, Nagamatsu, and Ohtsuka (1977) predicted which of six insurance policies agents would prefer to sell; while Nebeker and Mitchell (1974) and Matsui and Ohtsuka (1978) predicted the **145** leadership styles of supervisors in different settings and in different cultures.*

What is wrong with the between-individual approach for testing the theory? It does not take into account differences between people in ability, the difficulty of the jobs they perform, differences in the level of rewards they receive for their work, and various other things. The difference between these two approaches is subtle when first considered, but incredibly significant for the conclusions one reaches about the validity of the theory. Moreover, the between-individuals approach assumes that people who hold identical valence, instrumentality, and expectancy beliefs will respond identically to instruments designed to assess these constructs. Clearly, this assumption is dubious (Mitchell, 1974). As noted by Atkinson (1964) and Kopelman (1977), and the last person in a family to arrive at the dinner table is not necessarily the least hungry! So, to conclude that the theory is not very valid on the basis of research that utilizes an across (or between) individuals approach hardly seems fair.

Other Research Difficulties

In addition to the between/within problem just described, there have been a variety of other typical mistakes made by researchers interested in VIE Theory (Campbell and Pritchard, 1976). A complete discussion of these is beyond our present purpose, but brief mention can be made of a few:

1. The use of incorrect mathematical procedures for testing the interaction effects between effort and ability posited by the theory (see Arnold, 1981 for a way of dealing with this problem).
2. The use of supervisory ratings of *performance* as the criterion against which predictions of employee force is compared. The use of performance rather than effort has occurred because of the difficulty of assessing the latter. But since the theory purports to predict effort, and because effort is only one determinant of performance, the results of these studies have been negatively biased against the theory.
3. Low validity and reliability of valence, instrumentality, and expectancy measures (recall chapter two, and see de Leo and Pritchard, 1974). The effect of these problems has been to cause underestimates of the validity of the theory.
4. The use of cross-sectional research designs, in spite of the fact that the theory speaks of changes, at one point in time, of V, I, and E perceptions being predictive of changes of effort at some subsequent point in time (see Mayes, 1978a for a discussion of this problem and Lawler and Suttle, 1973 and Kopelman, 1979 for attempts to get around it).
5. Assuming that the valence, instrumentality, and expectancy beliefs people

---

*The interested student reader may wish to read of a study in which the researchers utilized a VIE model to predict the academic effort and performance of a sample of college students, employing a statistical technique to control for the between/within person problem (Mitchell and Nebeker, 1973).

hold are independent of one another, then multiplying these scores algebraically. It may be that these three beliefs are not in fact independent of one another, such that people may place higher valence upon outcomes that are believed more difficult to attain (recall our discussion of achievement motivation in chapter four). Multiplication assumes independence.

6. Assuming that people are, in fact, as rational as the theory would suggest, for all aspects of their behavior, when, in fact, we know that people have limited cognitive capacities and that much of human behavior is habitual and subconscious (Locke, 1975; Mayes, 1978b; Staw, 1977; Simon, 1957).

Conclusion

The self-correcting cycle of research activity we examined in chapter two has raised questions about these and other common problems in the research on VIE Theory, and the more recent studies have taken many of them into account. As a result, it appears that VIE Theory may be a more valid representation of work-related attitudes and behaviors than has been concluded by many authors who have surveyed studies that were fraught with the problems identified above. In short, we conclude that the situation for VIE Theory may be similar to that for Maslow's need hierarchy theory (recall chapter three), Equity Theory (chapter six), and maybe even Herzberg's two-factor theory (recall chapter two): although there have been many studies conducted with the intention of testing its validity, only recently have there been many appropriately-conducted studies, leaving us with grounds for optimism that the theory is a reasonably valid model of the causes of work behavior.

THE PATH-GOAL THEORY OF LEADERSHIP

VIE Theory has inspired a formal theory of leadership called the *Path-Goal Theory*. In a nutshell, this theory suggests ways that leaders can make work groups more effective through the impact they can have on employee beliefs about valences, instrumentalities, and expectancies. More specifically, the theory discusses the ways in which leaders may use any of at least four types of behavioral styles to influence employee satisfaction, the acceptance of the leader by employees, as well as employee beliefs that effort can result in performance, and that performance will result in desired rewards (House and Mitchell, 1974).

The four leadership styles considered are the following:

1. *Directive*—meaning the leader structures the work, assigns tasks, clarifies his role with his subordinates, and creates and enforces standards of performance.
2. *Supportive*—the leader shows genuine respect for employee needs and status, attempting to make the work more pleasant. Such a leader treats subordinates as equals, and is friendly and approachable.

147

3. *Participative*—the leader consults with subordinates about problems and decisions that must be made, and takes subordinates' suggestions into account when possible.

4. Finally, *achievement-oriented* leadership involves a style in which the leader sets challenging goals, and shows confidence that subordinates can reach their goals.

Path-Goal Theory assumes that individual managers are capable of exhibiting more than one of these styles, depending upon the circumstances. In other words, it is a mistake to assume that a particular manager is simply a participative leader, or a *supportive type.* In fact, the theory suggests the types of conditions under which it is more appropriate for a leader to employ each of these various behavioral styles. Based on VIE Theory, it is assumed that the effective leader will behave in ways that recognize and arouse employee needs for the types of outcomes that the leader has at his disposal, and then attempt to increase the payoff to employees for successful performance when it occurs. Moreover, the successful leader will try to influence subordinate expectancy beliefs, by assisting with the accomplishment of difficult tasks, and by clarifying ambiguous task assignments. Finally, the effective leader will attempt, where possible, to make the distribution of rewards contingent on the successful accomplishment of work. To summarize,

> . . . the motivational functions of the leader consist of increasing the number and kinds of personal payoffs to subordinates for work-goal attainment and making paths to these payoffs easier to travel by clarifying the paths, reducing road blocks and pitfalls and increasing the opportunities for personal satisfaction en route (House and Mitchell, 1974, quoted from Downey, Hellriegel, and Slocum, 1977, p. 226).

Limitations of space prevent a more elaborate treatment of the Path-Goal Theory here. The interested reader can trace the development of the theory by reading Evans (1970, 1974), House (1971), House and Dessler (1974), and House and Mitchell (1974). Research testing the theory has been reported by Dessler and Valenzi (1977), Downey, Sheridan, and Slocum, (1976), Greene (1979), Schriesheim and De Nisi (1981), Schriesheim and Schriesheim (1980), and Schriesheim and Von Glinow (1977), among others. In general, the research on the theory seems to be increasingly more supportive as the theory itself becomes more elaborate, and as the instruments and methods used to test it become more refined. Path-Goal Theory holds a great deal of promise as further work is done on it.

IMPLICATIONS OF VIE THEORY FOR MANAGEMENT

We noted in chapter five that beliefs about work (or about life in general) are based on the individual's perceptions of the surrounding environment, and that these perceptions are influenced by information stored in the person's memory. It is assumed here that valence, instrumentality, and expectancy beliefs are established and influenced in the same manner as are other beliefs. Therefore, it also follows that because beliefs may not be valid or accurate, the person's behavior may not seem appropriate to observers. And it also follows that because these three beliefs are merely beliefs (as opposed to intentions), they may not result in behavior at all, or at least, they may not result in any specifically predictable behaviors. They should, however, influence an individual's *intentions* to act certain ways. Accordingly, a number of implications follow from VIE Theory for any supervisor who wishes to try to "motivate" his staff. Many of these suggestions were implicit in the foregoing discussion of the Path-Goal Theory.

Expectancy-Related Factors

First, in order to generate positive expectancy forces, the supervisor must assign his personnel to jobs for which they are trained, and which they are capable of performing. This requires that the supervisor understand the skills, strengths, and weaknesses of each of his subordinates, as well as the nature of the skill requirements of the jobs to which he is assigning them. If people are assigned to tasks that they are not capable of performing, according to VIE Theory, their expectancy perceptions will be low, and we will not expect to see them trying to perform.

Consider how difficult it is, in practice, for supervisors completely to appreciate the skill requirements of the jobs their employees must perform, and to recognize that it is the level of skills of the *employees* vis à vis the jobs, not their own skill levels, that matter. Jobs often change with time and as incumbents come and go, making it difficult to keep track of what they require. In addition, supervisors who have performed some or all of the jobs under their purview may forget how difficult these jobs are to newcomers, so they may either overestimate or underestimate the difficulty level of jobs for any of these reasons. Finally, it is important to recognize that employees' skills and abilities change over time, both as a result of formal training and education, as well as from the natural consequences of maturation and simple work experiences.

But adequate skill levels are not sufficient to assure positive expectancy perceptions. In addition, the employee must *believe* that the other circumstances surrounding his effort are favorable and conducive to his success. For example, the supervisor must be sure that machinery and equipment are in good repair, and that the employee's own staff, if any, are trained and capable of being of assistance. Likewise, there must be sufficient budget to make successful **149** performance possible. In short, the job must be capable of being performed by an employee if we are to expect the employee to try to perform it, and—more importantly—the person must perceive that it is so. But countless practical factors can combine to make it very difficult for any supervisor to accurately estimate the expectancy beliefs held by particular employees about specific jobs; accordingly, they make it difficult for supervisors to fully implement the implications that follow from the expectancy component of VIE Theory. More will be said about these matters in chapter twelve.

Of particular importance for supervisors is the structuring of the expectancy beliefs of newcomers to a work setting (Hall, 1976). Managers often take a "sink or swim" approach with new employees, assigning them work duties that are too difficult, given their relative lack of familiarity with the rules, procedures, and the myriad other circumstances that must be understood in order to make work efforts successful. An alternative approach is to under-challenge newcomers, requiring them to work through a tedious series of trivial jobs before being given any real challenge. Recent college graduates often complain of this treatment upon landing their first jobs after graduating, and, as a result, turnover among recent graduates is usually very high (Mobley, 1982). A third approach, the desired one, is to strike a balance using a combination of achievement-oriented, supportive, and directive leadership styles (as defined in the previous section), attempting to make the newcomer's initial experiences challenging and successful. Success experiences are necessary for developing strong expectancy beliefs, and for maintaining a positive self-concept about one's work—a feeling of competence, self-determination, and high self-esteem (cf. Deci, 1975; Hall, 1976; Korman, 1970, 1976).

Instrumentality-Related Factors

In order to operationalize the concepts of instrumentality and valence, supervisors must make sure that positively valent rewards are associated with good job performance, *and that their employees perceive this connection.* In practice, this also is difficult for a number of reasons. Most supervisors have a limited stock of rewards available to them for distribution to their subordinates. Company policies with regard to pay and benefits are usually restrictive, for the good reasons of control and the maintenance of equity. Further, union contracts are generally quite clear about the bases of reward distribution and often require that pay and other rewards be based on seniority rather than merit, further restricting the capacity of individual supervisors always to know who their meritorious employees are. This problem is especially common among managerial, professional, and technical personnel, in whose jobs good performance is normally very hard to measure, even when someone tries diligently to do so. As a result of these and other practical difficulties, implementing the instrumentality implications of VIE is often (perhaps usually) very difficult.

Valence-Related Factors

Where does the notion of valence fit into practice? VIE Theory would prescribe that those rewards which are distributed for good performance should be the types of things that employees desire. All that we know from common sense, as well as that which we have learned from research into human needs (see chapters three and four), tells us that different people have different need profiles at different times, so it follows that different outcomes will be rewarding for different people at different times. Hence, even the same outcome (such as a job transfer to another city) may be positively valent for some people, while being negatively valent for others. And to the extent that satisfied needs tend to lose their capacity to motivate behavior (as is suggested by the need theories discussed in chapters three and four), we can expect certain organizationally-distributed rewards to be satisfying and perhaps motivating for a particular individual in some circumstances, but not so in other circumstances. Hence, older employees often have no desire to meet and befriend new employees on the job: their relatedness needs are already well met and secured by interactions with old friends and acquaintances. In short, implementing VIE and Path-Goal concepts, with regard to providing valent outcomes for work, can be very difficult in practice.

Individual Organizations

One leading authority has discussed the importance of attempting to reward individuals with outcomes that are best suited to their individual needs (Lawler, 1973, 1976). His suggestions entail comprehensive analyses of both the employees and the jobs in organizations, followed by the careful assignment of people to those jobs in which they will find outcomes they desire, *especially as a consequence of good performance.*

A notable attempt to structure rewards on a more-or-less individualized basis can be found in the concept of *cafeteria-style* compensation plans (Lawler, 1966; Nealy, 1963; Schuster, 1969). The general design of these plans is for the individual employee to be allotted a fixed dollar sum of compensation that she can distribute according to her own preferences across a variety of forms of compensation, including salary, and any of a number of fringe benefits, deferred earnings, stock options, and the like.

151

Cafeteria-style plans have not, however, been widely adopted; in large measure because of a number of practical considerations that were discussed above (Belcher, 1974). For example, these plans tend to make payroll accounting procedures more complicated and more expensive to administer (Hettenhouse, 1971). In addition, there seems to be some belief on the part of management groups that employees should be required to invest their earnings in at least some amount of protection from insecurity (such as long-term disability and health insurance), whether they desire to do so or not. Another problem concerns the fact that many group life and health insurance plans are priced according to the number of persons in an organization who subscribe to them. Therefore, any sort of compensation system that allows some people to opt out of a group plan may result in higher premiums for those who opt into group coverage, thereby discouraging the individual decisions to opt out. Yet another difficulty that can arise from cafeteria-style plans results when employees elect to take all or most of their compensation in the form of cash, thereby threatening the relationship of internal equity between job level and pay level in the eyes of the employees involved (see chapter six). Finally, Belcher (1974) suggests that some of the negative reactions to cafeteria plans arise from a fear that if compensation were completely individualized, the infinite number of combinations and blends that are possible would be completely unmanageable, but that it should be possible to offset this fear by arranging a limited number of combinations from which individuals may choose. It may be, according to Belcher, that it is not necessary to *totally* individualize compensation plans. In fact, a study by Mahoney (1964) supports this view.

Another problem usually encountered by managerial attempts to individualize employee rewards in a fashion consistent with VIE Theory concerns the difficulty of accurately determining the actual *needs* of individual employees. The reader is asked to recall the discussion in chapter three, in which the risks of inferring need states from observations of another person's behavior were examined. Managers simply may not be able to accurately determine the needs of their employees, so they must rely on techniques such as attitude surveys and one-on-one discussions to learn about employee *values*.

The distinction between needs and values may appear academic, but it is more than that. Rewards may be satisfying, according to Locke (1976), as long as they correspond with employee values and are not inconsistent with employee needs (recall chapter five). But when employee values deviate from needs (meaning that people desire things that are not actually conducive to their best interests), organizational reward systems aimed at fulfilling employee values may not be at all beneficial, for either the individuals involved or for the organization as a whole. So, for example, certain employees may indicate that they desire greater responsibility and decision making power in their jobs. This stated preference reflects first a value—something the individuals *believe* will be good for themselves. In many cases, this value, if attained, will in fact satisfy needs—in this case, greater responsibility may be instrumental for fulfilling growth needs. In other cases, however, employees find that greater responsibility on their jobs is burdensome, stressful, and very frustrating: not everybody benefits from having responsible jobs, as will be discussed in chapter eleven.

The point of all this is that attempts to structure organizational reward systems in accordance with VIE Theory require that managers determine, somehow, what their subordinates want, and that they then proceed to tie job performance to the distribution of those outcomes. As noted above, systematic attempts to do this are frequently undertaken with the aid of employee attitude surveys; therefore VIE Theory may serve to guide the construction of such surveys, as we will see.

The Content of Employee Surveys

While a complete discussion of the design and use of employee attitude surveys is beyond our present purpose, VIE Theory clearly has a number of implications for this process. Specifically, rather than including only questions dealing with employee attitudes (as is commonly the case), greater benefit can be gained from seeking insight into the nature of employee beliefs, particularly beliefs about whether people feel it is typically possible to convert effort into performance, and whether rewards are seen as being tied to performance and as being equitable (Lawler, 1967b). In addition, more can be learned from enquiring *why* employees hold high or low expectancy and instrumentality beliefs, as well as why they believe the distribution of rewards is seen as inequitable, should that be the case.

The reader who is interested in greater detail about the construction of employee surveys is referred to recent books by Nadler (1977) and Dunham and Smith (1979). Detail concerning the administration of surveys in organizational settings is provided by Williams, Seybolt, and Pinder (1975).

Summary

The point here is that even those managers and supervisors who understand VIE Theory, and who are capable of distilling practical implications from it for application on their jobs, are usually severely handicapped by countless practical features of organizations, work **153** groups, union contracts, standard practices and policies, history, and precedents. More importantly however, we must remember that even if managers are able to structure work settings and reward distribution systems so as to comply with the implications of VIE Theory and the Path-Goal model, they will not be successful unless their policies and practices result in beliefs and perceptions, on the part of employees, which are consistent with high performance levels. For example, employees might not realize that rewards are, in fact, distributed in accordance with merit, even if that is actually the case. Likewise, employees may underestimate their chances of succeeding at a task, because they are not aware of the help that is available to them at the time. According to VIE Theory, it is beliefs that ultimately determine employee behavior, so unless managerial practices translate into beliefs that are favorable toward high job performance, beliefs will not result in employee intentions to perform well.

To conclude, VIE Theory offers a number of elegant implications for managerial practices aimed at generating and sustaining high levels of employee motivation. But putting these implications into practice can be difficult, because managers are often quite limited in the degree of control they have over the practical factors that must be manipulated in order to totally determine their employees' expectancy, valence, and instrumentality beliefs, and thereby influencing their intentions to perform well. Again, more attention will be directed in chapter twelve to how practical constraints, such as those discussed here, can influence the application of VIE Theory and other approaches to work motivation.

WHERE DO WE STAND?

In chapter five, we learned about beliefs, attitudes, and intentions, as well as how these constructs are formed, transformed, and converted into behavior. In this chapter and the one preceding it, we have examined two formal theories of work motivation which assume the cognitive/perceptual model of human functioning (Walter and Marks, 1981), and posit that beliefs and attitudes are the ultimate causes of behavior. However, these two theories posit the importance only of beliefs and attitudes about work—beliefs and attitudes about inputs, outcomes, equity, expectancies, valences, and instrumentalities. Both Equity Theory and VIE Theory (as well as the Path-Goal leadership model) assume that these constructs are responsible for arousing and directing work effort through the development of intentions. But we know that beliefs and attitudes do not totally determine intentions, and that intentions do not always result in predictable, specific behavior. Therefore, Equity and VIE beliefs cannot be expected to automatically result in specific work behaviors. And, as the research evidence presented above and in the last chapter has shown, neither Equity Theory nor VIE Theory is totally capable of predicting levels of work effort or decisions either to participate in, or to withdraw from, organizational settings. In the next chapter, however, we will address an approach to employee motivation that takes employee intentions as its point of departure, and because the connection between intention and behavior is more direct than that between either beliefs or attitudes and behavior, we will see that this approach has proven somewhat more successful, by comparison.

INTENTIONS AND MOTIVATION
8 Goal Setting and Management by Objectives

Ah, but a man's reach should exceed his grasp, Or what's a heaven for?
—Robert Browning

Chapters six and seven have presented formal theories of work motivation that assume a cognitive/perceptual model of human nature (Walter and Marks, 1981). More specifically, both Equity Theory and VIE Theory assume that people's perceptions of their work environments cause them to form beliefs and attitudes (about inputs and outcomes, or valences, expectancies and instrumentalities, respectively), and that these cognitions, in turn, instigate and direct various work-related behaviors.

The reader will recall from chapter five, however, that the general connection between cognitive factors on the one hand, and behavior on the other, is quite tenuous; but that the linkage between intentions, per se, and behavior is more direct than that between either beliefs or attitudes and behavior. In other words, intentions, once formed, are more likely to be useful for predicting and explaining behavior than either beliefs or attitudes (Fishbein and Ajzen, 1975). It is suggested that the limited predictive validity of both Equity Theory and VIE Theory can be explained, in part, accordingly. Moreover, it would follow that if any cognitive theory is to be predictive of behavior, it will likely be one that bases its predictions on *intentions* (rather than either beliefs or attitudes). In fact, there *is* such a theory, and the purpose of this chapter is to present and discuss it.

More specifically, this chapter consists of three main sections. In the first section, we will briefly examine the formal theory of intentional behavior as proposed by Ryan (1970). The second part of the chapter will then review the related work on *goal setting,* as developed by Locke, Latham, and their colleagues. As one might anticipate from the reasoning in the previous paragraph, we will see, in fact, that goal setting enjoys more scientific support than either Equity Theory or VIE Theory as a predictor of work effort and performance.

Finally, we will briefly review a managerial technique known as *Management by Objectives* (MBO)—a technique which draws heavily (but not exclusively) from the principles of goal setting. We will address the disparity between the general success of goal setting programs, per se, and that of Management by Objectives, and speculate on the future of MBO in work organizations.

To begin then, what are intentions, and how are they formed?

THE THEORY OF INTENTIONAL BEHAVIOR

The fundamental theory of motivation underlying current work on goal setting assumes that people's *intentions* are an important factor in explaining their behavior, although not the only factor, as illustrated in Figure 8-1 (Ryan, 1970). For example, the theory does not reject needs as a force in initiating action, although it assumes that needs influence behavior primarily through the effect they can have on the individual's intentions.

According to the theory, the analysis of behavior can be broken down into four interrelated stages or levels (Ryan, 1970). Each level helps explain the one that follows it. So, as mentioned, the most immediate level of explanation consists of the intentions people hold: individuals strive to act intentionally, pursuing whatever goals they have in mind. Whenever circumstances permit, behavior that is consistent with those intentions can be expected.

FIGURE 8-1   A Simplified Representation of the Four Levels of Causality of Behavior

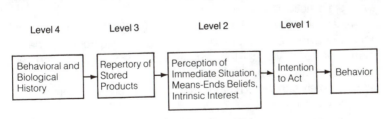

The second level of explanation consists of three sets of factors that influence the person's intentions. These are: (1) the person's perceptions concerning means-ends relationships (as in VIE Theory, whether the person believes that certain acts will result in certain out- **157**

comes); (2) the level of intrinsic interest or attractiveness of the act being contemplated; and (3) the appropriateness of the act in the particular social and physical setting in question (Ryan, pp. 26–27). The person's perceptions with regard to these three factors constitute the most important determinants of the person's intentions to act.

The reader may notice the similarity between these three factors and the elements of VIE Theory (discussed in the last chapter), Fishbein and Ajzen's theory of attitudes and behavior (as presented in chapter five), and even the theory of intrinsic motivation that was presented in chapter four of this book. The point is that it is possible to invoke other bodies of cognitive motivation theory to help understand the origins of human intentions to behave in Ryan's theory.

The third level of explanation consists of those factors that influence the three factors comprising level two. More specifically, level three factors consist of explanations for why people perceive things the way they do, why they find particular acts intrinsically interesting, and so on. The theory assumes that people become ". . . equipped with many prepared ways of perceiving, anticipating, and conceiving the world and their own activity" (Ryan, 1970, p. 28). People have ready-made reactions to stimuli in their environment, reactions that are the result of past history and learning. Ryan conceives of these as repertoires—as stored *products* that are invoked in particular settings to make sense of the environment. These products consist of factors such as needs, values, preferences, plans, rules for behaving, and so on. At this third level of causal explanation, understanding behavior consists both of understanding the contents of the person's repertoire, as well as the principles concerning which elements of it will be used in particular situations. It consists of seeking patterns in the person's reactions to situations—patterns in the way the individual perceives means-ends relationships, patterns in the types of activities she finds intrinsically interesting, and patterns in the way she deems particular types of acts as more or less appropriate, both practically and socially.

Finally, the fourth level of explanation in Ryan's theory of intentional behavior consists of the historical and developmental background of the individual—the background that explains why the person's repertoire is formed as it is. For Ryan (1970), this level is the most remotely connected with actual behavior, and therefore of least interest in his theory.

For Ryan, in short, a person's intentions are the most immediate determinants of that person's behavior. In view of the critical importance of intentions in his theory, let's take a closer look at the nature of human intentions.

The Nature of Intentions

Fishbein and Ajzen (1975) define an intention as a special form of belief; that is, an intention is a belief linking a person (the object of the belief) with a behavior (which is the attribute of the belief). As we saw in chapter five, beliefs can vary in strength; thus, we can speak of the strength of an intention as the strength of the person's beliefs (in probabilistic terms) that he will actually behave in a particular manner. In more common terms, an intention is a conviction to act, a predilection to behave a certain way.

According to Ryan (1970), it is possible to consider a number of different dimensions of intentions—aspects that can be used to characterize them. For example, we might consider the degree of freedom of choice involved in the intention (the degree to which people are forced to behave by factors beyond their control, as opposed to the degree to which people feel they will behave in a particular manner, when and where they want).

Likewise, it is possible to consider the content (or direction) of an intention. For example, an intention may pertain to locomotion (going somewhere), to modifying something (such as baking a pie, firing an employee, or organizing a union). Alternatively, an intention may pertain to communicating something to someone, seeking a skill, or acquiring new knowledge. The point is that there are many different types of intentions people can hold, dealing with convictions to act in an infinite number of ways toward any of an infinite number of objects. The reader is reminded of the importance of the specificity of an intention, however, in making predictions of particular acts (recall chapter five and see Ajzen and Fishbein, 1977).

In summary, the basic concept underlying Ryan's theory is that intentions are the most immediate and most important causes of behavior. To understand the origins and nature of people's intentions requires that we understand the way that people view the world around themselves. In turn, in order to understand why people perceive things the way they do, we must understand the nature of stored products such as their needs, values, norms, and so on. Finally, in order to understand why individuals hold particular repertoires of such products, we must examine their backgrounds. It bears repeating that various other theories discussed in this book can be used to help understand the factors at each of these various levels of explanation, and that, consistent with the model linking beliefs, attitudes, and intentions to behavior (Fishbein and Ajzen, 1975), intentions, once they are formed, are the most immediate causes and predictors of actual behavior.

Because of space limitations, the foregoing discussion of the ba- **159** sic theory of intentions is brief and considerably oversimplified. The interested reader is referred to Ryan's (1970) book for more detail. Nevertheless, now that the elements of the theory of intentional behavior have been introduced, we can examine the tenets of the theory of goal setting.

GOAL SETTING

The most fundamental tenet of Goal Setting Theory* is that goals and intentions are responsible for human behavior. In this context, goals mean the same thing they meant in chapter four, where the frustration model was presented: a goal is something that a person tries to attain, achieve, or accomplish. In work settings, goals may take the form of things such as a level of job performance, a quota, a work norm, a deadline, or even a budgetary spending limit (Locke, Shaw, Saari, and Latham 1981).

The second major tenet derives logically from the first: if goals determine human effort, it follows that *higher* or *harder* goals will result in higher levels of performance** than easy goals. Moreover, the third tenet of the theory holds that *specific* goals (such as "reducing employee turnover by 20 percent within six months") are seen as resulting in higher levels of effort than vague goals such as "let's cut back turnover as much as possible."

A fourth tenet of the theory is that incentives such as money, feedback, competition, and the like will have no effect on behavior unless they lead to the setting and/or acceptance of specific, hard goals.

Notice again that this approach to work motivation relies heavily on the same cognitive/perceptual model of human functioning that underlies both VIE Theory and Equity Theory: in order for a person to have a goal, he must be aware of his surroundings and be fully cognizant of the meaning of what constitutes his goal. Behavior is intentional (Ryan, 1970)—it results from the deliberate adoption of one or more conscious choices of action. People engage in acts that are consistent with their intentions and goals.

---

*Its major proponents often refer to goal setting as a set of techniques rather than a formal theory (Locke, 1975). Notwithstanding their view, we will refer to the concepts and propositions related to goal setting as a theory, for two reasons. The first reason is that the goal setting framework is as coherent and well grounded as most other approaches presented under the rubric *theory* in this book. The second reason is consistency with the terminology used with reference to other theories presented in other chapters.

**In chapter one we made a distinction between work effort and performance—an important distinction that has been maintained throughout the rest of the book. And, although the concept of central interest in this book is work motivation (as manifested in effort), most of the theory and research on goal setting focuses on *task performance*. Accordingly, we will concentrate on performance as the outcome of primary interest in this chapter, with a reminder that effort is only one of many determinants of job performance in real work settings (see also chapter twelve).

Goal Difficulty and Task Difficulty

At first blush, these basic elements of Goal Setting Theory may seem trivial and self-evident. On the other hand, their simplicity is profound, and leads logically to a number of important corollaries for application in work settings.

The most important implication of the basic tenets of the theory concerns the most appropriate level of goal difficulty for maximum performance. A critical distinction must be made between task difficulty and goal difficulty, however, before we can proceed. According to Locke et al. (1981):

> Since a goal is the object or aim of an action, it is possible for the completion of a task to be a goal. However . . . the term goal refers to attaining a specific standard of proficiency on a task, usually within a specified time limit (p. 126).

Therefore, two people could be given the same task (such as to recruit twenty new sales representatives to the firm), but one person could have a much more difficult goal than the other; for example, being given half as much time as the other to achieve the goal. Same task, different goals. The theory predicts that to the extent that he is committed to it, the person with the harder goal will perform to a higher standard. The difficulty of the goal—not the difficulty of the task, per se—is seen as the critical determinant of effort level.*

The empirical evidence in support of the goal difficulty hypothesis is impressive. Edwin Locke, Gary Latham, and their colleagues have conducted dozens of experiments in both laboratory (Locke, Cartledge, and Knerr, 1970) and field settings (Latham and Yukl, 1975) to show that hard goals result in higher levels of performance than do easy goals (Locke et al, 1981). The tasks included in the laboratory experiments have ranged from chess problems to arithmetic problems, card sorting, brainstorming, prose learning, and data coding, among others.

The field studies have also been diverse in nature, and equally compelling. In one such experiment, for example, Latham and Baldes (1975) had forestry truck drivers set goals pertaining to the amount of wood they hauled on each load to their woodyard. Goals were set and measured in terms of the weight of each load, as a percentage of each particular truck's gross vehicle weight. Enough extra wood was hauled as a result of the goal setting program over a nine-month period that it would have cost the company $250,000 to have purchased the trucks that would have been needed to achieve the same increment in performance without the program.

In another experiment, Latham and Kinne (1974) showed how a

---

*On the other hand, more difficult tasks, per se, sometimes can contribute to higher performance, as a consequence of the greater learning hard tasks can foster (Campbell and Ilgen, 1976).

one-day goal setting training program resulted in both higher productivity and lower absenteeism among a sample of independent
loggers over a twelve-week period. In short, there is abundant evidence from advocates of this school of thought that difficult goals
result in higher performance than easy goals.

Contrast with other theories. Notice however that the goal
setting prescription regarding the optimum level of task difficulty dif-
fers from that derived from both VIE Theory (which would suggest
that motivation is maximized when expectancy beliefs are at a maximum) and McClelland and Atkinson's view (recall chapter four) that
achievement motivation is maximized when the individual perceives
the task to be of *moderate* levels of difficulty. The differences among
these three theories on this matter are dramatic, and of critical importance to anyone who wishes to apply motivation theory, either to the
design of tasks or the assignment of people to tasks.

On the one hand—as noted above—proponents of Goal Setting
Theory offer considerable empirical support for their position. On the
other hand, advocates of both VIE Theory and achievement motivation offer compelling evidence of their own. It may be that the
decision-making processes posited by VIE Theory are most useful
for predicting the level of goal accomplishment a person will pursue
in situations where the person is not committed, a priori, to any particular goal, but that once commitment is gained, performance is determined by the level of difficulty of the task (Cartledge, 1973; Locke,
1975). Moreover, it may be that tasks which are perceived as too
difficult lose their capacity to gain a person's commitment, thereby
supporting the achievement motivation position that tasks of moderate levels of difficulty are most motivating (Locke, et al., 1970).

The few studies that have addressed the differences among the
three perspectives on this matter have yielded contradictory results,
making it premature, at present, to offer a final word on the issue (cf.
Atkinson, 1964; Janz, 1982 with Dachler and Mobley, 1973; Locke
et al., 1970; and Mento, Cartledge, and Locke, 1980). The position
adopted here is that further, carefully controlled experimental research is required to identify the types of people for whom, and the
types of situations within which, the predictions made by each theoretic perspective most consistently apply.

Goal Specificity

In chapter five it was noted that higher degrees of specificity in an
intention will be associated with more accurate levels of prediction of
actual behavior (Ajzen and Fishbein, 1977). Likewise, an important
tenet of Goal Setting Theory is that higher levels of performance
result when goals are made specific. According to Ajzen and

Fishbein (1977), intentions can be made more or less specific with regard to the nature of the act involved, the target of the act, as well as in terms of the time and circumstances in which the intended act might occur. As we will see, managerial techniques based on the goal setting literature instruct practitioners to be as specific as they can with regard to each of these four dimensions. In short, the theory says that in addition to being difficult, goals should be specific.

Again, the evidence is persuasive. Employee performance is consistently higher when goals are formulated in terms such as, "Increase market share eight percent per annum," "Sell thirty pounds of peaches by noon," or "Increase my grade-point-average by one full grade by final exams," than it is when the target, the time, or the circumstances are not specified (Locke et al., 1981).

The Role of Incentives

If, as the theory states, goals or intentions determine behavior, what about all that we know from research and common experience about the influence of incentives (or even threats) on performance? According to Locke (1968), incentives are effective for influencing behavior *only to the extent that they influence the goals people strive to achieve.* In other words, incentives work only if they change a person's goals and intentions, or build commitment to those they already hold.

For example, consider the effects of competition—it is a form of motivational device used by many managers, coaches, teachers, and even parents. Why is competition effective for changing behavior, or increasing performance?

There are at least two reasons why competition may result in higher levels of performance, according to the theory. One is that competition may serve to build commitment on the part of the individual to the task, and to the goal of winning at the task: remember that the person must be committed to a goal in order to strive toward attaining it. However, a second feature of competition—particularly "stiff" competition—is that it serves to make the goal (winning) more difficult than it might otherwise be.

What about deadlines? Common experience (as well as research evidence) shows that people tend to get a lot more accomplished when they are facing deadlines. In fact, some people seem to thrive under the pressure of meeting deadlines for their work! Why might this be so? For the theory of goal setting, the answer is relatively simple: a deadline serves the same function as making a goal harder than it would be without it, and—the theory states—harder goals result in higher performance levels. To illustrate, a study by Latham and Locke (1975) showed that the performance levels of **163** wood-harvesting crews increased dramatically when restrictions were placed on the number of days during which pulp and paper mills would buy the wood they hauled. In the same way that Parkinson's Law (Parkinson, 1957) states that work expands to fill the time that is made available for it, this research, and the goal setting principle on which it is based, suggest that people's work pace will increase according to the level of difficulty they attribute to the task to be accomplished.

Other incentives would seem to influence motivation levels in a similar fashion. Money is probably the most widely used incentive; Goal Setting Theory would suggest that it will motivate higher levels of performance only to the extent that it results in higher levels of commitment by the individual to the task involved. In chapter seven we noted the importance, for example, of tying pay to good job performance, as well as the importance of having employees recognize the connection between merit and payment. And, in chapter six, we noted that rewards must be viewed as equitable in order to result in positive attitudes toward work. The relationship between these two principles and the use of incentives, from a goal setting perspective, should be clear: if a monetary incentive is not seen as contingent on performance, and/or if it is not seen as equitable, it is less likely to commit the individual to a goal of high performance. In short, principles of Equity Theory and VIE Theory help us understand the role of incentives, of all sorts, from the goal setting point of view.

Participation in Goal Setting

Should employees participate in the goal setting process? There are a number of conceptual reasons why higher levels of motivation and performance may result when the employee involved has participated with her supervisor in the setting of work goals (Mitchell, 1973). First, participatively set goals may sometimes be harder than goals set unilaterally by one's superior. Secondly, an employee who has participated in goal setting is more likely to be ego-involved in the successful attainment of those goals: because they are somewhat responsible for the type and levels of the goals they are pursuing, employees will be more desirous of seeing them fulfilled. A third possible reason that participation may result in higher performance is that the employee is able to gain a better understanding through participation of the reasons behind her goals as well as of what to do in order to successfully strive toward goal attainment.

In spite of the intuitive appeal of these arguments, however, the evidence that addresses them is somewhat mixed (Locke et al., 1981). For example, Latham, Mitchell, and Dossett (1978) found that although a group of scientists and engineers who participated in the setting of goals tended to set harder goals than were set for a comparable group by a supervisor, the two groups did not differ significantly in actual performance levels. Moreover, other studies have shown that when the difficulty level of a goal is held constant among groups, people whose goals are assigned to them seem to perform as well, on average, as people who have participated in the setting of their work goals (Latham and Saari, 1979a; Latham and Steele, 1983; Latham, Steele, and Saari, 1982). There is some evidence, nevertheless, that participation in goal setting contributes to greater understanding of task requirements (Latham and Saari, 1979b), which, in itself, may be conducive to superior job performance when supervisors are not readily available for consultation with their subordinates. Moreover, it may be that the general level of supervisory supportiveness is more important than participation, per se (Latham and Saari, 1979b), although the exact nature of the role of supportiveness in the goal setting process is less well understood than other facets of the theory (Locke et al., 1981).

The Role of Feedback

We will spend considerable time in chapters ten and eleven examining the importance of providing employees with knowledge of the results of their efforts. In the meantime, however, we must mention the critical role of feedback in goal setting contexts. The evidence on the matter suggests that both goals and feedback to the individual about his performance vis à vis those goals, are necessary in order to sustain high levels of employee performance. In other words, neither the provision of feedback, nor the setting of goals is sufficient for motivating performance—the two provisions are both required (Bandura and Cervone, 1983; Locke et al., 1981).

Why Does Goal Setting Work?

Why does goal setting seem to be so effective as a motivational strategy? The authors of a recent review (Locke et al., 1981) offer four reasons, reminding us that the concept of motivation is used to explain the *direction, amplitude* (level of effort), and *duration* (or persistence) of behavior (recall chapter one of this book). Notice in the following paragraphs how the fundamental tenets of goal setting relate to these facets of motivation.

First, goals direct attention and action. They identify the target of intended behavior (Ajzen and Fishbein, 1977), and, if they are stated specifically (as is recommended), the focus of the individual's effort becomes well defined. Likewise, the requirement that goals be made difficult relates directly to the effort level and persistence aspects of the motivation concept. If a goal is hard, it will normally re- **165** quire more effort, over a longer period of time, in order to be attained.

Finally, Locke and Latham (1984) offer a fourth explanation. They note that goal setting usually requires the development of strategy. In other words, when people contemplate a goal, they must also consider means for its attainment, especially when that goal is seen as difficult. For example, in the aforementioned study in which truck drivers set higher goals pertaining to the capacity to which they loaded their trucks (Latham and Baldes, 1975), many of the drivers involved made recommendations concerning how their trucks might be modified to facilitate their attempts to carry more lumber. It may be that harder tasks are more likely to stimulate more strategy development than easy tasks; likewise, it makes sense that the more specific the task goal, the more likely it is that people will devise specific techniques to achieve it.

In addition to the four reasons offered by Locke and his colleagues (1981) for the success of Goal Setting Theory, however, is the reason suggested at the beginning of this chapter. If one adopts the approach of Fishbein and Ajzen (1975 and chapter five of this book), it makes considerable sense that goal setting is a comparatively successful theory of work motivation. Recall that, according to Fishbein and Ajzen (1975), perceptions influence beliefs, which, in turn, typically result in evaluative *attitudes*. These attitudes then may or may not result in intentions to act, depending upon a number of factors. Nevertheless, in the casual chain linking perceptions, beliefs, attitudes, and intentions with behavior, intentions, once developed, are clearly the cognitive elements most closely connected with behavior. In fact, we can view the others (perception, beliefs, and attitudes) merely as factors that contribute to the development of intentions, but only imperfectly (cf. Mento et al., 1980).

In other words, beliefs and attitudes contribute to the development of intentions, but they do not totally shape or determine them. Therefore, to the extent that beliefs and attitudes are only partially related to a person's intentions (for the reasons discussed in chapter five), they will not be as effective as that person's *intentions* in predicting behavior. And, to repeat a point made earlier in this chapter, it follows that theories such as Equity Theory and VIE Theory which rely on beliefs and attitudes (which are merely *predictors* of intentions to act) cannot be as valid as goal setting, which takes intentions, per se, as its point of departure for predicting behavior.

The linkages between perceptions, beliefs, attitudes, intentions, and work behavior from the three cognitive theories are presented graphically in Figure 8-2. (The reader is urged to refer to chapter five of this book for a more complete discussion of these relationships.) In short, examination of the relationships represented in Figure 8-2 helps explain the limited potential predictive and explanatory capacity of the theories presented in the last two chapters, and suggests why Goal Setting Theory fares better by comparison.

FIGURE 8-2: Summary of Relationships Among Beliefs, Attitudes, and Intentions in Three Cognitive Theories

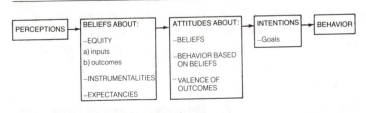

An Assessment of Goal Setting Research

There is little doubt that the research which has been conducted on goal setting has generally been far more rigorous and free of methodological error than that which has been conducted on any of the other theories and approaches presented in this book. There are a number of reasons that may explain this, but two seem especially important.

First, the theory itself is relatively simple by comparison with other theories of work motivation. For example, there are no requirements to develop psychometric measures of cognitive factors such as expectancies, valences, or instrumentalities. Likewise, the theory does not require the measurement of needs, as is the case in Maslow's and Alderfer's hierarchical models (recall chapter three). Time lags do not seem to play the important (but indefinite) role in goal setting that they entail in VIE Theory. In short, the theory is comparatively simple and requires testing procedures that are accordingly simple, and less subject to many of the types of methodological difficulties that have hindered the refinement of other theories presented in this book.

A second probable reason for the relatively high quality of goal setting research is that a limited number of researchers have been involved in it. Whereas countless people have conducted research into Equity Theory and VIE Theory, for example, only a limited number of individuals have been involved in the majority of the studies of goal setting. The recent review of Locke, Shaw, Saari, and Latham (1981) shows that Locke and Latham and their colleagues have carried the ball almost exclusively in developing this theory over the years. One result of this focused and ongoing attention by these researchers has been the development of a set of research techniques and testing procedures (or experimental paradigms) that have proven to be effective and relatively sound from a scientific point of **167** view. This author is not aware of any radical attacks on the research methods used by this relatively small school of scholars—attacks of the sort that have regularly been leveled at research into need hierarchy theory (e.g., Bandura, 1977; Mitchell and Moudgill, 1976; Salancik and Pfeffer, 1977), Equity Theory (see Carrell and Dittrich, 1978 and Pritchard, 1969), and VIE Theory (cf. Campbell and Pritchard, 1976), for example. The cumulative experience in both laboratory and field settings, by a limited number of people, must account for part of this.

Conclusions

The foregoing pages have provided a brief summary of the research and theory on goal setting. The relationship between this work and the theory of intentional behavior, presented at the beginning of this chapter, should be clear. Likewise, the relationship between the notions of goal setting, as they have just been described, and the managerial technique we will discuss in the remainder of this chapter, should also be apparent.

At the time of this writing, it seems safe to agree with Locke and his colleagues that "The beneficial effect of goal setting on task performance is one of the most robust and replicable findings in the psychological literature" (1981, p. 145). But it is important to reiterate the important difference between a lack of scientific support on the one hand, and negative evidence on the other; this point is of more than mere academic interest. Its relevance here is that it may be that other need-oriented and cognitively based theories are more valid than we are capable of demonstrating by normal scientific means (this argument has been raised in the discussion of several of the theories presented to this point in the book). As mentioned above, it would appear that the propositions derived from Ryan's theory of intentional behavior are more easily operationalized, measured, and tested than are propositions derived from many of the other theories we have examined to this point, thereby making it easier to demonstrate the validity of this approach.

Likewise, two other points of balance are in order. First, it must be noted that the scope of Goal Setting Theory is more focused than that of both the need-based theories presented in chapters three and four of this book and the other two cognitive/perceptual theories presented in chapters six and seven. So, whereas these other theories might be applied to understanding people's career choices, their attitudes with regard to voting for a union, or their decisions to work for one organization rather than another, Goal Setting Theory addresses only the problem of employees' performance levels. One might expect, other things being equal, that a more limited-range theory should do a better job, scientifically, than one with a broader range of focus (Merton, 1968; Pinder and Moore, 1980).

Secondly, while we note that Goal Setting Theory has been exposed to more research in field settings than have most other theories of work motivation, it is important also to note that the most compelling evidence in support of the theory still derives from laboratory and/or simulated work settings. There is very little in the way of *long-term* field research that addresses the validity of Goal Setting Theory *in its pure form,* without the contaminating influences of other managerial programs (such as those which accompany Management by Objectives, for example). Rather, that field-based research which does exist (e.g., Latham and Yukl, 1975) is derived from comparatively short-term field studies (most of which are supportive of the theory) or from formalized MBO programs that entail encumbrances not related to Goal Setting, per se, but that have caused such programs frequently to fail (as we will see shortly).

Notwithstanding these remarks, Goal Setting Theory has demonstrated more scientific validity to date than any other theory or approach to work motivation presented in this book. Moreover, the evidence thus far indicates that it probably holds more promise as an applied motivational tool for managers than does any other approach, especially when it is combined with a number of principles of behavior modification (as we will see in chapter ten).

Before leaving our discussion of goal setting, it is worth noting again the potential this theory has for integrating many of the other theories presented in this book (including some approaches and techniques that are still to be presented). Ryan's (1970) theory suggests the important role needs may play in determining the *repertoires* people develop for interpreting stimulus situations. Similarly, the work of Fishbein and Ajzen (1975) and Ajzen and Fishbein (1977) suggests how cognitive theories that rely on beliefs and attitudes (such as Equity Theory and VIE Theory) contribute to the explanation of behavior: their primary function is to provide a basis for predicting a person's intentions, not the direct prediction of behavior, as such.

Finally, it stands to reason that managerial programs that explicitly attempt to influence employee intentions *should* be more effective for influencing employee behavior than are programs designed to influence beliefs and attitudes. We will go on to examine Management by Objectives, a popular managerial technique that attempts to do just that.

MANAGEMENT BY OBJECTIVES

One of its leading proponents has claimed that Management by Objectives (MBO) is the predominant form of management in today's business and government organizations, and that this ap- **169** proach to management has been subjected to as much scientific investigation as any other (Odiorne, 1979). A cursory examination of the managerial literature confirms the widespread popularity of MBO, at least in terms of the number of organizations that have adopted it in some form or another. Likewise, as we saw in part one of this chapter, the scientific literature on goal setting (the major body of research and theory related to a central aspect of MBO) suggests that, in fact, many of the basic elements of MBO do rest on considerable scientific support. In the following sections, we will briefly examine MBO and discuss a number of issues related to it.*

Origins of Management by Objectives

Although thinkers dating back to the classical philosophers have held that human effort is (or should be) goal directed (Odiorne, 1979), the modern origins of MBO seem to be found in the work of Peter Drucker with General Motors and General Electric (Greenwood, 1981). Whereas earlier management theorists had assumed that objectives are an important part of managing, they placed little emphasis on the origins and consequences of objectives in organizational settings. It was Drucker who recognized the problematic nature of objectives and built an approach to management that centers primarily upon them (Greenwood 1981).

What is MBO?

In actual practice, there are almost as many varieties of MBO as there are organizations that claim to have adopted it. In other words, the specific features of MBO and MBO-like programs vary from one organization to another, sometimes causing confusion over just what is and what is not MBO. One recent comprehensive study of this matter has concluded that MBO can best be defined as:

> A managerial process whereby organizational purposes are diagnosed and met by joining superiors and subordinates in the pursuit of mutually agreed goals and objectives, which are specific, measurable, time bounded, and joined to an action plan; progress and goal attainment are measured and monitored in appraisal sessions which center on mutually determined objective standards of performance (McConkie, 1979, p. 37).

This definition will be adopted in this chapter and elsewhere throughout this book.

---

*Space constraints prevent a detailed treatment of the topic, but the interested reader can learn more from texts devoted exclusively to MBO by Carroll and Tosi (1973), Migliore (1977), Odiorne (1979), and Raia (1974). We will begin by defining MBO and identifying some of its most common features.

Some Specific Features of MBO Programs

As noted above, the specific characteristics of MBO and MBO-like programs vary in practice from one setting to another, although, in most cases, the two most essential features of such programs are: (1) a system for establishing work-related goals; and (2) some type of procedure for assessing the individual's performance vis à vis those goals after a specified period of time. Beyond these two very basic characteristics, however, there is less unanimity in practice about what constitutes MBO.

Nevertheless, McConkie (1979) has found varying degrees of agreement among a sample of experts concerning the following general statements *about the goal setting aspect of MBO:*

1. Objectives should be reviewed periodically.
2. The time period for goal accomplishment should be specified.
3. The indicators of results should be quantifiable if possible; otherwise they should at least be verifiable.
4. Objectives should be flexible, changing as circumstances change.
5. Objectives should include a statement of an "action plan" for how they will be accomplished.
6. Objectives should be prioritized, some being agreed upon as more important than others.

There is less agreement among the experts, however, concerning a variety of issues related to the *performance assessment* aspect of MBO programs. For example, whether employees should assess their own performances against their goals or whether the superior should be involved in the assessment process is one matter about which there exists some difference of opinion (McConkie, 1979).

In short, MBO, in common practice, usually consists of a set of procedures for the setting of individual goals on the basis of broader organizational goals, and the subsequent evaluation of individual performance in terms of the degree of accomplishment of these goals. The specific nuances with regard to the participation of subordinates in the goal setting and performance evaluation processes vary across organizations, as well as between units within particular organizations.

Functions Potentially Served by MBO

One of the leading advocates of MBO (Odiorne, 1979) has identified a variety of functions this system might be expected to serve, including the following:

1. Reduction of aimless activity and the wasting of time and other resources.
2. Reduction of conflict between superiors and subordinates as a result of greater clarity of each other's responsibilities.

171

3. Improvement of individual performance and overall organizational effectiveness.
4. Improvements in employee morale, employee development, quality of work, and delegation.
5. Improvement in the capacity of the organization to change and adapt.

In fact, it is claimed that MBO can help deal with a number of common problems faced by managers, such as deciding upon who is to receive pay increases, how many people should report to a particular individual, the types of people who should report to a given manager, the types and amount of information that should be communicated to subordinates, as well as the amount of delegation and decentralization that is most desirable in a particular situation. In short, advocates of MBO, such as Odiorne, believe that it is more than merely a set of techniques and procedures; rather it is viewed as a total system of management, even as ". . . a way of thinking about management" (1979, p. 52).

Basic Stages in MBO

MBO can be broken down into four basic steps. First, managers at each organizational level confer and negotiate with each of their subordinates to determine organizational and personal objectives for some upcoming period of time (such as six months or a year). In practice, the degree to which the subordinate actually participates in this goal setting process varies (as mentioned above), depending upon the personal styles of both the superior and subordinate, as well as upon the degree to which they try to adhere to strictly prescribed MBO principles (which normally advocate participation).

Secondly, the subordinate prepares an action plan that spells out how he will attempt to achieve the agreed-upon goals. These action plans may or may not be reviewed by the superior. Once agreed upon, however, the objectives and action plans guide the employee's work behavior during the following (and agreed-upon) period of time.

The third stage consists of a performance review by the superior and the subordinate of the latter's progress toward the objectives that were set at the beginning of the period. This performance review, in effect, replaces more traditional methods of performance appraisal practiced in many organizations. In fact, problems with traditional methods were largely responsible for the rapid growth in popularity of MBO and MBO-like programs. One classic paper, for example, points out how traditional performance appraisal systems place supervisors in the untenable position of "playing God" with subordinates: invariably, the supervisor finds himself passing judgment on the personal worth of the subordinate (McGregor, 1957). As a result of the unpleasantness that naturally results from such a process, performance appraisal seldom accomplishes its purposes of constructively evaluating an employee's job performance; rather it generates defensive reactions on the part of the subordinate, and/or attempts by the supervisor to avoid the process entirely. Accordingly, MBO was proposed as an alternative, because it requires that the superior and the subordinate focus attention on the *behaviors* and *accomplishments* of the employee, in terms of objectives that the employee helps establish. The result, according to McGregor (1957), is a more analytic process, which is impersonal and objective, and that makes constructive assessment more possible.

Finally, the fourth stage of most MBO programs is the setting of new objectives by the superior and the subordinate for the following period of time.

Cascading. One general feature that is prescribed by advocates of MBO is that the goals which are set at each organizational level should be consistent with the goals set at other hierarchical levels. More specifically, the goals set at the highest level of the organization should be stated in relatively general terms, which can subsequently be translated into increasingly more specific terms at each lower level. The process of distilling increasingly more specific objectives as one moves down the hierarchy is referred to as *cascading* (see Raia, 1974).

For example, an organization might have the objective of increasing profits by 10 percent over the next two-year period. This somewhat general objective is then interpreted into more specific goals for managers at lower levels of the firm. The vice president of administration of the company might, for instance, generate objectives with his boss (the president) that have to do with cutting costs, whereas the vice president in charge of sales may translate the general organizational profit goal into more specific objectives concerning sales levels and market penetration. Each of these v.p.'s would then, in turn, derive even more specific objectives with each of their own subordinate managers. So, to continue the example, the v.p. of administration might collaborate with his employment manager to set goals dealing with the reduction of the cost associated with turnover and the recruitment of new staff. The employment manager, in turn, would then generate goals with each recruiter and personnel interviewer, concerning specific techniques for reducing turnover and recruitment costs. Naturally, the specific objectives derived at each level will vary from one department to the next, depending upon the type of work performed (e.g., sales, marketing, production, and so on).

173

Assumptions Underlying MBO

MBO programs rely upon a number of assumptions (Barton, 1981). First, it is assumed that an organization may have more than a single objective. In fact, of course, most organizations have multiple objectives (Gross, 1965). The hypothetical firm in the above example, for instance, may have objectives dealing with new product development, the improvement of its corporate image, and diversification into different markets. Likewise, it is assumed that particular employees at each level of the organization may have more than one objective, and that objectives at any given level may result in more than one sub-objective at subsequent lower levels.

Secondly, it is assumed that when they are achieved, the various sub-goals at each level cumulatively contribute to the achievement of the goals at each successive higher level, ultimately to the attainment of the organization's goals at their broadest levels (such as increasing profits by 10 percent over a two-year period).

Thirdly, the use of an MBO program implies an organization's strategy and tactics are to be found in (and consist of) its goals and the action plans that derive from those goals. The means-ends linkages generated by an MBO program comprise organizational strategy and are the primary basis for organizational policy. It is in this sense that MBO has the potential to be much more than merely a goal setting and performance appraisal system.

Finally, it might be assumed that, ideally, the goals that result from an MBO program should be mutually compatible—they should not be counterproductive and mutually antithetical. In practice, of course, this is not normally the case. In fact, the opposite is more common: organizational goals are commonly incompatible (Daft, 1983). For example, the hypothetical organization mentioned above may find that its goals of increasing profits and expanding markets interfere with its goal of improving its reputation in the community. Likewise, university students often feel that university goals dealing with research and publication activities are inconsistent with objectives pertaining to quality instruction in the classroom. This is sometimes the case, but not necessarily. Barton (1981) has recently discussed the problem of incompatible goals in MBO settings and has presented an approach for dealing with it.

How Effective is MBO in Practice?

Now that we have looked at some of the claims made in support of MBO, as well as a number of its principal characteristics, it is appropriate to examine the scientific evidence concerning the actual value and effectiveness of these programs. Just how effective is MBO?

174   A recently published review of 185 case studies, surveys, quasi-experiments, and true experiments helps provide an answer—an answer that is less than totally encouraging, but one that will sound familiar to those who have read the earlier chapters of this book. In a nutshell, this review found an inverse relationship between the level of scientific rigor used in evaluative studies of MBO, and the degree of support claimed for the program studied (Kondrasuk, 1981) In other words, if researchers employ carefully constructed experiments designed to rule out alternative explanations for their findings, the results tend to be less than favorable for MBO. On the other hand, in one-shot case studies in which no control groups are used, and in which the basic fundamentals of experimental design are violated, MBO appears to have been effective.

By itself, of course, poor research does not provide grounds for concluding that MBO is ineffective; it merely makes it difficult to assess its value with any degree of confidence. Nevertheless, the high rate of failure of MBO programs among organizations that have adopted it (cf. Schuster and Kindall, 1974), and the evidence that is available (such as it is), indicate that MBO has failed to demonstrate the value to organizations that one might expect from it. Thus, Kondrasuk (1981) concludes that MBO is probably more likely to succeed in the private sector than in the public sector, in work settings that are removed from the customer, and in the short run, rather than over long periods of time. In short, MBO may hold considerable potential promise in theory, but its actual value, to date, has fallen short of this potential.

MBO and Goal Setting

It was argued earlier in this chapter that goal setting has demonstrated more validity than any other theory of work motivation, and that goal setting techniques constitute one of the two most common (perhaps universal) features of MBO programs. In view of the success of goal setting, per se, one might find the lower rate of success among formal MBO programs paradoxical, or even contradictory.

It is important to repeat that while goal setting techniques constitute an integral element of virtually all MBO programs, there is more to MBO than simple goal setting. As noted earlier, the performance review process is also an important element of MBO, as are the techniques of cascading and the formalization of strategy, tactics, and policy. It would appear, therefore, that the transformation of the relatively simple principles of goal setting (as developed by Ryan, Locke, and Latham, for example) into formal MBO programs, has resulted in some difficulties (cf. Ford, 1979; Muczyk, 1978; Reddin, 1971). In fact, there is an abundant literature dealing with the reasons most commonly responsible for MBO failures. Let us now take **175** a brief look at some of these reasons, in order to see what can be learned from them.

Some Common Causes of Failure of MBO Programs

There seem to be two general sets of causes of failure of MBO programs. The first set is concerned primarily with political issues at the implementation stage, while the second set entails behavioral reactions of organizational members, after MBO has been installed.

Politics at the implementation stage. Organizations are typically very political social systems, featuring struggles among individuals and coalitions of individuals for power, influence, and resources (Bacharach and Lawler, 1980). According to Jamieson (1973) and Odiorne (1979), failure to recognize and take the political reality of an organization into account at the time of the implementation of an MBO program, is bound to result in the failure of such a program. What are some of these factors?

First, there is the organization's power structure. Moving from a non-rationalized form of management to one that is explicitly designed to be as rational as MBO is bound to threaten those individuals inside the organization who already hold influence, often unofficially, over the way things are done. To formalize the setting of goals and the planning of policy in a broad-based fashion naturally challenges the power of those who have previously ''had the boss's ear,'' and is bound to result in resistance from those individuals. Similarly, when power is diffused among more than one camp, the potential for political maneuvering, ''horse trading,'' and coalition formation (either in support of or against innovations such as MBO) is high. The result can often be difficult for any program that is introduced into such a climate.

On a related point, it must be remembered that MBO, properly practiced, entails the sharing of power between superiors and their subordinates at all levels. Oftentimes, managers at one level may be willing to encourage the involvement of their subordinates (in the setting of goals and action plans, for example) only as long as they receive a similar degree of downward power sharing from their own superiors. Therefore, unless managers see more influence being passed downward to their levels from above, they are naturally going to fear that heavy participation by their own subordinates may make them redundant in the organizational hierarchy. As a result, the actual sharing of power is often an on-again, off-again sort of affair that can make a sham out of serious attempts to operate an MBO program.

A third factor (one that is related to the first two) might be seen as **176** a general resistance to change that can be anticipated whenever massive organizational change of any sort is attempted (see chapter four). For example, changes in cost accounting procedures, salary systems, and even the design of jobs that often accompany MBO, naturally threaten those people who believe (correctly or without justification) that they stand to lose something from the changes. Foot dragging and active resistance can be expected from such persons. Related to this problem is the one that normally occurs when tasks are reassigned: people who have tasks removed from themselves to be incorporated into other people's jobs naturally fear a loss of power, particularly when those tasks are central to the work flow, require particular expertise, and/or are concerned with dealing with any of the major problems facing the organization (Hickson, Hinings, Lee, Schneck, and Pennings, 1971).

A fourth factor noted by Odiorne (1979) is that people in organizations are often more loyal and committed to their immediate work unit than they are to the larger organization, per se. Thus, employees who must start to set formal objectives for the first time may comply only to the extent that they believe the objectives being set are going to benefit their work unit, per se. Otherwise, the loftier goals of the organization, as a whole, may not receive active support and participation during attempts to cascade them into specific objectives for particular groups.

Another political consideration has to do with possible individualists (often managerial, professional, and technical people, according to Odiorne) who are trained to be single-minded and independent. When people of this sort are confronted with a program that they view as being overly routine, bureaucratized, and limiting of their professional freedom, they can be expected to resist it.

In short, failure to recognize and accommodate the political realities within an organization may be sufficient grounds for the failure of the system before it ever really has a chance to get started. However, while managing these political factors at the implementation stage may be necessary for the effectiveness of MBO, it does not appear to be sufficient to assure success. The point is that, once installed, a number of other factors can function to limit the effectiveness of an MBO program. Let's take a brief look at some of the more common of these.

Post-implementation problems for MBO. In order to survive once it is installed, an MBO program requires a number of other necessary conditions. One of these is the quality of the organization's management information system: without the capacity to set goals and reliably monitor the performance of individuals and groups against those goals, an MBO program cannot be effective.

A second key factor is the leadership style of the organization's **177** managers. If an organization has had a history of autocratic decision making throughout its structure for some time, the participatory style normally required to make MBO effective is less likely to be adopted, particularly if the organization in question has been relatively effective as a consequence (or in spite) of its characteristic style. Especially critical is the skill of managers at conducting participatory interviews with their subordinates at the goal setting and performance review stage (Jamieson, 1973). Unless managers are trained and able to be creative, supportive, and nonthreatening when they jointly set goals and (especially) when they evaluate the performance of their subordinates against those goals, the organization will not derive the potential benefits that MBO offers. The ongoing, active support of MBO by senior executives is universally acknowledged as necessary for its success.

Similarly, key management personnel must not be adverse to the idea of planning: many organizations are quite effective in spite of an emphasis on future-oriented planning, particularly long range planning. MBO requires a mentality that fosters planning at various intervals into the future, so unless managers are willing and able to engage in such an approach to managing, MBO will have limited success.

In addition, job descriptions and the operationalization of those descriptions constitute an area of potential risk to MBO (Jamieson, 1973; Stroderbek and Plambeck, 1978). First, job descriptions must be kept current; otherwise managers and their subordinates will not have a sound base for determining the types and levels of goals that should be set. On the other hand, it is seldom possible to translate all of the elements of a job into specific goals, so care must be taken that those aspects of an individual's job that cannot be set into goals are not ignored (Levinson, 1970). For example, if sales representatives set sales figures for the coming year with their supervisors and attempt to reach their goals, care must be taken to assure that other aspects of the individuals' jobs (such as customer relations, inventory control, and the training of their own junior staffs—functions that are harder to quantify) are not ignored.

Managers sometimes have difficulty formulating objectives with their employees, even when those objectives are easily quantified (Jamieson, 1973). Thus objectives may be set too high or too low, or stated with insufficient precision (with regard to level or time frame, for example). In addition, it is not always possible to translate goals set at the upper end of an organization into more specific goals that can direct the activities of lower-level employees on a day-to-day basis (such as a goal to improve corporate image, for example).

178   Ideally, managers and subordinates should strive to set goals that incorporate the objectives of the organization with the goals of the individual employee (Levinson, 1970). In practice, of course, this is not always possible, so the subsequent commitment of the individual to the pursuit of his work goals is often less than might be desired.

Another problem has to do with the fact that much of the work performed in any organization is accomplished through the efforts of *groups,* rather than through the work of single individuals. Therefore, the interdependencies between an employee and other people around him in the workplace must be recognized, both when goals are established, as well as when performance is being reviewed. In some instances, it may be desirable to set goals for groups of employees, rather than for single individuals.

It is often found that as the initial enthusiasm for an MBO program starts to wane (for any of the reasons mentioned above), the daily practice of the program becomes less and less well maintained: managers and subordinates delay goal setting and performance review interviews, and/or conduct them in a half-hearted manner, simply for the sake of appeasing the personnel department. Often there is an increase in the level of authoritarianism in the setting of goals: newly converted democratic managers gradually revert to their true underlying autocratic styles. Sometimes the emphasis at the appraisal stage reverts to assessing the personal traits of the subordinates, rather than their objective accomplishments vis à vis their goals.

The tying of rewards to goal attainment in MBO sometimes discourages innovation and risk taking, and instead, encourages conservative goal setting, interpersonal rivalries, and factionalism (Ford, 1979). Sometimes the goal setting and appraisal practices are extended too far down the hierarchy, to levels where the nature of the work does not justify their use. The result is a proliferation of paper work and a rejection of the program altogether. Sometimes the pursuit of established objectives causes an inflexibility of activities that prevents the organization from exploiting opportunities that arise during the middle of an MBO time period.

In short, MBO requires a degree of monitoring and control to assure that it is not eroded over time in favor of managing by fiat, managing on a crisis-to-crisis basis, and/or managing with an evaluative style that discourages employees and managers alike from taking a forward looking, positive approach (Jamieson, 1973).

The ethics of MBO. One final reason some MBO programs gradually break down may be because of what some employees see as unethical and unfair aspects of such programs. Questions of ethics are relevant in both the goal setting and the performance eval- **179**

uation stages of MBO (Pringle and Longenecker, 1982). For example, the overly zealous implementation of an MBO program may coerce some employees into a requirement to participate in the setting
of goals when they have no desire to do so: not everyone wants to
participate in the planning and control functions of their own work
(Cherrington and England, 1980). On the other hand, ethical problems arise when employees are led to believe that they will be invited
to participate in the setting of their own goals, and the evaluation of
their own performance, but then, after seeing the program in actual
operation, recognize that their inputs are either discredited, ignored,
or unsolicited altogether. In an earlier paper, the author noted:

> MBO programs are often simply legitimized systems of phony participation, in
> which the fiction is maintained that the subordinate is making a real input into
> planning work objectives and procedures. Such situations smack of Machiavel-
> lianism and are quickly self-defeating (Pinder, 1977, p. 388).

But other ethical issues may also be involved. The strong prescription to quantify objectives (as we have mentioned earlier) may
force employees to focus on only parts of their jobs, ignoring other
elements, such as concern for other people, adherence to moral
standards of conduct, and commitment to principles of fair play. In
fact, one study found that the requirement to quantify goals was the
most commonly mentioned problem attributed to MBO programs,
among a sample of employees who worked under such systems
(Stein, 1975).

Earlier, the problem of assessing individual performance in jobs
in which the individual is interdependent with other employees was
mentioned. Apart from its practical dimension, this problem has
moral implications as well: failure to take the effect of factors beyond
the control of an individual into account, while deciding the level of
reward or punishment that person is to receive by the organization,
is blatantly unethical.

There are also ethical considerations related to the performance
assessment aspect of MBO programs (Pringle and Longenecker,
1982). To the extent that employees are evaluated exclusively on the
ends of their efforts (i.e., the degree of attainment of their goals) and
not on the *means* they use to achieve those goals, they may be compelled to engage in behaviors that are less than ethical.
Longenecker and Pringle (1981) note:

> . . . setting very difficult goals and then applying pressure to reach these goals
> creates conditions favorable to producing unethical behavior. Is it always clear
> to personnel that they are expected to attain goals only within the confines of
> ethical performance? Or, is the emphasis upon goals so intense that attention is
> directed to the goals and not to means of achieving those goals? (p. 89)

The sort of pressure Longnecker and Pringle mention can become all the more intense, of course, to the degree that the employee influences the goals to which he is committed. Failure to accomplish one's own goals, and living with the consequences of such failure, is akin to being hoisted on one's own petard (Levinson, 1970).

Summary

In short, if the basic principles of goal setting are to have a chance of being successful in work organizations, they must be accompanied by a host of organizational conditions, preparations, and (often) adjustments. The widespread application of MBO during the 1960s and 1970s in ignorance of these necessary organizational preconditions lead to failures in the majority of organizations that tried it (Reddin, 1971; Schuster and Kindall, 1974). It would appear that organizational scientists have a better understanding of individual differences and the nature of human intentions to behave than they do of the critical features of organizations in which work behavior takes place. Accordingly, even the more successful theories of work motivation (such as goal setting) will provide limited scientific validity and practical value for managers until more is learned about the "press" of characteristics of organizational settings (recall chapter two and see chapter thirteen).

Other Forms of Participatory Management Programs

Before we leave our discussion of goal setting and Management by Objectives, it is important to note that there are a variety of other formalized programs in work organizations, involving varying degrees of participation by subordinates in the setting of goals and the design of organizational policy. These programs differ along a number of dimensions, such as the degree to which they involve some form of performance evaluation, the use of committee structures, and the level of involvement of employees in policy making (for example, do representatives sit with the most senior executives in decision making, or interact only on a one-to-one basis with their immediate supervisors?).

Limitations of space prevent a discussion of these various participatory programs here. The interested reader is referred to Cummings and Molloy 1977; Strauss, 1982; Wall and Lischeron, 1977; and the entire edition of *Human Relations* (1976, vol. 29, no. 5) for representative treatments of the literature dealing with participation of employees in management, and to a paper by Dachler and Wilpert (1978) in which a variety of key dimensions of participation programs are delineated. **181**

CONCLUSION: THE PROGNOSIS FOR MBO

It has been argued in this chapter that MBO and programs like it that rely on goal setting have held considerable potential as managerial tools for increasing employee motivation and organizational control, but that, in practice, much of this potential has failed to materialize. In light of the foregoing analysis, we might ask about the future of MBO in management.

Perspectives on this question vary, of course, depending upon who holds them. Nevertheless, it is useful to recall the conclusions reached by Kondrasuk (1981), who has recently summarized the research on MBO effectiveness. His analysis suggests that MBO seems to be more effective in the private sector than in the public sector, in the short run (as opposed to the long run), and in work settings that are buffered from customers. When we consider these conclusions in light of observations made by two organizational theorists—Hofstede (1978) and McCaskey (1974)—we are able to understand them more clearly, as well as gain some basis for speculating about the future facing MBO and MBO-like programs.

Hofstede (1978) has noted that in order to be effective, MBO and other managerial control programs like it, require three necessary conditions. First, it must be possible to identify standards that represent the organization's objectives, presumably at all of its levels. Secondly, it must be possible to actually measure performance against these standards. Finally, it must be possible for the organization to implement any changes that are needed, to close whatever gaps are observed, when actual performance is compared with objectives.

In addition to Hofstede's (1978) observations, consider an argument raised by McCaskey (1974). According to McCaskey, *organizational planning does not necessarily require the setting and pursuit of goals.* Instead, he claims, there are some situations in which it is more appropriate to plan by identifying *domains* and *directions* that the organization wishes to pursue. A *domain* is a general area in which the organization wishes to operate (such as the production and sale of heavy equipment, or the provision of medical care to low-income families). A *direction* consists of an individual's (or of an organization's) *tendencies* and favored styles of perceiving and acting (1974, p. 283). In other words, planning without goals consists of deciding the general arena of activities in which the organization will operate and the general style of operations that will be undertaken. But it avoids setting targets and goals; the means are more important than the ends, and it is recognized that the organization may wish to change course at any time on the basis of its interactions with its environment.

According to McCaskey (1974), this type of planning is most appropriate in the following types of circumstances:

1. When it is too early in the organization's existence to set agreed-upon goals.
2. When the organization's environment is unstable and highly uncertain.
3. When members of the organization cannot build enough trust or agreement among themselves to make it possible to agree upon goals.
4. When the people involved, because of a high tolerance for ambiguity or a preference for risk and excitement, prefer the uncertainty and flexibility that is most likely in the absence of goals.

It is always difficult to forecast the future, and organizational theorists have been no more successful at it than any other futurists, but the creative application of the points raised by Hofstede and McCaskey helps explain some of the reasons for the comparative success of MBO in the types of settings noted by Kondrasuk (1981).

First, it stands to reason that MBO has been more successful in short run intervals than it has been over longer periods of time. There are increasing odds that the appropriateness of goals, and action plans in pursuit of those goals, will diminish as more and more time transpires after they are established. The total amount of change in the environment facing any organization will grow as a function of time, and, as noted by McCaskey (1974), change and uncertainty make goal setting risky and inappropriate.

What about Kondrasuk's (1981) observation that MBO has been more effective in contexts that are removed from customers? The activities of the organizations and individuals in any organization's environment are the major sources of uncertainty facing that organization. It is easier to program activities within one's own organization than it is to predict (let alone control) events beyond its boundaries (Thompson, 1967). Therefore, there is little wonder that MBO—which requires a degree of stability in the environment—fares better in contexts that are buffered from customers (whose tastes, expectations, and demands are constantly subject to change).

Now consider the superior performance of MBO in the private sector (as opposed to the public sector), and the three necessary conditions identified by Hofstede (1978): the setting of standards, the measurement of performance, and the capacity to change so as to bring performance into line with standards. It is generally much more feasible to set standards and measure performance against those standards in private enterprise than it is in government and public organizations (Bower, 1977). Consider, for example, the comparative ease of setting objectives for production, sales, inventory levels, and market penetration, as opposed to setting goals for the provision of social services. While surrogate measures are often **183** used in public (and service) organizations as a means of monitoring activity, these measures are often crude and relate primarily to inputs rather than outputs. As a result, the behavior of bureaucrats often becomes directed more toward "looking good" on input measures than toward actually pursuing the overall goals of the bureau or agency (e.g., Blau, 1963; Merton, 1968). In other words, goal attainment becomes more important than performance, as such.

Likewise, even in those cases in government organizations where standards can be set and performance can be assessed, the political realities facing public organizations often prevent ameliorative action from being taken. In addition, many of the problems governments tackle (such as reducing inflation or increasing trade with other countries) are almost intractable. Even within private sector organizations, it has been noted that the setting and quantification of goals is one of the most commonly mentioned complaints about MBO programs (Stein, 1975).

The point is that the very nature of government organizations and the work they seek to accomplish violate the three necessary conditions identified by Hofstede (1978) for the effectiveness of MBO and programs like it. A similar argument can be made for service organizations in the private sector.

What about the future? Again, forecasting what organizational life will be like in the coming years is difficult, but, based on the reasoning provided by McCaskey and Hofstede, we might anticipate that MBO will be less likely to succeed to the extent that:

1. The movement away from production and toward service industries continues (recall chapter one).
2. Scarcity and competition make organizations more vulnerable to collapse and make consensus among organizational members less common.

As we have mentioned, Odiorne (1979) is a leading proponent of MBO. He predicts that MBO will be most popular in the future in large, divisionalized companies, where performance is most easily measured and accountability is most easily established. In addition, he predicts continued use of MBO in the sales and production departments of smaller organizations. (Compare these predictions with Hofstede's observations about the necessity to set standards, measure performance, and change behavior in response to performance deficiencies.) Finally, Odiorne anticipates greater participation in MBO among staff departments (such as industrial relations and personnel) than has occurred in the past. Hofstede's analysis would not support this prediction.

In contrast to Odiorne's relatively positive outlook, however, there are also a number of critics who—after witnessing the tremendous gap between the promise and the general success of MBO—

conclude that MBO is a thing of the past. Ford (1979) for example, concludes the following:

> The fact is, the results of MBO have been a whole lot less than have been promised in theory. Whether the problem is in the concept or the implementation is an unresolved question. It is probably a combination of both. . . . MBO has generally not succeeded; devoting more effort to it to make it better is probably a waste of time. Other new managerial techniques will follow. If MBO is to leave us any kind of legacy it will be to serve as a guideline to what mistakes these new concepts should avoid (p. 53).

In short, organizational theory suggests that, if it is to survive in the future, MBO and programs related to it may require a number of special circumstances—circumstances that may or may not be likely. A greater understanding of organizations, per se, will be necessary, and once it is attained, it will then have to be integrated with our knowledge of individual behavior. Chapter thirteen will address this issue in more detail.

The legal imperative. Before closing speculation on the probable future of MBO and related managerial programs, it is worth noting briefly that employment law in the United States (and, to a lesser degree, in Canada) constitutes an important factor that must be taken into consideration. If organizations turn away from results-oriented assessment programs such as MBO in favor of more traditional performance appraisal systems, they run the risk of violating the law with regard to discrimination against groups that are protected by legislation such as the 1964 Civil Rights Act (in the U.S.) and The Canada Code (in Canada).

A detailed treatment of these issues is well beyond the scope of this book: the interested reader is referred to Latham and Wexley (1981) for a discussion of how United States law relates to performance appraisal in American organizations. In a nutshell, however, the point is this: the use of a performance appraisal instrument, for all intents and purposes, is little different from the use of any other psychometric instrument for making personnel decisions (Lazer, 1979). Therefore, if decisions made on the basis of that instrument impact adversely on protected groups (such as women or minorities, for example), the organization that uses it is subject to litigation. It then behooves the employer to demonstrate that the instrument in question is valid (that it really measures what it purports to measure). In the case of a performance appraisal instrument, this means showing that it actually measures performance on the essential aspects of the job in question. In view of the difficulty of assuring that performance assessment with the use of conventional techniques is both reliable and valid (cf. Latham and Wexley, 1981), results-oriented approaches, such as MBO, will continue to be attractive in the future. **185**

In balance, while the sort of organization theory analysis presented above may suggest that less or limited use will be made of MBO and programs like it in the future, the legal realities facing employers in the 1980s may occasion continued reliance—even expanded reliance—upon such programs. It will be necessary, therefore, for organizational scientists and managers to develop and utilize better understanding of ways for making programs such as MBO viable in practice.

OPERANT LEARNING AND WORK BEHAVIOR 9

Men are the sport of circumstances, when the circumstances seem the sport of men.

—*Lord Byron*

In contrast to the cognitive/perceptual model of human functioning (Walter and Marks, 1981) that underlies the theories of work motivation presented in the three previous chapters, there is one major approach (or set of approaches) to work motivation and behavior that rests primarily upon the *learning* model of human nature, presented in chapter three. This approach, variously referred to as behaviorism, behavioral learning theory, or operant conditioning, avoids reliance upon concepts such as perceptions, beliefs, attitudes, intentions, and motivation for understanding and predicting human behavior. Instead, the major tenet of the behaviorist approach is simply that behavior is a function of its consequences. While proponents of this school do not deny that people have needs, beliefs, attitudes, values, intentions, and the like, they do not invoke such concepts either to study or to influence human behavior. To quote B. F. Skinner,* the eminent psychologist whose work has been a foundation of this school:

---

*It must be noted at the outset that there is no single, unified school of modern behaviorism, notwithstanding the common tendency to assume that there is (Mahoney, 1974, p. 9). Rather, a continuum of schools of behaviorism exists, representing a number of perspectives differing among themselves in a variety of ways, the most important of which having to do with the role and importance of cognitive processes in human learning and behavior (Kazdin, 1978; Mahoney, 1974, chapter two). Accordingly, although we draw most heavily from B. F. Skinner's behaviorism in this chapter and the one that follows, the reader is cautioned that—even by his own admission—Skinner (1974) does not represent *the* voice of all behaviorism. Our reliance on his work here is based on three things: (1) the fact that it is at least as well known as any other school of behaviorism; (2) its obvious importance in modern psychology in general; and (3) the fact that it, more than any other brand of behaviorism, is most often cited by organizational scientists in particular.

When we say that a man eats *because* he is hungry, smokes a great deal *because* he has a tobacco habit . . . or plays the piano well *because* of his musical ability, we seem to be referring to causes. But on analysis these phrases prove to be merely redundant descriptions. A single set of facts is described by the two statements: 'He eats' and 'He is hungry.' . . . The practice of explaining one statement in terms of another is dangerous because it suggests that we have found the cause and therefore need search no further (1953, p. 31).

To apply this perspective to the types of behaviors we have considered in the previous three chapters would imply that to state that an employee works hard because she is loyal to her company does not really explain anything; it merely repeats the same information. The important thing is the behavior: the individual either works hard or she doesn't. Skinner writes:

We may . . . be disturbed by the fact that many young people work as little as possible, or that workers are not very productive and often absent [from their jobs], or that products are often of poor quality, but we shall not get far by inspiring a 'sense of craftsmanship or pride in one's work,' or a 'sense of the dignity of labor'. . . . Something is wrong with the contingencies which induce men to work industriously and carefully (1971, p. 157).

Again, adherents to this school do not deny that people experience emotions, or that they perceive things in their environments and formulate beliefs. But they consider these hypothetical factors as merely *accompanying* behavior, not causing it. In one of his early books, Skinner (1953) wrote:

The objection to inner states is not that they do not exist, but that they are not relevant in a functional [causal] analysis. We cannot account for the behavior of any system while staying wholly inside it; eventually we must turn to forces operating upon the organism from without (1953, p. 35).

Hence, an employee may experience what he calls pride in his work or satisfaction with his employer, but these feelings simply accompany the behavior of the individual on his job—they do not cause it, or account for it.

Even the concept of motivation is questioned by many behaviorists when the term is used to imply some sort of internal *causal* force that cannot be observed directly (Luthans and Ottemann, 1977). To attribute behavior to motivation as in the statement "Barry works hard at his job because he is a highly motivated fellow," is as redundant as the examples of eating, smoking, and piano playing found in the quotation at the top of this page. Motivation does not cause behavior—the contingencies of the environment do.

On the other hand, behaviorists often use mentalistic terminology out of necessity, convenience, and for descriptive purposes (Skinner, 1974). For example, a behaviorist who says "Barry is motivated," does not mean to imply that any real or physical entity called motivation exists in great quantity within Barry and causes him to work hard; instead, the behaviorist would be utilizing the term *motivated* to descriptively summarize Barry's behavior. It is the process of reifying concepts (such as motivation) from descriptive terms into terms that imply the existence of inferred behavior-causing entities that is rejected by behaviorists (Craighead, Kazdin, and Mahoney 1976).

The purpose of this chapter, and the one which follows it, is to present the *behavioral* approach to understanding work behavior and work-related problems. In the present chapter, we will examine a number of the principles of operant behavior that have the most relevance to the central topic of this book. Space limitations prevent us from examining all of operant psychology, however. The interested reader is referred to Skinner (1953, 1971, 1974) for three very readable and characteristic treatments. As we proceed, examples from work settings will be presented to illustrate the meaning and significance of operant concepts and techniques, including the somewhat controversial topic of punishment. Then, in chapter ten, we will introduce behavior modification, a branch of applied psychology that draws heavily on operant conditioning principles, but which includes a variety of cognitive concepts as well. In chapter ten we will see that behavior modification and the principles of operant psychology have a lot to offer our understanding of work effort and performance.

To begin then, what are the basic tenets and concepts of operant psychology?

OPERANT BEHAVIOR AND OPERANT CONDITIONING

According to Skinner and most of those who have followed in his tradition, it is useful to categorize behavior into two general types. One type is referred to as *respondent behavior,* which consists of acts that are reflexive, or unlearned. Sneezing or jerking one's knee when it is tapped with a doctor's hammer are examples. Respondent behavior occurs in *response* to something in the environment.

The second general category of behavior consists of most of the important acts human beings display. These are learned behaviors that *operate* on the environment to generate consequences, hence they are called *operant behaviors.* Whereas respondent behavior is elicited by a prior stimulus, operant behavior is *emitted* to produce a consequence. The environment acts upon the individual to produce respondent behavior, while operant behavior consists of the individual acting upon the environment.

For example, an employee who is confronted by a hostile supervisor may witness an increase in heart beat, a pair of sweaty palms, and a flight response. The stimulus that caused these behaviors is **189** the boss and the "nervous" reactions are respondent behaviors. Alternatively, the employee may approach his boss with a view to making peace and mollifying him. This action would be classified as operant behavior—it is initiated by the individual to operate on a part of his environment—in this case, his boss.

What is Operant Conditioning?

Operant conditioning is the process of changing the frequency or probability of occurrence of operant behaviors as a result of the consequences that follow them. For example, the employee who *successfully* applies diplomacy to the problem with his superior will be more likely to try this sort of (operant) behavior again in similar circumstances in the future. Alternatively, the negative consequences of his attempt at diplomacy may teach him not to try it again. The mechanisms through which the future probabilities of operant behaviors are influenced are referred to as *reinforcement* and *punishment*. (We will return to them shortly.)

Functional Analysis and Contingencies

Most of the important behavior we observe in organizations is learned, either before or after individuals enter them. This learning occurs in the context of stimuli, or cues, made up of such things as the organization's structure, the work group, the supervisor, the job description, telephone calls, and so forth. Operant learning occurs when people behave in response to these cues in certain ways, and in turn, when consequences follow from their behaviors.

The process of breaking behavioral events down into their antecedents, the behavior itself, and the consequences which follow it is called *functional analysis*. All three elements must be examined in order to understand behavior (Skinner, 1969). Important organizational consequences include the approval or disapproval of coworkers, money, fatigue, promotions, and the many other things that we have referred to as *outcomes* in previous chapters. When consequences such as these are directly tied to certain behaviors, they are said to be *contingent* upon those behaviors. For example, commission is a form of *pay* that is directly contingent upon the volume of product sold by a sales person. Similarly, fatigue is usually contingent upon hard work. Finally, when consequences bear no relationship to behavior they are said to be noncontingent upon that behavior, as is the case, for example, in pay schemes (such as salaries) under which people are paid simply with the passage of intervals of time. We will return to functional analysis later in this chapter, after we examine in more detail the concepts of contingency and the consequences of behavior.

190

The Consequences of Behavior

According to the operant conditioning approach, behavior occurring in a particular context can be followed by any of three types of consequences. These are referred to as reinforcement, punishment, and neutral stimuli. *Reinforcement* is defined as a consequence of behavior that increases the probability that an act will occur again in the future. *Punishment* is a consequence of behavior that reduces the probability of further occurrences of the act. Finally, it is sometimes the case that neither reinforcement nor punishment is contingent upon an act—in other words, there is no change in the person's environment as a consequence of his behavior. When this occurs, the act tends to cease. For example, a person who repeatedly puts a coin into a candy machine and receives nothing in return tends to stop investing in the recalcitrant machine. As a second example, a whining child who is ignored tends (eventually) to stop whining. Finally, an employee who wisecracks his superior will tend to stop if no one (including his work mates) provides him with any reinforcement. The process of disconnecting a behavior and the consequences that formerly reinforced it is referred to as *extinction* (Craighead, Kazdin, and Mahoney, 1976).

The law of effect. The relationship between contingent consequences and operant behavior is summarized in the *Law of Effect.* Although the general gist of this law appeared as early as a century ago in the writings of Herbert Spencer (1870), its first formal articulation was made by Thorndike (1911):

> Of several responses made to the same situation, those which are accompanied or closely followed by satisfaction to the animal will, other things being equal, be more firmly connected with the situation, so that, when it recurs, they will be more likely to recur; those which are accompanied or closely followed by discomfort to the animal will, other things being equal, have their connections with that situation weakened, so that, when it recurs, they will be less likely to occur. The greater the satisfaction or discomfort, the greater the strengthening or weakening of the bond (p. 244)

Thorndike was aware of the fact that many of his critics would object to his reliance on subjective terms, such as satisfaction and discomfort (they sound very cognitive), so he explained further:

> By a satisfying state of affairs is meant one which the animal does nothing to avoid, often doing such things as attain and preserve it. By a discomforting or annoying state of affairs is meant one which the animal commonly avoids and abandons (Thorndike, 1911, p. 245).

The Law of Effect has been subjected to a variety of attacks over the years on numerous logical, philosophical, and empirical grounds. A review of these issues is beyond our present purpose. Suffice it to say that its modern form, the *Empirical Law of Effect* (of   **191** which there are more than one version), remains one of the most important tenets of behaviorism today. In a nutshell, the Empirical Law of Effect states that ". . . the consequence of a response is an important determiner of whether the response will be learned" (Wilcoxon, 1969, p. 28). In other words, people tend to do those things that they find positive and they tend not to do those things that they learn to be aversive. Hence, if an employee associates high rates of pay with high levels of job performance, she will tend to behave in ways that she has learned are conducive to high performance.

When a behavior occurs and is followed by a desirable consequence, that behavior is said to be *reinforced* (meaning strengthened). The odds will increase that the person will behave in a similar fashion on future occasions that are similar. On the other hand, if the behavior results in aversive consequences, that behavior will be less probable in future similar circumstances, and it is said to have been punished. But desirable and undesirable consequences in organizations are only partially contingent upon the behavior or the performance of employees. Accordingly, we can consider a range of relationships that may exist between behavior and its consequences. These behavior-consequence relationships are referred to as *schedules of reinforcement,* and the control of these schedules constitutes the application of operant conditioning in work organizations, educational institutions, clinical settings, and the like.

Schedules of Reinforcement

The simplest type of reinforcement schedule is referred to as *continuous.* When every instance of a particular behavior is reinforced, the schedule is defined as continuous. However, if reinforcement is provided after only *some* occurrences of an act, the schedule is defined as *intermittent,* or *partial.*

Continuous and intermittent schedules each have some important characteristics, and some important differences. First, new learning occurs fastest when the behavior being acquired is reinforced continuously. For example, a new employee who is learning how to set up a jig on a lathe will learn more quickly if he is reinforced *every* time he does it correctly. On the other hand, behavior that is reinforced by a continuous schedule for an ongoing period of time is more susceptible to extinction when, for whatever reason, the reinforcement stops or fails to occur following any particular occurrence of the act. Moreover, once a behavior has been learned, it will occur at higher frequency levels (and perhaps more intensely) when it is reinforced intermittently. So, for example, employees who have been taught to be polite to customers through the use of continuous reinforcement will be more likely to continue being polite if their su-

FIGURE 9–1: Intermittent Reinforcement Schedules

		Basis of Distribution of Reinforcement	
		Occurrence of Behavior	Passage of Time
Constancy of Schedule	Fixed	Fixed Ratio 1	3 Fixed Interval
	Variable	2 Variable Ratio	4 Variable Interval

pervisors decrease the frequency of reinforcement for courteous behaviors to an intermittent schedule.

Types of intermittent schedules. It is possible to administer intermittent reinforcement a variety of ways. Sometimes reinforcement occurs only after the emission of a certain number of the desired behaviors; in other words, it is possible to assure that the reinforcement is contingent only upon *behavior.* Such schedules are called *ratio* schedules, because reinforcers are dispensed according to some proportion of the instances when the behavior occurs (such as every fourth time, for example). Alternatively, it is possible to administer reinforcement following the passage of certain periods of time, such that, for example, the first desired response following the designated period (say, one hour) produces a reinforcer. Schedules of this sort are called *interval* schedules.

Aside from whether they are granted on the basis of some ratio with the occurrence of behavior or whether they occur only after the passage of time, we can also consider intermittent reinforcement on the basis of whether the ratio or the time interval used is constant, or changing and variable.

Hence, we can consider the four different types of reinforcement schedules illustrated in Figure 9-1.

Let's consider some examples of these various types of intermittent reinforcement. A *fixed ratio* schedule is one in which the reinforcement follows every n'th occurrence of an act. For instance, an employee who is paid a fee after every fourth delivery of materials to a warehouse is being reinforced under a fixed ratio arrangement (see Cell 1). Notice that continuous reinforcement is a special case of a fixed ratio schedule in which the ratio is 1:1. However, if the employee is paid *on average* every fourth time, but not every fourth time, per se, we would say he is being compensated according to a *variable ratio* schedule (Cell 2 of Figure 9-1).

As an illustration of how interval schedules might work, consider **193** a sales representative who is being encouraged by her sales manager to make follow-up visits with her customers. If the sales manager acknowledges only those visits that occur at the beginning of every month, for example, and ignores those visits made by the sales rep during the middle of the month, the manager is using a fixed interval schedule (Cell 3), in which the interval is, of course, one month. However, if the manager reinforces only those customer visits undertaken by the rep after one week, then three days, then four weeks, then eight days (and so on), he would be employing a variable interval schedule (see Cell 4). In short, the passage of a particular period of time is necessary for the administration of a reinforcer or punisher under an interval schedule, but it is not sufficient: in addition, once the designated interval has passed, the person must perform the act which is being encouraged or discouraged.

Once a behavior has been learned, it can be encouraged through the careful use of intermittent schedules. Ratio schedules are superior to interval schedules for this purpose (because they are directly contingent upon the occurrence of the desired acts without the necessity of the passage of time), and variable ratio schedules are more effective than fixed ratio schedules. Notice that under a variable ratio schedule (such as what we find in slot machines, for example), the person knows that he will be "paid off" every n'th time, on average, but he is never sure whether any specific occurrence of his behavior will be rewarded. Moreover, once the desired act has been acquired and developed, a variable ratio schedule can be made more lean or "stretched," meaning that the ratio of reinforcements to occurrences of the behavior can be reduced. For example, after we train a sales representative to be courteous to customers by using a continuous (or nearly continuous) schedule, we can reduce the ratio of reinforcements to occurrences of polite behaviors by reinforcing, say, every fifth or sixth occurrence on average, and then eventually cutting back on the frequency of reinforcements so that, on average, the ratio of reinforcements to behaviors becomes smaller and smaller. In practice, it becomes increasingly less necessary to reinforce behavior after it is learned.

In summary, we can state the following about reinforcement schedules: (1) new learning is acquired most rapidly when it is conducted under a continuous schedule of reinforcement; (2) however, once a behavior has been acquired, it is best to begin reducing the frequency of reinforcements to some form of intermittent schedule, because they are more resistant to extinction; (3) ratio schedules result in higher levels of performance of an act than interval schedules, because the former are entirely behavior-based, whereas the latter are based on both time and behavior; and (4) the highest rates of behavior occur under variable (as opposed to fixed) ratio schedules.

While the foregoing discussion has focused on schedules of reinforcement, we must note that punishment also occurs according to either continuous or intermittent schedules as well, although the effects of punishment under these alternative schedules are different from the effects of reinforcement. More will be said about punishment later in this chapter.

Negative Reinforcement

Organizational scientists and managers have tended to misuse behavior modification terminology and concepts, sometimes impeding the advancement of this approach to work behavior (Heiman, 1975; Mawhinney, 1975). Perhaps the best example of this concerns the misuse of the concept of negative reinforcement.

Negative reinforcement is not punishment. Like positive reinforcement, negative reinforcement *strengthens* the probability that a person will perform an act. By definition, punishment reduces such a probability. In fact, punishment refers to the presentation of an aversive agent or event, or the removal of a positive agent or event following a response, reducing the probability of that response in similar future circumstances. In order to be considered punishment, however, the act of either adding or removing an agent must result in a reduction in the frequency of occurrence of the act.

Notice that what some people find punishing may be reinforcing for others. For example, some people enjoy an evening at the opera, whereas, for others. . . . But while positive reinforcement involves the *application* of some circumstance (such as a pat on the back or a Friday afternoon off work), negative reinforcement entails the *removal* of some circumstance that was previously part of the environmental context. For instance, being permitted to return to day shift as a consequence of good performance on night shift is a negatively reinforcing consequence of effective job behavior for those employees who find night work aversive. Being transferred from a remote outpost as a consequence of good work is another example of negative reinforcement (for many people at least). Notice that the things which are negatively reinforcing for some people may not be negatively reinforcing for others, just as what some individuals find positively reinforcing may have no impact on the behavior probabilities of other individuals. (For example, many people are not bothered at all by the winter weather in Winnipeg and Minneapolis!)

We can classify the concepts of positive reinforcement, negative reinforcement, and punishment quite simply by considering whether **195**

FIGURE 9–2: A Summary of Reinforcement and Punishment

Effect on Frequency of Behavior	Consequence	
	Applied	Removed
Increases	Positive Reinforcement	Negative Reinforcement
Decreases	Punishment by Application	Punishment by Removal

the consequence which follows an act increases or decreases the frequency of the act, and whether it is applied or taken away. See Figure 9-2.

Reinforcers: The Agents and Events of Reinforcement

Now that we have discussed the nature of reinforcement and punishment and have differentiated between positive and negative reinforcement, let's take a closer look at those consequences that are reinforcing to people—the reinforcers. As will be shown shortly, there are a variety of things that can be reinforcing, although it must be reiterated that different individuals will have their behaviors made more frequent (reinforced) by the administration of different types of positive and negative reinforcers.

Primary and secondary reinforcers. An agent or event that increases the probability of an act is referred to as a *reinforcer.* Many reinforcers (such as food and water) are called *primary reinforcers* because they are reinforcing unto themselves; an individual does not need to learn of their reinforcing value. People who are hungry and thirsty can derive reinforcement from food and water, without having them linked to any other reinforcers. On the other hand, certain reinforcing agents and events acquire their capacity to increase the probability of particular behaviors through their learned association with other (primary) reinforcers. These are called *secondary reinforcers.* Money is the most important example in organizational settings. By itself, pay has no primary reinforcement capacity, but people quickly learn that pay can be used to acquire those things that do possess primary reinforcing value (such as food, shelter, status, and so forth). It is important to recognize, however, that not all primary reinforcers will always have the capacity to reinforce behavior. For example, food may lose its capacity to change a person's behavior if the person is not hungry. Likewise, potential secondary reinforcers, such as praise, may not have the same reinforcing power for some people as they do for others.

Generalized conditioned reinforcers. Some reinforcers are particularly potent for influencing the probability of the occurrence of behavior because they are themselves reinforcing. Again, money is a good example: because of the fact that it becomes associated, through learning, with a wide variety of other consequences that have either primary or secondary reinforcement value, it is particularly reinforcing. Attention and the approval of other people are other examples of such *generalized reinforcers* (Skinner, 1953), because they are usually accompanied by physical contact, praise, kindly remarks, and support of various other forms, including the possibility of the provision of primary reinforcers (such as physical warmth or food).

Behaviors as reinforcers: The *Premack Principle*. The reinforcers discussed to this point have all been stimuli of some sort or another—stimuli that are either provided or removed contingent on behavior. However, it is possible for *behaviors* to have reinforcing qualities of their own. That is, permitting an individual to work at a favored task contingent upon the completion of a less-preferred task can actually increase the probability that the individual will engage in the former task. This phenomenon is called the *Premack Principle* (Mawhinney, 1979; Premack, 1971).

For example, an employee who dislikes the paper work associated with inventory control, but who does enjoy using new inventory to build retail sales displays, might be reinforced to keep better inventory records (and to keep them more up to date) if opportunities to participate in the design and construction of displays was permitted only upon the completion of inventory work. And, like all of the other reinforcers that have been discussed, this activity reinforcer can be administered according to either a continuous reinforcement schedule, or any of the intermittent schedules that were discussed above.

The multiplicity of reinforcers. It is important to recognize that social situations can include many sources of both reinforcement and punishment for people. Work settings are no exception. In fact, the application of behavior modification principles, for either understanding or influencing employee behavior, must recognize that the organization's official reward system (or reinforcement system in operant conditioning terms) is only one of several systems that can dispense reinforcements and punishments for individuals. For example, employees who work in groups quickly learn that co-workers can control both reinforcers (in the form of social acceptance and **197**

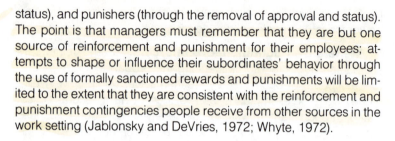

status), and punishers (through the removal of approval and status). The point is that managers must remember that they are but one source of reinforcement and punishment for their employees; attempts to shape or influence their subordinates' behavior through the use of formally sanctioned rewards and punishments will be limited to the extent that they are consistent with the reinforcement and punishment contingencies people receive from other sources in the work setting (Jablonsky and DeVries, 1972; Whyte, 1972).

Behavior Shaping

Sometimes the behavior we want to encourage in others is so complex that it does not occur spontaneously, in pure form. Complex behaviors that consist of a number of elements (such as swinging a golf club properly) may be developed, however, if successive approximations to them are reinforced. In other words, we begin by reinforcing behaviors that bear even the slightest resemblance to the behavior we ultimately wish to develop. Continuous and variable ratio schedules are used initially, but the *standard* required for reinforcement increases as the person proceeds, meaning that behaviors increasingly closer to the final one become required in order for a reinforcement to be earned—a sort of successive approximations approach.

So, for example, an employee who has had difficulty interacting with customers would initially be reinforced for even the slightest attempts to be friendly, such as smiling at them, or at least not leaving the room when customers enter. After a while, however, positive reinforcement would be received only for more friendly behaviors, such as asking customers whether they need service. Desirable behaviors are reinforced while irrelevant or inappropriate behaviors are extinguished. Eventually, the employee can be placed on a variable ratio schedule of reinforcement for performing the ultimately desired acts, and the ratio gradually reduced. This process is referred to as *behavior shaping.* Many of the acts we perform every day, such as driving a car, writing a letter, and being a parent, are learned through behavior shaping; they are far too complex to learn all at once.

Functional Analysis

It was noted earlier in this chapter that a functional analysis explains behavior by looking at both the conditions that precede it and the consequences that follow it. To this point, we have focused largely on the consequences of behavior. What about the antecedents?

Prompts. A reinforcement not only increases the probability of the behavior it follows, but also contributes to bringing that behavior under the control of whatever stimuli are present when the behavior occurs (Reynolds, 1975). In other words, when a particular act occurs and is reinforced in the presence of a certain type of stimulus, the presence of that stimulus, by itself, can increase the frequency of the act (or *prompt* it).

For example, a manager's instructions to a group of employees can set the group in motion. A parent's gesture to her child can often control the child's behavior (but not always, of course). When a particular prompt (or *cue*) initiates behavior that is subsequently reinforced, it is called a *discriminative stimulus*. A discriminative stimulus "sets the occasion" for behavior to unfold; it increases the probability that a behavior will follow. It signals the fact that a reinforcement may be following, although, by itself, it does not actually elicit behavior. Nevertheless, after such a stimulus has been associated with enough reinforcement experiences, it can take on reinforcing qualities of its own, permitting the individual to learn elaborate sequences of behaviors called *chains.*

Chaining. A chain is a series of behaviors that are linked together by stimuli that act both as reinforcers and as discriminative stimuli. A chain starts with the presentation of a discriminative stimulus. When the person responds in the appropriate manner in the presence of that stimulus, a reinforcer follows. This reinforcer often serves, however, as a second discriminative stimulus, which makes the next appropriate response more probable (but not definite). Likewise, if the response that results is appropriate, it, in turn, is followed by reinforcement which then prompts a third behavior. The sequence can go on and on until, ultimately, a primary or secondary reinforcer results that is sufficient to put an end to the sequence and to reinforce all of it.

As an example, consider the writing of a business letter to order a shipment of new raw materials for a production shop. The original discriminative stimulus might simply be the time of year (such as the end of September, when orders are normally placed), or a frantic telephone call from a foreman who is worried that the present inventory of materials is close to exhaustion. The chain which follows might be composed of a number of responses, such as uncovering a typewriter, putting a fresh sheet of paper in the roller of the typewriter, creating and typing the letter, preparing an envelope and sealing it (with the letter enclosed, of course), putting postage on the envelope, and depositing the letter in the mail slot early enough to make the morning's mail pick up. The stimulus that follows each behavior (such as a bare typewriter, a finished letter, an addressed envelope, and so on) prompts the next behavior in the chain, each of which, in turn, is reinforced by the stimulus which follows that. Ultimately, of course, the entire chain may be reinforced a week later by the arrival of new materials, and by an end to the incessant reminders of the worried foreman.

Notice that each of the behaviors in the chain can be, by itself, composed of a chain of smaller behaviors. For instance, the very act of putting a fresh sheet of paper in the roller mechanism of a typewriter consists of a sequence of smaller micro-behaviors, tied together in a sequence that has proven more or less successful in the past.

Discrimination learning. Not every discriminative stimulus, or prompt, results in reinforced behavior. In the context of some stimuli, a particular behavior may be reinforced, while in the context of other stimuli, the same behavior may not be reinforced. For example, uttering a curse may result in the chuckles of one's work mates, but pays off less well when one's spouse is present. People learn to discriminate among stimulus conditions in which particular acts are reinforcing and in which others are punishing. Accordingly, we can make use of this sort of learning by increasing or decreasing the probability of behaviors, by applying or removing the antecedent cues with which they are associated.

Let's look at an example. When a telephone rings (a discriminative stimulus), we are prompted to answer it, because previous experiences of a similar sort have generally been reinforcing. Each sub-act in the chain that constitutes answering the phone sets the stage for the one which follows. For instance, picking up the receiver is reinforced by hearing an open line, which, in turn, prompts the act of saying "Hello," which, in turn, is reinforced by the knowledge of who has called. Notice that the same behavior (lifting the receiver and saying hello) is not likely to occur without the presence of the initial discriminative stimulus (the ringing of the telephone's bell).

In summary, many behaviors consist of chains of less complex behaviors. Each of the elements of each chain sets the stage for, and simultaneously reinforces, other behaviors that follow from them. Functional analysis is the process of breaking an individual's behavior patterns down into a series of *antecedent-behavior-consequence (A-B-C)* linkages for analysis. Only through a study of the specific cues that prompt a behavior, as well as of the particular reinforcers that follow it, can we understand behavior, let alone influence it.

Generalization

In the foregoing section, it was stated that people discriminate among stimulus conditions before behaving in certain ways. But human learning includes the opposite process as well. It is called *stimulus generalization.*

200   Students in university are aware of the virtues of the different pedagogical techniques their professors use to teach them material. It is often said that cases are useful teaching (and learning) devices because they are more realistic or hands-on than are lectures or discussions of concepts and ideas. However, the best solution to one case may not be the best solution for any other case, either in reality or in the classroom setting.

Notice that if the process of discrimination went too far, the behavior of students would be idiosyncratic for every different problem they encounter. As a result, many professors try to have their students generalize their learning from one situation to another. In other words, students strive to recognize similarities among stimulus situations (such as case problems) so that they can invoke behavioral solutions that were learned in the context of one problem, to deal with problems that are different to varying degrees (e.g., House, 1975). The skills of eating spaghetti are quite similar to those of eating linguine, so a gourmand who learns how to eat the former should also be proficient at eating the latter, through the process of stimulus generalization. Likewise, the behaviors necessary for negotiating with a union steward over an incipient grievance, are similar to (but not identical with) those needed to negotiate a raise in pay from one's own boss. Similarity between antecedent contexts is a matter of degree, but effective functioning in our culture requires that we generalize our antecedent-behavior-consequences linkages from one setting to others that are sufficiently similar in important ways.

People also learn how to generalize the *responses* they make to stimuli. In other words, while stimulus generalization entails learning how to invoke the same behavior in response to a variety of similar antecedent conditions, *response generalization* entails learning to employ behaviors that are similar to one another in a given situation. To the extent that one behavior is similar to another one (such as smiling and laughing), when one of the acts is reinforced, the other is also more likely to be reinforced.

An example from the work setting might be as follows: a supervisor instructs an employee to act safely when using dangerous equipment. The behaviors associated with "acting safely" are then reinforced. Other behaviors, such as speaking more quietly on the shop floor, keeping the work area clean, or even helping other employees improve the safety of their behaviors may also result. The employee's safety-related skills have generalized in this example to other behaviors that, for some reason, hold some similarity for the individual involved. Research in behavior modification shows that it is not always possible to predict the exact form that response generalization may take for a given individual. Two people may be reinforced for performing the same act, but then generalize that act to entirely different subsequent behaviors.

201

In short, the analysis of operant behavior reveals that learning does not occur in a unique cue-unique behavior-unique reinforcement fashion. Rather, people respond to general similarities among stimulus situations using behaviors that have been learned in other circumstances. Likewise, the reinforcement of particular behaviors in situations may result in the reinforcement of other, similar behaviors in the same context.

Looking Ahead

To this point, the emphasis has been on influencing the probability of behavior through positive means. But we know that punishment also can be used to change the occurrence of behavior. Let's take a look at punishment and the nature of formal discipline procedures typically found in work settings.

PUNISHMENT

Of the three types of consequences that can result from behavior, none is more ubiquitous in nature and more controversial in practice than punishment. (Recall from our earlier discussion that reinforcement and extinction are the other two.) We learn a great deal from being punished. Skinner notes, for example:

> A child runs awkwardly, falls, and is hurt; he touches a bee and is stung; he takes a bone from a dog and is bitten; and as a result he learns not to do these things again (1972, p. 60).

Likewise, punishment and the fear of it are very common in day-to-day experience in organizations (Arvey and Ivancevich, 1980), largely because it is reinforcing to those who use it (e.g., Mayhew, 1979). In fact, the heavy reliance on punishment in the usual practice of management provided much of the impetus for the introduction of operant conditioning techniques (with their emphasis on *positive* reinforcement) into the management literature (see Aldis, 1961 and Nord, 1969). Yet, in spite of its ubiquity in work settings, very little work has been done to formally study the nature and consequences of punishment at work (Arvey and Ivancevich, 1980).

Defining Punishment

Recall that punishment is defined in terms of the impact it has on behavior. More specifically, punishment is:

> . . . the presentation of an aversive event or the removal of a positive event following a response which decreases the frequency of that response (Kazdin, 1975, pp. 33–34).

202 It is important to remember that different people find different events punishing, just as differences exist among the things people find reinforcing. "Different strokes for different folks!" As a result, the conscious administration of punishment in organizational settings can be difficult: for example, while some employees find being assigned to night duty punishing, others favor night work (Frost and Jamal, 1979). Moreover, notice that the simple administration of aversive stimuli does not constitute punishment, according to this definition. Many negative things can occur in the workplace, but unless they are related to behavior and have the effect of reducing the future occurrences of that behavior, they cannot be classified as punishment, per se.

The Effects of Punishment

It was stated above that the use of punishment has been controversial. Most of this controversy results from the actual and imagined effects it has on people. Skinner was responsible for giving punishment "a bad name" in some of his early work, and many people accepted his position without question for many years, advocating the use of positive reinforcement instead, whenever possible. More recent evidence, however, suggests that punishment, although complex in its effects on behavior, can be effective. In fact, it has been particularly useful in clinical settings as a therapeutic mechanism for dealing with a variety of deviant behaviors (Kazdin, 1975).

A recent review of the literature has suggested that many of the adverse consequences traditionally attributed to it have not actually been demonstrated in research conducted *in work organizations,* per se, and that it is premature to discard punishment as a managerial technique (Arvey and Ivancevich, 1980). For example, conventional wisdom has held that punishment results in attempts to "get back" at the punishing agent, or at least to avoid it. In organizational settings, this would imply that punishment will result in deliberate attempts to seek revenge on a punishing supervisor, through acts such as physical aggression toward the supervisor or the work (displaced aggression). Alternatively, the conventional wisdom suggests that a punished employee will withdraw from the work setting, either physically or psychologically (see chapters four and five).

Another belief about punishment is that its effects generalize to discourage behaviors similar to those being punished, but that are not intended to be discouraged. For example, it would be assumed that punishing an employee for aggressively questioning a client might generalize to reduce the likelihood that the employee will act in such a manner toward suppliers and competitors.

A third criticism has been that punishment never totally eliminates a behavior. Rather, it has been assumed that punished behav- **203** ior tends to disappear only when the punishing agent is present, and that it often reappears when surveillance is discontinued. The implication is that managerial systems based on punishment require close supervision and all of the costs associated with it. (One wonders, for example, whether "reformed" criminals are ever sorry for their crimes, or whether their sorrow results only from having been caught and punished!)

In short, there have been a variety of dysfunctional side effects attributed to the use of punishment for changing human behavior, but the research evidence underlying these beliefs is sparse, particularly as they relate to work settings.

The Ethics of Punishment

One interesting criticism raised about the use of punishment concerns its morality: is it ethical to punish another person? It is worthwhile to note that punishment can be of either of two varieties: retributional and backward looking or corrective and forward looking. It may be that punishment that is intended to attain revenge is less ethical and less civilized than is punishment that is intended to prevent the individual from behaving in undesired ways in the future.

Moreover, it is also useful to distinguish between punishment and the use of coercion (Walter and Marks, 1981). Whereas punishment involves the application of aversive consequences or the removal of positive consequences for behavior, coercion goes further. Coercion entails the extralegal use of threats, fear, terror, violence, and often the application of naked force. Coercion involves the misuse of power between two people, or between a power figure and his followers (Cook, 1972). For example, the college professor who extorts sexual favors in exchange for grades is employing coercion, as is the supervisor who threatens to systematically assign an employee to unpleasant tasks if that employee participates in union-organizing activities.

In short, it seems that coercion and retributional punishment are generally viewed in our culture as less ethical than punishment which is administered equitably, within the bounds of legitimate authority, and with a view to preventing further occurrences of dysfunctional or harmful behavior.

Making Punishment Effective

McGregor (quoted by Sayles and Strauss, 1977) noted years ago that in order to be effective, punishment should occur in practice, as similarly as possible, as it occurs in nature. In fact, he coined the *Hot Stove Rule* to summarize his belief. According to this rule, the most effective punishment is that which is immediate, contingent upon behavior, intense (meaning not too severe, but not without some pain), consistent, impersonal, and informational. In addition, an alternative to the punished act should be available. Hence, when a person touches a hot stove, what happens? The burn which results is punishing, and it is felt immediately. It results from an unfortunate *behavior* (rather than from the passage of time or random events). If the stove is at all hot, the pain is intense. In addition, hot stoves play no favorites—they are impersonal and consistent, punishing anyone who touches them, every time they are touched. And the experience tends to be informational: that is, people normally infer quickly the cause of their suffering. Finally, there are usually alternatives to touching hot stoves, such as moving away and avoiding them in the future.

In short, according to McGregor, punishment in organizations should have all of these features in order to be effective. The review of the literature mentioned above (Arvey and Ivancevich, 1980) reconfirms most of McGregor's wisdom about punishment, and adds that it is most effective when the punishing agent (such as a supervisor) has relatively close and friendly relations with the punished individual, when the agent explains the reason for the punishment to the person, and when the individual understands what the contingencies for punishment will be in the future. Finally, when alternatives to the punished behavior are positively reinforced, it is less likely to occur in the future (Arvey and Ivancevich, 1980).

Alternatives to Punishment

Although, as we have said, punishment occurs frequently on a day-to-day basis in organizations, and may be more effective at eliminating behavior than has traditionally been believed, many supervisors would prefer to avoid using it when it is not necessary. Accordingly, a number of alternatives may be effective in some circumstances. One is to ignore the undesirable behavior, and/or remove those aspects of the person's environment that reinforce it, thus bringing about extinction. Another alternative is to positively reinforce behaviors that are incompatible with the undesired ones. For instance, many effective teachers have learned that reinforcing quiet, constructive study and play behavior can reduce the problems created by boisterous students. Finally, it is often possible to combine these tactics into a careful form of environmental engineering. For example, many organizations in which smoking in particular rooms or offices is unwanted have found it beneficial to provide specially-designated areas where smoking is permitted. Rather than displaying signs that say, "No Smoking Allowed" in restricted areas, they post signs saying, "Smoking Allowed in This Area" in those places where it is deemed appropriate. Many restaurants make active use of this ap-   **205** proach. Likewise, it may be possible to reduce the amount of graffiti that is written on the walls of a washroom, or work area, if paper and pencils are provided in those areas as an alternative. The objective of environmental engineering is to anticipate the types of dysfunctional behaviors that might occur in particular settings, and to take steps to make them impossible, or at least, nonreinforcing.

Organizational Discipline and Punishment

How do formal discipline policies and practices in work organizations compare to the principles of the hot stove? In many cases, not very well. For example, it is difficult in practice to make punishment immediate. This is particularly the case when policies require a series of appeals and quasi-legal investigations after a charge is laid. For example, more than a year and a half passed at a major Canadian university recently, between the time when it was first alleged that a senior professor was misusing government research funds, and the beginning of the period of suspension meted out as punishment for the offense.

Compounding the problem, of course, is the difficulty of distributing punishments so that they are consistent and perceived as equitable. Consistency can be difficult to achieve for a number of reasons. One of these is that different people are often responsible for distributing punishment. For example, the same employee may be susceptible to the approval and discipline of more than one supervisor, even though such reporting relationships violate the principle of unity of command. Sometimes an employee is punishable by his own superior, as well as by his superior's boss.

A number of other factors can influence the consistency of the punishment administered by the same individual, including, for example, the mood of the supervisor* (Goodstadt and Kipnis, 1970) and the value of the employee to the organization (Rosen and Jerdee, 1974c). Likewise, a variety of factors in the work context can influence the degree to which accidents or mistakes are attributed to the individual employee (as opposed to factors beyond the employee's control). Hence, if supervisors are aware of the consequences of inappropriate employee behaviors, they are more likely to assume that the behavior will occur again, and more likely to assume that the employee is responsible both for the behavior and for the outcome that follows from it (Mitchell and Kalb, 1981). Further, supervisors who have had experience working on a job are more likely to attribute mistakes made on that job to external factors beyond the em-

---

*For a behaviorist, of course, the mood of the supervisor does not *cause* his use of discipline. Rather, the aversive behavior of the subordinate is the discriminative stimulus that occasions the use of discipline; the boss's mood is merely an accompanying (or *collateral*) emotional reaction.

ployee's control. As a result of these and other factors, the same supervisors can make differing interpretations of the culpability of their employees, and, as a result, administer different types and amounts of punishment for the same misbehavior (Mitchell, Green, and Wood, 1981). The point here is that although hot stoves may be consistent in the way they punish, supervisors in complex work settings often are not.

Are discipline procedures intense? Generally, formal discipline policies are more *progressive* than immediately intense. This is commonly the case in unionized work settings, in which collective agreements may restrict the intensity of the punishment that can be meted out by supervisors. One writer, in fact, has proposed a method of progressive discipline that he claims can obviate many of the negative side effects that have traditionally been attributed to punishment (Huberman, 1964). This approach entails a series of disciplinary measures which are applied following each transgression by a particular employee. For example, the first offense results in a casual reminder of the rules and a "note of correction." The second occurrence results in a private discussion in the boss's office. The third offense also results in a talk with the supervisor, and includes a discussion of possible reassignment. Continued infractions result in suspensions, first with pay, then without. Ultimately, the employee is dismissed.

While programs of this sort are common in organizations, they do violate the purely psychological prescriptions concerning the intensity of punishment. On the other hand, they favor the goals of consistency and impersonality, and—as a result—are more defensible on legal grounds (cf. Fox, 1981). Finally, they tend to be more readily accepted because of their apparent humanity and reasonableness.

Discipline in Arbitration Decisions

Arbitration decisions in unionized work settings have been studied to determine whether they are progressive and *corrective* or retributional, intense, and *authoritarian* (using the term employed by the author of the study). The results suggest that corrective and retributional decisions are almost equally common although there are a number of offenses that tend to result more frequently in punitive decisions. These offenses are insubordination, illegal striking, and dishonesty (Wheeler, 1976).

Conclusion

To summarize, punishment is a major facet of the managerial styles employed in work organizations. It can be a very effective means of **207** quickly eliminating undesired behaviors, so it is reinforcing to managers who employ it. A number of unintended side effects have been attributed to the use of punishment, although there is very little evidence that these occur in work settings among adults. In practice, disciplinary procedures tend to have features that make them only partially similar to the most effective forms of punishment found in nature, and formal organizational policies, as well as arbitrator decisions, seem to support this divergence, probably because nature's style of punishing people is deemed too harsh by civilized people.

OPERANT CONDITIONING AND VIE THEORY

At this point it may be instructive to compare and contrast the operant conditioning approach to that of VIE Theory. First, we have mentioned many times the fact that, *in their pure forms,* the two approaches make entirely different fundamental assumptions about human nature and the causes of behavior. VIE Theory attributes behavior to internal beliefs and attitudes, while behavior modification rejects internal constructs in favor of the antecedent stimuli and external *consequences* of behavior. *

Secondly, both theories include the notion of probabilities, but in different ways (Petrock and Gamboa, 1976). VIE Theory speaks of the subjective probabilities in the minds of people in the form of expectancies and instrumentalities. Operant conditioning speaks of the probabilities and frequencies of behaviors occurring as a consequence of the reinforcements and punishments that result from behavior.

Both theories advocate that rewards (or reinforcers) be administered contingently upon behavior, as soon as possible after the desired behavior occurs. Notice, however, that operant conditioning holds variable ratio schedules to be the most motivating in the long run, once a behavior has been learned, whereas VIE Theory would suggest that instrumentality beliefs should be strongest when rewards are *always* tied to performance (as under a continuous reinforcement schedule). Research on this issue involving workers has been largely mixed and inconclusive, if only because of the difficulty of controlling reinforcement/reward schedules carefully in real work settings (cf. Latham and Dossett, 1978; Saari and Latham, 1982; Yukl and Latham, 1975; Yukl, Latham and Pursell, 1976; Yukl, Wexley and Seymore, 1972).

To this point, we have used the terms *reward* and *reinforcement* somewhat interchangeably. In fact, however, it is important to differ-

---

*On the other hand, both theories assume that humans are basically hedonists who seek to maximize pleasure (or at least survival potential) and minimize pain.

entiate between the two concepts. The term *reward* implies a set of subjective reactions experienced internally—it is rooted in the cognitive/perceptual model of human functioning. On the other hand, *reinforcement* implies that a behavior is made more probable, or more frequent, by its consequences; no mention of internal states or perceptions is involved. In short, choice of either term implicitly indicates whether an individual assumes the importance of internal or external factors as the primary causes of behavior.

Until recently, there has been a tendency for operant conditioning to focus on extrinsic outcomes rather than intrinsic ones, if only because the former are objective, measurable, and do not require the invocation of need concepts. On the other hand, VIE Theory has devoted considerable attention to the role of both intrinsic and extrinsic rewards, especially since these two types of motivation were both formally recognized in Porter and Lawler's (1968) revised expectancy model. Recently however, some behaviorists have attempted to provide operant conditioning interpretations of the impact of extrinsic reinforcement on *intrinsic motivation* (e.g., Mawhinney, 1979).

In balance, we can conclude that the differences between the two approaches are of more theoretical importance than they are of practical significance (Petrock and Gamboa, 1976). Both theories would propose that rewards (or reinforcers) be linked with performance (or desired behaviors). Both schools would suggest that reward/reinforcement contingencies feature outcomes that people desire or value. Finally, both acknowledge the importance of the context of behavior; the behaviorists, because they hold the antecedents and consequences of acts to be their cause, and the VIE theorists (e.g., Lawler, 1973), because they recognize that features of the work environment are important for structuring expectancy and instrumentality beliefs which, in turn, result in intentions to act.

A GLANCE AHEAD

The purpose of the present chapter has been to introduce some of the most important principles of operant psychology, laying the foundation for a treatment of the application of these principles to the problem of work motivation and behavior. The purpose of the following chapter will be to examine the techniques of behavior modification, and the relatively new approach to work motivation referred to as *Organizational Behavior Modification*.

10 WORK BEHAVIOR MODIFICATION

I don't believe in circumstances. The people who go on in this world are the people who get up and look for the circumstances they want.
—G. B. Shaw

The purpose of this chapter is to extend our treatment of operant psychology by introducing behavior modification and, more specifically, an approach to work motivation known as *Organizational Behavior Modification.*

At the outset, it is necessary to repeat the caveat that appeared at the beginning of chapter nine concerning the multiplicity of schools of behaviorism. The point is that there are a number of approaches to behaviorism and behavior modification, differing among themselves on the issue of the nature of cognitive processes (such as thinking, for example) and the role of these processes in explaining behavior (Mahoney, 1974). For example, B. F. Skinner and his followers have long acknowledged that people perceive, form beliefs, think, have emotions, and so on (e.g., Skinner, 1974), but—as we noted in chapter nine—they treat these processes as caused by the same types of environmental events that determine behavior. Such internal processes and private events are collateral products of people's environmental histories, not the causes of their behavior.

Other behaviorists, however, seem to attribute more of a causal role to internal, cognitive processes, although the introduction of any particular such process into the analysis is generally based on the demonstrated *utility* of the concept in explanation (cf. Craighead, Kazdin, and Mahoney, 1976; especially pp. 49–50 and pp. 134–152). Thus, whether the inclusion of a cognitive element into the analysis of behavior represents a legitimate interpretation of operant psychology (such as that developed by Skinner), or whether it represents an *addition* to operant psychology, depends upon one's perspective, and especially, upon the precise role attributed to that concept.

The significance of this diversity of views of behaviorism for our present purpose is that the treatment provided in this chapter cannot possibly represent the *only* approach, or the "best" approach. Rather, what follows is the author's interpretation, one that is heavily influenced by (but not totally the same as) the approach taken by Craighead et al. (1976). It is likely, therefore, that this presentation will not meet with the full approval of many adherents to the behaviorist paradigm, but it is hoped that it will reasonably reflect many, or most, of the tenets of that approach held in common among them. The interested reader is referred to Craighead et al. (1976), Kazdin (1978), and Skinner (1974) for three differing points of view.

The chapter will consist of three main sections. First, we will define behavior modification and briefly examine a number of cognitive processes that are currently included as part of modern behavior modification. As a means of avoiding the philosophical and theoretical issues raised in the above caveat, these cognitive processes will simply be presented and defined, without regard to whether they are inherently part of operant psychology, or additions to it.

In the second part of the chapter, we will examine Organizational Behavior Modification, a field concerned with the application of behavior mod to the problems of particular interest in this book—employee motivation and behavior.

Finally, we will review a number of issues—some of them controversial—that pertain to operant psychology, behavior modification, and their application in organizational settings. To begin, however, we will define behavior modification in general terms.

BEHAVIOR MODIFICATION

What is Behavior Modification?

On the basis of the diversity of views discussed in the foregoing paragraphs, it is not surprising that there is no universally agreed upon definition of behavior modification. Nevertheless, for the sake of discussion, the following definition is borrowed from Kazdin (1978, p. ix) and adopted for use in this book:

> . . . the application of basic research and theory from experimental psychology to influence behavior for purposes of resolving personal and social problems and enhancing human functioning.

Notice that this definition would imply that knowledge from *all* branches of experimental psychology constitutes the knowledge base of behavior modification, without regard to the particular schools involved. The definition also implies that behavior modification is not a fixed or final set of techniques; rather, as new research and theory are developed in the various schools of psychology, the knowledge base and techniques of behavior modification will continue to change accordingly (Craighead et al., 1976).

Nevertheless, it is clear that the principles of operant psychology discussed in chapter nine constitute an important part of behavior modification (if not all of it). In addition to the principles presented in chapter nine, however, current behavior modification also includes a variety of other principles and processes, many of which are of a cognitive nature. Those of interest to us here are referred to as attention, mediation, anticipation, problem solving, attribution, feedback, modeling, goal setting, and self-management. We will examine each of these processes in the following sections.

Attention

Even if we adopt the assumption that behavior has its antecedents and consequences in the environment, we must recognize that people are usually faced with a vast array of environmental events and contingencies, and that we are simply not capable of monitoring them all. Instead, we tend to restrict our focus to subsets of the environment, including subsets of all of the possible antecedents to behavior and subsets of all of its possible consequences. Two people in the same situation may concentrate their attention on different aspects of the environment and behave differently as a result. Therefore, while one employee may be particularly inclined to stay abreast of his supervisor's moods, another may not recognize the fact that the same supervisor tends to have shifts in mood from one day to the next. Likewise, some employees are more susceptible to the reinforcements and punishments they receive via the *informal* system of the organization, while others concentrate on the rewards and punishment administered by management. In short, it is the environmental events *to which people attend* that determine their behavior (Craighead et al., 1976, p. 135).

Mediation

As people experience the cues that prompt behavior and the consequences that are contingent upon it, they learn. However, the material that is learned can be organized into symbolic mental structures in an orderly fashion that facilitates recall and recognition, or it may not be so organized. Different people employ different mental techniques for organizing the things they have learned, such as mnemonics, poems, and various other types of associations. ("The way I remember the name of my boss's wife is that it is the same as my mother's!") Current behavior modification recognizes the role played by such mental processes in human behavior.

Anticipation

Why do some people take an umbrella to work with them in the morning, even when it is not raining when they leave home? Why do people abandon sinking ships? The answer is that human beings often anticipate events, including those they have already experienced in the past (such as being caught in the rain without an umbrella), as well as those they may not have experienced before (such as going down with a ship). The point is that learning from the past—be it personal learning or vicarious learning—causes people to anticipate reinforcement and punishment from their future behavior.

Problem Solving

When an individual behaves in a certain way in response to a challenge or task, the reinforcement or punishment that follows will influence the probability that the person will behave the same way in the future when confronted with the same situation, and we say that a behavior has been learned. On the other hand, we noted in the previous chapter that it is not necessary for people to experience antecedent-behavior-consequence contingencies for all possible, specific circumstances they may encounter. People develop the capacity to generalize somewhat from one situation to another. In other terms, we tend to develop problem solving skills which make it possible to consider an array of potential behaviors for dealing with problem situations, as well as select the one(s) that are most likely to be effective.

Attribution

People observe events around themselves and make inferences about the causes of those events. The events may be the antecedents that provide the operant conditioner's *prompts* or *cues* for behaving, or they may be the consequences of the operant behaviors that follow the cue. Alternatively, the event may be something that has little to do directly with the individual in question. The point is, people tend to be naive psychologists, trying to determine why things happen the way they do (recall chapter three, and see Heider, 1958). In the work setting, managers frequently make attributions about the reasons for the quality of the work of their subordinates, **213** attributing it either to hard work and effort (or a lack thereof), or to factors that are beyond the control of the employees involved (see Mitchell et al., 1981 for a formal theory pertaining to this sort of process).

Feedback

Feedback is the provision of information to a system about its output. In human terms, it consists of telling individuals something about their behavior, in either quantitative or qualitative terms. The provision of feedback is one of the most potent and most common elements of behavior modification, particularly when applied to work settings (Prue and Fairbank, 1980). Often, feedback is combined with the setting of goals, and in fact, the feedback usually consists of information concerning the employee's progress toward those goals.

To illustrate, a large textile company wished to reduce the average length of time its truck drivers spent at stops when they moved materials and merchandise between its various locations. They conducted a study to determine a baseline length of time against which the success of their intervention could be measured. They found that the average stop was taking sixty-seven minutes. They then set a company goal of forty-five minutes per stop, and began a three-stage program in which average stop time per terminal was fed back to the managers and employees of the terminals. The feedback was combined with reinforcers ranging from simple "thank-yous," to certificates and photographs of the employees with plant managers.

The first stage of the program lasted nineteen weeks and employees received feedback and reinforcements weekly. The second stage lasted eighty weeks, and saw feedback and reinforcement provided every two weeks. The third stage consisted of the provision of feedback and reinforcement on an average of every four weeks, on a variable interval schedule (recall chapter nine). Finally, a post-check of the company's performance three and one half years later showed that average time per stop was approximately thirty-seven minutes—well below the preintervention average, and better even than the goal set at the beginning of the intervention. As a result of the project, the firm realized considerable savings through an overall increase of 12 percent in the amount of internal transportation of materials (Runnion, Johnson, and McWhorter, 1978). The point here is that feedback, even without other reinforcers, can usefully influence employee behaviors, although, as we saw in chapter eight, it is most effective when it leads to the setting and/or acceptance of specific goals.

214   **Advantages of feedback.**   Of all the performance improvement mechanisms used in behavior modification, feedback is usually the most inexpensive and generally the most easy to employ. It costs little, in most circumstances, to tell employees how well they are doing. Further, feedback is usually a more positive means of gaining behavior control than are punishment and discipline, consistent with the positive orientation of the philosophy of behavior modification. Finally, feedback is usually more feasible than other behavior mod practices in organizations with internal constraints concerning the distribution of rewards and punishments. Union agreements, for example, may limit the use of money as a reinforcer, but seldom prohibit management from telling rank and file employees when they are performing well on their jobs.

In short, feedback has a number of advantages in behavior modification efforts, accounting in large part for its popularity in such programs (Prue and Fairbank, 1980). It is important to note that while feedback may be reinforcing (i.e., increasing the frequency of behavior), it is conceptually distinct from reinforcement, per se. The reason, of course, is that information fed back can also reduce the frequency of behavior, thereby qualifying for the formal definition of punishment in some situations.

Dimensions of feedback.   There are a number of aspects of feedback that must be taken into account when considering its use in behavior modification. Of particular interest is whether the feedback is provided to the individual in public or in private. One summary of the evidence on this matter has concluded that private feedback is desirable when: (1) the performance of the person receiving it is low; (2) supervisors have the necessary interpersonal skills to deal with subordinates on a one-to-one basis; (3) there are enough resources (such as supervisory time) to provide it; (4) workers are in close proximity to their supervisors; and (5) the individual receiving it is being compared to his own baseline performance or some designated standard (Prue and Fairbank, 1980).

Another consideration is the means used to deliver feedback. It can be provided verbally, in written form, by mechanical means, or by the individual himself as he keeps record of his own behavior and performance. There are costs and benefits associated with each of these approaches. For example, self-monitoring implies trust of the individual and includes the employee in the intervention program. Verbal feedback can be quick and inexpensive to administer. Written feedback can help with the keeping of records for ongoing assessments of performance improvements.

Also of concern is the *content* of the feedback, or the standard that is implied in the message. For example, is the individual's performance to be compared with that of other people (such as her

215

work group), with her own previous performance, or with some external standard or goal? The reader is reminded of the value of specifying hard and specific goals, as we discussed in chapter eight, and is referred to Prue and Fairbank (1980), who have reviewed a variety of specific issues that should be taken into account to plan the content of the feedback that is to be provided to employees.

The timing of feedback is often important. Ideally, feedback should be provided as soon as possible after the behavior about which information is being fed back, although people vary in their capacity to effectively wait to learn how well they are doing at a task. Immediate feedback is particularly valuable when it pertains to a task that the individual is learning for the first time, and/or when the task involved is complex. It would seem that feedback should be made contingent upon behavior rather than the passage of time, per se, as is the case with reinforcement, but there is little research evidence on this point at present.

Who should give the feedback? It stands to reason that the greater the prestige of the person who provides it the more attention will be paid to feedback, although there are circumstances where this may not necessarily be the case. For example, the trustworthiness of the person, his capacity to deliver reinforcers and punishments, his expertise, sincerity, and the nature of the relationship between the person delivering the message and the person receiving it also should be taken into account.

Further detail about considerations relevant to the nature and use of feedback is provided for the interested reader by Anderson (1970), Greller (1978), Prue and Fairbank (1980), and Walter and Marks (1981).

Modeling

In chapter nine we discussed the development of complex behaviors from simpler ones through the process referred to as behavior shaping. It was noted there that a great deal of human behavior is the result of behavior shaping; in fact, shaping continues throughout our lives, as we become increasingly more sophisticated in dealing with our environments.

On the other hand, Bandura (1969, 1977) and others have noted that many complex behaviors seem not to require the time and ongoing *personal* experiencing of reinforcement and punishment entailed in shaping processes. Instead, they note that some complex behaviors can often appear all at once for the first time. The primary means by which this occurs, according to Bandura, is through identification processes—we watch others and learn from them.

For example, a new employee in a grocery store may stand beside an experienced clerk to observe how vegetables are trimmed and prepared for display. After watching the several microsteps involved in efficiently trimming and wrapping a head of lettuce, for example, the experienced clerk may say to the newcomer, "Here, you try." Of course the rookie may not be as proficient as the veteran upon the first attempt, but a little shaping (of both the lettuce and the rookie's behavior) can normally overcome the problem and, before too long, the entire behavioral sequence has been learned.

Primary modeling mechanisms. There are three basic means through which people model their behavior after others. The first one is called imitation, and was illustrated by the example of the lettuce trimmer in the previous paragraph. Notice that the person whose behavior is being modeled need not actually be alive or present for learning to take place. In fact, training films are commonly used in organizations to demonstrate how relatively complex acts are performed.

A second form of modeling involves the use of behavior that already exists in the person's repertoire but that is cued (or prompted) by the behaviors of others around him. For example, employees in a work setting may be much more likely to engage in clownplay when one of their informal leaders does so than would normally be the case. Although this aspect of modeling is similar to imitation, the difference has to do with whether the behavior being displayed by the individual is new (which is the case in imitation), or whether it is already known by the person but prompted by the behaviors of other people in his environment.

A third modeling mechanism is vicarious identification with the *consequences* of the behaviors of other individuals. Public punishment in the days of old capitalized on this process: several people could "learn" about the consequences of illegal acts, without having to perform those acts and incur the costs personally. Thus, if we see others being reinforced for behaving in certain ways, we may be more likely to behave in similar fashion ourselves, almost as if we had experienced the reinforcement firsthand.

Notice that it is possible for modeling to result in the learning of behavior (either new behavior or old behavior in new circumstances), without that behavior actually being put into practice. Whether people actually employ the behaviors they observe depends upon a number of things, including who the model is and the consequences that the model incurs as a result of the behavior. Research indicates that people are more likely to imitate the behavior of models who are high in prestige or expertise (Craighead et al., 1976, p. 107).

Other Cognitive Elements of Behavior Modification

In addition to the cognitive mechanisms discussed in the foregoing sections, current practice in behavior modification employs a variety of others as well. Most of these have been less relevant to programs designed to deal with work problems, so they will not be treated here. The interested reader is referred to textbooks by Bandura (1969, 1977), Craighead et al. (1976), and Kazdin (1975) for more detail on them. However, before we turn our attention to Organizational Behavior Modification, per se, brief mention must be made of two more.

Goal setting.   The first of these is goal setting. Many of the applications of behavior modification to work settings have included some form of goal setting (Locke, 1978) as a means of improving performance over baseline rates (of behaviors such as attendance, performance, work quality, and so on). The reader is referred to chapter eight of this book for greater detail on the concepts and techniques of goal setting.

Self-management.   A final cognitive process that is included in many behavior modification settings is referred to as self-management. Basically, self-management is a process by which a person selects, from among those response alternatives that are available at a particular time, those that otherwise would not be chosen (cf. Erez and Kanfer. 1983; Mills, 1983; Thoresen and Mahoney, 1974). In a sense, self-management consists of overriding one's natural predilections in favor of pursuing goals that are less naturally favored.

In its most general form, self-management entails a three-stage sequence in which the individual monitors his own behavior, evaluates that behavior against some standard, and then administers reinforcers or punishment to himself on the basis of the evaluation (Kanfer, 1980). So, for example, an employee who has been instructed by his supervisor to reduce the amount of material he wastes in a construction site might be taught methods for actually measuring the amount of scrap he throws away or the number of times he actively makes use of materials that have been discarded by himself or someone else. The evaluation stage follows closely, of course, as the employee will normally be immediately aware of how well his performance measures up to the standards he or his employer have set for him.

The third stage, the self-administration of either reinforcement or punishment, is somewhat more complex. For example, the person may voluntarily deny himself certain normal pleasures (such as a routine coffee break) if he notices that he is not making progress toward his goal. Alternatively, if he manages to make considerable use of discarded materials on a given morning, he may then administer any of a number of desirable consequences to himself, such as making a phone call to a friend, taking an extra long lunch hour, or merely uttering statements to himself such as, "That's better!"

Summary

The foregoing discussion has briefly introduced a number of processes and techniques that are commonly employed by psychologists in behavior modification settings. When combined with the basic methods of operant conditioning and those of other schools of psychology, these techniques have proven highly effective in influencing a wide array of human behavior in educational, clinical, and rehabilitation settings. Of particular interest to the main topic of this book, however, is the use of behavior modification in applied work settings. Therefore, we turn our attention in the following sections to *Organizational Behavior Modification.*

ORGANIZATIONAL BEHAVIOR MODIFICATION

Since Aldis (1961) and Nord (1969) first suggested the application of the principles of operant conditioning to work organizations, there has been a gradual increase in the popularity in what has come to be called *Organizational Behavior Modification* (sometimes referred to as *O.B. Mod* or *Organizational Behavior Management*). In fact, an entire journal—the *Journal of Organizational Behavior Management*—is devoted to disseminating knowledge about the application of these principles to managerial problems and reporting research conducted within the O.B. Mod framework. It is important to repeat, however, that while operant psychology is the most important parent discipline underlying O.B. Mod, the actual techniques applied by its practitioners include concepts such as those discussed in the foregoing sections of this chapter (Fredericksen and Lovett, 1980; Luthans and Kreitner, 1975; Miller, 1978).

Managing Behavioral Contingencies at Work

Managers who wish to apply O.B. Mod must, in simple terms, learn how to diagnose and influence the antecedents and the consequences of the behavior of their employees. Luthans and Kreitner (1974, 1975) have proposed a general sequence for accomplishing this, called *Behavioral Contingency Management.* It consists of five basic steps.

First, the manager must identify those employee behaviors which are detrimental to job performance. It is important that the **219** manager be precise about exactly which behaviors are undesirable and need to be dealt with, and, if possible, that they be countable.

The second step is to actually count the frequency of the problematic behaviors, establishing a *baseline* that can be used to determine the effectiveness of the manager's subsequent intervention. The count may be made by the manager or by the employee himself (recall our earlier discussion of self-monitoring). Often, tally sheets are designed for this purpose, or managers sometimes merely sample the behavior of their personnel, checking how frequently they engage in the behavior in question during randomly selected periods of time. Wrist counters or the judicious application of memory are recommended in cases when it is probable that the employee will change his behavior if he knows that his supervisor is observing and recording it (cf. Whyte, 1972).

The third step is to identify both the conditions that are antecedent to the behavior, as well as the consequences that reinforce it. For example, the author once observed a number of work groups in a plant in which steel containers were manufactured. Foremen in each of the groups often complained that employees of the other groups stole parts and materials for use on their own projects. (The word they used, of course, was "borrowed.") Upon investigation, it was learned that most of the borrowing occurred toward the end of every month. Moreover, the foremen whose workers conducted the informal requisitions managed to keep their cost figures low, while assuring that their project deadlines were met. (The consequences for victimized foremen were exactly the opposite, of course.) Here, the antecedent of the dysfunctional behavior (borrowing) was the time of the month in which it occurred. The consequences? A formal reward system that reinforced the foremen for in turn reinforcing his staff for raiding the supplies and materials of the other work groups!

Petrock (1978) has suggested a useful means for analyzing the consequences of employee behavior for contingency management. He notes that most on-the-job behavior is of either of two varieties: job-related or non-job-related. Moreover, each of these types of behavior can result in either positive or aversive consequences. Finally, regardless of whether they are positive or aversive, the consequences of employee behavior can be classified according to three important dimensions:

1. Whether the impact is on the employee or the organization (or both).
2. Whether the consequences are immediate or delayed.
3. Whether they are certain and highly contingent upon the behavior, or somewhat random and only partially contingent upon behavior.

Therefore, the management of employee behavior requires that the supervisor identify both the reinforcing and punishing consequences that accrue to the employee, for both those behaviors that are deemed desirable, as well as those that are undesirable (from a managerial point of view). Clearly, individuals will engage in desirable behavior on the job when it results in a positive net balance of reinforcing consequences, rather than a balance of punishing consequences. On the other hand, when employees find work demands result in more unpleasant outcomes than positive ones, we can expect that rules will be broken or ignored or that employees will actively engage in practices that are more reinforcing than is compliance with management's desires.

According to Petrock, the punishing consequences of desired work behavior are usually personal (rather than organizational), immediate, and directly contingent on those behaviors. For example, wearing safety equipment is often uncomfortable, obeying formal rules can be inconvenient, and doing things by the book is often a "hassle." On the other hand, the reinforcing consequences of desired behavior are frequently personal, delayed (rather than immediate), and contingent upon behavior, making desirable behavior less attractive in many cases than undesirable behavior. In short, Petrock suggests that supervisors who wish to influence the behavior of their employees must carefully identify and attempt to balance the positive and aversive consequences of both positive and negative behaviors, and then take steps to assure that desired behaviors result in more positive, and fewer aversive consequences than undesired behavior.

It is important to reiterate that many work behaviors are often reinforced informally by the social system of the workplace, in spite of the fact (or often *because* of the fact) that management officially discourages them.

The third step in behavioral contingency management is the selection of an intervention strategy (Luthans and Kreitner, 1975). These can include the application of any of the following, alone or in combination: positive reinforcement, negative reinforcement, punishment, or extinction. The manager tries to make the chosen consequence contingent upon the behavior she is trying either to reinforce or eliminate. There are a variety of factors that can (and should) influence the precise strategy selected, such as the nature of the job, the organization's structure, history and precedents, union contracts, and other, more informal agreements. The manager or the employee continues to record the frequency of occurrence of the behavior in question. If the intervention is effective, the undesirable behavior will decrease in frequency (or cease altogether), and more favorable behaviors will take their place.

The final step is to evaluate the intervention by observing whether the desired behavior actually becomes more frequent, **221**

while undesired behavior becomes less frequent. Without evaluation, a manager cannot tell whether her attempt to change her employee's behavior has been successful. If it has not been successful,
further remedial steps might then be possible (such as reexamining
the antecedents or changing the consequences or the schedules by
which they are administered).

In short, Luthans and Kreitner's (1974, 1975) five step approach
follows consistently from the operant conditioners' suggestions for
functional analysis, focusing upon the antecedents and consequences of behavior, as well as upon the nature of the behavior itself.

The Positive Approach in O.B. Mod

While O.B. Mod makes use of reinforcement as well as punishment,
the emphasis is on the application of *positive* control measures wher-
ever possible. Luthans and Kreitner (1975, p. 84) summarize this
view:

> Reinforcement is the key to operant learning theory and the most important prin-
> ciple of behavior modification. The simple fact is that positive reinforcement,
> contingently applied, can effectively control human behavior. . . . With the possi-
> ble exception of the contingency concept itself, the understanding and appro-
> priate use of positive reinforcement is most important to success in O.B. Mod.

The trick, of course, is to identify those things that people find positively reinforcing, for as has been noted repeatedly, different people
find different consequences reinforcing.

Identifying reinforcers. How can we identify the consequences that particular individuals find positively reinforcing? Strictly
speaking from an operant conditioning perspective, the only appropriate way is to conduct functional analyses of people's behavior:
that is, to observe the antecedent conditions in which behaviors occur, the specific behaviors themselves, and the consequences of
those behaviors, with a particular view to noticing increases or decreases in the frequencies of the behaviors of interest.

For example, if a manager notices that a particular employee engages in clownplay when he has too little work to do (the antecedent
condition), and that he seems to attract the attention and support of
his coworkers when he does so, thereby increasing his propensity to
act in such a manner (the reinforcement effect), the manager might
infer that the individual's behavior can be influenced by the contingent application (or withdrawal) of interaction with his peers. That is,
if social interaction is reinforcing to the employee, chances for social
interaction might be adopted by the supervisor as a contingent consequence for encouraging the individual to perform tasks on the job.

222 Just as we can observe the brand of beer people prefer at the pub when they are thirsty, so we can make inferences about the specific nature of other reinforcers of a particular individual's behavior.

In practice, however, it is not possible to observe all the consequences of every employee's acts, and to observe whether these consequences function to increase or decrease the occurrence of specific behaviors. Therefore, other means are more feasible and more frequently used to identify reinforcers. One method is simply to ask people what they desire from their work (recall our discussion of attitude surveys near the end of chapter seven).

There are a variety of standardized instruments for inquiring about the types of things people desire from their work. One of these is the *Minnesota Importance Questionnaire* (Gay, Weiss, Hendel, Dawis, and Lofquist, 1971). Another is referred to as the *Job Orientation Inventory* (Blood, 1973). In common practice, however, employee *attitude* surveys normally feature a number of tailor-made questions pertaining to the types of potential reinforcers that may be more or less idiosyncratic to the organization involved.

A third approach to identifying reinforcers is through the use of trial and error: the manager simply tries a variety of outcomes contingent upon desired employee behavior and observes whether they actually function to reinforce (make more frequent) the behaviors in question. There are a wide variety of potential reinforcers in some organizations, while in others managers are limited by organizational policies, precedents, or formal agreements (such as union contracts) in the types of things they can offer employees in return for behavior (see chapter twelve). Nevertheless, Luthans and Kreitner (1975) suggest several categories of potential reinforcers that might be available in practice. Their categories, with examples, are:

1. Consumables: beer parties, Easter hams.
2. Manipulatables: wall plaques, watches.
3. Visual and Auditory: piped-in music, redecoration of work environment.
4. Tokens: money, stocks, vacation trips.
5. Social: solicitations for suggestions, smiles.
6. Activity Based: job with more responsibility, time off, work on a personal project with pay (recall the Premack Principle).

The point is that there are a variety of outcomes creative supervisors might attempt to employ as reinforcers with their staffs, although in virtually all organizations there are constraints of one sort or another. But the desire is to find something positive rather than to rely on negative influences such as punishment or threat of punishment.

Applications of O.B. Mod

There is some agreement that the application of operant conditioning principles to the modification of human behavior has been much **223** more successful, to date, in controlled laboratory settings, than it has in real, ongoing field settings (e.g., Repucci and Saunders, 1974). Moreover, of those applications which have been attempted in real settings, the most common have tended to involve the modification of the behavior of either children, prisoners, or the mentally ill—people over whom the behavior modifier (or therapist) typically has considerable legitimate authority and control (Argyris, 1971). There are fewer reported applications of behavior modification in ongoing *work* organizations, although, as suggested previously, they are becoming increasingly more common (cf. Scott and Podsakoff, 1983).

Generally, these applications have been of four main varieties: (1) programmed instruction, particularly for the hard-core unemployed; (2) modeling (for purposes of training); (3) improving work behaviors such as performance, safety, and attendance; and (4) advertising research (Babb and Kopp, 1978; Locke, 1977; Schneier, 1974). Because of limitations of space, we will restrict our focus here to those programs that have been specifically directed at the improvement of job performance, safety, and attendance.

Improving job performance.   One of the earliest and best-publicized applications of Organizational Behavior Modification consisted of the work that was undertaken in the early 1970s by Emery Air Freight (Dowling, 1973b). The Emery experience is worthy of note for at least two reasons. First, it was billed as one of the pioneering attempts to apply the principles of operant conditioning to work motivation. Secondly—and perhaps more importantly—it has been the source of some controversy that illustrates the conflict that exists between cognitive and operant conditioning schools of thought on the issue of work motivation and performance. Accordingly, let's take a quick look at the study itself.

Management at Emery investigated a large number of the firm's operations and concluded that there were widespread differences between actual employee practices on the one hand and the practices that were prescribed and intended by company policy on the other. For example, it was found that customer service representatives were much slower than desired in responding to customer enquiries about freight rates, flight schedules, and other issues. Management had employees monitor their own performance and record how well they were doing on measurable standards. Goals were set to increase performance levels, and constant feedback and positive reinforcers were provided for improvements.

Emery saved an estimated $3 million, over a three-year period as a result of their program (Dowling, 1973b). They expanded it into various other parts of their operation, including areas such as operations, sales and sales training, and shipping. Initially, the most commonly used reinforcer was praise, but eventually it began to lose its capacity to reinforce desired behavior. In fact, it understandably became a source of irritation. Therefore, supervisors began using alternative reinforcers such as assigning employees to pleasurable tasks upon the completion of less desirable ones (again, recall the Premack Principle discussed in chapter nine), time off, freedom to attend business luncheons, letters sent home praising the employee, and so on.

The need at Emery to expand the range of reinforcers used raises an important point. *Reinforcers* are reinforcing, by definition, only when they actually increase the frequency of a behavior or set of behaviors. Therefore, a supervisor, parent, teacher, or other individual who is attempting to modify someone else's behavior must remember that different outcomes reinforce different people. (We discussed this issue near the end of chapter seven, in the context of individualized reward systems from the point of view of VIE Theory.) The point is that certain outcomes, particularly praise, may become transparent, appear phony, and manipulative, and thereby lose their capacity to influence behavior (Staw, 1977). In fact, such consequences may become punishers. In short, supervisors and other behavior modifiers must be careful to monitor the *actual* reinforcing power of those things they distribute contingent on behavior, otherwise, rather than reinforcing behavior, they may find they are punishing those behaviors they are attempting to encourage.

As suggested above, the Emery Air Freight experiment has become the focus of controversy since it was first reported. The controversy concerns whether the design and execution of their program actually constituted an example of operant conditioning, per se. Some critics, while not disputing the success of the program, have argued that operant psychology, by itself, cannot account for what happened. Rather, because the employees involved were required to set goals, monitor their own performance improvements, and accept feedback about those improvements, a strict operant psychology explanation is insufficient to explain the results. Instead, a more cognitively based explanation—particularly that associated with Goal Setting Theory—has been offered (e.g., Locke, 1977, 1978, 1979).

The position taken here is that identifying and crediting the formal theory most responsible for Emery's success, are less important than the fact that what they did—whatever it was—worked. Moreover, other studies that have applied various blends of goal setting, feedback, and positive reinforcement have subsequently also been effective for improving employee performance.

For example, various combinations of goal setting, feedback, **225** and reinforcement have been used in a wide array of organizational settings to improve the job performance of work groups as diverse as clerks in a small grocery store (Komaki, Waddell, and Pearce, 1977), mountain beaver trappers (Latham and Dossett, 1978; Saari and Latham, 1982), discipline engineers (Ivancevich and McMahon, 1982), telephone service crews (Kim and Hamner, 1976), truck drivers (Latham and Baldes, 1975; Latham and Kinne, 1974; Runnion, Johnson and McWhorter, 1978; Runnion, Watson and McWhorter, 1978), salespeople (Miller, 1977), and others (see Andrasik, 1979 and Hamner and Hamner, 1976 for two reviews of these and other studies). In short, it is clear that these techniques can be useful for the improvement of job performance of many occupational groups, although there is still some debate concerning which of the various ingredients (goal setting, feedback, or reinforcement, for example) are the most important (see Locke, 1978 and Ivancevich and McMahon, 1982 for two discussions of this issue).

Improving safety and reducing accidents. Organizational Behavior Modification has demonstrated considerable promise recently for reducing accidents in a variety of work settings. For example, Komaki, Barwick, and Scott (1978) identified a set of "desired safety practices" in two departments of a wholesale bakery in which accidents had become an increasingly serious problem. Employees were shown slides of both safe and unsafe behaviors associated with getting their work done (thereby providing a basis for behavior modeling), and were asked to discuss the safe and unsafe aspects of the acts depicted in the slides. Feedback was provided by the use of a chart that reported the frequency of occurrence of safe behaviors, showing graphically how the employees' safety performance improved over the pre-study baseline period. In addition, supervisors provided verbal reinforcement to those employees whom they saw engaging in the desired behaviors on the job.

As a result of these three intervention components (behavior modeling and instruction, feedback, and reinforcement), the proportion of safely conducted behaviors increased from 70 percent to 96 percent in one department, and from 78 percent to 99 percent in the other. Moreover, the company's employees seemed favorable toward the program.

Similar O.B. Mod interventions have been effective for improving safety and reducing accidents in other settings. For example, Komaki, Heinzmann, and Lawson (1980) enhanced the safety record of a sample of civic vehicle maintenance workers, using a combination of behavior modeling, instruction, and feedback, finding that the feedback was necessary to keep the program effective after the early modeling and instruction phases were completed. Finally (although this does not exhaust the list of possible examples), Haynes, Pine, and Fitch (1982) reduced the accident rate of a sample of urban bus drivers, using a combination of feedback, competition, and monetary and non-monetary incentives.

In short, accident control and safety management seems to be one area that is especially amenable to the techniques of O.B. Mod.

Reducing absenteeism.   The control of employee absenteeism is another area in which O.B. Mod has shown some degree of promise (see chapter five for a discussion of the costs of absenteeism to work organizations). Although many of these studies have been criticized for being of relatively short duration and for not reporting cost/benefit data (Schmitz and Heneman, 1980), there have been enough studies with encouraging results to suggest that further attempts are warranted (see, for instance, Kempen and Hall, 1977; Nord, 1970; Orpen, 1978; Pedalino and Gamboa, 1974; and Kopelman and Schneller, 1981). Two recent studies, in fact, have suggested that the combined application of positive reinforcement and punishment may be particularly effective for controlling employee absences (Kempen and Hall, 1977; Kopelman and Schneller, 1981).

To summarize, there are a number of work-related behaviors that seem more or less amenable to modification by the principles of O.B. Mod. On the basis of the studies reported here, as well as others that have not been discussed, it appears that programs featuring goal setting—in conjunction with feedback and/or positive reinforcement—are most frequently associated with success. In fact, blends of goal setting and other behavior modification principles and techniques (such as those mentioned at the beginning of this chapter) seem to be more effective in applied work motivation settings than any other theory or set of techniques discussed in this book.

The Quality of O.B. Mod Research

Throughout this book we have seen that much of the research that has been conducted to test the validity or the applied utility of various theories has been flawed in one way or another, leaving us with only a partial understanding of the relative merits of these theories and of the techniques that follow from them. Although research into the application of operant principles in work organizations has been underway for only a few years, it is worthwhile to consider it in the same light. Accordingly, one author (Andrasik, 1979) assessed twenty reported applications of behavior modification to organizational problems and concluded that:

1. Researchers tended *not* to report the reliability of the measures they used (of such things as absenteeism).

2. All of the twenty research reports contained baseline data, making it easy to determine the extent of the impact of the interventions.

3. About 60 percent of the studies permitted the reader to isolate the cause-effect connections that resulted from the various elements of the interventions.

4. Only four (20 percent) of the studies reported follow-up data attesting to the ongoing impact of the intervention.

In addition to these four major dimensions, the reviewer noted other important features of the twenty studies (Andrasik, 1979). All of them reported benefits to the organizations involved that outweighed the implementation costs incurred, and many reported impressive savings in actual dollar terms. Moreover, the interventions were well received by most of the organizational participants involved, with a few exceptions. Finally, he noted that none of the studies permitted a comparative evaluation of behavior modification applications with other, nonbehavioral techniques.

In balance, when one considers the fact that behavior modification has only recently been systematically introduced to the practice of management (compared to the introduction of other theories and approaches discussed in this book), and takes into account the difficulties of conducting rigorous research in ongoing organizational settings, we can conclude that tests of the value of behavior modification have been reasonably well conducted and supportive of the behavior modification approach. There is little doubt that when management consistently links positive reinforcers to desired employee behaviors and either punishes or ignores undesired employee behaviors, individuals are likely to try to do those things supervisors desire on the job.

CONTROVERSY AND BEHAVIOR MODIFICATION

Of the theories of work motivation discussed in this book, Herzberg's two-factor model has doubtlessly been the most controversial (recall chapter two). Second in controversy, however, must be the theory and applications that have come from operant psychology for application to organizations. Since the relevance of operant conditioning for understanding and managing organizations was first mentioned by Aldis (1961), Nord (1969), Luthans and Kreitner (1975), and others, there has been a sequence of controversies ranging from the theoretical and the philosophical through to the operational and ethical. While a complete presentation of the controversies involving behaviorism in organizations is beyond the scope of this volume, brief mention will be made of a number of the issues, along with references that will be useful for the reader who wishes to pursue any of them further.

228

Antibehaviorist Polemics

The majority of the controversies that have been directed at operant conditioning and behavior modification, per se, have pertained to the ethics of controlling human behavior, and to the allegation that to do so with the help of applied psychology is denigrating to human beings. Let's take a closer look at this issue.

The ethics of control. Is it unethical to apply techniques for the explicit purpose of influencing the behavior of other people? What about the sanctity of human nature and the freedom we have all fought to attain and protect? Who has the right to control another person's behavior, to determine what they can and cannot do? These questions constitute the crux of one of the most important attacks that has been leveled at Skinner and his followers.

Typically, the reply is as follows. Because of the fact that human behavior naturally can result in only one or more of three possible consequences—reinforcement, punishment, or extinction—all people are both conditioned and conditioners. In Skinner's own words, "We all control, and we are all controlled" (1953, p. 438). From the time we are born and begin to behave, we all find that our acts result in either positive or aversive consequences. The world is a giant Skinner box in which people formally and informally administer rewards and punishments to one another. Children who are reprimanded by their parents for speaking out of turn are affected with the same degree of external control as children who accidentally cut themselves when they fall on sharp rocks. Control is natural; it is unavoidable. It is constant and ubiquitous. To deny that control is everywhere in nature is to ignore reality, so to refuse to exercise control is to defer it to others. In short, the formal application of procedures to reinforce or punish behavior is little different from what occurs in the absence of such procedures, so we are collectively better off by consciously learning about and utilizing the laws of behavior to make life as safe and comfortable as possible (see Rogers and Skinner, 1956 for a debate on these issues).

Related to this issue is the fact that much of the research that has lead to our knowledge of operant and respondent behavior has been conducted upon animals. Critics react negatively to the application of animal-based knowledge to human behavior—are we no better than, or different from animals? Defenders of operant psychology recognize that human behavior is more complex than animal behavior, but argue that much of it is ultimately determined by similar underlying principles. Animals have been used merely for the obvious reasons of humanity, cost, and convenience.

A third fundamental attack on operant psychology pertains to the issue of human rationality. To claim that human behavior is **229** merely a function of its consequences ignores the rational side of human nature, and with it, the free will that humans exercise. In other words, critics argue that people have consciousness and the capacity to think, reason, and choose among alternatives. While not denying the importance of the consequences of human acts, these critics propose that Skinnerian psychology denies any role to human cognition, and thereby treats us merely as automatons, or mindless creatures, without the capacity to behave with volition. We noted earlier in this chapter that current schools of behavior modification openly admit the importance of rational processes (e.g., Craighead et al., 1976; Mahoney, 1974), so some peace has been made on this point. Nevertheless, there are still some behaviorists who retain the position that internal processes, such as cognition, are useless for understanding behavior: they cannot be observed or measured, so they certainly cannot be influenced. To attribute human behavior to internal processes is both redundant (for the reasons discussed at the beginning of chapter nine) and unscientific.

On the other hand, critics of strict behaviorism claim that it is no more scientific to attribute behavior to environmental factors with a philosophy that, "If it works, we should use it," than it is to posit the importance of unobservable internal events. They argue that it is as scientific to rely on internal (albeit hypothetical) causes of human behavior as it is to rely on unobservables to explain the nature of physical entities and phenomena. Who has observed an electron, for example?

The point here is this: the radical behaviorist and cognitive/perceptual approaches constitute two incommensurate sets of fundamental beliefs regarding human nature. In their pure forms, they cannot be reconciled. On the other hand, recent eclectic approaches claim that each of these perspectives has something to offer an understanding of human nature—neither is totally correct nor incorrect (Fedor and Ferris, 1981; Hitt, 1969; Walter and Marks, 1981). Further, it makes little difference to the person with applied intentions (such as parents, teachers, therapists, or managers), which approach is adopted. In fact, the success of behavior modification techniques that utilize both behaviorist and cognitive concepts illustrates that the difference between the two points of view holds more importance for philosophy, religion, and barroom debate than it does for applied problem solving (cf. Bandura, 1977).

Criticisms of organizational behavior modification.   In addition to many of the general issues we have just examined, there are a few points of controversy that relate to the application of operant psychology and behavior modification *to applied work set-*

tings. As we will see, some of these are practical in nature while others are ethical.

First, we can ask whether it is ethical to control the work behavior of human beings, particularly in view of the democratic social structure in which we live, and the fact that work is such an important element of human existence. One answer to this question, of course, is that employees are free to come and go from one work setting to another, choosing the work that they find features the level of managerial control that is most comfortable, recognizing that some form of control is always unavoidable (for the reasons presented earlier). Furthermore, how can one have organized work effort without some degree of formal control? How can our economy and our society, as a whole, function and be competitive without some system of control? When people go to work for an employer, they implicitly (sometimes explicitly) resign themselves to the authority of the formal control system implemented by that employer.

A related question concerns the observation of work behavior (Luthans and Kreitner, 1975). Is it ethical to monitor, sometimes surreptitiously, the work behavior of others, with a view either to measure it (for establishing a baseline before intervention) or to watch whether it changes in response to intervention? Still another question concerns whether it is possible to gain reliable measures of the work behavior of employees when they are aware that they are being measured (Whyte, 1972). Let's take these one at a time.

First, it is usually quite difficult in practice to gain realistic assessments of the work rate of employees when those employees realize they are being observed. This is especially so when the purpose of the observation is to set standards for performance and payment under piece-rate pay systems. Therefore, managers who desire to gain reliable information about the rates and levels of employee behavior and performance might benefit, in some settings, from the use of spy-like techniques.

Moreover, defendants of O.B. Mod argue that if the benefit to be gained by the appropriate setting of standards and the fair monitoring of performance is to be conducive to employee welfare, then such observation is justified. In other words, these particular ends justify the means used, within reason, of course (see Luthans and Kreitner, 1975, p. 185). Besides, managers have always observed the work performance of their employees; O.B. Mod merely formalizes the process, and employees should be made fully aware that their behavior will be monitored with a view to managing it.

Several *practical* issues related to O.B. Mod have been raised by critics. One concerns the problems of gaining reliable measurement, as just discussed. Another concerns the difficulty of determining what is reinforcing and punishing for particular employees, and then making it feasible to dispense these reinforcers in such a way that is economically viable and equitable. (More will be said about this in chapter twelve.)

A number of other practical issues deserve mention, issues dealing particularly with the *implementation* of O.B. Mod programs. One of these has to do with administrative procedures and the red tape that often accompanies any form of organizational action. If the organization involved in an OB. Mod intervention requires that the attempt be burdened with formal procedures that encumber the interventionist, his effectiveness will be limited accordingly.

Another problem has to do with the language that is used by both the interventionist and the employees involved. On the one hand, precision of communication is necessary in order for professionals to communicate effectively with one another. In fact, operant terminology has been particularly subject to misuse and misinterpretation (Mawhinney, 1975). On the other hand, excessive jargon and the use of buzzwords can alienate employees and managers whose cooperation is essential for the success of programs (Murphy and Remnyi, 1979).

Still another practical issue concerns the *time* that is granted by management for change to occur and manifest itself. On the one hand, management groups are reinforced to participate in enlightened managerial techniques when they show a payoff (especially in dollar terms). On the other hand, because of the many complexities of the dynamics in organizations, positive results sometimes take a while to become evident. While this problem is not unique to applications of O.B. Mod, they certainly do apply to them.

In short, some critics have claimed that behavior modification has proven to be much more effective in settings where the interventionist has held a position of high authority and control over those whose behavior has been modified, as is the case, for example, in prisons, mental institutions, and even school settings (Argyris, 1971). The control over outside influences that can interfere with the strict application of the measurement, reinforcement, and punishment of behavior in these types of settings is most similar to that which is possible in the laboratory settings in which the principles of operant psychology were first developed. But when these techniques are taken to actual work settings in organizations that feature constraints such as traditions, suspicions, unions, budgets, and impatient management groups, they are much less easy to install and make effective (see Murphy and Remnyi, 1979 and Reppucci and Saunders, 1974). We will explore the importance of these practical constraints in more detail in chapter twelve, and see that they are problematic for the application of other theories of motivation as well.

CONCLUSIONS

A cursory reading of the literature on work motivation and be-havior suggests that, when compared to the many need-oriented and cognitively based theories, the behaviorist approach occupies somewhat of a minority position. To date, there seems to have been less research and fewer theoretic papers and books published on Organizational Behavior Modification than there have been devoted to these alternative approaches.

On the other hand, there is evidence that increasingly more work is being done within the behaviorist camp on topics related to work motivation and behavior. Moreover, with the increasingly higher levels of reconciliation between the behaviorist and the cogni-tive schools (as is witnessed, for example, in current O.B. Mod work), it would appear that operant conditioning and behavior modification will continue to grow in importance in the future. In fact, a decade ago, two eminent industrial psychologists—John Campbell (1971) and Marvin Dunnette (1976)—both paid tribute to the accomplish-ments made by behaviorism in understanding work-related prob-lems. The years since their positive evaluations of this approach have shown their endorsements to have been justified and suggest that O.B. Mod will become even more widely accepted in the years to come.

11
INTRINSIC MOTIVATION THROUGH THE DESIGN OF JOBS

Challenge is the core and mainspring of all human activity. If there is an ocean, we cross it; if there's a disease, we cure it; if there's a wrong, we right it; if there's a record, we break it, and finally, if there's a mountain, we climb it.

—*James Ramsey Ullman*

Work is accomplished in organizations by the assignment of people to jobs. Consequently, an important element of the process of managing organizations consists of effectively matching people and jobs. The most frequently used general strategy for accomplishing this matching has been to select from external labor markets those individuals who seem to have the abilities necessary to perform the jobs that need to be filled (e.g., Arvey, 1979; Dunnette, 1966; Schneider, 1976). Alternatively, a second strategy is to train and develop those individuals who are already employed by the organization, so as to make them capable of effective performance of vacant jobs (e.g., Bass and Vaughan, 1966; Wexley and Latham, 1981). In fact, the business of selecting people from external labor pools and that of training members of the organization's internal labor pool constitute two of the major functions in the management of human resources.

TWO STRATEGIES

Notice that both of these strategies assume, implicitly, that people must either be found or changed to *fit* the jobs that need to be filled: they both assume that jobs are somehow immutable. In a sense, these strategies—especially the training approach—seem to assume that people are more maleable and changeable than are organizational jobs. In many cases, especially those in which the nature of the work is heavily determined by technology, this assump-

234

tion is well-founded. On the other hand, it is possible in many other cases to accomplish the effective matching of people to jobs by adopting an alternative assumption that does not treat jobs as fixed, but rather that sees work as capable of being defined and/or redefined to fit the abilities and needs of the people who must perform it. This second approach is fundamentally different from the first, although, in practice, the matching of human beings to work can be accomplished through a combination of both strategies.

Rationale for the Second Strategy

The last twenty years have witnessed the development of a number of specific types of techniques and programs, whose purpose is to capitalize on the second of the two matching strategies mentioned above. That is, they seek to effectively combine people and jobs by designing or redesigning jobs to match people, rather than the other way around. Let's take a look at some possible reasons behind the recent emergence and popularity of these job changing techniques before we examine the techniques themselves.

Some people are less maleable than jobs. One reason for the recent interest in changing jobs to match people, is the realization on the part of many managers that it is often easier, cheaper, and more rewarding to alter jobs than to alter people, particularly adults. Formal personnel selection and training programs are costly and of only limited success. In addition, the legal constraints posed by equal employment regulations have added extra cost and practical anxiety to an exclusive reliance on traditional strategies of selection and training (e.g., Arvey, 1979; Pinto, 1978).

Modern employees are better educated and more affluent. A second reason for the new concern for changing jobs to match people lies in the fact that, on average, today's workforce is different from that of previous generations for whom work was designed according to the principles of scientific management (Taylor, 1911) and/or the classical principles of management (Massie, 1965). The key differences are educational and economic: on average, the modern workforce is both better educated and more affluent than workforces of previous times (O'Toole, 1981). These differences hold a number of important implications:

a) Employee needs for existence are less salient, thereby making growth needs comparatively more active than they were in previous times (recall chapter three).
b) Higher education levels result in greater demands for growth need satisfaction from the job.
c) As a result of the combined effects of (a) and (b) above, dull, repetitive work is

235

more frustrating to a greater proportion of the workforce than was the case in previous times (Cooper, Morgan, Foley, and Kaplan, 1979; Hoerr, 1978).

d) Absenteeism, tardiness, turnover, sabotage, and unionization activity result from need frustration at work (see chapters four and five), making it comparatively more expensive for management to design work according to classical principles and expect employees to respond accordingly.

Work requires flexibility. The shift in western economies away from production and toward service industries (Malkiel, 1979), and the parallel increase in the number of managerial, professional, and technical jobs in these economies, has made it more necessary than it was in previous times for employees to be more autonomous and self-directing on their jobs. In other words, more and more jobs require flexibility, spontaneity, and creativity, and defy rationalization and strict routinization.

In short, there are a variety of reasons behind the recent emergence of techniques such as job enrichment, job enlargement, power sharing, and employee participation. In fact, the major intention of many of these programs is to address problems created by the phenomena listed above. Specifically, these programs are largely intended to provide intrinsic satisfaction and motivation experiences through working: they are designed to make it possible for employees to derive more growth need satisfaction, both from doing their work and from doing it well (recall chapter four). The purpose of the present chapter is to examine the current theory, research, and techniques associated with job design and redesign.

Because of its length, this chapter will be broken into four major parts. Part one will present a discussion of the role of job design in instigating intrinsic motivation, focusing on four current theoretical approaches. The issue of individual differences in employee reactions to job enrichment will be discussed in part two. In part three, a number of the practical aspects of job redesign strategies will be presented and discussed. Finally, part four will summarize the scientific evidence that attests to the validity of these approaches for generating intrinsic motivation, as well as to their practical value as managerial techniques.

To begin then, how does the design of work relate to the potential satisfaction of employee growth needs?

PART ONE: INTRINSIC MOTIVATION THROUGH JOB DESIGN

In chapter four, Deci's (1975) concept of intrinsic motivation was presented. It was explained there that intrinsic motivation consists of energy expended, first to increase and then to reduce a person's levels of arousal, challenge, and incongruity. People are viewed as seeking levels of stimulation in their environments that provide degrees of both physiological and psychological arousal that are neither too low, nor too high, for their personal preferences. An emphasis on the *physiological* basis for understanding job design is desirable from a *scientific* point of view, because it permits an objective, quantifiable insight into the impacts of jobs on people without the necessity of relying on subjective self-report explanations of employees. On the other hand, there are a variety of difficulties associated with a strictly physiological approach—difficulties that make such an approach hard to put into managerial practice. Therefore, a greater understanding of how jobs might be sources of motivation can be gained if we consider *both* physiological and psychological perspectives on the matter, rather than adopting only a single view. Further, we will see that the two approaches are generally quite consistent with one another, such that a practical manager who relies, of necessity, on cognitive and perceptual models of job design will in most cases enact policies that are consistent with those that would follow from a strict physiological perspective. Therefore, let's look first at the design of jobs from the point of view of the physiologically-based activation theory, as proposed by Scott (1966).

ACTIVATION-AROUSAL THEORY

The principal thrust of the activation theory approach to job design is that jobs are, in themselves, sources of activation for the people who perform them. Activation is ultimately conceptualized as ". . . the degree of excitation of the brain stem reticular formation" (Scott, 1966, p. 11). Certain properties of any stimulus object or setting (such as a job), generate greater levels of activation and arousal. In particular, the intensity, variation and variety, complexity, uncertainty, novelty, and meaningfulness of objects and situations are of special importance. Therefore, a job that has little variety, few component tasks, little novelty, and no uncertainty or unpredictability, will be less activating than a job which features the opposite characteristics. That is, jobs that feature elements of novelty and change, unpredictable requirements, and multiple tasks, other things being equal, should be comparatively quite capable of generating arousal.

Notice that the theory does not suggest that more activation is better. Instead, it suggests that these characteristics of work determine the overall levels of arousal experienced by the employee. But the level of arousal most comfortable for a particular employee is the critical issue. Again, too much stimulation is dissatisfying, as is too little. When an employee encounters a work situation in which the stimulation level is either *slightly* higher or *slightly* lower than her preferred **237** level, she will enjoy it. For example, not having to attend a regularly scheduled meeting may make a manager's day a bit less hectic than normal, and therefore somewhat more satisfying than usual. Likewise, a spontaneous gathering of colleagues in a person's office, followed by an unusually brisk flurry of telephone calls may be viewed as exciting and pleasurable.

On the other hand, *extreme* deviations from the person's optimum arousal level are aversive and instigate efforts to restore normalcy, through either generating or reducing stimulation. Daydreaming, clownplay, and kibitzing on the job are often examples of the former, whereas escape behaviors such as tardiness or malingering are often examples of the latter. Employees can often increase or decrease the stimulation of a job situation by actually modifying the content or flow of the work itself. For example, ways of increasing stimulation would include informally trading jobs with other employees, reversing the sequence of certain tasks, or designing new techniques for performing tasks. Alternatively, breaking complex jobs down into constituent elements, or simply postponing or ignoring certain parts of a job, are examples of means for reducing job-related stimulation. The point is that workers can often adjust the level of activation provided by a job, or create means of magnifying or reducing the degree of arousal a job provides them. As a result of the efforts a person expends to adjust stimulation levels closer to what is "normal," that person's performance at whatever other tasks he is doing usually suffers. In balance, therefore, the relationship between activation level and task performance is best summarized by an inverted U, such that performance of a job is compromised when the job is too dull or too hectic for the individual involved (Yerkes and Dodson, 1908).

Individual Differences in Arousal Preference

People differ at least three separate ways in the amount of stimulation and arousal they prefer (Korman, 1974). First, for a given time of day, some individuals desire greater stimulation and resultant activation than others. Students who share housing accommodations with friends who seem perversely "night people" or "morning types," are aware of the fact that individuals can vary considerably between themselves as to when they seek and enjoy stimulation and activity from their surroundings.

Secondly, a given individual varies across the period of a day in the level of stimulation he finds desirable. A common pattern is for people to prefer relatively low levels of noise and commotion early in the morning, before a sufficient quantity of caffeine has been in-

238

gested. Later in the day, greater levels of excitement are desired until bedtime approaches when, again, less excitement is preferred. But this pattern is not universal, by any means.

A third form of individual difference that pertains to activation-arousal theory is a tendency for people to adapt, within limits, to progressively higher or lower levels of stimulation at particular times in a day. Whereas a junior clerk comes to accept relatively little stimulation from his entry-level position, he manages to desire and seek increasing levels of stimulation as he is promoted upward through a series of jobs that involve increasingly higher levels of stimulation, and as a result, higher levels of overall arousal.

In short, people vary a great deal, both between themselves, as well as within themselves, in terms of their preferred levels of stimulation. These differences are of vital importance in understanding how to use arousal theory to design jobs, but as will be discussed in the next section, they make the *formal, precise* application of the theory by managers virtually impossible.

The Value of the Optimum Arousal Approach

In a sense, Scott's (1966) activation-arousal theory provides a number of very simple suggestions for job design. Specifically, this approach suggests that job-related motivation will be maximized when the job is neither too complex nor too simple for the employee; therefore, jobs should be designed for people so as to feature optimum, balanced levels of complexity, novelty, and stimulation.

But applying this advice in practice is far from easy, for a number of reasons. First, it is not possible for job design specialists (let alone line supervisors) to gain *precise* measures of either the level of stimulation a job generates, or of the effect that particular objective stimulation levels (even if they could be determined) have on a particular employee. Moreover, the between-person and within-person differences in arousal preferences add to the problem: how are managers to appreciate the differences among their employees in their preferred levels of arousal for particular times of the day? Further, how can a job be designed such that it arouses greater activation in the employee at precisely those times of day that match the individual's preferences for more or less arousal? And finally, how can a manager accurately measure the changes that occur for particular individuals in their preferred levels of arousal as they change and adapt to sequences of job assignments, as described earlier? In brief, the precise adoption and application of this approach to job design seems impossible in practice. On the other hand, it would be a mistake to discard or ignore it altogether, for several reasons.

First, as mentioned earlier, the optimum arousal approach provides a relatively sound physiological basis for understanding why and how other approaches to job design function as they do. As will be shown in the following sections of this chapter, a variety of other general strategies for job design have been advanced, most of which offer concrete detail concerning how jobs should be designed for the purpose of making them intrinsically motivating, but little in the way of ultimate explanations as to *why* their prescriptions can be motivating for employees. While the optimum arousal approach is not fully consistent with all other formal theories of job design, it is consistent with enough aspects of these other approaches to provide us with some biological insights into how the design characteristics of jobs may influence people.

A second major value of the optimum arousal approach is that its principles can be kept in mind by managers for their use on an *informal* day-to-day basis, both as a guide to the assignment of people to jobs, as well as a basis for understanding effective and ineffective job behaviors and attitudes. In other words, although it is impossible for managers to calibrate stimulation and arousal levels precisely (as argued above), it is possible for managers to pay attention, in a less formal fashion, to the differences among their people in the levels of challenge, excitement, and activity they seem to desire. Moreover, it is desirable for mangers to fully appreciate the differences among the jobs that fall under their purview in terms of the types and amounts of challenge, excitement, and activity they entail—especially for an employee who is newly assigned to perform them.

A third point of value of this theory (one that is related to the second), is that the concepts it provides can be useful both for explaining certain personnel problems after they occur, and/or preventing such problems before they occur. For example, the so-called Peter Principle (Peter and Hull, 1969) suggests that promotion systems in organizations tend to advance people upward in hierarchies, until they are ultimately assigned to jobs at which they are not competent. There is little *scientific* evidence in support of this proposition, but it does fit the observations of many of us and therefore holds some intuitive appeal. To the extent that the Peter Principle has any validity, the mechanisms described in the optimum arousal approach help us understand it. Translated into terms of the theory, the Peter Principle might be paraphrased as follows:

> There is a tendency in many organizations, in which promotions and transfers are based on merit, for employees eventually to be moved into jobs in which the level of physiological and psychological stimulation featured in these jobs is high enough to arouse activation levels that are sufficiently too great in comparison to

employees' preferred levels. When this happens, these employees are motivated to reduce activation through avoiding or reducing the net stimulation generated by the job, thereby limiting their effective performance of these jobs.

A related example concerns the use of job transfers as a means
of fostering experiential learning for the sake of developing employees so as to prepare them to take over senior level positions in geo-
graphically dispersed organizations. It may be that the stimulation
and traumas associated specifically with undergoing a move, per se
(see Brett, 1981), can add to the increment in arousal that normally
accompanies a job reassignment (such as a promotion) that does
not entail geographic mobility, thereby resulting in net levels of activation that are dysfunctional for experiential learning to occur (Pinder and Walter, 1984).

In short, the two preceding examples illustrate that a manager
need not be a physiological psychologist to benefit from the key concepts provided by Scott's (1966) activation theory approach to job
design. And, as we will see in the following sections, managers who
explicitly attempt to follow the guidelines of other formal theories of
job design will inadvertently be adhering to much of the advice that
Scott's theory would propose.

SUBJECTIVE APPROACHES TO JOB DESIGN

Because of the practical difficulties of operationalizing and applying the formal, physiological activation theory approach described above, both organizational scientists and practitioners have
devoted much more attention to theories of job design that avoid the
physiological concepts found in Scott's theory, in favor of alternative
approaches that rely on the subjective perceptions of people about
job characteristics. These *subjective* theories of job design seem
easier, both to researchers who wish to construct theories without
monitoring brain activity, as well as to managers who simply wish to
match people and jobs in an enlightened fashion.

The following sections will present the central ideas found in
three of the most popular and well understood of these so-called
subjective approaches: Herzberg's Two-Factor Theory, Hackman
and Oldham's Job Characteristics approach, and Staw's Expectancy Theory approach. Less emphasis will be placed here on Herzberg's model, since it received so much detail in chapter two. Following the descriptions of these three models, we will examine both
their scientific status, as well as their respective "track records" in
real world settings. The interested reader is referred to reviews by
Steers and Mowday (1977), Davis and Taylor (1979), Griffin (1982),
Hackman and Oldham (1980), or Cummings and Molloy (1977).   **241**

The Two-Factor Theory

The so-called Motivator-Hygiene (or Two-Factor) theory of work attitudes and motivation was presented and discussed in detail in chapter two. In that chapter, it was argued that the asymmetry posited by the theory to exist between the origins of job satisfaction and job dissatisfaction has made the theory very controversial, so much so that it has fallen into disrepute with many critics. But it was also argued in chapter two that it is not always necessary to totally adopt or reject a theory of work motivation in order to be influenced by it; rather, sometimes it is wise to accept certain elements of a particular theory, while reserving judgment on or rejecting other, less defensible elements. This seems to be the case for Herzberg's Motivator-Hygiene theory. Specifically, it is not necessary to accept Herzberg's notions of the independence and asymmetry of positive and negative job attitudes to accept (and benefit from) the advice provided by the theory for job design.

Herzberg (1966) was among the first industrial psychologists to explicitly consider and write about the notion of human growth needs. Although his theory borrowed somewhat from Maslow (1943), it was not identical to Maslow's theory, and made substantial additions to it. (For example, Herzberg rejected Maslow's notions of hierarchical differences in prepotency among human needs.) The point is that Herzberg's theory argues that jobs must feature a number of characteristics in order to permit them to arouse and then satisfy growth needs. To repeat in part the discussion of chapter two, jobs should permit achievement as well as recognition for that achievement; they should be interesting to perform; they should permit feelings of growth through advancement; and they should provide feelings of responsibility for the employee executing them. In short, jobs should feature those factors Herzberg, Mausner, and Synderman (1959) came to call the *motivators*.

In summary, it is not necessary to assume that the absence or removal of these job characteristics does not result in low job attitudes. But there is some evidence that when jobs are changed so as to build in higher levels of these factors, positive consequences can accrue for both the employee and the organization (Ford, 1973; Paul, Robertson, and Herzberg, 1969). Few of Herzberg's toughest critics deny this.

The evidence to support Herzberg's job design suggestions will be presented later with the results of other job redesign strategies.

The Job Characteristics Approach

Perhaps the most popular current perspective on job design is that which has been developed by Richard Hackman, Greg Oldham, and their associates. Their approach is similar to that of Herzberg's, insofar as it proposes a set of features that should be built into jobs in order that they be satisfying and motivating, although the two approaches differ somewhat with regard to the specific characteristics of work that make it desirable. The interested reader is referred to the early work of Turner and Lawrence (1965), and Hackman and Lawler (1971), and, especially, to chapter three of Hackman and Oldham's (1980) recent book.

Elements of the theory.   According to Hackman and Oldham (1980), an employee will experience *internal motivation* (a concept very similar to that of intrinsic motivation, as was described in chapter four of this book) from his job when that job generates three *critical psychological states* in him. First, the employee must feel personal *responsibility* for the outcomes of the job (such as its levels of quantity and quality). Second, the work must be experienced as *meaningful.* That is, the employee must feel that his efforts "count" or matter somehow, to someone. The third critical psychological state in the Hackman/Oldham model is knowledge of the actual results of the person's own work efforts. In other words, an employee should be aware of how effective he is in converting his effort into performance (using VIE Theory terms from chapter seven): he should have a *knowledge of the results* of his efforts.

In short, jobs should be designed, according to Hackman and Oldham, so as to generate experiences for the employee of meaningfulness, responsibility, and a knowledge of the results of one's effort.

Notice that Herzberg's model of job design would agree completely with Hackman and Oldham's requirement for feelings of responsibility, and that Herzberg's achievement and advancement for achievement factors are consistent with Hackman and Oldham's suggestion concerning knowledge of results, insofar as knowledge of one's success is necessary for feelings of achievement to occur, while, in addition, advancement often serves as a formal recognition of positive results. Briefly then, there is some degree of consistency between the two approaches with regard to the role of responsibility and knowledge of results in the design of motivating work.

The question remains: How can jobs actually be designed to make it possible for employees to experience these three critical psychological states?

Generating experienced meaningfulness.   For Hackman and Oldham, three specific *core factors* of jobs are particularly important for making work feel meaningful. The first factor is referred to as *skill variety,* which is defined as:

243

The degree to which a job requires a variety of different activities in carrying out the work, involving the use of a number of different skills and talents of the person (Hackman and Oldham, 1980, p. 78).

The need for competence (White, 1959) expresses itself, in part, by behaviors that involve exploring and investigating the environment, as was explained in chapter four. One aspect of this searching and exploring entails the use and development of the person's various skills and abilities. Accordingly, Hackman and Oldham propose that jobs which require the use of multiple talents are experienced as more meaningful, and therefore more intrinsically motivating, than jobs that require the use of only one or two types of skills. Notice too, that the exercise of numerous skills would likely result in the stimulation of a greater number of the employee's senses, thereby resulting in higher overall levels of activation and arousal. (See Schwab and Cummings, 1976 for a discussion of the issue of the stimulation of multiple sensory modalities when designing jobs.)

Hence, the inclusion of task variety as an element of job design is consistent with the concept of growth need satisfaction, as well as with the more physiological approach taken by activation theory. It is *not* consistent, however, with Herzberg's approach, which refers to the simple addition of tasks as *horizontal job loading* or as *job enlargement* (as opposed to job enrichment). This difference between the Hackman/Oldham approach and that of Herzberg is crucial because, as will become evident in the following sections, the addition of varied tasks to a job can be one practical means of generating some of the other key features prescribed by both theories.

A second job characteristic that is seen as contributing to experienced meaningfulness is referred to as *task identity,* which is defined as:

The degree to which a job requires completion of a ''whole'' and identifiable piece of work . . . doing a job from beginning to end with a visible outcome (1980, p.78).

In recent years the popular press has paid considerable attention to the worker *alienation* that results from repetitious jobs in which employees perform the same simple operations hundreds or thousands of times every day, with only a minimal understanding of how the work they do relates to ''the bigger picture.'' For example, auto assembly workers who install the same three or four parts to the hundreds of partially constructed cars that pass their work stations every month have little understanding of how those few parts fit in with the effective functioning of the completed vehicle.

Work is experienced as more meaningful, according to Hackman and Oldham, when employees are capable of gaining a greater

244   understanding of how their jobs fit in with those of other employees, and with the completion of an integral unit of product or service. So, for example, the famous curvilinear assembly lines used in Scandinavian auto assembly plants are designed, in part, to permit employees to participate in much larger subsections of finished automobiles, than is possible in conventional straightline assembly plants in North America (Gyllenhammar, 1977).

How does the notion of task identity fit with the other viewpoints presented here? On the surface, providing task identity, per se, does not seem particularly relevant for the satisfaction of the major growth needs we have examined. On the other hand, insofar as stimulus complexity and meaningfulness determine the stimulating capacity of objects and events (Fiske and Maddi, 1961; Scott, 1966), a job with task identity should be more stimulating from the point of view of activation theory. Finally, Herzberg's approach would probably admit that task identity contributes to the motivator factor referred to as interesting work.

The third factor that makes work more meaningful is referred to as *task significance,* defined as:

> The degree to which the job has a substantial impact on the lives of other people, whether those people are in the immediate organization or in the world at large (1980, p. 79).

Thus, for example, munitions employees during World War II worked long, hard hours in miserable production plants, maintaining high levels of motivation and morale because of the important contribution they knew they were making to the war effort (Turner and Miclette, 1962).

The task significance component of Hackman and Oldham's *experienced meaningfulness* concept is harder to relate to other job design approaches than are the skill variety and task identity components, with the possible exception that performing work perceived as significant might contribute to the satisfaction of esteem needs (both the need for the esteem of others, as well as for a positive regard of one's self).

In short, Hackman and Oldham's (1980) theory suggests that experienced meaningfulness is important for a job to arouse intrinsic motivation and that it, in turn, requires that the work be integrated, important, and demanding of the use of multiple skills and abilities.

Generating experienced responsibility. Whereas three core job factors are seen as contributing to feelings of meaningfulness, only one factor—*autonomy*—is required for an employee to experience the psychological feelings of *responsibility*. Autonomy is defined as:

245

The degree to which the job provides substantial freedom, independence, and discretion to the individual in scheduling the work and in determining the procedures to be used in carrying it out (Hackman and Oldham, p. 79).

Autonomy and responsibility have long been recognized as important facets of employee motivation and satisfaction. They are explicitly recognized in Herzberg's two-factor theory (see chapter two), McClelland's (1961) theory of achievement, and deCharms' (1968) thinking about pawns and origins (recall chapter four of the present volume). Moreover, autonomy was treated as a separate category of higher-order need by Porter (1962, 1963) in his adaptation of Maslow's need hierarchy for studying managerial job attitudes. From the point of view of activation theory, it is reasonable to assume that people who are responsible for their own job outcomes will be more fully activated than people who share responsibility for success or failure on the job with others.

The point is that Hackman and Oldham's suggestion that autonomy (and the responsibility feelings it fosters) are motivating is quite consistent with the other perspectives and approaches to job design which we have considered here.

Generating knowledge of results. The third critical psychological factor in Hackman and Oldham's model is referred to as *knowledge of results*. They see two basic types of *feedback* as the essential determinants of the degree to which an employee understands how well he is doing on the job. The first type of feedback comes from the job itself, such as that which occurs when a worker assembles an alarm clock and tests it to see whether he has put it together properly. The second type comes from other people, such as one's superior, who informs the individual as to how well he is doing on the job. Hackman and Oldham recognize the role that both forms of feedback can have for providing knowledge of results, but stress the importance of designing jobs so that they regularly provide the former type—feedback from the job itself.

Why would we expect that feedback from the job itself would be more motivating than that which is mediated by other people, such as one's supervisor? One reason is that when the feedback comes from the person's own observation of how well she is doing, it often comes *immediately* after the employee has done the work. Secondly, this form of feedback is not as susceptible to the interference that can result from a variety of social-psychological processes (such as those that have to do with the perceived credibility of the source of the message, or the relative power of the sender of the message), as compared to that of the employee who receives it. In short, feedback from the task itself is simple, direct, and impersonal, and seems to be

a more powerful means of providing motivating information than is

— Person - for fit

FIGURE 11–1: The Job Characteristics Theory

Parameters

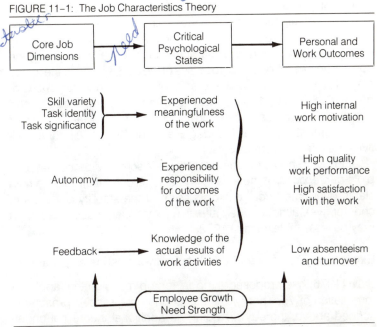

feedback from outside sources (Ilgen, Fisher, and Taylor 1979; Ivancevich and McMahon, 1982).

The importance of feedback for intrinsic motivation is explicitly recognized in Deci's Cognitive Evaluation Theory (recall chapter four), in which it was seen as critical for either enhancing or reducing the person's feelings of competence and, subsequently, the person's level of intrinsic motivation or, alternatively, affecting the person's locus of causality and subsequent intrinsic motivation. Likewise, a strong desire for task-related feedback is one of the most important traits displayed by males who are high in achievement motivation (McClelland, 1961). Feedback can clearly affect a person's level of self-esteem as well, depending upon whether it is favorable or unfavorable. Finally, from the perspective of activation theory, feedback from a task may, itself, contribute to both the complexity and novelty of that task for the individual.

A full summary of the critical psychological states, as well as the major core factors seen as producing them, is provided above in Figure 11-1.

Measuring the dimensions. Hackman and Oldham have developed an instrument called the *Job Diagnostic Survey* (JDS) which is used, among other things, to assess what they refer to as the overall *motivating potential score* for any particular job. Perceptions of the job incumbent are used to calculate the amount of skill variety, **247**

task identity, task significance, autonomy, and feedback found in a job. When combined, scores on these dimensions enable a job analyst to assess the degree to which a job may be capable of arousing intrinsic motivation for particular individuals. Detail concerning the content and psychometric properties of the JDS is beyond the scope of this book. The interested reader is referred to Hackman and Oldham (1975, 1976, 1980), and Hackman, Oldham, Janson, and Purdy (1975) for greater detail on the development of the theory and the instrument, as well as to Aldag, Barr, and Brief (1981) for a positive assessment of the JDS itself.

Finally, it should be noted that there is some evidence that people's *perceptions* of these task characteristics of their jobs remain stable over time (recall our discussion of the stability of beliefs in chapter five), although their affective (emotional) reactions to them may be less stable (Griffin, 1982).

Expectancy Theory and the Job Characteristics Approach

Staw (1976) has proposed a model for job redesign that applies a formulation of VIE Theory to the Job Characteristics Approach described above, thereby providing an additional theoretical understanding of why certain features of jobs may arouse intrinsic motivation. The form of VIE Theory Staw adopts, is that which was previously proposed by House (1971) and House, Shapiro, and Wahba (1974). (The reader is referred to chapter seven of this book for a detailed treatment of VIE Theory, in its more basic forms.)

In essence, this model explicitly recognizes the fact that overall work motivation can be determined by both intrinsic and extrinsic factors (recall chapter four). More importantly, the model delineates the separate effects of two specific types of intrinsic motivation: (1) that which is associated with simply doing a job; and (2) that which is associated with effective achievement of the job. Specifically, the House et al. (1974) expectancy model can be represented as follows:

$$M = IV_a + (P_1)(IV_b) + \sum_{i=1}^{n} (P_{2i})(EV_i)$$

Where:

M = total task motivation

IV_a = intrinsic valence associated with *task behavior*

IV_b = intrinsic valence associated with *task accomplishment*

EV_i = extrinsic valences associated with outcomes for task accomplishment

248 P_1 = perceived probability that one's behavior will lead to task accomplishment

P_{2i} = perceived probabilities that one's task accomplishment will lead to extrinsically valent outcomes.

A number of features of this model deserve highlighting. First, the reader is reminded of the crucial distinction between *valence* and *importance:* it is the *expectation of the satisfaction* associated with an outcome that attracts the individual to engage in a task. Secondly, the strength of the valence associated with *task behavior* for an individual (IV_a, above), rests largely with the strength of the person's need for competence (see chapter four). In simple terms, it consists of the enjoyment people anticipate receiving from merely attempting a task, regardless of how successful they expect to be at it. The reader is reminded of Murray's (1938) belief (see chapter three) that satisfaction consists of the pleasure of the process of reducing need-related tension, in addition to the pleasure of the feeling one has once the need has been satisfied. The first component of the House, Shapiro, and Wahba model is consistent with this element of satisfaction.

On the other hand, the strength of the intrinsic valence associated with *task accomplishment* (IV_b, above), will be determined largely by the strength of the person's need for achievement. Therefore, the net force attributed to the achievement component of the model is seen as being determined by the same mechanisms described in the discussion in chapter four: overall achievement-oriented motivation is determined largely by the person's perception of the probability of task success. Tasks that are anticipated to be either too easy or too difficult arouse little achievement motivation, because the intrinsic thrill of mastering an easy goal is small, whereas difficult goals are judged to be unattainable, thereby discouraging the individual from attempting them. In short, the achievement-related component of the Staw/House et al. model requires that the anticipated probability of success and the anticipated thrill from succeeding both be considered. Moreover, because of the inverse relationship between perceived probability of task success and this form of valence, the net motivational force associated with achievement outcomes will be maximized when the person perceives the odds of success as moderate.

The last component of the model refers to the same sort of instrumentality x valence combinations for extrinsic outcomes as were described in the treatment of VIE Theory given in chapter seven. But our purpose here is to focus on the intrinsic elements of the model and how they are relevant to the design of jobs. Accordingly, no more will be said here about the extrinsic aspects.

Independence of the intrinsic components. As presented, the model implicitly assumes that the two forms of intrinsic **249**

FIGURE 11-2: Expectancy Theory Approach to Intrinsic Motivation

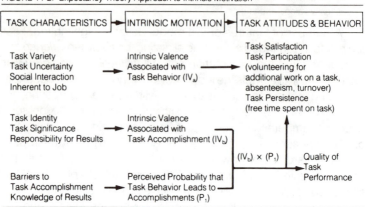

motivation are independent of one another. So, for example, it suggests that a person could continue to expect to derive pleasure from engaging in a task, even if he constantly fails at the task. Hall's theory of career success experiences (Hall, 1976) and the impact they can have on feelings of competence and self-esteem suggests that this may not in fact be the case (also see Bandura, 1982). Instead, Hall suggests, repeated success experiences at a task may, to a certain limit, serve to increase a person's attraction toward the task, whereas continual failures eventually reduce the individual's affinity for it. Nevertheless, Staw's adaptation of House, Shapiro, and Wahba's (1974) expectancy theory to job design provides a theoretical rationale for a number of prescriptions for the design of work. These are summarized in Figure 11-2.

Design implications from the expectancy model. Figure 11-2 suggests that overall task motivation can be influenced if a job is designed so as to affect the intrinsic valence of doing it, the intrinsic valence associated with succeeding at it, and the person's perceptions of her chances of succeeding. Specifically, the figure suggests that jobs which feature a variety of different tasks, jobs that are not overly routine, and jobs that require the employee to interact a great deal with others will, ceteris paribus, have a greater likelihood of appealing to employee needs for competence: that is, they will foster relatively high levels of the intrinsic valence associated with doing the task. In other terms, such tasks will tend to be comparatively enjoyable, and satisfaction will result from the very act of doing them and reducing the tension associated with the need for competence.

Figure 11-2 also suggests that the valence associated with success at a job will be comparatively high when the person sees it as comparatively high in Hackman and Oldham's (1980) *task identity* and *task significance* dimensions, and when the person expects that he will be largely responsible for his success or failure at the job. In other words, an individual will expect a greater thrill from accomplishing a job goal when he believes that his efforts (as opposed to luck or the efforts of other people) determine success or failure, and when he is able to see how his accomplishments fit into "the greater picture," and that they are of value to the organization or to someone associated with it.

Intuitively, this argument makes sense. But recall that net achievement-oriented motivation also depends heavily on the person's judgments about whether he will be able to perform the task (as discussed above, as well as in chapter four). Figure 11-2 illustrates that a host of factors in the job itself, or in the context of the job, can serve to influence the employee's views about his likely ability to perform it. The interactive nature of the valence associated with achievement (IV_b) and the perceived probability of achievement (P_1) in determining the individual's overall achievement-oriented motivation is reflected in Figure 11-2.

PART TWO: INDIVIDUAL DIFFERENCES IN REACTION TO JOB ENRICHMENT

In this chapter it has been argued so far that a major purpose of job design strategies such as job enrichment, is to structure work activities so as to make them intrinsically motivating and satisfying. As discussed in chapter four, however, we know that people differ considerably in terms of the strength of their growth needs—the basic needs that, when aroused, account for what is called intrinsic motivation. In addition, an earlier section of the present chapter discussed the complexity of the difference, both between people, as well as within individuals, in terms of the levels of stimulation they desire from their environments (including their jobs). To the extent, therefore, that individual differences exist in the strength of the needs and preferences people have for the outcomes job enrichment can provide, it should follow that enriched jobs will be more attractive to (and more highly motivating for) some people than others. In other words, we would logically expect considerable individual differences between people in their attitudinal and behavioral reactions to so-called *enriched* work. In fact, many of the theories of job design available today explicitly recognize the fact that many people view their jobs as secondary sources of need satisfaction, and simply do not desire to work in jobs that feature high levels of challenge and responsibility. **251**

Job enrichment is not for everyone. Let's take a brief look at the role attributed to individual differences in the theories discussed above.

Herzberg has often been criticized for ignoring the role of individual differences in the motivation styles people display, although later statements of his theory readily acknowledge that certain people are *abnormally* preoccupied with the satisfaction of hygiene needs, for various reasons (see Herzberg, 1976, chapter two).

Likewise, the early research of Turner and Lawrence (1965) on the motivational characteristics of jobs suggested that employees from rural backgrounds respond much more positively and favorably to job enrichment than employees with urban backgrounds do.

The work of Hackman and Lawler (1971) followed directly from that of Turner and Lawrence, although Hackman and Lawler (1971) attempted to measure the strength of the growth needs of each of the *individuals* in their study, reasoning that a more precise prediction of the effects of job enrichment could be gained by considering individual need states, rather than a person's general sociological/geographic background. Their reasoning made logical sense, and their empirical results provided support. There were higher correlations between the existence of enriched job characteristics and outcomes such as intrinsic motivation, job satisfaction, and attendance among employees with high growth need strength than among employees who were low in growth needs. Later studies by Wanous (1974), Brief and Aldag (1975), and Giles (1977) added further support to Hackman and Lawler's conclusions, and the current theory of job design forwarded by Hackman and Oldham (as described earlier in this chapter) includes provisions for assessing the strength of employee needs for growth before implementing changes to their jobs (Hackman and Oldham, 1980, p. 118).

But, as often is the case, the matter is not so simple. A review of the evidence by White (1978a) concluded that the majority of studies in which employee responses to job design were found to depend upon employee traits, of some form or another, failed to hold up in replication studies. That is to say, sometimes a particular variable (such as the strength of employee growth needs) determined the effect of job characteristics on work outcomes, but sometimes those same variables failed to make any difference. White (1978a) concluded that individual difference factors that influence the impact of worker responses to job characteristics are situation specific. In other words, certain variables may be important in some situations, whereas other variables may be important in other situations, where jobs are designed to be enriched. A separate review of the evidence by Pierce and Dunham (1976) reached essentially the same conclusion. White added strength to his argument by showing in a vast study of his own (White, 1978b) that not one of seventy-three different individual variables he investigated consistently affected the impact of job characteristics on employee responses! A disappointing state of affairs, to say the least.

Other researchers, such as Dunham (1977), and Sims and Szilagyi (1976), have attempted to show that *organizational* factors (as opposed to individual factors) may determine whether job enrichment has positive consequences for employees. But still, the results are very inconsistent and inconclusive. It may be that the most accurate and most practical way of predicting whether job enrichment will have positive benefit for a particular individual, is simply to ask the person, as Cherrington and England (1980) did in a recent study, how much he desires enriched work, rather than relying on less direct predictors such as work values or need states.

In conclusion, there is abundant evidence that not everybody desires to work at jobs that feature the enriching characteristics proposed by the theories described in this chapter. But it is still very difficult to predict which categories of people will, or will not, benefit from and enjoy job enrichment. Surrogate measures such as assessments of individual needs and personality traits are unreliable predictors, although simply asking the people involved, directly, about their desire for job enrichment may be useful. Readers interested in greater detail concerning this issue are referred to a thorough review by Cummings (1982).

PART THREE: PRACTICAL ISSUES IN JOB ENRICHMENT

Now that a number of theoretical approaches to job redesign have been discussed, there are a variety of practical issues that deserve attention—issues that are important for understanding how job enrichment might be employed in real settings, as well as for explaining some of the successes and failures job enrichment has encountered in the field.

This part of the chapter consists of two sections. The first section provides a few practical clues for identifying specific work settings that might benefit from formal job enrichment. The second section of the chapter will examine a number of practical constraints that can make the implementation of enrichment difficult, and which can even be responsible for its failure in settings where they are not appropriately dealt with.

WHERE MIGHT ENRICHMENT BE APPROPRIATE?

Drake (1974) has identified a number of preliminary clues that might help identify situations in which job enrichment *may* be of value. When found, these indicators do not necessarily imply that **253** jobs should (or can) be enriched, but they are intended to suggest that some consideration of enrichment may be warranted.

1. *Repetition of the same functions.* If an operation is performed at one point in a work flow, and then repeated by someone else later in the same flow, *it may be* that the two jobs involved are not sufficiently different to justify their separation into two jobs. Perhaps the jobs can be combined into a single job that features more stimulation, variety, meaningfulness, and feedback than is possible in either of the separate jobs.

2. *Unusual reporting relationships.* People whose jobs require them to report to more than one supervisor will encounter role conflict (see chapter twelve), and probably not enjoy as much autonomy as they might otherwise experience from their jobs. On the other hand, a high frequency of one-to-one reporting relationships may suggest that many employees are expected to perform the menial and unmotivating tasks that are neglected or discarded from the jobs of their superiors.

3. *Layering.* Some organizations feature multiple levels of authority among jobs in which the work performed is basically identical. For example, allowing low level employees to provide refunds to customers up to a certain maximum amount, and requiring successively higher amounts to be passed upwards in the organization's structure, limits the potential for employee feelings of responsibility, autonomy, and to a lesser extent, knowledge of results. Similar sounding job titles such as *Junior File Clerk, Intermediate File Clerk, File Clerk,* and *Senior File Clerk,* may signal the existence of layered functions that might be rearranged for the sake of job enrichment.

4. *"Super-gurus" and "trouble shooters."* The smooth functioning of many work settings often relies heavily on the existence of a small number of "gurus," who seem to know virtually everything about the company, its customers and suppliers, and all other aspects of the operation. Such people are, of course, very important and usually very powerful as a consequence of their wisdom. Moreover, they are often quite jealous about their roles and unwilling to share their knowledge. But their monopoly often robs other employees of responsibility, meaningfulness, and autonomy in the work they perform, while leaving the organization as a whole vulnerable to their departure.

5. *Special checking or inspection jobs* may not be necessary. Permitting employees to check the quality of their own work adds potential task meaningfulness, autonomy, and knowledge of results to their jobs.

6. *Excessive number of job titles.* Drake (1974) suggests that if the ratio of people to job titles in a work setting is not at least 5:1, it may be the case that the work is too fractionated, and that enrichment may be appropriate.

7. *Pools.* Drake (1974) also suggests that the existence of pools of people performing similar work such as typing, keypunching, or word processing is a signal that certain people in the organization are casting off the routine (and boring) parts of their jobs onto other people. On the other hand, operators in such a pool may receive more variety and task identity than do operators who work for only one or a few individuals.

8. *Liaison personnel.* Highly differentiated organizations often require special individuals to coordinate and integrate activities that involve more than one group (Lawrence and Lorsch, 1969). Whereas entrusting such special functions to particular individuals may facilitate integration, it may also impoverish the motivational potential of those jobs being integrated, depriving them of task significance, task identity, and skill variety.

254

9. *The existence of several jobs requiring the same equipment* suggests that the work being done on these jobs is too highly specialized and fractionated. Is it possible that a single job (with many incumbents) might be created that combines all the tasks that were previously assigned to many different jobs, thereby providing potential for higher levels of skill variety and task identity?

It is interesting to note that information concerning most of these clues can be gathered from documents such as union contracts, personnel manuals, organization charts, and organizational folklore.

To summarize, there are a variety of characteristics of organizational structure that may suggest places in which jobs might benefit from enrichment and/or restructuring. After noting such clues, the interested manager would have to proceed to investigate more thoroughly the potential for and feasibility of job redesign. Some aspects of this feasibility assessment are the topic of the next section.

Implementing Job Enrichment

As two of the leading proponents and developers of the theory and practice of job enrichment, Oldham and Hackman (1980) have recently recognized that taking this theory and putting it into effective practice can be very difficult, because of the constraints that are often encountered in real organizational settings (as opposed, say, to artificial research settings). Changes in job design cannot usually be implemented without changes in (or at least accommodation to) other elements of the organization and its various programs and procedures. In fact, many early failures of job redesign programs can doubtlessly be blamed on failures to recognize these other organizational considerations.

Obstacles in Implementation

What, then, should be attended to in addition to the diagnosis of jobs and people for the sake of successfully installing job enrichment? Oldham and Hackman (1980) have identified a number of constraints to the effective installation of such programs, including the following:

1. *The technological system* (that is, the basic nature of the production or work process). The assembly line is a classic example of a technology that drastically curtails the degree to which jobs can feasibly be enriched. Any type of work process that depends heavily on the use of particular machinery will typically be very expensive to modify—perhaps prohibitively so (cf. Anderson, 1970).
2. *Personnel systems,* such as job analysis and the development of more or less rigid job descriptions, which are often enshrined in labor-management collective agreements, can limit the feasibility of job enrichment. Enriching jobs means changing jobs, and seldom only one or two at a time. Tradition, bu-

reaucratization, and formal agreements such as those just mentioned, can make this sort of change very difficult.

3. *Control systems* (such as budgetary and accounting systems or production and quality control reporting systems) can also impede job redesign efforts, because by nature, they are often designed to limit individual discretion, autonomy, and flexibility. Groups that traditionally have been responsible for these control functions are often quite resistant to giving them up.

4. *Training programs* must be available that can permit whatever levels of effort are induced by the enriched work, to result in useful performance. Otherwise, the motivated effort created by the work will be frustrated and result in the types of frustration responses we examined in chapters four and five, undermining the acceptability of enrichment among those who must implement it.

5. *Career development practices* must also be appropriate. For example, we noted in the last section that job enrichment may not be appropriate for all employees; some people neither want, nor are capable of handling, the challenge and responsibility enrichment entails. Without career development strategies (such as transfers or reassignments) to accommodate or effectively deal with employees unsuited for job enrichment, frustration, job dissatisfaction, and resentment can be expected, and one can anticipate limited benefit from job enrichment programs.

6. *The levels of pay and the methods of payment* are also important. Equity Theory (see chapter six) would predict that increased levels of pay would be expected by employees who perceive the increases in responsibility that result from enrichment to constitute additional *inputs* they must make to their jobs. Alternatively, employees who perceive enrichment as resulting in greater satisfaction (or in greater outcomes), may not make such pay demands. One practitioner with considerable experience in job enrichment has suggested that if the redesign of jobs is done properly, employees do not necessarily demand more money for the responsibility added to their positions. In fact, he notes that most job evaluation programs in organizations are designed to easily deal with the added levels of responsibility and skill levels that can result from enrichment, should the issues be raised (Caulkins, 1974). Nevertheless, there has been very little research directed toward the issue of pay *level* implications of job enrichment, although there is some theoretical basis to worry that the *form* of payment is important. Recall from chapter four that Deci's (1975) Cognitive Evaluation Theory suggests that contingently paid money (as in piece-rate pay plans) may undermine intrinsic motivation—the very goal sought by enrichment programs. Finally, whether the pay is distributed on an individual, group, or organization wide basis, must be compatible with the means by which the work is accomplished (i.e., by individuals, groups, or by overall organizational performance).

Other authors, such as Sirota and Wolfson (1972), have noted different obstacles to the installation and success of job enrichment. While these other factors are a bit more subtle than those noted by Oldham and Hackman, they are no less critical. For example, it is often very difficult to overcome the long-standing biases and beliefs held by many managers concerning the virtues of job design according to the classical principles of previous times (cf. Massie,

1965). But even when traditional beliefs are successfully challenged in principle, it is still necessary to educate managers in the theory and techniques of job enrichment, so that they can provide the types and amounts of support that are necessary for success.

Additionally, managers who consider job enrichment for their organizations often expect to see real returns on the financial investments involved in unrealistically short periods of time. Demanding evidence of return on investment is fine, but the payoffs that are possible (although not guaranteed) from enrichment interventions seldom appear immediately. Moreover, an honest "sales job" by someone proposing that an organization venture into job enrichment cannot *promise* meaningful return on investment—whether it be in the long or short run. Such promises simply are not founded, especially now after so many attempts have been observed to fail. It is no wonder that many mangers who are concerned with costs and profitability are skeptical about allowing enrichment changes in their organizations. To make matters worse, unless top management is at least somewhat enthusiastic, any new enrichment attempt is bound to fail—a sort of self-fulfilling prophecy of disaster.

Another barrier to effective installation of job enrichment can be a generalized fear of the unknown among those who will be affected most heavily—especially middle managers, who often expect that such programs will undermine their authority and possibly make them redundant. ("If I give away all my power to my subordinates, what need will there be for *me* in this organization?") There is also a natural tendency on the part of many managers to accept the idea of enrichment in abstract terms, but to deny that it might be feasible, or even necessary, in their own organizations.

Sirota and Wolfson (1972) also note the tendency among many job enrichment specialists to be dogmatic in the techniques they use, either to diagnose or to install enrichment strategies. There are many cases where the particular problems facing an organization require eclecticism on the part of the interventionist (Sandler, 1974), yet successful applications brought about by one method, naturally tend to encourage the continued use of that same method.

Unions and job enrichment. There is at least one other set of factors that can influence the effective installation of job redesign: labor unions and the collective bargaining process. While the majority of formal job enrichment programs have been conducted in nonunion settings or among only the nonunion personnel in organizations where unions are represented (Schlesinger and Walton, 1976), there have been a number of instances where formal enrichment has been attempted in the midst of unionized settings. It would be an oversimplification to say that labor unions have a typical or unitary attitude about such programs (Donahue, 1982), but there are a number of issues that normally must be dealt with when a union is involved.

First, it is often the case that union leaders are wary about job enrichment (and other formal programs aimed at improving the quality of work life). This wariness comes from the concern that their own positions may be undermined. That is, to the extent that the enrichment design entails greater responsibility and autonomy for dealing with job-related problems, union stewards may fear that their traditional role as representatives of the rank and file may be diminished. A second common concern for labor officials is that the union membership may perceive any joint union-management cooperation over the planning and installation of enrichment with suspicion that they are "in bed" with management.

Unions are often suspicious that programs such as job enrichment are simply newfangled methods of "speed-up" designed primarily to extract higher levels of productivity per man-hour of labor. Often, this sort of suspicion has been well-founded. Unions may accept managerial prerogatives to redesign work, so as to make more efficient use of capital equipment and other resources, but rarely agree to programs they perceive as designed primarily to increase productivity through exploitation of their membership (Schlesinger and Walton, 1976).

But perhaps the biggest difficulty in successfully installing programs such as job enrichment in unionized settings is the fact that by its very nature (in North America, at least), the labor-management relationship is adversarial rather than cooperative—hardly the sort of relationship to foster collaboration and joint decision making (Ephlin, 1973).

In summary, it is commonplace to argue that organizations are systems, and that change in certain of their parts necessitates changes in other parts (e.g., Katz and Kahn, 1978). Oldham and Hackman (1980), and Sirota and Wolfson, (1972) have provided specific illustrations of the meaning of this concept: job enrichment cannot effectively be implemented without regard for various subsystems in the organization's structure, policies, and practices. Pursuant to the discussion presented in chapter two, it is unfortunately the case that the precise nature of the interdependencies among new managerial techniques (such as job enrichment) and other organizational considerations, are not appreciated until a significant number of costly and disappointing failures are experienced. This raises the question of the validity of the theory (or theories) of job enrichment, and of their "track records" in applied organizational settings.

PART FOUR: THE VALIDITY AND UTILITY
OF JOB ENRICHMENT

In chapter two, the twin issues of validity and applied utility were introduced as they relate to theories and techniques from behavioral science. Apropos that discussion, we can now ask about the scientific validity and applied utility of the predominant approaches to job enrichment. Just how good are they?

The Validity of Job Enrichment Theory

Sadly, there is no *simple* answer to this question, although there are a variety of answers pertaining to the different approaches that are available. First, the author is not aware of any empirical tests or applied applications of the Staw/House, Shapiro and Wahba model presented above, although there are myriad tests of various expectancy theories, if not the precise one underlying Staw's model. The reader is referred to chapter seven for a summary of the evidence concerning Expectancy (or VIE) Theory.

Likewise, there are no specific empirical tests of the activation/arousal theory approach to job design, per se, with the possible exception of a study reported by Standing (1973), who found that steel mill inspectors who were particularly high or low on a measure of cognitive complexity (which may be a surrogate measure for preferred activation levels), were more satisfied with various aspects of their jobs than were inspectors (performing virtually the same job as the others) who attained moderate scores on the cognitive complexity scale. More direct tests of Scott's theory have not been conducted, in large measure because of the obvious difficulties involved in operationalizing it.

The bulk of the research and applied evidence, therefore, pertains to Herzberg's approach and the job characteristics model of Hackman, Oldham, and their colleagues. A complete study-by-study review of the evidence is beyond the scope of this chapter, but a brief summary of the evidence is appropriate here. The interested reader is referred to the following sources for more detail: Davis and Taylor, 1979; Hackman, 1977; Hackman and Oldham, 1980; Luthans and Reif, 1974; Fein, 1974; Yorks, 1979; Cummings, Molloy, and Glen, 1977; and Gyllenhammar, 1977.

Until the mid-1970s, the majority of the job enrichment programs attempted in North America were based on Herzberg's Motivator-Hygiene Theory, or on some variant of the so-called sociotechnical approach of Davis and his colleagues (see Davis and Taylor, 1979; Kelly, 1978). The early literature reporting these projects was generally quite positive and encouraging (e.g., Ford, 1973; Paul, Robertson, and Herzberg, 1969), although it is probable that **259** most of the failures and disappointments were less likely to be reported. Nevertheless, Herzberg-inspired job enrichment programs have enjoyed a reasonable track record, in spite of the limited and/or unknown validity of the theory behind them (recall chapter two). As has been stressed earlier, the concept of asymmetry between what Herzberg calls motivators and hygiene factors is less important for the practical purposes of job redesign than the fact that jobs which feature the so-called motivators seem to result in more favorable consequences than those which do not.

Since the mid-1970s, new theories, such as the Job Characteristics Approach described above, have emerged and have influenced organizational development via job enrichment. How valid is the Job Characteristics Approach? As has been the case so many times in this book, the best answer to this question is that the scientific validity of this theoretical model is unknown, in spite of the considerable amount of research that lies behind it.

The reason for this conclusion is that much of the research that generated and sought to test the validity of the Job Characteristics Approach has been flawed by problems in design and execution (Arnold and House, 1980; Roberts and Glick, 1981). For example, the theory holds that *changing* jobs so as to build in higher levels of the core factors (task identity, skill variety, and so on), will result in *increases* in intrinsic motivation and job satisfaction, and *reductions* in employee withdrawal behaviors, such as absenteeism. Yet the majority of the research pertaining to the theory has not, in fact, shown that changes in job design at one point in time result in changes of the sort predicted at a later point in time. Instead, most of the studies have been synchronous, or cross-sectional, meaning that measures of job characteristics have been gathered and correlated with measures of employee reactions that were gathered at the same point in time. Thus, while the evidence based on data of this sort have revealed encouraging simultaneous associations between the strength of the core factors on the one hand, and favorable employee reactions on the other, it cannot, by itself, support the type of *causal* claims made by the theory. (The reader will recall from chapter seven that a similar problem has characterized much of the research associated with VIE Theory.) In addition, the research has featured a number of other shortcomings which, collectively, reduce the conclusiveness of the findings and leave uncertainty about the actual validity of the Job Characteristics Approach. Nevertheless, theories often gain popularity, even hegemony, in spite of weaknesses in the research on which they are based (Bourgeois and Pinder, 1984) and it is important to remember that failure to unequivocally support a theory of this sort does not necessarily imply it is

260

wrong. Hackman, Oldham, and their colleagues have made a contribution, and time and further research will reveal how valuable that contribution is.

Benefits of Job Enrichment

It was stated earlier that the most important goal of job enrichment was to increase and sustain intrinsic motivation among employees. Presumably, higher levels of intrinsic motivation will be accompanied by higher levels of performance and job satisfaction, as well as reduced levels of withdrawal, such as absenteeism and turnover. What is the evidence in this regard? Does job enrichment deliver the sorts of things it was hoped it might deliver?

With some exceptions, the research which might have provided an answer to this question has not been as well conducted as one might have hoped (as was mentioned above). It is very difficult to establish sufficient experimental control in real organizational settings to permit either a researcher or a manager to rule out all possible explanations for observed changes in employee behavior when an experiment has been attempted. Moreover, as was suggested earlier, there is more chance that we will see and hear about the supposed successes, than we will about applications of job enrichment that have failed. These considerations aside, what evidence there is on the matter, suggests that *job enrichment is probably much more useful for influencing employee attitudes than it is for improving performance levels* (e.g., Orpen, 1979). Thus, enriched work may contribute to organizational effectiveness indirectly through the impact it has on the consequences of healthy work attitudes much more than directly through increases on employee productivity, *per se* (Dowling, 1973a).

Although research into the matter has tended to be of questionable quality (Griffin, Welsh, and Moorhead, 1981), it seems that positive changes in work attitudes are not usually accompanied by increases in productivity as a consequence of job enrichment. There may be a number of reasons for this, but there are two that seem most plausible.

First, the reader is reminded of the tenuous relationship that exists between beliefs, attitudes, intentions, and behaviors (see chapter five). Changing jobs so as to change employee perceptions of task characteristics (as is proposed by Herzberg, Staw, and Hackman and Oldham) can be expected to have only a very indirect impact on employee effort levels, because beliefs must be positively evaluated and then converted into specific intentions to act. As we saw in chapter five, some beliefs about particular stimulus objects **261** will be positive, while others are negative for a given individual. In the case of job redesign attempts, this means that employees may perceive many things about *enriched* jobs, some of which seem desirable, others of which may seem aversive. Presumably, here is where it was hoped that individual differences in growth need strength would be important: people high in these needs were assumed to assess their beliefs about enriched jobs favorably. But models such as that of Hackman and Oldham (1980) fail to take into account the possibility that employees will hold beliefs about enriched jobs other than those pertaining only to their capacity to satisfy growth needs. As a result, it may be that not all beliefs that are generated by enriched work are positively evaluated. Consequently, there is a diminished likelihood that net perceptions of enriched work will lead to the types of intentions that are necessary to instigate the sort of behavior that is required for higher levels of performance. In short, any model that tries to build predictive bridges between employee *beliefs,* on the one hand, and employee *behaviors,* on the other, overlooks the important intermediary roles of attitudes and intentions, (Fishbein and Ajzen, 1975) and will result in only limited predictive effectiveness accordingly.

A second reason why enrichment may not easily result in increases in job performance has to do with the fact that many factors can operate to dampen the conversion of employee effort (even if it *is* increased by enrichment) into performance. A number of the specific impediments that can interfere with enrichment programs have already been discussed in this chapter. In addition to them, there are the myriad other organizational factors that can absorb some of the impact of motivated effort on performance levels, as we will see in chapter twelve.

In conclusion, one can argue that increased job satisfaction and possibly reduced levels of withdrawal may be the major benefits that are potentially attainable from enrichment efforts; and that these positive benefits seem attainable without any accompanying cost in productivity to management (e.g., Dowling, 1973a). Accordingly, one might argue that job enrichment is a desirable strategy for management to adopt. But there is too little solid evidence to claim that enrichment results in higher levels of effort or job performance, per se.

Criticisms of Job Enrichment

In the previous section it was argued that a healthy skepticism must accompany any assessment of the success of job enrichment, because of the difficulties that researchers and managers naturally encounter when trying to gain the sort of rigorous experimental control that is necessary in order to demonstrate that observed changes in employee attitudes and behavior can be attributed to enrichment attempts.

In addition to this set of criticisms, however, there have been a number of others aimed at job enrichment in general, based on a variety of other considerations of a nonscientific nature. One of these has to do with the problem of individual differences, as we have discussed them earlier in this chapter. Briefly, the argument from this quarter is that job enrichment is not for everyone: some workers would much prefer increases in pay, job security, and working conditions (Fein, 1974), or social interaction (Reif and Luthans, 1972) from their jobs, rather than the more amorphous things attributed to job enrichment. Further, Katz (1977, 1978, 1980) argues that some people will benefit from enrichment much more at some stages in their careers than they will at other stages. For example, newcomers to a job setting will be primarily oriented toward establishing the social ties that will assist them in becoming established and making sense of their new surroundings, while employees who have been at their jobs for long periods of time will be oriented toward pay, security, and other factors that Herzberg would refer to as satisfying hygiene needs. For Katz, only those employees who have been established in their jobs for moderate periods of time will be likely to benefit from the potential outcomes offered by enrichment.

Another criticism concerns the *application* of job enrichment, the argument being that this technique has been treated as only the last in a series of programs, distilled from behavioral science for application to management problems as a sort of panacea (Hackman, 1975; Pinder, 1977, 1978, 1982). When this occurs, management groups are prone and/or susceptible to adopting job enrichment without carefully first establishing that the problems being addressed, if any, are the sorts of problems for which the technique might be appropriate.

Finally, there are critics who suggest that job enrichment is doomed to failure as a means of really increasing the quality of working life because it, like most or all other management techniques, takes as given the very socio-economic conditions that give rise to organizational problems for human beings—the nature of the fundamental means of ownership and distribution of wealth. This radical attack (Jenkins, 1975; Nord, 1977; Nord and Durand, 1978) holds that no managerial technique will cure the ills caused by work designed according to the principles of classical management and scientific management, because they do not address the most basic cause of these ills—the fundamental assumptions made by the capitalist system itself.

263

CONCLUSIONS

In conclusion then, we can say that job enrichment has been one of the most popular and most written about new applied techniques based on behavioral science. We can also conclude that the more recent scientific and managerial experience with job enrichment has not been as impressive or as encouraging as were the earlier indicators. It is clear that any hope that job enrichment would help make work universally more humane, and help make the work force more productive, simply has not been realized. But it is also clear that much of the research which has been done to develop and test new approaches to job redesign, has not been of sufficient quality to permit an accurate estimate of either the validity of the scientific theories involved or of the applied utility of the techniques that arise from those theories (Hackman, 1977). But the reader must not be too critical of either the theories or of the scientists who have attempted to develop them. As we saw in chapter two, it is extremely difficult to conduct research in real organizational settings that permits us to generate unequivocal evidence in support of the validity or utility of behavioral science ideas. As has been the suggestion in many other parts of this book, it may be that the theory (or theories) of job enrichment is, in fact, more valid and of more potential applied utility than we are presently capable of demonstrating.

SUMMARY AND ISSUES OF APPLICATION 12

Thinking is easy, acting is difficult, and to put one's thoughts into action is the most difficult thing in the world.

—Goethe

The first chapter of this book argued that work motivation is a critical issue that has important implications for the quality of life we can enjoy in Western society. Each of the subsequent ten chapters has then presented one or more perspectives on work motivation and discussed the implications of those perspectives for the management of human resources.

A number of themes have been recurrent throughout the ten foregoing chapters. One of these themes is that virtually all of our knowledge of work motivation consists of theory, and that, in turn, each of these theories is more or less well grounded in the empirical observations of organizational scientists and/or practicing managers. Accordingly, we have examined both the quantity and the quality of the evidence concerning the validity of each theory, recognizing that the net value of the evidence available for each approach places natural limits on the degree to which we should permit it to influence our thinking about work motivation.

A second theme that has underpinned the analysis thus far is that each of the major theoretic approaches to work motivation (and the managerial techniques that derive from them) is predicated upon important assumptions concerning the fundamental nature of human beings. In chapter three, for example, we saw that scientists and philosophers have advanced a wide array of perspectives on the essence of human nature, although subsequent chapters of the book have shown that three of these viewpoints have provided the foundation for most extant formal theories of work motivation: the view that humans are wanting (or fulfilling) animals (chapters three and four); the view that they are rational/perceptual animals (chapters five through eight); and the view that humans are learning creatures (chapters nine and ten).

Each of these three fundamental sets of assumptions reveals something about human nature, as do each of the formal theories of work motivation we have discussed in this book. On the other hand, each approach offers a different variety of concepts, terminology, and applied managerial techniques to understand and assimilate, making it difficult to gain an integrated view of work motivation, and leaving the student/reader who has applied goals somewhat unclear concerning which theories and managerial techniques are most tenable and useful.

The present chapter will attempt to deal with some of these problems. Specifically, part one will briefly summarize the most important applied propositions about work motivation that seem founded on the basis of theory and research from each of the three perspectives on human nature identified above. The particular propositions to be associated with each perspective are those that seem most tenable to the author at the time of this writing: different students of the field might offer different lists, depending upon their differing evaluations of the theory and research that is presently available. Moreover, future research and theory construction will amend lists such as the one that follows, for, as was argued in chapter two, such is the nature of behavioral and social science. Nevertheless, the propositions to be listed are intended to reflect the most important applied implications of the theories associated with each of the three views of human functioning: they are intended to provide the best justified and potentially most useful of the many thoughts that derive from each perspective. Toward the end of part one of the chapter, we will address the issue of which theory of work motivation is the most correct, the most valid, or the most useful. It will be argued that while some current theories seem to enjoy more support than others, it is likely that different theories are more useful in different situations than others.

Then, in part two, we will examine an apparent paradox relating to the application of our knowledge of work motivation. In brief, the paradox is this: most of the conclusions we have reached from our theories seem relatively simple, at least in principle. On the other hand, everyday experience in most work organizations reveals that there are still wide variances in the effort expended and performance levels attained by employees, and that even enlightened managers (defined here as those who are familiar with behavioral science theory and research) often seem unable to utilize their knowledge of the principles of motivation to make our organizations more efficient and effective. In short, why aren't these apparently simple principles put to use more often than appears to be the case? To help explain this paradox, the discussion will turn to a number of important features of work organizations that can serve to limit the impact of well-intended attempts to apply the basic principles of work motivation to the management of employee performance. We will see that there are a host of practical constraints found within most work organizations—constraints which can limit the amount of control that enlightened, well-intentioned managers can have on the motivation levels of their subordinates.

To begin, let's briefly summarize the most important applied principles that derive from the three major perspectives on human nature discussed in this book, beginning with the view that human beings are wanting, fulfilling creatures.

PART ONE: SUMMARIZING THE PRINCIPLES

Humans as Needing Animals

The most important applied points that follow from the theory and research predicated on this model of human nature are the following:

1. Internal needs, some of which are innate and some of which are learned, are ultimately responsible for instigating and directing human behavior.
2. There are a variety of human needs; they operate in differing degrees of strength for different people, as well as in varying levels of strength for particular individuals at different times.
3. It is difficult to assess the strength of needs directly; they are hypothetical constructs, the existence of which can be inferred only from observing behavior.
4. Certain human needs are more powerful in instigating and directing behavior than others, although there is less than total agreement about the comparative strength of the various nonphysiological needs (which are widely viewed as the least prepotent of all).
5. Since there is no one-to-one correspondence between particular needs and particular behaviors, it is difficult to make inferences about the operation of particular needs in other people on the basis of observations of their behavior.
6. Needs that have been attended to tend to lose their capacity to arouse and direct behavior.
7. Most behavior is determined by the force of more than one need.
8. Intrinsic motivation can be defined as motivation directed at satisfying a set of what are referred to as *higher-level* needs, including needs for achievement, self-esteem, competence, and self-actualization.
9. The need for achievement is most likely to motivate behavior when the individual perceives a moderate (or "fifty-fifty") degree of chance of success at the task.
10. To varying degrees, people have a need to be treated equitably and to treat others equitably.

11. People can be expected to vary in the degree of equity they find in the same reward/punishment circumstances; equity is "in the eye of the beholder."
12. Equality of treatment, therefore, does not assure equitable treatment.
13. Frustration is the situation in which behavior that is intended to achieve certain goals for the sake of meeting a need (or needs) is blocked.
14. Some blockages are external to individuals; others result from characteristics of the people themselves.
15. There are a variety of common human reactions to frustration, including aggression, regression, denial, and goal displacement (to mention a few).
16. These various types of reaction to frustration manifest themselves in different ways in different people, often making it difficult to diagnose or recognize frustration-related behavior.

Again, other students of work motivation might quarrel with the inclusion of some of these points or with the exclusion of others. Accordingly, the reader is referred to chapter three and chapter four, —and to a lesser extent, chapters six and eleven—for more detailed discussions of the rationale behind each of these and other points of work motivation that follow from the view that humans are wanting, fulfilling creatures.

Next, let's take a similar look at the most important applied principles that follow from theory and research predicated on the assumption that people are perceptual, rational creatures.

Humans as Perceiving/Rational Animals

This fundamental assumption underlies the bodies of theory presented in chapters five, six, seven, eight, and in part, eleven. Although these three major theories (Equity, VIE, and Goal Setting) share the view that behavior results from human perceptual and cognitive processes, they often make disparate suggestions about work motivation. Consequently, only the most conclusive and well-founded principles from the cognitive theories will be presented here. What applied principles do these theories hold in common?

1. Human beings are conscious animals. They perceive their environments and process information gathered from that environment. Beliefs and attitudes formed on the basis of this information provide the ultimate causes of behavior, but intentions are the most immediate causes.
2. Accordingly, the most effective means for changing volitional behavior is to alter people's perceptions, and accordingly, their beliefs, attitudes, and—of most importance—their intentions.
3. Perceptions of equity (or inequity) are based on the individuals' perceptions of the exchange relationships they have with other individuals or organizations (such as their employers), and may be heavily influenced by the perceptions they have regarding the nature of exchange relationships others have with those same individuals or organizations.
4. Sufficiently high levels of perceived inequity will motivate attempts to restore equity.
5. Strong feelings of inequity result in withdrawal behaviors if efforts to alter the exchange relationship fail.

6. People can be expected to alter their perceptions of exchange relationships if behavior aimed at actually changing them fails, and if withdrawal is not possible.
7. As a result, absenteeism, turnover, and psychological withdrawal are commonly observed among people who feel inequitably treated.
8. People's perceptions of the difficulty of tasks that confront them determine, in part, the level of their motivation to engage in those tasks, although different theories make different suggestions about the optimal level of perceived task difficulty.
9. The degree of satisfaction expected from work-related outcomes influences the motivation to engage in a task; expected satisfaction—not actual satisfaction—is what matters.
10. The strength of the connection perceived between positively evaluated outcomes and work performance is a major determinant of work motivation, as is the strength of the connection perceived by the individual between work performance and the receipt of negatively evaluated outcomes.
11. Specific task goals result in higher levels of performance than do vague goals or instructions to "do your best."
12. Incentives influence work motivation only to the extent that they influence people's intentions to act.
13. People's perceptions of the value of work-related outcomes, their beliefs about the strength of the connection between these outcomes, and their beliefs about the likelihood of being capable of performing at a certain level determine their *intentions* to strive toward that level of performance, and as noted above, intentions are the immediate causes of behavior.

Perhaps the most important differences we observed among the three major cognitive theories pertain to the optimal levels of perceived task difficulty. The reader is referred to chapters eight and eleven for detailed discussions of this issue. Also important, at least on a theoretical level, is the issue of the optimal relationship between the level of payment (or other outcomes) people receive and their motivation to work. Equity Theory predicts that people who are overpaid while working under a piece-rate pay schedule will minimize their effort as a means of restoring equity, while VIE Theory predicts that people in such situations will work hard to maximize their overall outcomes. However, on a practical level, and on the basis of the bulk of the research, it would appear that the VIE Theory prediction on this matter is the more tenable.

Humans as Learning Creatures

The third of the three most important models of human functioning underpinning current approaches to work motivation is that provided by behaviorism, particularly as developed by B. F. Skinner and his followers. Chapters nine and ten discuss the operant conditioning approach and Organizational Behavior Modification, respectively. What are the most important and well-founded applied implications from the theory and research rooted in this perspective? **269**

1. Behavior is determined by its antecedents and its consequences.
2. Behavior that is reinforced in the context of a particular set of antecedent circumstances is more likely to be emitted on future occasions in those (and similar) circumstances.
3. Behavior that is punished in the context of a particular set of antecedent circumstances is less likely to be emitted on future occasions in those (and similar) circumstances.
4. Most behaviors occur in chains, in which the consequences of an act reinforce that act and serve as cues that make it more likely that the person will subsequently emit certain other acts, which themselves have been reinforced in the past.
5. A complete understanding of behavior requires, therefore, a knowledge of its antecedents and its consequences, as well as of the form of the behavior itself.
6. Consequences can be distributed on the basis of either interval or ratio schedules; the latter are more powerful for influencing behavior than the former.
7. Continuous reinforcement is most effective for the acquisition of new behaviors.
8. Extinction occurs most rapidly among behaviors that have been reinforced by continuous schedules.
9. Higher levels of behavior result from variable ratio schedules than from any other schedule, once a behavior has been learned.

It is important to reiterate that lists such as the three which have been offered here are, to a considerable degree, arbitrary. It is hard to reach agreement about the amount of support that should be required for a body of theory before it or any of its tenets are proclaimed ready, or appropriate for application (cf. Bobko, 1978; with Pinder, 1977, 1978). Moreover, it is hard to state the principles that derive from each perspective at equal levels of specificity. So, for example, the lower absolute number of principles listed in association with the operant conditioning approach should not be interpreted as suggesting that Organizational Behavior Modification has less to offer than other perspectives; in fact, the discussion at the end of chapter ten argues explicitly that this definitely is not the case. In a nutshell, then, the thirty-eight points listed above (in addition to whatever corollaries that derive from them) provide a reasonable set of principles that may be used by those whose job it is to manage the motivation of the human resources at their command.

WHICH THEORETICAL APPROACH IS BEST?

Now that we have identified some of the most important applied propositions regarding work motivation that derive from each of the three philosophical perspectives on human nature, it is tempting to ask: "Which perspective is best?" or, more specifically, "Which theory is the most valid, the most correct, or the most useful?" Sadly, albeit predictably, there is no simple answer to this question. Each general perspective on human nature reveals a particular aspect of it (Walter and Marks, 1981); accordingly, each formal theory of work motivation has something to say about it as well (Steers and Porter, 1979). Yet readers with applied interests still need some guidance as to when and where to allow their managerial behavior to be influenced by the different approaches to work motivation. What help is available?

A Contingency Approach

Recent theorizing in organizational science has seen the emergence of what are called *contingency theories.* The fundamental idea underlying these approaches is that different circumstances necessitate the application of different theoretic ideas and/or different managerial strategies (cf. Lawrence and Lorsch, 1969; Moore, Johns, and Pinder, 1980; Shepard and Houghland, 1978). Accordingly, Mayes (1978b) and Staw (1977) have recently proposed contingency approaches to work motivation that suggest that different theories may be of differential value in understanding and influencing employee behavior in different types of work situations. Since Mayes' (1978b) approach is more fully articulated than Staw's (1977), we will focus upon it. Although his approach does not include all of the theories of work motivation presented in this book, it does offer considerable insight into the problem at hand: when should a manager place more emphasis (or faith) upon one particular theoretic perspective, as opposed to another?

According to Mayes (1978b), it is possible to characterize behavioral environments (such as work settings) using two continuous dimensions: (1) the degree of knowledge an individual has about potential outcomes from his acts; and (2) the degree of knowledge the individual has about the nature of the causal relationships that exist, if any, among major elements of that setting (such as the people, policies, and practices in the setting).

To illustrate the first dimension, consider a situation in which an employee is unaware that it is possible to earn extra time off work and bonus pay. Alternatively, consider another employee who *is* fully aware of the potential for time off and bonus pay, his knowledge coming, say, from having experienced these outcomes personally on several occasions.

To illustrate the second dimension, consider the degree to which an employee (such as a newcomer to a work setting, for example) realizes that her behavior will, in fact, make it possible for her to accumulate time off work and earn bonuses. It may be the case that an individual doesn't realize that her acts on the job are really *instrumental* for influencing the types and levels of rewards she receives **271**

FIGURE 12–1: Mayes' Four-Way Breakdown of Behavioral Environments

	Degree of Knowledge About Potential Outcomes	
Degree of Knowledge About Causal Relationships	Outcomes Well Known	Outcomes Unknown
Causal Relationships Well Known	Quadrant One	Quadrant Two
Causal Relationships Unknown	Quadrant Three	Quadrant Four

(recall chapter seven). For Mayes, the important thing is the person's level of *awareness* of both potential outcomes and the nature of the causal connections among them, making his contingency model an example of what we have called throughout this book, a *cognitive* approach.

Mayes suggests that it is possible to cross-classify work settings (or any other behavioral environment) according to these two dimensions, as is shown in Figure 12-1. Let's take a look at the situation, as it faces an employee, in each of the quadrants that can be identified if we categorize work settings according to his two dimensions.

In quadrant one, we have an employee who is quite aware of the situation: he has knowledge of both the outcomes that are potentially available, as well as a clear understanding of the relationships among the various persons, policies, actions, and other entities that constitute his work setting. In short, a person with cognitions such as those illustrated in quadrant one is quite knowledgeable about the nature of his work environment.

Mayes (1978b) proposes that VIE Theory would be most appropriate for understanding the behavior of employees in such a setting. Why? Because the person's knowledge about both outcomes and instrumentalities would make it possible to estimate the net subjective expected utility that the person would place upon various courses of action (such as levels of work-related effort) in such a setting (recall chapter seven). For example, if the employee realizes that superior performance results in opportunities for time off and pay bonuses, and if the person places high valence upon these outcomes, we might expect him, other things being equal, to pursue those outcomes by behaving in a manner that he believes will result in high levels of performance.

Research suggests that VIE Theory will be a better predictor of behavior in situations in which a person considers only a limited number of potential outcomes than it will be in cases in which the person considers a large array of possible consequences (Leon, 1979). On the other hand, when the person does take a large number of prospective outcomes into account, Goal Setting Theory (recall chapter eight) becomes relevant, according to Mayes. Specifically, he argues that a rational individual will categorize potential outcomes into classes and relate them to specific behavioral objectives, or goals, which then direct his behavior. But what about the other quadrants in Figure 12-1?

Consider quadrant three. Here we have the situation in which the person has knowledge about the outcomes that may be attainable, but much less knowledge about the causal connections that exist in the work setting and that may make it possible for him to attain them. (This type of knowledge is part of what was referred to as *savoir faire* in chapter one.) Mayes (1978b) notes that such a situation is common among employees who move from one organization to another, similar organization. Similarly, we might expect a quadrant three situation to confront an employee who is transferred from one region to another by his employer: there are frequently a *few* differences in the nature of the work group, the organizational climate and culture, and, in general, in "the way things get done" (Louis, 1980; Pinder and Walter, 1983). The point is that a person in such a setting faces some degree of ambiguity about the workplace, although time and early exploratory behavior, along with the advice of other people, will eventually clarify the situation in most cases (Walter and Marks, 1981).

Even more ambiguity exists for employees in quadrant four: here the person has no knowledge of either outcomes or the relationships that exist among things and events in the workplace. Such a situation is common among people who are new to work in general (such as recent college grads who enter the workforce for the first time), or who are newly hired by an organization in an unfamiliar industry.

Mayes (1978b) argues that a person's behavior in highly ambiguous situations (such as in quadrants three and four) is best predicted by the nature of the individual's internalized norms or values (recall part one of chapter eight). In addition, the person's reactions to the outcomes and treatment she receives in such ambiguous situations will be predicted best by an equity formulation in which the person's standard for comparison is an internal one, rather than one based on social comparison processes. Eventually, as the person functions in the new work setting and progresses from random experimentation through to more appropriate styles of acting (Walter and Marks, 1981), we can expect that learning will occur, and that behavior will be most accurately predicted by the principles of **273** operant conditioning. Moreover, an external comparison person (or a "comparison other") may then begin to serve as the reference point for the newcomer's equity attitudes, assuming, of course, that the individual's culture includes an equity norm (Mayes, 1978b).*

In short, Mayes' contingency approach provides one insightful way of integrating and combining some, although not all, of the theories of work motivation we have considered in this book. The model does not consider the role of employee needs, as such, and does not address Herzberg's Motivator-Hygiene Theory (see chapter two). Moreover, it gives comparatively short shrift to the role of Goal Setting Theory, particularly in light of the scientific merits of that approach (recall chapter eight). But it does provide some guidance, both for the researcher who wishes to reconcile various theoretical ideas and for the practitioner, who wishes to apply modern motivation theory to the management of human resources. Moreover, it suggests a general strategy for future research and theory development, as we will see in chapter thirteen.

Recapitulation

Let's return to the question that was asked earlier: which of the various theories presented in this volume is most correct, the most valid, and/or the most useful for managing human resources? The analysis just presented has attempted to provide an answer, albeit not a simple one. The point is that each of the various models of human functioning that have been identified by philosophers and psychologists has some degree of truth, something to say about human nature. As Walter and Marks (1981) note ". . . the whole is greater than the sum of the parts" (p. 57), meaning, of course, that the individual is more than what is reflected in any (or all) of the models that have been proposed to date. Accordingly, because formal theories of motivation—including work motivation—all rest on one or another of the various models of human functioning, it follows that human behavior (and, again, including human *work* behavior) is more than what is reflected in any single theory. Rather, each of the formal theories of work motivation presented in this book has something to say about the nature and origins of human motivation in general, and about human work motivation in particular. No one approach is right; no one approach is wrong. The enlightened management of human resources, therefore, requires that practitioners be familiar with all of the various theories that are available, and be capable of understanding the comparative strengths and weaknesses of these theo-

---

*Quadrant two is excluded from the analysis because it represents a somewhat impossible situation: one in which a person is knowledgeable about the causal elements in his behavioral environment, but unaware of the outcomes that can be obtained from such causal interactions.

ries, as well as the types of circumstances within which each theory may be the most revealing and, potentially, the most beneficial. This is no easy task, but then, as noted repeatedly here and in the observation of everyday life, human beings are not simple, and when working in complex organizational settings the patterns of their work effort are anything but simple.

PART TWO: ORGANIZATIONAL REALITIES AND THE APPLICATION OF WORK MOTIVATION THEORY

At several points throughout this book, the presentation of theories and techniques of work motivation has been followed by a discussion of the applied implications they hold for the management of human resources. We have seen in many cases, however, that the principles derived from theory cannot always be implemented as easily as one might wish, because of the practical circumstances found in many (or most) work settings. The fact of the matter is that work organizations are usually far more complicated than the comparatively controlled circumstances within which theories are generally developed and refined (Boehm, 1980), so they can often make the transfer of those theories to managerial practice difficult. The discrepancy we noted in chapter eight between the high level of scientific success of Goal Setting Theory and the modest levels of success of most MBO programs is perhaps the most dramatic example of the problem: organizational scientists interested in work motivation have under-emphasized the role of the contexts within which employee motivation is generated and expended. Recent papers by Mayes (1978b), and Freedman and Montanari (1980), constitute two notable exceptions, although neither of them provides as much detail as is needed for a complete understanding of the problem.

Accordingly, the primary purpose of this part of the chapter is to examine the impact that the contexts found in most organizations can have on the application of the principles of work motivation. For the sake of structuring the discussion and providing illustrations, we will utilize the list of principles provided earlier in this chapter. However, we must first rearrange the points in the list by noting that, for the most part, each of them is primarily concerned with one of the following considerations:

1. The nature and level of difficulty of the task, especially as it is perceived by the individual employee.
2. The degree to which work-related outcomes are contingent upon job effort and/or performance.
3. The level of satisfaction an employee derives, or expects to derive, from the attainment of these work-related outcomes.

275

Before beginning our exploration of the contextual impediments to implementation, a word of caution is in order. The multiplicity, ubiquity, and apparent intractability of the contextual factors to be discussed below may generate a sense of futility on the part of the reader—a belief that the theories of work motivation currently available have no applied value. Clearly, the creation of such a belief is not intended. In fact, abundant evidence has been provided throughout this book that many current theories of work motivation (and the techniques based upon them) do offer applied value to practicing managers, and that there are many examples of the useful application of these theories and techniques. Instead, our purpose in what follows is to argue that although the principles identified at the beginning of the chapter may seem simple (even self-apparent, in some cases), there are many powerful factors that can operate against their simple adoption and application to the problem of work motivation and human productivity, the importance of these issues notwithstanding.

To begin, then, what is there about formal work organizations that can make it difficult for a manager who wishes to do so, to influence work motivation through the application of the first set of principles identified above—those concerned with designing tasks and influencing task difficulty?

INFLUENCING ACTUAL AND PERCEIVED LEVELS OF TASK DIFFICULTY

There are a variety of factors that can constrain the impact individual managers can have on the objective levels of difficulty of the jobs under their purview, as well as the difficulty levels of those jobs as perceived by their subordinates. Some of these factors are characteristics of the managers and employees involved, while others are characteristics of the organization and its task environment.

Employee Characteristics

To begin, the reader is reminded of the discussion in chapter one of this book: the level of task-related ability possessed by the individual employee is an obvious first constraint. Moreover, ability is a multifaceted construct, such that any individual may have the abilities needed to perform one type of work, but not another. In addition, ability is not a fixed commodity: people are constantly acquiring new skills and capacities, both on and off the job.

Aside from lack of ability, there are countless other characteristics of employees, some of them transitory in nature, that can interfere with effective job performance. Anxiety, depression, or other counterproductive emotional states, alcoholism or other forms of substance abuse, family disturbances, and short-run physical illness are examples (Mitchell, Green, and Wood, 1981).

The employee's basic personality may also influence the level of difficulty he tends to attribute to certain tasks. In particular, the strength of the person's self-esteem may be particularly important. Korman (1970, 1971, 1974, 1976), for example, has developed a formal theory of work behavior in which self-esteem plays a central role. For Korman (1976), the net level of a person's self-esteem in a particular situation is determined by three general factors. The first is the individual's general, persistent level of self-esteem, a level that is somewhat independent of the situations in which he finds himself. Secondly, Korman believes that people have self-perceptions about their levels of competence at particular tasks or in particular settings. This component of self-esteem, of course, varies from one setting to another for a given individual. Finally, Korman holds that a person's net self-esteem in a given situation is also partially determined by the expectations of other people: to the extent that they think we are competent, need-satisfying, and able, and to the extent that they behave toward us in ways that indicate that they hold these beliefs about us, our level of net self-esteem in a given situation is increased accordingly.

According to Korman (1976), each of these three sources of self-esteem will show a positive association with performance, other things being equal. In other words, people who are high in these various components of self-esteem are more likely to perform well in task situations. Moreover, the relationship between task-related ability and actual job performance is hypothesized to be stronger among people who are high in self-esteem than among those who are lower in self-esteem. In other words, having the ability to perform a task may not be enough; it may help a great deal if you believe that you are capable of performing that task, and this belief is influenced both by your self-esteem with regard to the task in question, as well as by your more general characteristic level of self-esteem.

Supervisory attempts to influence the work motivation of employees through manipulating tasks and perceived task difficulty levels may also be confounded by other employee characteristics, such as the person's needs for independence (cf. Porter, 1962, 1963; Kerr and Jermier, 1978), competence (White, 1959), and achievement (McClelland, 1961).

A final employee characteristic that must be noted is the level of experience and personal familiarity of the supervisor with the task in question. It is natural for a manager who has performed a task himself sometime in the past to lose sight of the probable difficulty of that task for someone who is new to it.

277

In summary, the point is this: there are a variety of temporary and long-term characteristics of both employees and their supervisors that may interfere with the degree of actual influence a manager can have on the level of difficulty of a task, as it is perceived by his employees, thereby affecting the manager's capacity to influence motivation levels through the first of the three sets of principles identified earlier.

Organizational Characteristics

There are a number of characteristics of organizations that can heavily influence the degree of control supervisors can have over the objective level of difficulty of their subordinates' tasks, and, accordingly, over the level of difficulty of those tasks in the minds and eyes of their staffs. For example, the quantity and quality of information that is made available by the organization's communication system is important: for any but the most routine of jobs, employees cannot convert their effort into job performance unless they have sufficient information to tackle their work. In addition, the quantity and quality of the tools and equipment, materials, and supplies is also important, as is the time that is made available by the organization for the task to be accomplished. The nature of the physical work environment is also important: for example, work settings without enough (or too much) light and heat can make effective work performance difficult (Peters and O'Connor, 1980).

Budgets.   One very important organizational factor is budget: not only the amount of money that is available to undertake the work, but also the means by which employees must administer their budgets. On the one hand, budgets can provide structure and guidance to the work-related efforts of a work group. On the other hand, they can also be rigid and constraining, making it difficult for the manager in charge to be flexible in ways that make it possible to deal with changing circumstances (Hopwood, 1976). In many organizations, managers are restricted in the freedom they have to reallocate resources from one budgetary "line" to another. This sort of control may be useful in stable, highly predictable circumstances, but it can drastically limit the effectiveness of managers whenever change or instability occurs (such as when a machine requires unforeseen maintenance, for example).

The point is that if a budgetary system is rigid and constraining, it can make the work of employees more difficult than it would be if more flexibility and discretion were permitted.

Technology.   If we define technology as the means by which the inputs into a work organization are transformed into outputs, including the specific means by which raw materials are actually converted into goods and services (Perrow, 1967), then we can see how the dominant technology of an organization can severely limit the impact a supervisor can have on either the real, or perceived, levels of task difficulty within his work unit.

For example, economic considerations make assembly lines mandatory in the manufacture of some commodities, and there are limited variations possible once such an assembly line has been designed, constructed, and set into place. Many jobs, therefore, are quite limited in the extent that they can be redesigned or altered by a supervisor (Oldham and Hackman, 1980). Technologically constrained jobs can be unambiguous, routine, methodologically invariant (Perrow, 1967), and generally quite boring! Jobs of this sort can minimize the need for managerial supervision (Kerr and Jermier, 1978), and reduce to a bare minimum the control any supervisor can have on the levels of either the objective or the subjective difficulty of the work. Supervisors may have some degree of impact on employee motivation through other mechanisms, but virtually none through the influence they have on the design or redesign of jobs within technologies of this sort.

The relationship between technology and job characteristics was demonstrated in a study by Rousseau (1977), who classified nineteen production units into one of three technological categories. Ten of these units were categorized as having a *long-linked* technology, meaning that the output from one unit or job constitutes the input to another unit or job. Long-linked technologies are common in mass production settings, featuring stable jobs and minimal uncertainty as to how the work is to be performed (Thompson, 1967).

The remaining work units were classified as being either *mediating* or *intensive* technologies (Thompson, 1967). Mediating technologies are those in which a number of standardized processes are used to deal with inputs, the particular process selected depending upon the nature of the client or problem at hand. For example, the main activities in banking are classified as mediating: there is a finite variety of operations that are normally conducted, but the ones that are selected in a given case depend upon the customer's particular request. In intensive technologies, the procedures are determined exclusively by the unique requirements of the problem (or client) being served. Intensive technologies are characterized by high levels of employee discretion and problem solving, and the procedures to be followed change as the work is underway (Thompson, 1967). The work in a medical operating room is a classic example.

Once the nineteen units were classified according to technology, Rousseau had the employees in each rate their jobs according to the dimensions of the Job Characteristics Approach to job design **279** (recall chapter eleven and/or see Hackman and Oldham, 1980). The mean assessments of the jobs, in terms of the major task dimensions of the JCA, were then computed and compared across technological categories.

As predicted, there were substantial differences across technological types, in terms of the motivational potential of the jobs within each. For example, there was a lower average level of skill variety (see chapter eleven) reported in long-linked work settings than in either mediating or intensive settings. Likewise, task identity and autonomy were both higher, on average, in jobs with mediating technologies than in jobs with either long-linked or intensive technologies.

While Rousseau (1977) reports a number of other interesting findings, the main point for our purpose here is that different types of primary technology are associated with different types of individual jobs, limiting the amount of discretion a supervisor may have in altering those jobs to increase employee motivation. Based on Rousseau's findings, as well as everyday experience with long-linked technologies (as we find in assembly lines, for example), it is clear that these types of jobs are generally less inherently motivating, and probably less capable of manipulation by individual managers.

Unions. Before we leave our discussion of technology, brief mention should be made of the role of trade unions, particularly as they relate to the introduction of new technology in work settings. While there are no hard-and-fast rules in this regard, it is often the case that unions resist the introduction of new technologies, primarily for the sake of protecting the job security and/or the skill security of their members (Swan, 1982; Walton, 1975). The impact of such a policy, when effectively carried out, is to provide one more limitation to the capacity of managers to influence the level of task challenge and difficulty, the first of three general categories of variables revealed by the analysis in this book to be important in managing employee motivation levels.

Organizational structure. Organizational structure refers to the nature of the fixed reporting relationships found within an organization. For the sake of discussion, it is possible to distinguish between two broad aspects of structure—*superstructure* and *infrastructure* (Khandwalla, 1977).

Superstructure is what we see on organizational charts: it refers to the issue of who reports to whom, to the number of levels in the hierarchy, and to the nature and number of formally recognized departments or groups in the organization. Superstructure is the organization's formal "skeleton."

On the other hand, *infrastructure* refers to a number of characteristics that are harder to portray visually on a chart. Instead, infrastructure refers to a variety of characteristics of the organization that result, in part at least, from the nature of the superstructure. *Standardization* and *centralization* are two facets of infrastructure that are of particular importance to us here. *Standardization* refers to the degree to which work procedures are the same from one part of the organization to another. For example, its high levels of standardization explains why a McDonald's hamburger tastes essentially the same in Saskatchewan as it does in West Virginia. *Centralization* refers to the level in the hierarchy at which decision-making authority rests: centralized organizations are those in which all (or most) decisions are made at the top, while in decentralized organizations decisions are made by managers lower down in the hierarchy.

For our purposes, these are some of the most important elements of organizational structure that can influence the impact of supervisory attempts to influence employee motivation through task difficulty.

How and why is organizational structure important to the issue at hand? Consider infrastructure first. Highly standardized procedures, by definition, limit the amount of discretion a manager has in designing jobs and procedures for subordinates. To return to our earlier example, a first-line supervisor in a McDonald's outlet cannot permit an inspired employee to decide how to cook or garnish a "Big Mac"! Things are done by the book.

What about the centralization-decentralization dimension? Again, almost by definition: if decision making is delegated down the hierarchy to its lower levels, then individual managers may have some discretion in decision making, discretion that may pertain to the way work inside their units is accomplished. On the other hand, such discretion is limited to the extent that decision making is largely centralized and controlled by senior levels of management.

Now, let's look at the impact of superstructure. How might the nature of the formal "skeleton" of the organization relate to managers' capacities to influence the difficulty of jobs under their command? The answer lies, in large part, in the degree to which the formal structure contributes to two phenomena referred to as *role ambiguity* and *role conflict*. What is the meaning and significance of these terms?

Role ambiguity. Suppose employees are both highly motivated and highly able to do their jobs, but that they are often unclear as to what they are supposed to do, exactly, to perform the jobs effectively. Imagine an organization where change is so frequent and **281**

so significant, when it occurs, that its employees are often uncertain about what needs to be done, how to do it, and how they will be evaluated for their efforts.

This situation is referred to as *role ambiguity* (cf. House and Rizzo, 1972; Kahn, Wolfe, Quinn, Snoek, and Rosenthal, 1964). It is not an uncommon situation in most organizations, although some jobs seem more likely to feature it than others. One consequence of too much role ambiguity is, quite naturally, an inability on the part of the employee to convert all of her effort and ability into effective performance. One can hardly be expected to achieve work goals when the nature of those goals is vague and/or subject to constant change.

What causes role ambiguity? The most common cause (although not the only one) is change—change in organizational design (such as in reporting relationships), technology (how the work gets done), policies and procedures, or even change in personnel. Change is natural in all organizations and is quite healthy (Aldrich, 1980). But too much change, or too rapid change can make it difficult for people to monitor what is going on and how their job behavior should be adjusted in response. The point is that change and role ambiguity can make an employee's job more difficult than a supervisor intends it to be.

There have been a number of empirical investigations of the *consequences* of role ambiguity in organizations. Most of these studies have examined (and demonstrated) consistent negative effects of role ambiguity on employee work attitudes, such as job dissatisfaction, low job involvement, and propensity to leave the organization (cf. Hamner & Tosi, 1974; House & Rizzo, 1972; Ivancevich & Donnelly, 1974; Lyons, 1971). Although there is somewhat less hard evidence that role ambiguity is detrimental to job performance, the connection has received some empirical support (cf. Brief & Aldag, 1976; Miles, 1976; Miles & Perreault, 1976; Schuler, 1975) and makes intuitive sense: how can individuals perform effectively in roles in which the requirements for effectiveness are not clear to them?

In chapter eleven, it was argued that jobs designed with variety, responsibility, and a degree of inherent ambiguity can be more motivating than jobs that are highly routinized and programmed. Isn't this inconsistent with the arguments just presented? The reader is again reminded that motivation and performance are not the same thing: an ambiguous job may be highly motivating and, within limits, quite satisfying. But when too ambiguous, a job becomes incapable of being executed effectively on a regular basis. Moreover, there appears to be some evidence that people vary in the degree to which role ambiguity results in unfavorable job attitudes and reduced performance effectiveness (cf. Abdel-Halim, 1980; Lyons, 1971; Miles & Petty, 1975).

In summary, role ambiguity is natural in most work organizations because change itself is a natural phenomenon. A certain degree of role ambiguity is healthy for most individuals, because it represents challenge and variety in one's job—two factors which (as we saw in chapter eleven) have been found to be sources of motivation themselves. Moreover, there are considerable differences between people in the degree of clarity or ambiguity they experience (Miles & Perreault, 1976) and like (Cherrington & England, 1980) in their jobs. But, as is the case with all good things in life, when the point is reached where there is too little clarity on the part of employees concerning what is expected of them, we can expect to see their work behavior become less effective. Moreover, we can expect to see their satisfaction with their jobs decline as a result of the frustration that the ambiguity generates.

Role conflict. In addition to their work roles, almost all employees occupy roles outside of their jobs (such as father, wife, or fraternity brother). Sometimes these roles entail competing demands (or expectations) that are inherently incompatible (as in the case of a salesman whose job requires extensive travel, keeping him away from his family at times when he is needed to fulfill his roles of husband and/or father). This is an example of what is referred to as *inter-role conflict,* because the incompatible expectations arise from two or more different roles which the man simultaneously occupies. It makes intuitive sense that employees whose roles outside of their jobs make conflicting demands on their time and attention will tend, in the long run at least, to be less effective than those whose outside roles are not incompatible with the demands placed on them at work: "You can't please all of the people all of the time."

There are at least three other varieties of role conflict that can also make a job more difficult and prevent an employee's effort and ability from resulting in successful job performance. One is called *inter-sender* conflict, a situation that arises when two or more people with whom the employee interacts while fulfilling his work role "send" him expectations that are incompatible. This is where the organization's superstructure enters the picture.

For example, a foreman in an assembly shop often finds himself inundated by expectations of people from all parts of the organization. Moreover, the expectations one group of actors places upon him cannot always be met in ways that will satisfy everyone: his superiors want him to enforce the firm's work rules more judiciously, but his subordinates let him know that they expect him to be a bit lax and flexible. Quality control engineers expect him to stress the quality of **283** the work his unit produces, but at the same time his own boss wants him to stress quantity. For most assembly work, these two demands cannot simultaneously be satisfied. The foreman's own peers have norms for his behavior, norms that, if he violates them, will make the other foremen look too tough (or too lax) by comparison. The case of the foreman or first-line supervisor is a classic example of inter-sender conflict (Roethlisberger, 1945)—one that is made even more difficult when there is a union involved (due to the special role expectations emanating from shop stewards and collective agreements). University deans and department heads, charge nurses in hospitals, and first-line supervisors in all work settings commonly experience inter-sender role conflict. It can be a very stressful and dissatisfying experience—one that makes a job far more difficult than it might otherwise appear.

Sometimes a work role can require an employee to perform duties that are incompatible and in conflict with his basic values and views of what is right (in a moral sense, for example). Disciplining or firing another person is an example of a role requirement that many people find very distasteful and contrary to their personal values concerning discipline and punishment. Having to lie to one's colleagues to cover up a bad decision by one's superior is another example. This sort of incompatibility is referred to as *person/role conflict,* denoting that it consists of a clash between the expectations which his role makes with a set of expectations the employee makes of himself.

There is at least one other form of role conflict we must consider. Referred to as *intra-sender* role conflict, it involves cases where the same person (an employee's supervisor, for example) sends the individual conflicting messages (such as separate demands that the employee attend two different meetings at the same time). Inconsistent instructions from a supervisor who changes his mind or who forgets the nature of previous assignments he has given his staff are common causes of intra-sender role conflict which, like the other forms of role conflict described above, are stress inducing and frustrating for the affected employee.

What are the causes and consequences of role conflict? In the early research of Kahn and his associates (Kahn et al., 1964), role conflict was found to be more prevalent in boundary spanning roles (jobs where the employee interacts with people in other organizations). Role conflict was also more prevalent among middle managers than among lower-level managers or senior-level executives. Positions that require the supervision of personnel seem particularly likely to feature role conflict.

The consequences attributed to role conflict by the early Kahn et al. study and by others since (cf. House & Rizzo, 1972; Miles, 1976;

Miles and Perreault, 1976; Rizzo, House, and Lirtzman, 1970), include reduced performance effectiveness, and more frequently, reduced job satisfaction, reduced fondness for role senders (people in the employee's role set who make incompatible expectations), tension, stress, anxiety, and reduced communication with role senders.

The point here is that an organization's superstructure and infrastructure can affect the difficulty of jobs through the impact they have on the levels of role ambiguity and conflict experienced by job incumbents. Moreover, as important elements of both the superstructure and infrastructure of organizations, supervisors (at all levels) are responsible for most of the ambiguity and conflict found within work settings. Regardless of whether they are caused by an employee's immediate supervisor or by parts of the structure beyond that supervisor's control, the ambiguity and conflict in particular jobs can make those jobs more difficult (or more easy) than they are intended to be by those who design them and assign employees to them.

Recapitulation

In summary, there are a variety of characteristics of complex work organizations that can be beyond the control of individual managers, characteristics that can influence attempts to design jobs for subordinates in such a manner as to maximize the motivation levels of those subordinates. On the other hand, the summary of the theory of work motivation provided at the beginning of this chapter indicates that control of task design and difficulty levels is an important aspect of control of employee motivation, so enlightened managers concerned with the motivation of their human resources must grapple with the sorts of impediments and constraints discussed above.

INFLUENCING THE RELATIONSHIP BETWEEN PERFORMANCE AND REWARDS

One of the oldest, most important, and best-justified applied prescriptions for managerial behavior aimed at influencing employee motivation is to tie job-related outcomes (such as rewards and punishments) to job effort and/or job performance. As noted recently by Locke (1982), the concept of paying employees on the basis of their output for the purpose of motivating high levels of performance dates back at least as far as the early days of scientific management (Taylor, 1911/1967), probably even much further. In the terms we used in chapters nine and ten (where the operant conditioning approach was presented), it is suggested that reinforcers and punishers be administered according to a ratio schedule, contingent upon the occurrence of desired job behaviors. In the terms of VIE Theory, **285** the goal is to make performance *instrumental* for the receipt of rewards and the avoidance of undesirable consequences. Finally, although the principle is somewhat different from the perspective of Equity Theory, managers are directed to tie outcomes to employee inputs, so that employees feel that the ratios of outcomes they receive, in relation to the inputs they provide, are subjectively equal to the corresponding ratios they attribute to other people. In short, these three theories converge, more or less, in suggesting that managers do what they can to establish a relationship between performance (or at least effort) and work-related outcomes. On the surface, this idea seems quite simple and relatively straightforward. Yet, in practice, the principle is sometimes hard to effect. Why is this so?

There are a variety of reasons why it can be difficult in practice to tie rewards to performance in a manner that would satisfy the three theories mentioned above. Some of these reasons have to do with characteristics of the managers involved, while others have to do with characteristics of the subordinate. Still other impediments to tying rewards to performance relate to characteristics of the organization and to features of the environment in which it functions (Freedman and Montanari, 1980).

In the following sections, we will examine each of these general classes of practical factors that can make it difficult for managers to adhere to a policy of administering work-related outcomes strictly on the basis of employee performance. For the sake of discussion, the focus will primarily be upon the distribution of monetary rewards, although the general principle being examined pertains also to the distribution by managers of other types of rewards, as well as to negative work-related outcomes, such as reprimands, firings, demotions, and the like.

To begin then, let's look at a number of features of the environment within which organizations operate—features that can constitute practical constraints on the practice of tying rewards to employee job performance.

Environmental Variables

Numerous variables in the organization's environment can restrict the degree to which practicing managers can actually tie performance to rewards. One of these is the overall economic climate of that environment: in tough economic times, for example, managers may be more inclined to distribute those rewards that are available, especially monetary rewards, *equally* among their subordinates, without regard to performance differences or perceptions of equity (Freedman and Montanari, 1980). Equal treatment often seems most fair and less likely to generate conflict then equitable treatment.

Further, government regulations pertaining to minimum wages and other conditions of work place limits on the degree to which it is possible to link rewards to performance. Likewise, labor markets have a direct influence on pay levels, particularly the levels that are offered to attract new employees. Periodic fluctuations in the supply and demand for various types of personnel can necessitate the payment of high salaries and wages to new employees, often to the point of compressing the remuneration of current employees (see chapter six). Similarly, employees who hold lucrative offers from other employers in a "seller's market" can often force their superiors to increase pay levels beyond what would be required if a strict adherence to the pay-for-performance dictum were being followed.

Labor unions and collective agreements. There are a number of ways that the existence of a labor union can affect the practice of management in general (Swan, 1982), and the freedom of management to distribute rewards in accordance with performance in particular. For example, negotiated job classification schemes and jurisdictional agreements among unions themselves make it difficult for managers to freely assign employees to tasks as a means of rewarding good performance or punishing poor performance. Likewise, collective bargaining can influence the number and nature of rules that can be imposed upon employee behavior and supervisory discretion. But perhaps the major influence that collective agreements have on the ability of managers to reward performance concerns the role of seniority.

Seniority, performance, and rewards. Seniority is usually defined as the length of service an employee has with an organization, although, in some cases, it is defined in terms of the length of one's tenure within a particular job, department, or subunit. And, although seniority is a ubiquitous factor in unionized settings, it often plays a role in the management of nonunionized employees as well (Foulkes, 1980; Kochan, 1980).

Seniority tends to influence personnel management in two general ways (Kochan, 1980). The first is through the role it plays in benefit status, such as the distribution of pay, vacations, pensions, severance pay, and the like. In fact, it often *appears* that seniority is *the* most important determinant of pay in some organizations. For example, a recent survey of eight thousand hourly paid and salaried employees from forty different organizations in a wide variety of occupations and industries in British Columbia found a very strong association between pay and level of seniority (Painter, Sutton and Burton, 1982). As shown in Table 12-1, only at the highest levels of pay did the correlation between the two variables break down. **287**

TABLE 12-1: Relationship Between Seniority and Level of Pay
(from Painter et al., 1982)

	Mean Seniority in Months	Rank Order	(N)
< = $10,000	28.33	10	(4)
$10,001–15,000	43.32	9	(60)
$15,001–20,000	52.81	8	(805)
$20,001–25,000	84.82	7	(1804)
$25,001–30,000	117.25	6	(1400)
$30,001–35,000	140.74	5	(1089)
$35,001–40,000	160.92	4	(234)
$40,001–45,000	202.84	2	(110)
$45,001–50,000	192.65	3	(29)
>$50,000	241.90	1	(40)

The second general role played by seniority pertains to competitive-status provisions, which influence decisions such as who is promoted, laid off, transferred, or recalled first following a lay-off (Kochan, 1980). For example, a large U.S. study reports that seniority is an important provision related to promotion decisions in 90 percent of collective agreements in manufacturing and 43 percent of agreements in nonmanufacturing settings (U.S. Department of Labor, 1970). In fact, the use of seniority as a primary basis for allocating promotions explains the relationship between seniority and pay level noted above: the more senior employees in such situations are those who move into the higher-paying jobs.

It is relatively easy to understand why many employees (particularly senior ones) favor seniority as a determinant of their pay, benefits, and career opportunities. Seniority provisions protect their job security by reducing the threat of layoff, by increasing the chances of transfer or "bumping" rights, by minimizing the length of time they are laid off, and by influencing the levels of both severance payment and income supplements during periods of layoff (Kochan, 1980). (On the other hand, young, highly motivated employees often find that seniority arrangements prevent them from advancing as quickly as they might otherwise advance, so not all workers favor such arrangements.) Moreover, seniority is an objective criterion for reward distribution, one that is less likely to induce allegations of favoritism on the part of management.

The most important point concerning seniority for our present discussion has to do with its impact on job performance. Some people believe that seniority represents ability, more experienced employees being assumed to be more competent at their jobs than employees who are less senior, especially in the case of unskilled and semiskilled jobs. Likewise, there is some evidence that job satisfaction and seniority may be related, such that job attitudes diminish with age, to a point, and then grow more positive as employees grow older.

But the research evidence linking seniority with performance and job satisfaction is generally quite poor, leaving no *scientific* basis for assuming that seniority has these sorts of positive benefits (Gordon and Johnson, 1982). In fact, Kochan (1980, p. 367) has noted that the benefits of seniority provisions to management are the greatest in situations ". . . where individual differences in ability and motivation make little difference in job performance. The more variable the technology and skill requirements, or the more important individual discretion and motivation are in explaining variations in job performance, the more employers will seek to limit both the scope of the seniority unit and the weight assigned to seniority in promotion decisions."

Nevertheless, in spite of the fact that there is little solid evidence that seniority bears any real relationship with either employee attitudes or performance, many management groups—even when unions are not involved—still include seniority in their personnel management decisions (Foulkes, 1980). One reason for this is that seniority is easy to quantify and measure, giving it more of an objective quality than other decision criteria, such as ability or merit (Gordon and Johnson, 1982). As noted earlier, such objectivity can forestall allegations of favoritism and can be invoked as an indicator of management's desire to treat employees equitably, wherein length of service is considered an *input* in Equity Theory terms (Swan, 1982).

A second reason management groups often favor seniority is the continuity it can provide; seniority-based reward systems often feature lower rates of costly turnover, and—in many cases—provide older employees a greater sense of security and higher levels of commitment to the organization. Finally, as noted by Kochan (1980), seniority-based systems make it easier for management to engage in manpower planning; when seniority provisions largely or exclusively determine promotions, for example, it is relatively easy to predict which employees will be moving into which positions, and when.

In summary, the existence of a labor union in a work setting can radically affect the discretion of management in the control it has over its human resources (Slichter, Healy and Livernash, 1960; Swan, 1982). The formalization of seniority as an important basis of reward distribution—sometimes the only basis—constitutes the most significant aspect of labor unions from the point of view of the discussion at hand: how to manage the motivation levels of a work unit. **289**

Organizational Factors

There are a number of features of most work organizations that can limit the degree to which it is possible for them to adhere strictly to a policy of rewarding performance. Although space limitations prevent an exhaustive treatment of such factors, it is possible to discuss a few of them.

Budgets. Again, consider budgets and the budgetary processes that are common (almost universal) in work organizations. They can have a variety of influences on the motivation of people to perform, including both those people who set and administer them as well those who work within the budgetary constraints set by others (usually their superiors).

On the one hand, providing a unit's manager with a budget may constitute the setting of a specific goal for that individual, a goal toward which he is to strive during the following fiscal period. As we know from chapter eight, specific goals can be quite motivating for those who pursue them, particularly if those goals are difficult and accepted by the individual.

On the other hand, if a budget is too stringent (and therefore too hard to stay within), or too specific (such that it prevents flexibility in the reallocation of funds from one ''line'' to another), then it may be quite difficult for managers to differentially reward performance in a manner that is consistent with motivation theory. In either case, such a budget is clearly dysfunctional for the motivation of subordinates.

But what about the motivation of the manager who administers a budget? First of all, the allocation of budgets among units within an organization is a highly political affair, such that factors other than the merit or performance of a unit (such as a department) may help it to acquire a greater share of the available resources than would otherwise be the case (Pfeffer and Salancik, 1974). Aside from the influences of intraorganizational political processes, however, other factors determine the distribution of budget, including such things as selling seasons, product turnover rates, borrowing needs, raw material cycles, production cycles, labor availability, and a host of others, both inside as well as outside the organization (see Schwarz, 1981). The point is that it is not always the most effective managers (where effectiveness is measured in terms of organizational goal attainment) who are granted the largest budgetary shares for allocation within their units.

Finally, consider the role that budgets often play in the assessment of the managers who administer them. Since the metric of budgets is money, and since money is an easily measured commodity, budgetary goal attainment is a common basis for the appraisal of managers in work organizations (Latham and Wexley, 1981). As we noted in chapter eight in connection with the assessment of managers in MBO settings, exclusive reliance on *ends* (as opposed to means) can be both dysfunctional and unethical. Likewise, if managers are rewarded or punished simply on the basis of adherence to budgetary goals without regard to the means used to reach those goals, then managers at one level may reward managers below them for administering their budgets without regard to the differential merit of their own personnel.

In short, the point is that most organizations establish and operate under the guidance of budgets, and managers tend to do those things that they (themselves) are rewarded for doing. Certain features of budgets often reward managers for behaving in ways that are not entirely consistent with policies of distributing rewards in accordance with performance at all levels throughout the system.

Task interdependencies and group performance. A related problem has to do with the fact that so much of the work that is accomplished in many organizations results from the efforts of several individuals, often working at separate but highly interdependent jobs (Hopwood, 1976; March and Simon, 1958). Separating the production and operating costs attributable to particular individuals and units is a major problem in managerial accounting (Horngren, 1977), but one that must be dealt with if high performance is truly to be rewarded with bonuses and other benefits. Likewise, parceling out bonus money or other desirable consequences among members of a work group, all of whom have had something to do with the successful accomplishment of an organization's goals, is also a sticky problem. While there doesn't seem to be much empirical data to support such a claim, it would appear on the basis of day-to-day observation that the work being performed by humans (as opposed to robots, for example), is becoming more complex, and more interconnected. To the extent that this is true, careful enactment of policies of tying work-related outcomes to the levels of job performance of individuals will grow increasingly more difficult in the future.

Organizational goals and formal reward systems. Another factor is the nature of the organization's goals, either implicit or explicit, concerning the payment of its staff (Freedman and Montanari, 1980). For example, many organizations distribute pay in a manner that favors low levels of conflict or competition among members. Others prefer to distribute rewards to encourage poor performers to improve their contributions. Still others structure pay so as to retain valuable talent, particularly when they face shortages of critical types of labor.

Organizational goals favoring the minimization of conflict frequently give rise to policies of salary secrecy. Since these were dis-

291

cussed at length in chapter six, only brief mention need be made of them here. To the extent that, as research suggests is often the case, employees do not hold accurate perceptions about how much money other people earn and about the relationship between performance and rewards within their organizations, then the performance benefits promised by motivation theory will not be realized.

Likewise, different organizations base their formal pay programs upon different types of compensable factors (cf. Belcher, 1974). Therefore, high levels of educational requirements or dangerous working conditions may contribute to a pay structure in which merit seems to be of secondary importance in determining how much money people actually earn. Moreover, basic ''system'' rewards, such as fringe benefits and base pay levels can provide such high net levels of inducements to employees for merely belonging to an organization that it is difficult for the employer to offer further incentives above and beyond them (Staw, 1977). When these sorts of system rewards are high enough in level, employees are paid off merely for joining and staying with the organization, not for meritorious performance (Katz and Kahn, 1978).

The point is that, either intentionally or inadvertently, formal reward systems in organizations can often serve goals that are inconsistent with a policy of tying outcomes to performance (cf. Kerr, 1975, 1982).

Informal group norms and organizational culture. There is a rich literature, as well as abundant everyday experience, demonstrating that work settings are, above all, social settings within which people interact and work, frequently in formally designed groups. Moreover, aside from the formal work group structures established by management, informal groups usually emerge and flourish, groups based on common interests, interpersonal affinities, and mutual trust.

An important feature of group dynamics is the development of cohesiveness, the emergence of norms regarding behavior, and—depending upon the level of cohesiveness that does develop—more or less adherence by individual members to these behavioral norms (Moch and Seashore, 1981; Shaw, 1971). Adherence to group norms is developed and maintained by the administration of the group's social rewards and sanctions. Most people who have ever held a job will have witnessed and will understand this point, but the reader who wishes a colorful case example is referred to the formal report of the famous ''Hawthorne Studies'' (Roethlisberger and Dickson, 1939, especially chapter eighteen).

A behavior of particular importance in work groups is, of course, the work performed by individual members. Work groups tend to develop norms about how much work is appropriate, and will administer social rewards and sanctions so as to support those norms. Members who perform below the standard ("chisellers") may be forced by the group to "pull up their socks," while "ratebusters" are frowned upon and punished by other members of the group, particularly if the group is highly cohesive. But it is important to realize that there is no simple relationship between the level of cohesiveness in a work group on the one hand, and the level of performance of the group on the other. Instead, there *is* a relationship between the amount of cohesiveness within a group and the degree of *variance* that is observed among the group's members in terms of the amount of work they perform: highly cohesive groups tolerate lower variance than less cohesive groups. The actual average level of performance in a work group depends upon the group's attitude toward management, so that a fundamentally promanagement work group will, on average, produce at a high standard, while an antimanagement group will not (Seashore, 1954).

The importance of this phenomenon for the present discussion is this: managers must realize that employees, as social beings, respond to the rewards and punishments of the informal system according to the same basic laws of psychology that regulate their reactions to the formal reward systems controlled by management (Whyte, 1972). Therefore, individual employees will frequently behave in ways that will earn them the favor of the informal system, even at the cost of foregoing wages or of incurring retribution from the formal system. Even in situations where the amount of pay employees receive is determined by the amount of output they produce, people have been observed to restrict their productivity in order to adhere to group norms (e.g., Coch and French, 1948; Hickson, 1961; Roethlisberger and Dickson, 1939; Roy, 1952). In brief, managers may try to administer those work-related outcomes over which they have control in a performance-contingent manner, but it is important for them to realize that human employees live and work in a social world in which informal rewards and punishments can either encourage or discourage the very sorts of behaviors they attempt to promote.

Organizational scientists have recently recognized the importance of what has come to be called *organizational culture.* This term represents the prevailing values, beliefs, and expectations within an organization (Pondy, Frost, Morgan, and Dandridge, 1983; Schwartz and Davis, 1981). It is a relatively slow-changing feature of an organization, one that is rooted in its past, and one that constrains and guides the actions that can effectively be taken in the future. While a complete discussion of the meaning of this new concept is beyond the present purpose, it is clear that organizations differ dra- **293** matically in regard to important values concerning the way employees should be managed, as well as in regard to what can be expected of employees in return. So, for example, while one organization's culture may stress competition among its members for the attainment of recognition and other rewards, other organizations seem to be characterized more by norms of cooperation, collaboration, and team play.

It stands to reason that implicit cultural values regarding the means by which rewards and punishments should be distributed will play a central role in the actual distribution of those rewards and punishments. In fact, there is preliminary laboratory evidence from a study of undergraduate business students that managers who are rewarded as a result of the performance accomplishments of their subordinates are more likely, in turn, to reward those subordinates for their effective performance (Hinton and Barrow, 1975). While organizational cultures are not usually manufactured or contrived, they can be influenced and supported by the practices of both management and employees. The laboratory study mentioned above suggests that cultural norms of tying outcomes to performance may represent one important type of norm that is either consistent with an organization's culture or inconsistent with it. In the context of all the other practical constraints faced by policies of tying outcomes to performance, it is easy to understand why and how a value of actually rewarding merit may not be part of a particular organization's culture.

Turnover.   The discussion in this section has tended to focus on the one-to-one relationships between employees and supervisors, and the day-to-day distribution of rewards and punishments by the latter to the former. But we can also conceive of the issue of tying rewards and punishments to performance on a more long-term basis. That is, while it is often not possible to dispense work-related outcomes on a regular, daily basis, it is common in many organizations for employees to be granted promotions, vacations, desirable job assignments, and other favorable outcomes intermittently, and on the basis of performance "over the long haul." In fact, this is frequently the case in the distribution of benefits to managerial personnel. Thus, managers who have demonstrated superior performance over an extended period of time, combined with high levels of demonstrated loyalty to their organizations may be recognized by their superiors by favors, benefits, and recognition in the form of bonuses, promotion opportunities, and other outcomes. But, as was noted in chapter five, it can often be a mistake to assume that an organization will "remember" superior service and loyalty, if only because people come and go from organizational structures, for various reasons. The fact is that organizations do not have hearts, minds, and memories—individuals do. So employees may find that those people whom they have counted on to "take care" of them some time in the future in exchange for sacrifices they have made in the past, are no longer able (or willing) to reward such service. Deaths, retirements, demotions, and firings can quickly remove middle managers' mentors, leaving them with no one to influence the distribution of rewards in their favor, as they had hoped. In short, the coming and going of senior managers often makes it difficult for an organization to adhere closely to a policy of rewarding long-term merit.

Organizational effectiveness and profitability. Finally (although, again, the list is not exhaustive), the comparative ability of the organization to pay is always a factor. Low levels of profit in the private sector can lead to the exodus of talent away from those very organizations that need such talent, and into those that are already profitable. Likewise, limited budgets in public sector organizations often occasion an exodus of talent to private industry, where it is believed that the meritorious prosper.

In summary, there are many characteristics of formal work organizations—including their budgets and control procedures, their official and operative goals, the nature of task interdependencies, cultures and informal norms, turnover, as well as their current levels of profitability and effectiveness—that can affect the degree to which managers can influence employee motivation through linking rewards and punishments to performance, as prescribed by theory.

Managerial Factors

A third general category of variables that can interfere with attempts to tie rewards to performance consists of characteristics of the managers involved (Freedman and Montanari, 1980). Different managers hold different goals and values, of course, and these goals and values often pertain to the issue of how benefits and punishments ought to be distributed. For example, managers vary in their willingness to enforce rules and to apply discipline to subordinates for rule violations (Shull and Cummings, 1966). Other managers, out of a sense of humanity and fair play, prefer to distribute rewards (and/or punishments) on the basis of employee effort, or behaviors, rather than on the strict basis of performance, per se. Further, there is some evidence that males may be more likely than females to adhere to a norm of equity in distributing rewards, while the latter may more frequently be inclined to distribute rewards according to a norm of *equality,* particularly if the outcomes of that distribution are to **295** be made public (Kidder, Bellettirie, and Cohn, 1977; Leventhal, 1973).

Cognitive complexity.   One managerial characteristic that would seem especially important is cognitive complexity, a psychological construct related to the way people perceive things and process information. Specifically, cognitive complexity can be defined as consisting of three independent dimensions (Vannoy, 1965). The first of these has to do with the number of dimensions an individual takes into account when perceiving an object, a concept, or another person. More complex people take note of a greater number of aspects of the object in question (such as, for example, the height, weight, age, race, interests, and personal appearance of another individual), while less cognitively complex people pay attention to fewer dimensions (such as concentrating on the apparent race of the person, for example).

A second aspect of cognitive complexity pertains to the number of levels that are considered along each dimension. For instance, are we satisfied to know that an employee is an engineer, or would we prefer to differentiate among types of engineers, wanting to know whether a particular individual is a chemical engineer, a civil engineer, or a specialist in any of a number of other engineering subspecialties. More complex people make more distinctions among attitude objects than less complex people.

A third aspect of cognitive complexity concerns the degree to which a person can tolerate disorder, ambiguity, and contradictory information (see chapter four). Some people are much more at ease with clutter than others, whether that clutter is physical or psychological.

What is the relevance of all this for the present issue? Managers, like other people, vary in cognitive complexity. In order for managers to be able to operationalize the advice that rewards and punishments be made contingent upon performance, they must first be able to recognize and differentiate among the performance levels of members of their personnel. Cognitively complex managers will take more aspects of performance into account in forming these judgments, and be more likely to make finer, more sophisticated assessments of their people along each of the dimensions they consider. Moreover, the more complex managers will be more capable of tolerating "mixed signals" as they relate to the assessment of their employees. In short, the cognitive style of managers is a particularly important factor to be taken into account when we consider the practical aspects of distributing rewards in organizations according to performance.

Managerial work. But aside from the demographic and psychological characteristics of the would-be enlightened manager/administrator, it is also important to take into account the day-to-day realities of managerial work. Managers often tend to be very busy people who operate at a frantic pace. They tend to prefer quick interactions with other individuals on the job, and to prefer oral rather than written communications. They move from task to task quickly, with a minimum amount of time to contemplate and deliberate on matters (Mintzberg, 1973). In short, managerial work, by its very nature, can be almost antithetical to the practice of carefully assessing the performance of one's subordinates, along all of many dimensions and then distributing rewards and punishments according to a schedule that is closely correlated with merit, and that will be perceived as equitable by all who are concerned.

Of course, there are numerous *formal* methods by which supervisors can appraise the work of their subordinates, but most of these require considerable memory on the part of the supervisors, or the constant keeping of records on a minute-by-minute (or at least day-by-day) basis. Latham and Wexley (1981) offer a more complete discussion of the pros and cons of both traditional and behaviorally based formal approaches—approaches that all have in common, to varying degrees, the age-old problems of reliability and validity described in chapter two.

Employee Factors

Finally, it is important to realize that certain characteristics of employees themselves can have considerable influence on the degree to which their superiors reward and punish them in accordance with their performance. Several obvious factors come to mind—factors that have to do with biases on the part of managers, either for or against the individuals involved. These biases are frequently based on sex, race, or age considerations, and need not be conscious or deliberate. In fact, research has shown that age and sex often *do* influence the way supervisors treat subordinates (e.g., Rosen and Jerdee, 1976; Terborg, 1977).

Less obvious, however, are the nature and number of inputs an employee puts into his job, where *inputs* are defined in Equity Theory terms (recall chapter six).

Employee inputs. To illustrate, Dyer, Schwab, and Theriault (1976) asked a sample of managers to rate a variety of factors according to two considerations: (1) the degree to which these factors are actually involved in determining pay increases; and (2) the degree to which they *should be* involved in determining pay increases. **297**

The results were as follows. The managers reported that level of job performance, budgetary considerations, the nature of their jobs, the amount of effort they expend on the job, and their levels of training and experience were, in fact, the most important determinants of the amount of pay increases they received, while a similar set of factors were viewed as the factors that *should* be taken into account. However, when Dyer and his colleagues computed the differences between the degree to which a particular factor was viewed as actually taken into consideration and the degree to which it should figure in determining pay increases, the three factors with the greatest discrepancy were the cost of living, the nature of the job, and the level of job performance. In other words, of the many factors considered, these three considerations were viewed as being the most underemphasized in determining pay increments. The point is that performance was not only viewed as the most important determinant, it was also viewed by the managers as one of the three factors that should be given even *more* emphasis in the determination of their salary levels. On the other hand, the same sample of managers felt that two other factors—the cost of living and the nature of the job performance—ought to be given more weight than they normally receive. Therefore, while it may be that managers are in favor of being paid on the basis of performance, other nonperformance issues may influence their beliefs and attitudes about reward distribution, both as it relates to their own salaries, as well as to the rewards they make available to others.

Recapitulation

Although it is one of the best-justified prescriptions to derive from current theories of work motivation, the policy of tying work-related outcomes to employee job performance is, in fact, not widely practiced, even in organizations that purport to follow such a policy (Porter, Lawler, and Hackman, 1975). The primary reason for this discrepancy between what might be viewed as optimal practice (optimal, that is, from the point of view of motivation theory) and actual practice can be understood when one considers, as we have in the foregoing sections, the myriad practical constraints found in real organizational settings—constraints that originate in both the official and the informal structures and processes of actual work settings.* In short, theory is one thing, practice is another, notwithstanding the importance of putting that theory into actual practice.

---

*A study by Herman (1973), for example, shows how certain types of employee behavior can be predicted by attitudes, when that behavior is free from constraints. Although the behavior of interest in Herman's study was voting in accordance with one's attitudes toward unions in a certification election, it shows how practical constraints can cause a gap between attitudes and actual practice in work settings (recall chapter five of this book).

INFLUENCING EMPLOYEE SATISFACTION FROM
WORK-RELATED OUTCOMES

The third general category of applied principles which derives from the summary of current work motivation theories that appeared at the beginning of this chapter, pertains to the nature of employee needs, values, and goals, and to the distribution by managers of work-related outcomes that are seen by employees as both valent and equitable. In other words, this third set of principles deals with making use of individual differences in employee needs by providing rewards and punishments that are consistent with those needs, in such a way that employees feel that they are treated equitably.

The discussion in chapters three through seven of this book periodically touched upon a number of the practical difficulties that a manager can encounter while trying to implement these principles, so the following treatment of these difficulties will be comparatively brief. Nevertheless, we can ask the following question: "What are the practical constraints and impediments facing a manager who might wish to implement this third set of work motivation principles?"

There are essentially three potential problems confronting any manager who wishes to implement this set of work motivation principles. The first problem concerns the assessment of the nature and strength of a particular employee's needs, in any given situation. The second problem has to do with the amount of access managers have to the kinds of reinforcers and punishers that are needed to implement the principles. Finally, the third problem has to do with equity, especially the fact that different employees frequently perceive inequities in the distribution of rewards and punishments made by managers. Let's look at each of these concerns, one at a time.

Assessing Individual Needs

In chapter three we noted that people differ in the profiles of needs that initiate and direct their behavior. Moreover, we noted that these differences are of two major types: differences between people at a given point in time, as well as differences within particular individuals at different points in time. We also saw that it is difficult to determine the types and strengths of the needs that are operative within an individual, both because psychometric assessment is not feasible for practicing managers, and because informal assessment must rely on the observation of behavior. (Recall from chapter three that there is no one-to-one correspondence between needs and behaviors, and that people often tend to attribute their own needs to others.)

In short, the point is that it is quite difficult, in the day-to-day practice of management, to assign work-related outcomes in accordance with the third set of principles of work motivation, because first **299** of all, it is difficult for managers to gain reliable and valid assessments of the nature and relative importance of employee needs.

Managerial Access to Appropriate Outcomes

In order to implement the third set of work motivation principles identified at the beginning of this chapter, a manager must be capable of furnishing employees with the types of rewards (or reinforcers) that they desire. Given the wide variance in individual tastes and preferences (apart from the intra- and inter-individual differences in basic needs just noted), most managers are generally quite limited in the types and amounts of positive and negative consequences they can administer in practice, particularly within the context of a collective agreement.

Equity and Equality

The third major problem that managers frequently encounter when they attempt to distribute rewards on the job on the basis of performance concerns equity: how to assign rewards and punishments to various members of a work group in a manner that will be perceived as equitable by all who are concerned. As a complete discussion of these matters is presented in chapter six, only a brief summary will be provided here.

The essence of the problem is that equity exists only in the eye of the beholder. In other words, what may appear to one individual to be an equitable distribution of rewards may not appear so to another person in the same work setting. So, for example, while supervisors may feel that they have distributed financial, prestige, and job content rewards (such as those described above) among their employees in proportions that appear to them to be approximately in line with their perceptions of the differential inputs provided by members of their staffs, it is likely that many of their subordinates—particularly those who received fewer rewards—may not perceive the outcome to be as equitable as they see it. The reason for these differential impressions, of course, is that different people take into account different input factors, use different comparison standards, and have less than perfectly accurate perceptions of the types and amounts of outcomes others receive. Frequently, it would seem, managers adhere to a practice of distributing rewards *equally* among employees, a practice that violates Equity Theory-based prescriptions, but that is likely to obviate the problems that arise from social comparison processes in which people perceive that others have benefited more from the managers' kindness than they have.

Recapitulation

There are a variety of practical limitations to the degree to which managers can successfully implement many of the applied principles which fall into the third general category identified at the beginning of this chapter—those dealing with individual differences in employee needs, values, goals, and equity perceptions. As we found to be the case in our earlier discussions of the implementation of the first two sets of principles, it would appear to be one thing to understand these principles, but quite another thing to be capable of operationalizing them in ongoing work settings. Yet, if they are to be of any applied value to the management of human resources, these principles must be operationalized and utilized.

MOTIVATION IN THE PUBLIC SECTOR

Insofar as at least 20 percent of the U.S. workforce is employed in the public sector—the figure is at least 24 percent in Canada and 37 percent in the United Kingdom (Bird, Bucovetsky and Foot, 1979)—it is important that we take at least a brief look at the issue of the application of motivation theory in government organizations.

It seems that there are a variety of characteristics of government organizations, their environments, and their employees, that are relevant to the issue at hand (Bower, 1977; Newman and Wallender, 1978; Perry and Porter, 1982). For example, they are expected, typically, to pursue the goals assigned to them by elected bodies, often without due regard to the amount of resources at their disposal, whereas private sector organizations have more freedom to change goals, undertake new projects, and/or abandon old ones on the basis of the resources that are available. Moreover, it is frequently the case that the nature of politics necessitates that government agencies undertake programs without sufficient time and resources to permit them to succeed (Bower, 1977). Further, government managers must operate organizational structures that have been designed by other individuals and groups: we often hear, in fact, about the difficulty new government administrations have in gaining control over recalcitrant bureaucracies that were created and sustained by previous administrations.

In addition, while goal conflict is a common phenomenon in most organizations, it is almost a defining characteristic of many public sector organizations (Newman and Wallender, 1978). Imagine the difficulty, for example, of rebuilding a nation's military forces while at the same time reducing inflation, balancing the budget, and holding the line on interest rates! Nevertheless, large-scale goals of **301** this sort are translated into increasingly more specific, but no less mutually incompatible goals throughout government hierarchies. The point is that government organizations must be managed in ways that are fundamentally different from the way most successful private enterprises are managed (Bower, 1977), and many of these differences result in, or are accompanied by, significant differences in the "context for motivation" of public sector employees (Perry and Porter, 1982).

For example, centralized personnel selection procedures and government policies regarding tenure (or job security), heavily affect the freedom managers have in the assignment of personnel to jobs. Such policies and procedures may help explain why, for example, public sector managers are less satisfied, on average, than their private sector counterparts with promotion opportunities (see Perry and Porter, 1982 for a review of the evidence on this). Likewise, the formalized job classification procedures, seniority provisions, and centralized compensation programs of many public agencies prevent public managers from distributing pay on a performance-contingent basis to the same extent as is possible in the private sector (although, as we have seen, it is difficult even there).

There appear to be a number of features of the *jobs* in the public sector that have importance for the motivation of employees (Perry and Porter, 1982). For example, task meaningfulness (see chapter eleven) is frequently lower for public employees, who are primarily in the business of providing services, rather than producing material goods.

It is frequently very difficult to assess performance on jobs performed in the public sector: consider the assessment of the performance of police officers, social workers, and aldermen, for example. In order to tie rewards to performance, as we have repeatedly noted, it is first necessary to reliably assess performance along valid dimensions—a difficult task in so many public sector jobs, particularly those in which the task goals are incompatible, as mentioned above.

Earlier in this chapter, we discussed the impact of turnover among senior executives on the distribution of performance-contingent rewards. Consider this same issue as it relates to government organizations, in which top management come and go at regular intervals, on the basis of the pleasure of the electorate!

Finally (although this list of differences between public and private organizations is far from exhaustive), consider the impact that antigovernment sentiments (such as those that were so prevalent following the Watergate era) can have on the capacity of government agencies to attract talented, highly motivated personnel and to retain

302 them in positions which, in many cases, require them to interact with a chary, even jaded constituency. Are public prosecutors and defenders, for example, given the same respect today as they were before Watergate?

In summary, the point is that government organizations are not, and cannot be, run with management styles that would bring effectiveness to organizations in the private sector. Moreover, many of these inherent differences can serve to further restrict the capacity of managers to operationalize policies that are consistent with the most potentially useful principles of work motivation. Finally, the fact that government is the largest single employer in most nations of the world (and particularly the fact that the proportion of the workforce in most nations that is employed by government is actually growing), the application of the principles of work motivation to this segment of the workforce seems particularly important, albeit particularly difficult.

CONCLUSIONS: MANAGERIAL MOTIVATION
TO MOTIVATE EMPLOYEES

The main conclusion from the foregoing discussion is that work organizations are complex social systems that can make the application of the apparently simple principles of work motivation summarized at the beginning of the chapter very difficult to put into actual practice. The intention of the discussion has not been to suggest that theories of work motivation cannot, or should not, be applied in real work settings; rather, the point is that application is not as simple as we might wish, and the realities of organizational life help explain, in part, the limited degree to which enlightened managers of human resources are successful in deriving maximum productivity from their human resources.

In brief, the problem cited in chapter one remains: inflation, while slowing down at the time of this writing, is still high; unemployment is at postdepression record levels, and Western economies continue to operate with deficit budgets. And, to repeat the most important point made in the opening chapter of this book, work motivation may be only one factor among all the many determinants of productivity, itself only one determinant of economic well-being, but it is the only one over which the vast majority of practicing managers have any hope of gaining control. The problem is important, but the solutions are not simple, notwithstanding the apparent simplicity of the principles of work motivation provided by behavioral science.

As one means of understanding the gap between the importance of the problem and the difficulty of the solution, it is instructive to consider the motivation of practicing managers to apply theories of work motivation to their human resource problems. After all, such **303** attempts represent merely one type of intentional work-related behavior (Steers and Porter, 1979), and are likely to be repeated in situations in which they are rewarding to the managers involved.

Accordingly, consider the following short list of questions that might be raised to address the question: "Why do managers try, or fail to try, to implement current theories of work motivation within their work groups?" The list is not intended to be definitive or exhaustive; it is intended merely to be suggestive of the sort of analysis the student/reader might conduct to understand the gap between the simplicity of the concepts on the one hand, and the limited application of those principles in work organizations on the other.

1. If I were to try to apply current motivation theory in my organization, would I be successful? What factors would facilitate my attempts, and what factors might frustrate them?
2. If I were successful in applying these theories, what would happen to me, and to my organization? What would be the consequences of my attempts?
3. How much satisfaction or benefit would I derive from these consequences? How much trouble, pain, or cost would I derive from these consequences?*

The point is that it is frequently the case that any, or all, of the answers that would arise in response to these questions, would not favor the application of work motivation theory. If, for example, a manager feels that attempts on his part to apply the principles described in this book are not likely to be effective (for any or all of the multitude of reasons outlined earlier in this chapter), he may not wish even to try. In VIE Theory terms, of course, we would say that such a manager has low expectancy perceptions: he doesn't believe he can turn his attempt into *performance,* where performance is translated here to mean successful application of his knowledge of work motivation. Alternatively, it is entirely possible that a particular manager will feel that the constraints on his attempts to implement motivation theory are minimal, and that he would probably succeed if he were to try.

The second question, of course, pertains to instrumentality beliefs: "If I succeed in applying theory to my own work context, what will happen to me?" Or, alternatively, "What will be the consequences, for me and the organization, if I succeed in my attempt?" A manager may then consider any of a variety of possible outcomes, including things such as improved performance levels among members of his work group, increased overall organizational effectiveness, alienation from his peers (such as other managers made to look poor by comparison), and so on.

The third question has to do with valence. Depending upon the

---

*The reader who is familiar with chapter seven of this book will recognize that these questions arise from a VIE Theory approach to the problem.

manager's needs, of course, he will evaluate the various outcomes he anticipates to be contingent upon successful application as either positive, aversive, or of no consequence. If the organizational reward system rewards its managers for increases in the performance of its various work groups (see Hinton and Barrow, 1975), and if a manager believes that higher motivation levels will in fact result from his implementation attempts and eventuate into higher overall unit performance, he will be favorably disposed to trying to implement the theory. However, if the manager believes only trouble and grief will be forthcoming from his successful implementation, he is not likely to be bothered.

The point is that many organizations purport to be enlightened in the way they manage their human resources, and spend countless dollars either to attempt to actually be enlightened or at least to maintain appearances. But it is one thing to employ managers who have been trained in behavioral science, giving them an apparent mandate to make use of their training; it is another thing to structure the organization so that enlightened management is possible (the expectancy component), and so that successful application of behavioral science (as measured by increased performance, lower turnover, or whatever) is rewarded by things that the managers responsible for the performance desire.

In short, the widespread application of the scientifically based theories of work motivation to the problems of productivity facing Western economies will require that at least as much attention be paid to the design of organizations, as is paid to the prescriptions found in those principles. For, unless the context for the implementation of theory makes such implementation both possible and rewarding for managers, they are not likely to be motivated to try it. More will be said about the importance of organizational settings for work motivation in chapter thirteen.

13 CONCLUSIONS AND FUTURE DIRECTIONS

All universal judgements are weak, loose, and dangerous.

—*Montaigne*

A survey of recent reviews of the scientific literature on work motivation reveals that organizational scientists hold widely differing opinions concerning the rate of progress that is being made in our collective understanding of the topic.* For example, Steers and Porter (1979) and Campbell and Pritchard (1976) feel that we have learned a great deal about work motivation in recent decades, while others, such as Staw (1977), feel that little has been added to the knowledge base provided fifty years ago by early experimental psychologists. In fact, when one considers Locke's (1982) observation that the idea of paying employees on the basis of their performance dates back at least as far as the early days of scientific management (Taylor, 1911), probably further, and when we recognize that the fundamental issues of social comparison processes, and feelings of equity and inequity date back at least as far as the Bible (Matthew 20: 1-19), Staw's negative assessment of our collective rate of progress doesn't seem without foundation.

This author's view is that both the quantity and quality of useful new knowledge we have about work motivation are less than commensurate with the obvious importance of the issue, the frequency

---

*While the majority of the chapters of this book are addressed both to students and practicing managers on the one hand, and to organizational scientists on the other, the contents of this chapter are directed more toward the latter group than to either of the other two. The purpose of the present chapter is to evaluate, in general terms, the theory and research on work motivation and behavior, and to offer some suggestions for the future conduct of the scientific efforts devoted to the problem. Nevertheless, because practicing managers ultimately stand to benefit from the advancement of new motivation theories and techniques, the argument presented here may be of interest to them as well.

with which it is discussed by managers and in the media, and—especially—the volumes of research and formal writing that has been devoted to it since, say, 1965. To be clear, it is not that we don't know very much about the phenomenon, nor that we are not continuing to learn about it. Rather, the position taken here is that we seem to be adding increasingly smaller increments to our base of knowledge about work motivation and behavior, as more and more research is conducted into the topic.

One reason for this declining rate of progress has been suggested by Campbell and Pritchard (1976), who note that, collectively, we have tended to underutilize those theories that are available, both in the activities of science, as well as in the practice of management. How is this so?

The previous chapter of this book details numerous reasons why the theory of work motivation may be underutilized by practitioners (or at least why it may be of only limited effectiveness when it is applied): there are a host of practical constraints found in many organizations that can militate against successful implementation of the theory (or theories). In short, management groups cannot, and/or do not, make as much use of the principles of work motivation as they otherwise might.

Organizational scientists are also guilty of underusing and misusing current theories of work motivation, but in their own way. As has been noted repeatedly throughout this book, there have been many instances in which researchers have apparently either ignored, or misinterpreted, extant theories of work motivation when they have designed and conducted studies that purport to test them. The confusion that surrounded Herzberg's theory (recall chapter two), the chronic oversimplifications of Maslow's need hierarchy (recall chapter three), and the almost universal interpretation of VIE Theory as a between-person model (chapter seven) are examples.

But, progress in any science is generally a nonlinear affair, and the organizational sciences are no exception (Bourgeois and Pinder, 1984). This means that we cannot realistically expect to generate a constant rate of increase in knowledge and understanding for every unit of scientific energy that is invested. In the case of work motivation, it would appear that many of its most obvious features were noticed and understood early on, and that great strides were made in a short period of time. However it is one thing to observe general tendencies and to make universal observations about them—statements that, in balance, are false nearly as often as they are true. It is quite another thing to gain an understanding of the exceptions to the general rule, to learn about the nature of whatever individual differences and so-called *boundary conditions* that apply.

To illustrate, consider the early expectancy-valence theories, **307**

such as those introduced to organizational science by Georgopoulos, Mahoney, and Jones (1957), and Vroom (1964), and compare them to the more complex versions that were subsequently offered by theorists such as Porter and Lawler (1968), Graen (1969),
Lawler (1971, 1973), Dachler and Mobley (1973), and more recently, Kopelman and Thompson (1976). Each of these modifications of the basic model added one or more variables, aimed at taking into account some degree of what previously had been seen as
error variance, or unknown exceptions to the general expectancy-
valence formulation. Likewise, consider Equity Theory: it is one thing
to state that people develop feelings about the way they are treated
in comparison to the way they believe others are being treated; it is
far more difficult to go beyond that initial observation to attempt to
determine as Goodman (1974) did, for instance, when a person utilizes an internal equity norm or relies upon social comparison processes, and when they do, to predict with whom they will compare
themselves.

In balance, we can conclude the following. The obvious importance of work motivation, both to organizational science and to business and industry, has occasioned a proliferation of theory and research into the topic over the past quarter century. In fact, work
motivation must be the most written-about topic in the organizational
sciences (Staw, 1977). But much of the research that has been
conducted—both to develop new theories and to test previously existing ones—has been flawed by any of a number of problems. We
are left, therefore, with only a few studies actually attesting to the scientific validity and practical utility of most current theories of work
motivation and behavior. It is probably safe to conclude that current
work motivation theory is, for the most part, more valid than we are
capable of demonstrating. However, while new methodological
techniques, and the more careful application of existing ones, may
ultimately confirm or disconfirm the apparent validity of current theoretic approaches, it seems clear that *major new advances are not
likely within the bounds of current research frameworks.* Instead,
fundamentally new approaches seem warranted—approaches that
are even more radically different than those that have been suggested by other reviewers of this topic (such as, for example, Campbell and Pritchard, 1976; Hamner, Ross, and Staw, 1978; an Staw,
1977).

Suggestions for new approaches arise when we note common
important features of current approaches. Accordingly, consider
two features that are common to virtually all extant approaches to
work motivation, characteristics that may be placing natural limits on
the ultimate levels of validity and applied utility they can ever be expected to achieve. One of these common features is their attempt at

generality—virtually all of the theories we have examined in this book are intended to be of universal applicability, at least within the confines of this culture. The second common characteristic—one that is closely related to the first—is that, by and large, they tend to underemphasize the *contexts* within which work motivation occurs.

In the following sections, we will examine these two characteristics of current theory more closely, and propose the elements of a new general framework that corrects for the shortcomings inherent in them. It is hoped that the proposed framework will help guide future research and new theoretic approaches, leading to new advances in knowledge concerning work motivation and behavior.

To begin, let's take a look at the meaning and significance of the second of the two aforementioned limiting characteristics of current theory: their common tendency to underemphasize the context of work motivation.

THE CONTEXT OF WORK MOTIVATION

For many years, behavioral scientists have recognized, in principle at least, that the context within which human behavior occurs is a major determinant of the nature, intensity, and duration of that behavior (e.g., Lewin, 1938; Murray, 1938; Tolman, 1932). For example, much or most of experimental psychology has been concerned with the effects of specific environmental stimuli on animal and human behavior. Likewise, the consequences that accrue to the individual from the environment are seen by operant psychologists as the primary determinants of behavior. And, as we noted in chapter three, need theorists such as Henry Murray recognized that human needs, when they are in a state of readiness, can be induced by certain characteristics of the environment (called *press*).

Nevertheless, although the importance of environmental contexts has been recognized *in theory* for some time, only recently have psychologists begun to investigate the joint interaction between individual traits and contextual factors in a systematic way (cf. Bem, 1972; Bem and Allen, 1974; Bowers, 1973; Cronbach, 1975; Endler, 1975; Magnusson and Endler, 1977a; Mischel, 1968). Thus two new subdisciplines have recently emerged to explicitly consider person-by-context interactions—*Environmental Psychology* (Craik, 1970, 1977; Russell and Ward, 1982) and *Interactional Psychology* (Magnusson and Endler, 1977b). The point is that the study of the effects of situational contexts on human behavior is a relatively new concern, in spite of the fact that the obvious importance of such contexts has been recognized in principle for some time.

Similarly, although most theories of work motivation and behavior implicitly recognize the influence of contextual factors such as su- **309** pervisors and other features of the work setting, the bulk of the formal research and theory construction on the topic focuses upon characteristics of the individual rather than upon contextual factors. Thus, we have seen a variety of need-based theories that discuss the nature and functioning of human need states (chapters three and four), and we have noted the heavy intrapsychic orientation of the cognitive theories discussed in chapters five through eight. And, while we have noted that the operant conditioning approach holds that behavior is a function of its consequences, we hasten to observe that little is provided in the way of guidance by that approach to help us understand the specific aspects of behavioral contexts that are either reinforcing or punishing. The point is that, in comparison with many other subdisciplines in behavioral science, organizational science in general, and work motivation theory in particular, have tended to place most of its emphasis on understanding the nature of individuals, rather than on understanding the contexts within which individuals work.

Of course, as is the case with any generalization, there have been some notable exceptions to this global statement. In this particular case, one can cite the work of scientists such as Herzberg, Hackman, Oldham, and others who have studied the impact of job design on work-related motivation (see chapters two and eleven). Likewise, there have been some attempts to examine the relationship between certain organizational/structural characteristics on the one hand, and work attitudes and behavior on the other (e.g., Berger and Cummings, 1979; James and Jones, 1976; Porter and Lawler, 1965), but, for the most part, these have been few in number and not very conclusive. Accordingly, the general approach to future research to be presented shortly, will include systematic study of the contexts within which work motivation and behavior occur.

THE GENERALITY OF CURRENT APPROACHES

With Larry Moore, this author has argued elsewhere that the progress of organizational science has been impeded by the widespread attempts of its adherents to develop and advance general, universal theories before such generality has been justified (Pinder and Moore, 1979, 1980). Proposed as an alternative to the promulgation of universal theories of organizations and the behavior of people within them is the development of *middle-range* theories—theories that attempt to explain only certain segments of the total universe. In one sense, all of motivation theory, as we know it, is middle-range theory, because when viewed in the light of the rest of the discipline, it deals with only a limited set of phenomena (work motivation and behavior). On the other hand, there are other ways of generating middle-range theories pertaining to any particular phenomenon, and it has been the general neglect of organizational scientists to consider these approaches in the advancement of work motivation theory that may have contributed to the relatively low yield of new knowledge we have been acquiring on the topic in recent years.

An alternative approach is to generate categories of situations within which certain theories, or parts of a particular body of a theory, are intended to apply. The *contingency model* advanced by Mayes (1978b) and described in the previous chapter of this book constitutes the only serious attempt known by this author to implement such a strategy in the area of work motivation. The point is that, for the most part, virtually all of the theories presented in this book purport to have universal applicability, although—as we have seen—the evidence in support of most of them provides insufficient grounds for such claims. Thus, the various need theories all acknowledge that, although people differ in the strength of their needs, the same underlying sets of needs, in varying combinations, can ultimately explain all human behavior. Likewise, although some of the cognitive models include certain individual difference variables, they all suggest that the mechanisms leading to behavior on the job are pretty much the same for most of us, once these individual differences have been taken into account. Finally, the theories of goal setting and operant behavior may be the most universalistic of all: individual differences are seldom mentioned in treatments of Organizational Behavior Modification, and advocates of Goal Setting Theory imply that the dynamics of goal setting are ubiquitous in many or most other approaches to the problem (Locke, 1978)!

In summary, major new advances in work motivation theory will require the development of middle-range approaches that include, among other things, systematic attention to the context of work motivation and behavior. Such an approach is proposed below.

A PROPOSED FRAMEWORK FOR FUTURE RESEARCH

The general strategy being offered here consists of four basic steps:

1. A reconceptualization of the notion of work contexts.
2. The development of a taxonomy of work contexts based upon this reconceptualization.
3. The development of an empirical taxonomy of motivational types.
4. The development of middle-range theories of motivation and the eventual ascension to general models of work motivation and behavior.

Let's take a look at these steps, one at a time.

311

Reconceptualizing Work Contexts

As mentioned earlier, the few attempts to examine the concept of work contexts, in reference to work motivation, have consisted primarily of studies (and theory) dealing with the impact of particular features of the *jobs* that employees perform, or of investigations into the relationship between certain structural characteristics of organizations and work motivation. Moreover, as we noted at the time, the first approach has been moderately successful, but a bit narrow in focus, while the latter approach has generally not been very fruitful (Berger and Cummings, 1979, p.194).

Nevertheless, the author believes that both of these approaches have been justified in their objective, although each of them has been bound to be limited in value to the construction of theory concerned with work motivation and behavior. The reason for this belief is that, while both the immediate job and the larger organizational setting are important components of the context of work, any approach that considers only one of them will, obviously, be unable to take into account the important motivation-related features of the other. Thus, for the sake of future theory construction, the context of work must be taken into account at least as much as the nature of the human beings doing the work, and, in addition, it must be redefined to include relevant aspects of both the micro (related to the job) and the molar (related to the larger organizational setting) work environments.

One question that must be addressed if such an approach is to be pursued concerns whether objective features of jobs and organizations should be considered, or whether their subjective features should be utilized. On the one hand, the majority of the work that has looked at the impact of organizational characteristics on employee attitudes and behavior in the past has relied on objective features of organizations (such as number of hierarchical levels, for example). On the other hand, the most successful theories of job design (such as the Job Characteristics Approach that was presented in chapter eleven) have focused on the *psychological meaning* of jobs possessing particular design characteristics.

As noted by Schwab and Cummings (1976), there are a number of problems associated with a reliance on the subjective approach, such as: the potential for confounding the personal needs and perceptual styles of people with the way tasks are perceived and evaluated; the fact that such confounding, when it occurs, makes it difficult to isolate which objective features of the job are responsible for determining the reactions of employees; and, finally, the difficulty of extricating perceptions of the job from other intrapsychic characteristics of the people involved, such as their overall level of job satisfaction, for example. In short, exclusive reliance on the subjective impact of jobs and organizational characteristics entails a number of potential problems.

Recently, psychologists such as Magnusson and Endler (1977a), and Sarason (1977), have argued convincingly that understanding is needed of the relationships among three broad classes of variables: the contexts of behavior, the internal cognitive and affective processes of individuals, and behavior itself. Likewise, in the context of theory and research in work motivation, Campbell and Pritchard (1976) have stressed the importance of understanding intrapsychic processes, such as thoughts and affective reactions.

This author is sympathetic with both perspectives, but believes that the practical research difficulties noted by Schwab and Cummings will have to be overcome in order to permit the type of intrapsychic insight that Campbell and Pritchard feel is necessary. For example, while the particular substantive dimensions that have emerged from research in environmental psychology would likely be of limited usefulness in advancing knowledge about work motivation, per se, the conceptual and empirical approaches from that discipline (cf. Craik, 1970, 1977; Russell and Ward, 1982; Ward, 1977; Ward and Porter, 1980; Ward and Russell, 1981; Wohlwill and Kohn, 1976) might be of use in dealing with some of the problems identified by Schwab and Cummings (1976), and permit the eventual development of a formal taxonomy of work settings, the second step in the general approach being proposed here.

Developing a Taxonomy of Work Situations

The need to develop a formal taxonomy of situations for the sake of improving the prediction of individual behavior has been recognized for many years. For example, Dunnette (1963, 1966) argued that different types of people are bound to behave in different ways, depending, in part, upon the nature of the circumstances within which they find themselves. Moreover, the urgency of being able to make better-than-chance predictions of the behavior of political leaders during the time of a crisis on the basis of patterns exhibited by these individuals in similar circumstances has been cited as a specific example of the need for a taxonomy of behavioral situations (Fredericksen, 1972). The point is that to the extent that it is true that human behavior is, in fact, jointly determined by both intrapsychic and situational factors, then continued attempts to predict or explain behavior without taking contextual heterogeneity into account are bound to be frustrated, and theories such as those represented in this book **313** will continue to be of limited scientific validity and of limited applied value to practitioners. In short, the dimensions identified from a program of research, such as that mentioned above, could provide the basis for such a taxonomy.

Developing a Taxonomy of Motivational Types

The importance of individual differences in the prediction of human behavior has been recognized for some time (e.g., Cronbach, 1957; Owens, 1968, 1976; Tyler, 1965). In fact, the ubiquity of reliable differences between populations of people differing on the basis of age, sex, race, and other variables has led to the development of one of the two major schools of modern psychology (Cronbach, 1957).

In the area of work motivation, however, comparatively little use has been made of our knowledge about the reliable differences that do exist between groups of people, with a few notable exceptions. These exceptions include, for example, the work of Hackman and his colleagues, dealing with individual differences in reactions to job characteristics (Hackman and Oldham, 1980; Wanous, 1974), Herzberg's typology based on his two-factor theory of motivation (recall chapter two), and Schein's (1978) concept of the *anchors* upon which different people base their career choices and decisions. The point is that, although we widely recognize that different people behave in different ways—even when they are in the same situations—we have failed to determine the precise role of these interindividual differences in work motivation. Accordingly, the third step in the realization of the general strategy being proposed here, would be the development of a meaningful, motivation-related taxonomy of individuals, based upon objective demographic characteristics (e.g., Owens, 1976), intrapsychic traits such as needs (Alderfer, 1972) or cognitive style (e.g., Barnowe and Frost, 1982; Kolb and Plovnick, 1977), or both objective and intrapsychic factors.

Developing Middle-Range Theories

The fourth stage of the general approach being proposed would be to combine the work accomplished during each of the two previous stages. That is, middle-range theories of work motivation and behavior would be developed, each theory (or set of theories) pertaining only to limited types of people, in limited types of motivational circumstances.

The combination of the typology of motivational types, and the typology of motivational settings, is portrayed graphically in the matrix shown in Figure 13-1. The entries of the matrix consist of theories that would apply only to the limited combinations of people-by-

FIGURE 13–1: Representation of Construction of Middle-Range Theories of
Work Motivation and Behavior

Types of Individual from Stage 3	Types of Work Setting (from Stage 2)			
	Type 1	Type 2	Type 3	Type 4
Type 1	Theory 1,1	Theory 1,2	Theory 1,3	—
Type 2	Theory 2,1	—	—	—
Type 3		—	—	—
Type 4		—	—	—

settings that would be possible from the previous two stages. Some of these theories may be currently existing ones, found to be of particularly high levels of scientific validity and/or applied utility, for certain types of people, within limited types of work settings. Alternatively, the specific nature of whatever taxonomies of people and settings emerge from stages two and three (as described above), may suggest entirely new theories that would be of particular value in various of the cells shown in Figure 13-1. The point is that, initially, at least, an attempt would be made to build and confirm bodies of theory and applied techniques for each of the nonvacant person x situation intersections of the Figure. Then, in the same way that middle-range theories of other organizational phenomena might be combined as levels of understanding warrant (Pinder and Moore, 1979), these motivation theories might be combined and the total number of person-by-situation interactive models reduced, leading, ultimately, toward more general theories that can justify disregarding individual and situational differences. *

In conclusion, the proposed model constitutes a radical departure from current practice in the science-making activities devoted to the advancement of knowledge concerning work motivation and behavior. However, to the extent that the observation made at the beginning of this chapter is justified—that there is little *fundamentally* new in the theory of work motivation—radically new approaches are necessary. It is hoped that the new framework will provide the sort of guidance that is going to be needed before dramatic new discoveries are made into the problem of work motivation and behavior.

---

* The similarity between the proposed approach and Dunnette's (1963, 1966) modified model for personnel selection and placement must be recognized. In fact, in many ways, the two models are very similar, sharing an appreciation for the ubiquity of both individual and situational differences and proposing the development of interactive models that take the interactions between types of people and types of situations explicitly into account. The primary difference, of course, is that Dunnette's model was proposed for application to problems of personnel selection and placement, whereas the model being advanced here, is intended to assist the development of formal theories of work motivation and behavior. Ultimately, however, each aspires to assist the prediction of individual behavior in a specified work setting.

APPENDIX OF CASE STUDIES

CASES FOR DISCUSSION AND ANALYSIS

This section contains seven short case studies that can be approached using the concepts and theories discussed in this book. In fact, many or most of the cases can be analyzed using the ideas found in more than one chapter of the book, and it is instructive to revisit many of them several times, comparing the analyses suggested by the various theories, as well as the types of solutions that might emerge from each of them.

Two assists are offered to guide the use of the cases. The first assist is the table that appears on page 317. The table suggests which cases might provide useful illustrations of the concepts presented in the various chapters of the book. An X mark beside a chapter number and below a case number suggests that certain concepts in that chapter may be of particular value in approaching the case in question. (However, the reader may find that chapters other than those indicated are also of value in analyzing certain cases, and in guiding their solutions.)

Secondly, in addition to the table, each case is accompanied by one or more questions that are intended to suggest ways that they may be approached. Again, the questions following each case are not exhaustive of those that might be raised, but are intended only to be suggestive of the types of applications that can be made of the theoretical tools presented throughout the book. Unless otherwise noted, all cases were written by the author especially for this book.

A GUIDE TO THE CASES

	CASE NUMBER						
CHAPTER NUMBER	1	2	3	4	5	6	7
Two	X	X			X		X
Three	X	X			X	X	X
Four	X	X			X	X	X
Five	X	X		X		X	X
Six	X	X	X	X		X	X
Seven	X	X		X	X	X	X
Eight				X	X	X	
Nine	X	X			X	X	
Ten	X	X			X	X	
Eleven	X	X					
Twelve	X	X	X	X		X	X

CASE ONE: PAMELA JONES, FORMER BANKER

Pamela Jones enjoyed banking. She had taken a battery of personal aptitude and interest tests that suggested she might like and do well in either banking or librarianship. Since the job market for librarians was poor, she applied for employment with a large chartered bank, the Bank of Winnipeg, and was quickly accepted.

Her early experiences in banking were almost always challenging and rewarding. She was enrolled in the bank's management development program because of her education (a B.A. in languages and some postgraduate training in business administration), her previous job experience, and her obvious intelligence and drive.

During her first year in the training program, Pamela attended classes on banking procedures and policies, and worked her way through a series of low level positions in her branch. She was repeatedly told by her manager that her work was above average. Similarly, the training officer who worked out of the main office and coordinated the development of junior officers in the program frequently told Pamela that she was "among the best three" of her cohort of twenty trainees.

Although she worked hard and frequently encountered discrimination from senior bank personnel (as well as customers) because of her sex, Pamela developed a deep-seated attachment to banking in general, and to her bank and branch, in particular. She was proud to be a banker and proud to be a member of the Bank of Winnipeg.

After one year in the management development program however, Pamela found she was not learning anything new about banking or the B. of W. She was shuffled from one job to another at her own branch, cycling back over many positions several times to help meet temporary problems caused by absences, overloads, and turnover. Turnover—a rampant problem in banking—amazed Pamela. She couldn't understand, for many months, why so many people started careers "in the service" of banking, only to leave after one or two years.

After her first year, the repeated promises of moving into her own position at another branch started to sound hollow to Pamela. The training officer claimed that there were no openings suitable for her at other branches. On two occasions when openings did occur, the manager of each of the branches in question rejected Pamela, sight unseen, presumably because she hadn't been in banking long enough.

Pamela was not the only unhappy person at her branch. Her immediate supervisor, George Burns, complained that because of the bank's economy drive, vacated customer service positions were left unfilled. As branch accountant, Burns was responsible for day-to-day customer service. As a result, he was unable to perform the duties of his own job. The manager told Burns several times that customer service was critical, but that Burns would have to improve his performance on his own job. Eventually, George Burns left the bank to work for a trust company, earning seventy dollars a month more for work similar to that he had been performing at the B. of W. This left Pamela in the position of having to supervise the same tellers who had trained her, only a few months earlier. Pamela was amazed at all the mistakes the tellers made, but found it difficult to do much to correct their poor work habits. All disciplinary procedures had to be administered with the approval of Head Office.

After several calls to her training officer, Pamela was finally transferred to her first "real" position in her own branch. Still keen and dedicated, Pamela was soon to lose her enthusiasm.

At her new branch, Pamela was made "assistant accountant." Her duties included the supervision of the seven tellers, some customer service and a great deal of paper work.

317

The same economy drive that she had witnessed at her training branch resulted in the failure to replace customer service personnel. Pamela was expected to "pick up the slack" at the front desk, neglecting her own work. Her tellers seldom balanced their own cash, so Pamela stayed late almost every night to find their errors. To save on overtime, the manager sent the tellers home while Pamela stayed late, first to correct the tellers' imbalances, then to finish her own paper work. He told Pamela that as an officer of the bank, she was expected to stay until the work of her subordinates, and her own work, were satisfactorily completed. Pamela realized that most of her counterparts in other B. of W. branches were willing to give this sort of dedication; therefore, so should she. This situation lasted six months with little sign of change in sight.

One day, Pamela learned from a phone conversation with a friend at another branch that she would be transferred to Hope, B.C. to fill an opening that had arisen. Pamela's husband was a professional, employed by a large corporation in Vancouver. His company did not have an office in Hope; moreover, his training was very specialized, so that he could probably find employment only in large cities anyway.

Accepting transfers was expected of junior officers who wanted to get ahead. Pamela enquired at Head Office and learned that the rumor was true. Her training officer told her, however, that Pamela could decline the transfer if she wished, but he couldn't say how soon her next promotion opportunity would come about.

Depressed, annoyed, disappointed and frustrated, Pamela quit the bank.

Discussion Questions

1. Analyze this case from the point of view of the frustration model presented in chapter four, identifying Pamela's most salient work-related needs, goals, and the nature of the "barriers" that caused her frustration.
2. Describe Pamela's behavior in terms of VIE Theory. Why did she eventually elect to leave the bank?
3. Use the operant conditioning approach to explain Pamela's situation. How does your analysis differ from that suggested by VIE Theory?
4. Does Equity Theory help explain Pamela's behavior? How?
5. Which of the factors discussed in part two of chapter twelve of this book help explain what happened? What might be done about them?
6. What suggestions might you offer the personnel department at the B. of W. on the basis of Pamela's experience? (Be sure to let relevant theories guide your counsel.)

CASE TWO: JIM PRESTON, ALIENATED SALESMAN

Ever since the Atlas Electrical Supply Co. was bought out by Carey and Co., Jim Preston had been in a sales slump. A leading salesman for Atlas for the past twenty-eight years, Preston made a regular practice of enjoying handsome monthly bonuses in response to the company's incentive pay system. He had always been proud of the extra money, both as a symbol of his value to the company, as well as for the practical uses to which he had applied it. He often boasted about how the bonuses had helped him complete his mortgage several years early, as well as finance his daughter's education at the University of Toronto. In the four months since the new management took over, however, Jim's sales had fallen off sharply, along with his enthusiasm and company spirit, even though the bonus system was still being used. In fact, he had not collected a bonus in months. Sarah Powell, Jim's new supervisor since the takeover, was concerned. She held a series of informal discussions with Jim and several other sales personnel to try to get to the bottom of Jim's problems.

Mrs. Powell learned from her meetings that Jim resented being supervised by a woman who was younger than his own daughter—now a college graduate. He blew up at her during one of their meetings, yelling, "All of you new brass are the same—always trying to squeeze more out of the little guy. You think you know everything about selling! I was selling electrical parts and supplies before you or any of the other Carey supervisors were old enough to know what they are. Now you're telling me how to do my job. Why don't you get off my back? It's my business if I don't earn any bonuses!"

Sarah was startled by Preston's outburst, and concerned by his apparent resentment and hostility toward her. She learned that several of Preston's fellow salesmen, who were mostly younger than him, also resented him because of his resistance to the recent attempt to unionize the office staff. Several of them claimed that he was "a real company man," even though his sales figures didn't reflect it. She also learned that Jim was periodically re-

318

ceiving sales directives from Stan Campbell, Jim's former boss who had been moved laterally at the time of the takeover. Jim claimed he was never told clearly who his new supervisor was, now that the companies had merged.

After attending a luncheon meeting on job redesign, Sarah tried to "motivate" higher sales from Jim by adding to the product lines he carried, giving him a larger district to cover, and letting him move upstairs into a slightly larger office. She hoped that the changes would arouse new energy in Preston who, to her added frustration, seemed increasingly more preoccupied with his imminent retirement to a country town. Finally, Sarah asked Jim if he would like to retire early. He declined the offer, but Sarah recommended to her boss that they give old Jim "the golden handshake." Nothing else had worked.

Discussion Questions

1. Approach this case using the same questions that appear following the Pamela Jones case. Then, in addition, consider the following:
2. How does the reward system in the Carey Company differ from that of the Bank of Winnipeg, particularly with regard to concerns that might arise from Equity Theory, VIE Theory, and the practical constraints discussed in chapter twelve?
3. Contrast Jim Preston's salient needs with those of Pamela Jones. How do you explain any differences you find between them?
4. What would you have recommended to Sarah Powell, Jim's boss?

CASE THREE: THE SOLID STATE RECRUITING PROBLEM

In recent years the largest department of the faculty of engineering at a major Ontario university had been having great difficulty recruiting Ph.D.s qualified to teach solid state technology. Located near many television and electronics factories and government research installations, the university was facing a large demand for college graduates in the area of solid state technology. Class sizes were rising and both students and faculty were complaining that the higher student/faculty ratio was harming the quality of teaching. Faculty members also claimed that their research was suffering as well. Still, the community demanded engineers, and students responded to the demand by switching from other specialities into the solid state area. Growth in class sizes ranged between 10 and 20 percent per year.

The rising demand for s.s. engineers seemed to be widespread across the continent. Consequently, student/faculty ratios at most engineering schools were rising, as in the case of the Ontario school. In 1964, the faculty managed to hire Watson and LeClair, two uniquely qualified Ph.D.s in the solid state field, but their demand remained high! In 1965, the school was attempting to hire seven more Ph.D.s. Competition with other, more prestigious universities was fierce. However, because they liked the area and had family nearby, three new recruits joined the faculty in 1965. They came though at extremely high sal-aries, because in order to attract them the university had to outbid its traditional rivals in the east—Harvard, RPI, Cornell, McGill, and York.

It took no time for Watson and LeClair to learn "via the grapevine" that the 1965 recruits were joining the faculty at salaries starting twelve hundred dollars higher than they (the 1964 recruits) would be receiving, even after their 1965 raises. Each of the 1964 hirees went to the dean and demanded wage readjustments, threatening to quit if they were not granted. The dean was sympathetic but faced two other problems: first, to grant the two s.s. engineers the raises of two thousand dollars they were demanding would put their salaries away out of line vis à vis the salaries of other more senior instructors who were not in the solid state area. Secondly, the dean was facing an extremely tight salary budget, as well as increased pressure from the community and the university president's office concerning the "fat salaries" already being paid to faculty. The dean tried to get approval to meet the demands of Watson and LeClair (the 1964 men), but failed. Both quit and assumed higher-paying positions elsewhere. Further, when she heard that Professor LeClair had quit, Elizabeth French, one of the 1965 recruits, changed her mind and accepted a position at Cornell.

Class enrollments for 1966 increased 23 percent in the s.s. division.

[handwritten margin note: the 3 new recruit already was]

Discussion Questions

1. Analyze this case using Equity Theory and the issues discussed in chapter twelve. Adopt the point of view of each of the following people in your analysis:
   a. Watson   b. Elizabeth French   c. the dean of the school.
2. What advice would you offer the dean?

CASE FOUR: A QUIRK AT NARC

Barbara Wright felt uneasy about the conversation that was developing between two of the senior interviewers in the parking lot behind the National Attitude Research Company (NARC). Mary Kraus and Edna Hunt had somehow managed to obtain a copy of a memo to the vice-president from Sam Parker, the supervisor directly in charge of the thirty opinion research interviewers working for NARC. It seemed that, somehow, a number of the interview personnel were earning $2.50 per completed interview, while most of the others were being paid at the rate of $1.50 per interview. What was particularly annoying to Kraus and Hunt was the fact that the higher-paid people all happened to be young college graduates, hired in a batch very recently to help launch an opinion poll for a new client. Kraus and Hunt had worked for NARC for several years and had been earning the $1.50 rate for some time. Barbara Wright was one of the "new eggheads" who had been hired at the $2.50 rate. The hostility being expressed by the older interviewers suggested to Barbara that she would be well advised to stay clear of the conversation. She cherished her personal relationships with the older interviewers, and wanted to keep peace with them.

Discussion Question

Contrast the predictions that would be made about the motivation levels of Barbara Wright using Goal Setting, VIE Theory, Equity Theory, and O.B. Mod. Then, perform the same analyses as they pertain to Mary Kraus (or Edna Hunt). Do the perspectives offered by the various theories for these two people converge? Why or why not?

CASE FIVE: MARY THE MARTYR

The secretaries and clerk typists she supervised called her "Mary the Martyr." In many ways, she deserved the epithet. Mary Collins had been secretary to the vice-president of administration at J. R. Eves and Company for more than twenty years, although the exact number was something only Mary seemed to know—it was part of the image she projected of herself. She had seen five men occupy the office of vice-president over the years and managed, sooner or later, to develop an almost mother-son relationship with each of them. She protected her boss with fierce loyalty and judicious control of access to time on his official calendar and informal visits by his subordinates and the firm's other v.p.'s.

Mary always seemed to be in a rush. There was always a tenseness about her, an air of nervous anxiety that implied she was overworked and hopelessly behind schedule on her job duties. She was always the first member of the clerical staff into the office in the morning, and always the last to leave in the afternoon. A day never passed without an audible remark on her part concerning the long hours she worked. She mastered the skill of working phrases into her conversations with others, letting them know that she spent longer hours than they did in the office (e.g., "Last night, when I finally got out of here, I noticed how dark it gets by five-thirty—soon it will be Christmas!")

Eventually, each one of her bosses became so distracted by Mary's apparent state of overwork that they suggested her job be redesigned, transferring some of her duties to other people on the clerical staff. Each time the suggestion arose, however, Mary found a way of preventing any such change from occurring: there was always some reason why none of her chores could be redistributed to other workers. Oddly enough, the activity level surrounding her job seemed to dissipate for a few weeks after each attempt to change her job. But gradually, Mary would be seen more and more frequently in a state of frenzied panic and heard proclaiming, one way or another, that "the sky was about to fall."

Discussion Question

Analyze this case using O.B. Mod, and then use it and a goal setting approach to describe how you might manage the situation.

CASE SIX: THE LATE RANDY MOORE

Randy Moore was a likeable enough fellow. He always seemed to get the job done, and usually turned in high quality work. Moreover, he tended to get along reasonably well with the other employees at Rapid City Mortgage Company, as well as with the company's customers. Randy did have one annoying habit, however: he was always late for meetings, sometimes only a few minutes, sometimes much longer.

Whether it was a matter of meeting his friends for lunch, or attending the monthly meetings held by his boss to discuss customer accounts, Randy could be counted on to be late, usually arriving full of jokes, apologies, and—sometimes—explanations for his tardiness. Yet he never promised to change his ways, and he never did change them over the eighteen months during which Bob Knight was Randy's boss. After all, Randy usually managed to ascertain from others who had been on time for the meetings for which he was late,

what, if anything, he had missed. And he seldom permitted the fact that he had missed anything (as a result of his habit) to interfere with his day-to-day dealings with customers. Nevertheless, his lateness was disruptive and time-consuming, especially when it was necessary to brief him on what he had missed while the other clerks and supervisors in attendance waited. And recently, Bob Knight noticed that there were more and more occasions when Randy's absence hurt the flow of the agenda, because he was not there to provide information to the rest of the department concerning accounts under his care.

After talking to Randy about his tardiness and finding that their conversation had little effect, Bob Knight decided that another strategy was needed. He didn't wish to fire Randy, because the rest of his work behavior was acceptable, and as noted above, of good quality. But Bob was hard pressed to come up with another approach that seemed reasonable.

Discussion Questions

1. Contrast the explanations that would be offered for Randy's behavior by advocates of need theory, VIE Theory, and O.B. Mod. Discuss the major differences revealed in your analysis from the following two perspectives:
   a. The fundamental assumptions made by each theory regarding the essence of human nature.
   b. The types of solutions that each of these theories would propose.

CASE SEVEN: WOMEN LAZY, EXPECT SYMPATHY

TORONTO—The reason so few of the city's permanent employees are women is because "women are lazy and they expect sympathy and they want the jobs just because they're women," says Ald. Joe Piccinnini.

Discussing a recent study by the city's management services department which showed women account for only one-fifth of Toronto's 5,500 permanent employees, Piccinnini told the city executive committee Wednesday that women are underrepresented because few ever go to the trouble of

applying for jobs.

"They don't even bother to make applications, and yet they expect equal opportunity," he said. "Well, you're not going to get equal opportunity until you get out of bed, come down to city hall, and start applying."

The study, which Piccinnini said would alarm only "bleeding hearts," found that only 13 of 125 senior management positions in city departments are filled by women.

Canadian Press, 1982

Discussion Question

Discuss this case using MacGregor's concepts of Theory X and Theory Y (see chapters two and five), Equity Theory, and the practical matters described in chapter twelve.

REFERENCES

Abdel-Halim, A. A. Effects of person-job compatibility on managerial reactions to role ambiguity. *Organizational Behavior and Human Performance*, 1980, *26*, 193–211.

Adams, J. S. Toward an understanding of inequity. *Journal of Abnormal Psychology*, 1963, 422–436.

Adams, J. S. Inequity in social exchange. In L. Berkowitz (Ed.). *Advances in experimental psychology*. New York: Academic Press, 1965.

Adler, S. & Golan, J. Lateness as a withdrawal behavior. *Journal of Applied Psychology*, 1981, *66*, 544–554.

Ajzen, I. & Fishbein, M. Attitude-behavior relations: A theoretical analysis and review of empirical research. *Psychological Bulletin*, 1977, *84*, 888–918.

Aldag, R. J., Barr, S. H. & Brief, A. P. Measurement of perceived task characteristics. *Psychological Bulletin*, 1981, *90*, 415–431.

Alderfer, C. P. An empirical test of a new theory of human needs. *Organizational Behavior and Human Performance*, 1969, *4*, 143–175.

Alderfer, C. P. *Existence, relatedness, and growth*. N.Y.: The Free Press, 1972.

Alderfer, C. P. A critique of Salancik and Pfeffer's examination of need-satisfaction theories. *Administrative Science Quarterly*, 1977, *22*, 658–669.

Aldis, O. Of pigeons and men. *Harvard Business Review*, 1961, *39*, (4), 59–63.

Aldrich, H. E. *Organizations and environments*. Englewood Cliffs, N.J.: Prentice-Hall, 1980.

Anderson, J. Giving and receiving feedback. In G. W. Dalton, P. R. Lawrence, and L. E. Greiner (Eds.). *Organizational change and development*. Homewood, Ill.: Irwin, 1970.

Anderson, J. W. The impact of technology on job enrichment. *Personnel*, 1970, *47*, (5), 29–37.

Andrasik, F. Organizational behavior modification in business settings: A methodological and content review. *Journal of Organizational Behavior Management*, 1979, *2*, 85–102.

Andrews, I. R. Wage inequity and job performance. *Journal of Applied Psychology*, 1967, *51*, 39–45.

Angle, H. L. & Perry, J. L. An empirical assessment of organizational commitment and organizational effectiveness. *Administrative Science Quarterly,* 1981, *26,* 1-14.

Angle, H. L. & Perry, J. L. Individual and organizational influences on organizational commitment. *Work and Occupations: An International Sociological Journal,* 1982.

Argyris, C. *Personality and organization.* New York: Harper, 1957.

Argyris, C. Beyond freedom and dignity by B. F. Skinner, A review essay. *Harvard Educational Review,* 1971, *41,* 550-567.

Arnold, H. J. Effects of performance feedback and extrinsic reward upon high intrinsic motivation. *Organizational Behavior and Human Performance,* 1976, *17,* 275-288.

Arnold, H. J. A test of the validity of the multiplicative hypothesis of expectancy-valence theories of work motivation. *Academy of Management Journal,* 1981, *24,* 128-41.

Arnold, H. J. & Feldman, D. E. A multivariate analysis of the determinants of job turnover. *Journal of Applied Psychology,* 1982, *67,* 350-360.

Arnold, H. J. & House, R. J. Methodological and substantive extensions to the Job Characteristics model of motivation. *Organizational Behavior and Human Performance,* 1980, *25,* 161-183.

Arvey, R. D. *Fairness in selecting employees.* Reading, Mass.: Addison-Wesley, 1979.

Arvey, R. D. & Ivancevich, J. M. Punishment in organizations: A review, propositions, and research suggestions. *Academy of Management Review,* 1980, *5,* 123-132.

Atkinson, J. W. Towards experimental analysis of human motivation in terms of motives, expectancies, and incentives. In J. W. Atkinson (Ed.) *Motives in fantasy, action, and society.* Princeton: Van Nostrand, 1958.

Atkinson, J. W. *An introduction to motivation.* Princeton, N.J.: Van Nostrand, 1964.

Babb, H. W. & Kopp, D. G. Applications of behavior modification in organizations: A review and critique. *Academy of Management Review,* 1978, *3,* 281-292.

Bacharach, S. B. & Lawler, E. J. *Power and politics in organizations.* San Francisco: Jossey-Bass, 1980.

Bandura, A. *Principles of behavior modification.* New York: Holt, Rinehart, and Winston, 1969.

Bandura, A. *Social learning theory.* Englewood Cliffs, N.J.: Prentice-Hall, 1977.

Bandura, A. Self-efficacy in human agency. *American Psychologist,* 1982, *37,* 122-147.

Bandura, A. & Cervone, D. Self-evaluative and self-efficacy mechanisms governing the motivational effects of goal systems. *Journal of Personality and Social Psychology,* in press, 1983.

Barnowe, J. T. & Frost, P. J. Career decisions upstream from QWL: Personality and situational influences upon choice of business specialty. Unpublished manuscript, University of British Columbia, 1982.

Bartol, K. M. The sex structuring of organizations, a search for possible causes. *Academy of Management Review,* 1978, *3,* 805-815.

Barton, R. F. An MCDM approach for resolving goal conflict in MBO. *Academy of Management Review,* 1981, *6,* 231-242.

Bass, B. M. & Vaughan, J. A. *Training in industry: The management of learning.* Belmont, Calif.: Wadsworth, 1966.

Becker, H. S. Notes on the concept of commitment. *American Journal of Sociology,* 1960, *66,* 32-40.

323

Beehr, T. A. & Gupta, N. A note on the structure of employee withdrawal. *Organizational Behavior and Human Performance,* 1978, *21,* 73–79.

Behling, O., Labovitz, G. & Kosmo, R. The Herzberg controversy: A critical appraisal. *Academy of Management Journal,* 1968, *11,* 99–108.

Belcher, D. *Compensation administration,* Englewood Cliffs, N.J.: Prentice-Hall, 1974.

Bem, D. J. Constructing cross-situational consistencies in behavior: Some thoughts on Alker's critique of Mischel. *Journal of Personality,* 1972, *40,* 17–26.

Bem, D. J. Self-perception: The dependent variable of human performance. *Organizational Behavior and Human Performance,* 1967, *2,* 105–121.

Bem, D. J. Self-perception theory. In L. Berkowitz (Ed.), *Advances in Experimental Social Psychology, 6,* New York: Academic Press, 1972.

Bem, D. J. & Allen, A. On predicting some of the people some of the time. *Psychological Review,* 1974, *81,* 506–520.

Ben-Porat, A. Event and agent: Toward a structural theory of job satisfaction. *Personnel Psychology,* 1981, *34,* 523–534.

Berger, C. J. and Cummings, L. L. Organizational Structure, Attitudes, and Behaviors. In B. M. Staw (Ed.) *Research in Organizational Behavior,* Vol. 1, Greenwich Conn.: JAI Press, 1979.

Berlyne, D. E. The vicissitudes of aplopathematic and thebematoscopic pneumatology (or the hydrography of hedonism). In D. E. Berlyne and K. B. Madsen (Eds.), *Pleasure, reward, and preferences.* New York: Academic Press, 1973.

Betz, E. L. Need-reinforcer correspondence as a predictor of job satisfaction. *Personnel and Guidance Journal,* 1969, *47,* 878–883.

Bhagat, R. S. Conditions under which stronger job performance-job satisfaction relationships may be observed: A closer look at two situational contingencies. *Academy of Management Journal,* 1982, *25,* 772–789.

Bird, R. M., Bucovetsky, M. W. & Foot, D. K. *The Growth of Public Employment in Canada.* Montreal: Institute for Research on Public Policy, 1979.

Blair, J. M. Inflation in the United States. In G. C. Means et al. (Eds.), *The roots of inflation.* New York: Burt Franklin and Co., 1975.

Blau, P. M. *The dynamics of bureaucracy* (revised ed.). Chicago: University of Chicago Press, 1963.

Blood, M. R. Intergroup comparisons of intraperson differences: Rewards from the job. *Personnel Psychology,* 1973, *26,* 1–9.

Bobko, P. Concerning the non-application of human motivation theories in organizational settings. *Academy of Management Review,* 1978, *3,* 906–910.

Bockman, V. M. The Herzberg controversy. *Personnel Psychology,* 1971, *24,* 155–189.

Boehm, V. R. Research in the 'real world'—A conceptual model. *Personnel Psychology,* 1980, *33,* 495–503.

Bourgeois, V. W. & Pinder, C. C. The nonlinearlity of progress in organizational science. Unpublished working paper, Faculty of Commerce and Business Administration, The University of British Columbia, 1984.

Bowen, W. Better prospects for our ailing productivity. *Fortune,* December 3, 1979, 68–70, 74, 77, 80, 83, 86.

Bower, J. L. Effective public management. *Harvard Business Review,* 1977, *55,* (2), 131–140.

Bowers, K. S. Situationism in psychology: An analysis and a critique. *Psychological Review,* 1973, *80,* 307–336.

Brayfield, A. H. & Crockett, W. H. Employee attitudes and employee performance. *Psychological Bulletin,* 1955, *52,* 415–422.

Breaugh, J. A. Predicting absenteeism from prior absenteeism and work attitudes. *Journal of Applied Psychology,* 1981, *66,* 555–560.

Brett, J. M. The effect of job transfer on employees and their families. In C. L. Cooper and R. Payne (Eds.) *Current concerns in occupational stress.* New York: Wiley, 1981.

Brief, A. P. & Aldag, R. J. Correlates of role indices. *Journal of Applied Psychology,* 1976, *61,* 468–472.

Brief, A. P. & Aldag, R. J. Employee reactions to job characteristics: A constructive replication. *Journal of Applied Psychology,* 1975, *60,* 182–186.

Britton, J. & Gilmour, J. M. *The weakest link—a technological perspective on Canadian industrial underdevelopment.* Ottawa: Science Council of Canada, 1978.

Buchanan, B. Building organizational commitment: the socialization of managers in work organizations. *Administrative Science Quarterly,* 1974, *19,* 533–546.

Business Week. Boosting productivity at American Express, No. 2708 (October 5, 1981), 62, 64.

Calder, B. J. & Schurr, P. H. Attitudinal processes in organizations. In *Research in Organizational Behavior,* Vol.3, Greenwich, Conn.: JAI Press, 1981.

Campbell, D. J. & Illgen, D. R. Additive effects of task difficulty and goal setting on subsequent task performance. *Journal of Applied Psychology,* 1976, *61,* 319–324.

Campbell, J. G. Equal pay for work of equal value in the federal public service of Canada. *Compensation Review,* 1983, *15* (3), 42–51.

Campbell, J. P., Dunnette, M. D., Lawler III, E. E. and Weick, K. E. *Managerial behavior, performance and effectiveness.* N.Y.: McGraw-Hill, 1970.

Campbell, J. P. Personnel training and development. *Annual Review of Psychology,* 1971, *22,* 565–602.

Campbell, J. P. & Pritchard, R. D. Motivation theory in industrial and organizational psychology. In M. D. Dunnette (Ed.) *Handbook of industrial and organizational psychology.* Chicago: Rand McNally, 1976.

Caplan, R. D. & Jones, K. W. Effects of work load, role ambiguity and Type A personality on anxiety, depression and heart rate. *Journal of Applied Psychology,* 1975, *60,* 713–719.

Carmell, W. A. High court fails to address 'comparable worth' issue, but opens door a crack. *ABA Banking Journal,* 1981, *73* (9), 20, 23, 25.

Carrell, M. R. & Dittrich, J. E. Employee perception of fair treatment. *Personnel Journal,* 1976, *55,* 523–524.

Carrell, M. R. & Dittrich, J. E. Equity theory: the recent literature, methodological considerations, and new directions. *Academy of Management Review,* 1978, *3,* 202–210.

Carroll, S. J. & Tosi, H. *Management by objectives: Applications and research.* N.Y.: MacMillan, 1973.

Cartledge, N.D. An experimental study of the relationship between expectancies, goal utility, goals, and task performance. Ph.D. Dissertation, University of Maryland, 1973.

Cash, T. F., Gillen, B. & Burns, D. S. Sexism and 'beautyism' in personnel consultant decision making. *Journal of Applied Psychology,* 1977, *62,* 301–310.

Caulkins, D. Job redesign: pay implications. *Personnel,* 1974, *51* (3), 29–34.

Cheloha, R. S. & Farr, J. L. Absenteeism, job involvement, and job satisfaction in an organizational setting. *Journal of Applied Psychology,* 1980, *65,* 467–473.

Cherrington, D. J. & England, J. L. The desire for an enriched job as a moderator of the enrichment-satisfaction relationship. *Organizational Behavior and Human Performance,* 1980, *25,* 139–159.

Cialdini, R. B., Petty, R. E., & Cacioppo, J. T. Attitude and attitude change. *Annual Review of Psychology*, 1981, *32*, 357–404.

Coch, L. & French, J. R. P. Overcoming resistance to change. *Human Relations*, 1948, 1, 512–532.

Cofer, C. N. & Appley, M. H. *Motivation: Theory and research.* New York: Wiley, 1964.

Cohen, S. L. & Bunker, K. A. Subtle effects of sex role stereotypes on recruiters' hiring decisions. *Journal of Applied Psychology*, 1975, *60*, 566–572.

Condry, J. The role of initial interest and task performance on intrinsic motivation. Paper presented at the American Psychological Association, Chicago, 1975.

Cook, S. D. Coercion and social change. In R. J. Pennock and J. R. Chapman (Eds.), *Coercion*, Chicago: Aldine, 1972.

Cooper, M. R., Morgan, B. S., Foley, P. M. & Kaplan, L. B. Changing employee values: Deepening discontent? *Harvard Business Review*, 1979, *57*, 117–125.

Coyle, J. S. Scanning lights up a dark world for grocers. *Fortune*, March 27, 1978, 76–80.

Craighead, W. E., Kazdin, A. E. & Mahoney, M. J. *Behavior modification.* Boston: Houghton Mifflin, 1976.

Craik, K. H. Multiple scientific paradigms in environmental psychology. *International Journal of Psychology*, 1977, *12*, 147–157.

Craik, K. H. Environmental Psychology. In K. H. Craik, B. Kleinmuntz, R. L. Rosnow, R. Rosenthal, J. A. Cheyne, and R. H. Walters (Eds.) *New Directions in Psychology*, 4. New York: Holt, Rinehart, and Winston, 1970.

Cronbach, L. J. Beyond the two disciplines of scientific psychology. *American Psychologist*, 1975, 30, 116–127.

Cronbach, L. J. *Essentials of psychological testing.* New York: Harper and Row, 1970.

Cronbach, L. J. The two disciplines of scientific psychology. *American Psychologist*, 1957, *12*, 671–684.

Cronbach, L. J. & Gleser, G. *Psychological tests and personnel decisions.* Urbana, Ill.: University of Illinois Press, 1965.

Cummings, L. L. Organizational behavior. *Annual Review of Psychology*, 1982, *33*, 541–579.

Cummings, L. L. The brother-in-law syndrome: Inequity in everyday life. In L. L. Cummings and R. B. Dunham (Eds.) *Introduction to organizational behavior.* Homewood, Ill.: Irwin, 1980.

Cummings, L. L. & Schwab, D. P. *Performance in organizations: Determinants and appraisal.* Glenview, Ill.: Scott, Foresman & Co., 1973.

Cummings, T. G. and Molloy, E. S. (Eds.) *Improving productivity and the quality of everyday work life.* New York: Praeger, 1977.

Cummings, T. G., Molloy, E. S. & Glen, R. A methodological critique of fifty-eight selected work experiments. *Human Relations*, 1977, *30*, 675–708.

Dachler, H. P. & Mobley, W. Construct validation of an instrumentality-expectancy-task-goal model of work motivation: Some theoretical boundary conditions. *Journal of Applied Psychology*, 1973, *58*, 397–418.

Dachler, H. P. & Wilpert, B. Conceptual dimensions and boundaries of participation in organizations: A critical evaluation. *Administrative Science Quarterly*, 1978, *23*, 1–39.

Daft, R. L. *Organization theory and design.* St. Paul, Minn.: West, 1983.

Dalton, D. R. Turnover and absenteeism: Measures of personal effectiveness. In R. S.

Schuler, D. R. Dalton & J. M. McFillen (Eds.) *Applied readings in personnel and human resource management.* St. Paul: West, 1981.

Dalton, D. R. & Todor, W. D. Turnover turned over: An expanded and positive perspective. *Academy of Management Review,* 1979, *4,* 225–235.

Dalton, D. R. & Todor, W. D. Turnover: A lucrative hard dollar phenomenon. *Academy of Management Review,* 1982a, *7,* 212–218.

Dalton, D. R. & Todor, W. D. Antecedents of grievance filing behavior: Attitude behavioral consistency and the union steward. *Academy of Management Journal,* 1982b, *25,* 158–169.

Dalton, M. *Men who manage: Fusions of feeling and theory in administration.* New York: Wiley, 1959.

Davidson, D., Suppes, P. & Siegel, S. *Decision making: An experimental approach.* Stanford: Stanford University Press, 1957.

Davis, L. E. & Taylor, J. C. (Eds.) *Design of jobs.* Santa Monica, California: Goodyear, 1979.

Davis, T. R. V. & Luthans, F. A social learning approach to organizational behavior. *Academy of Management Review,* 1980, *5,* 281–290.

deCharms, R. *Personal causation.* N.Y.: Academic Press, 1968.

Deci, E. L. Effects of externally mediated rewards on intrinsic motivation. *Journal of Personality and Social Psychology,* 1971, *18,* 105–115.

Deci, E. L. Intrinsic motivation, extrinsic reinforcement and inequity. *Journal of Personality and Social Psychology,* 1972, *22,* 113–120.

Deci, E. L. *Intrinsic motivation.* N.Y.: Plenum Press, 1975.

Deci, E. L. Notes on the theory and metatheory of intrinsic motivation. *Organizational Behavior and Human Performance,* 1976, *15,* 130–145.

Deci, E. L. & Porac, J. Cognitive evaluation theory and the study of human motivation. In M. R. Lepper & D. Greene (Eds.) *The hidden costs of reward.* Hillsdale, N. J.: Lawrence Erlbaum Associates, 1978.

deLeo, P. J. & Pritchard, R. D. An examination of some methodological problems in testing expectancy-valence models with survey techniques. *Organizational Behavior and Human Performance,* 1974, *12,* 143–148.

Dessler, G. & Valenzi, E. R. Initiation of structure and subordinate satisfaction: A path analysis test of Path-Goal Theory. *Academy of Management Journal,* 1977, *20,* 251–260.

Dittrich, J. E. & Carrell, M. R. Organizational equity perceptions, employee job satisfaction, and departmental absence and turnover rates. *Organizational Behavior and Human Performance,* 1979, *24,* 29–40.

Donahue, T. R. Labor Looks at Quality of Work Life Programs. Keynote address delivered at a conference on labor participation. Amherst, Mass.: Labor Relations and Research Center, University of Massachusetts, 1982.

Dowling, W. F. Job redesign on the assembly line: Farewell to blue-collar blues? *Organizational Dynamics,* 1973a, *2* (1), 51–67.

Dowling, W. F. At Emery Air Freight: Positive reinforcement boosts performance. *Organizational Dynamics,* 1973b, *2* [1] 41–50.

Downey, H. K., Hellriegel, D. & Slocum, J. W. (Eds.) *Organizational Behavior: A Reader.* St. Paul, Minn.: West, 1977.

Downey, H. K., Sheridan, J. E. & Slocum, J. W. The Path-Goal Theory of leadership: A longitudinal analysis. *Organizational Behavior and Human Performance,* 1976, *16,* 156–176.

Drake, J. A planner looks at job enrichment. *Planning Review,* 1974, *2* (4), 7, 30–31.

327

Dreher, G. F. The role of performance in the turnover process. *Academy of Management Journal,* 1982, *25,* 137–147.

DuBois, P. *Sabotage in industry.* Hammondsworth: Penguin Books, 1979.

Dunham, R. B. Reactions to job characteristics: Moderating effects of the organization. *Academy of Management Journal,* 1977, *20,* 42–65.

Dunham, R. B. & Smith, F. J. *Organizational surveys: An internal assessment of organizational health.* Glenview, Ill.: Scott, Foresman and Co., 1979.

Dunnette, M. D., Arvey, R. D. & Banas, P. A. Why do they leave? *Personnel,* 1973, (May-June), 25–39.

Dunnette, M. D. & Kirchner, W. K. *Psychology applied to industry.* New York: Appleton-Century-Crofts, 1965.

Dunnette, M. D. A modified model for test validation and selection research. *Journal of Applied Psychology,* 1963, *47,* 317–323.

Dunnette, M. D. *Personnel selection and placement.* Belmont, Calif.: Wadsworth, 1966.

Dunnette, M. D. & Bass, B. M. Behavioral scientists and personnel management, *Industrial Relations,* 1963, *2* (3), 115–130.

Dunnette, M. D. Mishmash, mush, and milestones in organizational psychology: 1974. In H. Meltzer and F. R. Wickert (Eds.) *Humanizing organizational behavior.* Springfield, Ill.: Charles C. Thomas, 1976.

Dunnette, M. D. Performance Equals Ability and What? (Tech.Rep. 4009; ONR Contract No. N00014-68-A-0141) Minneapolis: University of Minnesota, Center for the Study of Organizational Performance and Human Effectiveness, 1972.

Dunnette, Marvin D. Aptitudes, abilities, and skills. In M. D. Dunnette (Ed.) *Handbook of industrial and organizational psychology.* Chicago: Rand McNally, 1976.

Dyer, L. and Parker, D. F. Classifying outcomes in work motivation research: An examination of the intrinsic-extrinsic dichotomy. *Journal of Applied Psychology,* 1975, *60,* 455–458.

Dyer, L., Schwab, D. P. & Theriault, R. D. Managerial perceptions regarding salary increase criteria. *Personnel Psychology,* 1976, *29,* 233–242.

Edstrom, A. & Galbraith, J. R. Transfer of managers as a coordination and control strategy in multinational organizations. *Administrative Science Quarterly,* 1977, *22,* 248–263.

Edwards, P. K. Attachment to work and absence. *Human Relations,* 1979, *32,* 1065–1080.

Endler, N. W. The case for person-situation interactions. *Canadian Psychological Review,* 1975, *16,* 12–21.

England, P. & McLaughlin, S. D. Sex segregation of jobs and male-female income differentials. In R. Alvarez and K. G. Lutterman (Eds.) *Discrimination in organizations.* San Francisco: Jossey-Bass, 1979.

Ephlin, D. F. The union's role in job enrichment programs. In Gerald G. Somers (Ed.) *Proceedings of the Twenty-Sixth Annual Winter Meeting.* Madison, Wisc.: Industrial Relations Research Association, 1973.

Erez, M. & Kanfer, F. H. The role of goal acceptance in goal setting and task performance. *Academy of Management Review,* 1983, *8,* 454–463.

Evan, W. M. and Simmons, R. G. Organizational effects of inequitable rewards: Two experiments in status inconsistency. *Administrative Science Quarterly,* 1969, *14,* 224–237.

Evans, M. G. The effects of supervisory behavior on the path-goal relationship. *Organizational Behavior and Human Performance,* 1970, *5,* 277–298.

Evans, M. G. Extensions of a path-goal theory of motivation. *Journal of Applied Psychology,* 1974, *59,* 172–178.

Faltermayer, E. Who will do the dirty work tomorrow? *Fortune,* 1974, *89* (1), 132–138.

Fedor, D. B. and Ferris, G. R. Integrating O.B. Mod with cognitive approaches to motivation. *Academy of Management Review,* 1981, *6,* 115–125.

Fein, M. Job enrichment: A reevaluation. *Sloan Management Review,* 1974, *15* (2), 69–88.

Feldman, D. C. The role of initiation activities in socialization. *Human Relations,* 1977, *30,* 977–990.

Feldman, D. C. The multiple socialization of organization members. *Academy of Management Review,* 1981, *6,* 309–318.

Feldman, J. M. , Reitz, H. J. & Hiterman, R. J Alternatives to optimization in expectancy theory. *Journal of Applied Psychology,* 1976, *61,* 712–720.

Festinger, L. A. A theory of social comparison processes. *Human Relations,* 1954, *7,* 117–140.

Festinger, L. A. *A theory of cognitive dissonance.* Evanston, Ill.: Row, Peterson, 1957.

Fishbein, M. Attitude and the prediction of behavior. In M. Fishbein (Ed.) *Readings in attitude theory and measurement.* New York: Wiley, 1967.

Fishbein, M. & Ajzen, I. *Belief, attitude, intention, and behavior.* Reading, Mass.: Addison-Wesley, 1975.

Fiske, D. W. & Maddi, S. R. *The functions of varied experience.* Homewood, Ill.: Dorsey, 1961.

Fleischman, E. A. A relationship between incentive motivation and ability level in psychomotor performance. *Journal of Experimental Psychology,* 1958, *56,* 78–81.

Florence, S. P. Stagflation in Great Britain. In G. C. Means et.al. (Eds.), *The roots of inflation,* New York: Burt Franklin and Co., 1975.

Flowers, V. S. & Hughes, C. L. Why employees stay. *Harvard Business Review,* 1973, *51* (4), 40–60.

Ford, C. H. MBO: An idea whose time has gone? *Business Horizons,* 1979, *22* (12), 48–55.

Ford, R. N. Job enrichment lessons from A. T. & T. *Harvard Business Review,* 1973, *51* (1), 96–106.

Foulkes, F. K. *Personnel policies in large nonunion companies.* Englewood Cliffs, N.J.: Prentice-Hall, 1980.

Fox, A. C. Progressive discipline: Policy and process. *EEO Today,* 1980–81, *7,* 332–342.

Fredericksen, L. W. and Lovett, S. B. Inside organizational behavior management. *Journal of Organizational Behavior Management,* 1980, *2,* 193–203.

Fredericksen, N., Jensen, O., Beaton, A. E., & Bloxom, B. *Prediction of organizational behavior.* N.Y.: Pergamon, 1972.

Fredericksen, N. Toward a taxonomy of situations. *American Psychologist,* 1972, *27,* 114–123.

Freedman, S. J. & Montanari, J. R. An integrative model of managerial reward allocation. *Academy of Management Review,* 1980, *5,* 381–390.

French, E. G. Effects of interaction of achievement, motivation, and intelligence on problem solving success. *American Psychologist,* 1957, *12,* 399–400.

Freund, W. C. Productivity and inflation. *Financial Analysts Journal,* 1981, *37* (4), 36–39.

Fromm, E. & Xirau, R. (Eds.) *The nature of man.* New York: MacMIllan, 1968.

Frost, P. J. & Jamal, M. Shift work, attitudes, and reported behavior: Some associations between individual characteristics and hours of work and leisure. *Journal of Applied Psychology,* 1979, *64,* 77–81.

Galbraith, J. & Cummings, L. L. An empirical investigation of the motivational determinants of task performance: Interactive effects between instrumentality-valence and motivation-ability. *Organizational Behavior and Human Performance,* 1967, *2,* 237–257.

Gannon, M. J. & Henrickson, D. H. Career orientation and job satisfaction among working wives. *Journal of Applied Psychology,* 1973, *57,* 339–340.

Garland, H. Effects of piece rate underpayment and overpayment on job performance: A test of equity theory with a new induction procedure. *Journal of Applied Social Psychology,* 1973, *57,* 325–334.

Garland, H. & Price, K. Attitudes toward women in management and attributions for their success and failure in a managerial position. *Journal of Applied Psychology,* 1977, *62,* 29–33.

Garner, W. R. The acquisition and application of knowledge: A symbiotic relationship. *American Psychologist,* 1972, *27,* 941–946.

Gay, E. R., Weiss, D. J., Hendel, D. H., Dawis, R. V. & Lofquist, L. H. *Manual for the Minnesota Importance Questionnaire.* The Minnesota Studies in Vocational Rehabilitation: XXVIII. Minneapolis, Minnesota, 1971.

Georgopoulos, B. C., Mahoney, G. M. & Jones, N. W. A path-goal approach to productivity. *Journal of Applied Psychology,* 1957, *41,* 345–353.

Giles, W. F. Volunteering for job enrichment: A test of expectancy theory predictions. *Personnel Psychology,* 1977, *30,* 427–435.

Gold, B. *Productivity, technology, and capital.* Lexington, Mass.: Lexington Books, 1979.

Goodman, P. A. & Friedman, A. An examination of Adams' theory of inequity. *Administrative Science Quarterly,* 1971, *16,* 271–288.

Goodman. P. S. An examination of the referents used in the evaluation of pay. *Organizational Behavior and Human Performance,* 1974, *12,* 170–195.

Goodstadt, B. & Kipnis, D. Situational influences on the use of power. *Journal of Applied Psychology,* 1970, *54,* 201–207.

Gordon, M. E. & Johnson, W. A. Seniority: A review of its legal and scientific standing. *Personnel Psychology,* 1982, *35,* 255–280.

Gorn, G. J. & Kanungo, R. N. Job involvement and motivation: Are intrinsically motivated managers more job involved? *Organizational Behavior and Human Performance,* 1980, *26,* 265–277.

Graen, G. Role making processes within complex organizations. In M. D. Dunnette (Ed.), *Handbook of industrial and organizational psychology.* Chicago: Rand McNally, 1976.

Graen, G. Instrumentality theory of work motivation: Some experimental results and suggested modifications. *Journal of Applied Psychology Monograph,* 1969, *53,* No.2, Part 2.

Gray, J. L. The myths of the myths about behavior mod in organizations: A reply to Locke's criticisms of behavior modification. *Academy of Management Review,* 1979, *4,* 121–129.

Greenberg, J. & Leventhal, G. S. Equity and the use of overreward to motivate performance. *Journal of Personality and Social Psychology,* 1976, *34,* 179–190.

Greene, C. N. Questions of causation in the path-goal theory of leadership. *Academy of Management Journal,* 1979, *22,* 22–41.

Greene, D. & Lepper, M. R. Effects of extrinsic rewards on children's subsequent intrinsic interest. *Child Development,* 1974, *45,* 1141–1145.

Greenwood, R. G. Management by Objectives: As developed by Peter Drucker, assisted by Harold Smiddy. *Academy of Management Review,* 1981, *6,* 225–230.

Gregory, M. S., Silvers, A., & Sutch, D. (Eds.) *Sociology and human nature.* San Francisco: Jossey-Bass, 1978.

Greller, M. M. The nature of subordinate participation in the appraisal interview. *Academy of Management Journal,* 1978, *21,* 646–658.

Griffin, R. W. A longitudinal investigation of task characteristics relationships. *Academy of Management Journal,* 1982, *24,* 99–113.

Griffin, R. W. *Task design: An integrative approach.* Glenview, Ill.: Scott, Foresman and Co., 1982.

Griffin, R. W., Welsh, A. & Moorhead, G. Perceived task characteristics and employee performance: A literature review. *Academy of Management Review,* 1981, *6,* 655–664.

Grigaliunas, B. & Weiner, Y. Has the research challenge to motivation-hygiene theory been conclusive? An analysis of critical studies. *Human Relations,* 1974, *27,* 839–871.

Gross, B. What are your organization's objectives? *Human Relations,* 1965, *18,* 215.

Guilford, J. P. *The nature of human intelligence.* New York: McGraw-Hill, 1967.

Guion, R. M. *Personnel testing.* New York: McGraw-Hill, 1965.

Guzzo, R. A. Types of rewards, cognitions, and work motivation. *Academy of Management Review,* 1979, *4,* 75–86.

Gyllenhammar, P. G. How Volvo adapts work to people. *Harvard Business Review,* 1977, (July-August), *55* (4), 102–113.

Hackman, J. R. & Lawler III, E. E. Employee reactions to job characteristics. *Journal of Applied Psychology,* 1971, *55,* 259–286.

Hackman, J. R. & Oldham, G. R. Development of the job diagnostic survey. *Journal of Applied Psychology,* 1975, *60,* 159–170.

Hackman, J. R. & Oldham, G. R. Motivation through the design of work: Test of a theory. *Organizational Behavior and Human Performance,* 1976, *16,* 250–279.

Hackman, J. R., Oldham, G. R., Janson, R., & Purdy, K. A new strategy for job enrichment. *California Management Review,* Summer 1975, 57–71.

Hackman, J. R. On the coming demise of job enrichment. In E. L. Cass and F. G. Zimmer (Eds.) *Man and work in society.* New York: Van Nostrand Reinhold, 1975.

Hackman, J. R. Work Design. In J. R. Hackman and J. L. Suttle (Eds.) *Improving life at work.* Santa Monica, California: Goodyear, 1977.

Hackman, J. R. & Oldham, G. R. *Work redesign.* Reading, Mass.: Addison-Wesley, 1980.

Hall, D. T. *Careers in organizations.* Pacific Palisades, Calif.: Goodyear, 1976.

Hammer, T. H. & Berman, M. The role of noneconomic factors in faculty union voting. *Journal of Applied Psychology,* 1981, *66,* 415–421.

Hamner, W. C. & Hamner, E. P. Behavior modification and the bottom line. *Organizational Dynamics,* 1976, *4* (4), 3–21.

Hamner, W. C. & Tosi, H. Relationship of role conflict and role ambiguity to job involvement measures. *Journal of Applied Psychology,* 1974, *4,* 497–499.

Hamner, W. C. & Foster, L. W. Are intrinsic and extrinsic rewards additive: A test of Deci's Cognitive Evaluation Theory of task motivation. *Organizational Behavior and Human Performance,* 1975, *14,* 398–415.

Hamner, W. C. & Smith, F. J. Work attitudes as predictors of unionization activity. *Journal of Applied Psychology,* 1978, *63,* 415–421.

Hamner, W. C., Ross, J. & Staw, B. M. Motivation in organizations: The need for a new direction. In D. W. Organ (Ed.) *The applied psychology of work behavior.* Dallas: Business Publications, 1978.

331

Harvey, J. B. & Albertson, D. R. Neurotic organizations: Symptoms, causes, and treatment. (Part 1). *Personnel Journal,* 1971, *50,* 694–699.

Haynes, R. S., Pine, R. C. & Fitch, H. G. Reducing accident rates with organizational behavior modification. *Academy of Management Journal,* 1982, *25,* 407–416.

Hebb, D. O. Drives and the C.N.S. (central nervous system). *Psychological Review,* 1955, *62,* 243–254.

Heider, Fritz. *The psychology of interpersonal relations.* New York: Wiley, 1958.

Heilman, M. E. & Kram, K. E. Self-derogating behavior in women—fixed or flexible: The effects of co-worker's sex. *Organizational Behavior and Human Performance,* 1978, *22,* 497–507.

Heiman, G. W. A note on 'operant conditioning principles extrapolated to the theory of management.' *Organizational Behavior and Human Performance,* 1975, *13,* 165–170.

Heneman, H. G. III & Schwab, D. P. Evaluation of research on expectancy theory predictions of employee performance. *Psychological Bulletin,* 1972, *78* (1), 1–9.

Herman, J. B. Are situational contingencies limiting attitude-job performance relationships? *Organizational Behavior and Human Performance,* 1973, *10,* 208–224.

Hershey, R. Coming—a locked in generation of workers. *Personnel,* 1973, *50* (6), 23–29.

Herzberg, F. Motivating people. In P. Mali (Ed.) *Management handbook,* N.Y.: Wiley, 1981.

Herzberg, F., Mausner, B., Peterson, R. O. & Capwell, D. F. *Job attitudes: Review of research and opinion.* Pittsburgh, Psychological Service of Pittsburgh: 1957.

Herzberg, F., Mausner, B. & Snyderman, B. B. *The motivation to work.* New York: Wiley, 1959.

Herzberg, F. *Work and the nature of man.* Cleveland: World Publishing Co., 1966.

Herzberg, F. One more time: How do you motivate employees? *Harvard Business Review,* 1968, *46* (1), 53–62.

Herzberg, F. Motivational types: Individual differences in motivation, in F. Herzberg (Ed.) *The Managerial Choice,* Homewood, Ill.: Dow Jones-Irwin, 1976.

Hettenhouse, G. W. Compensation cafeteria for top executives. *Harvard Business Review,* 1971, *49* (5), 113–119.

Hickson, D. J. Motives of workpeople who restrict their output. *Occupational Psychology,* 1961, *35,* 111–121.

Hickson, D. J., Hinings, C. R., Lee, C. A., Schneck, R. E. & Pennings, J. M. A strategic contingencies' theory of intra-organizational power. *Administrative Science Quarterly,* 1971, *16,* 216–219.

Hinton, B. L. & Barrow, J. C. The superior's reinforcing behavior as a function of reinforcements received. *Organizational Behavior and Human Performance,* 1975, *14,* 123–143.

Hitt, W. Two models of man. *American Psychologist,* 1969, *24,* 651–658.

Hoerr, J. A warning that worker discontent is rising. *Business Week.* June 4, 1979, no.2588, p.152, 156.

Hofstede, G. The poverty of management control philosophy. *Academy of Management Review,* 1978, *3,* 450–461.

Hom, P. W., Katerberg, R. & Hulin, C. L. Comparative examination of three approaches to the prediction of turnover. *Journal of Applied Psychology,* 1979, *64,* 280–290.

Homans, G. C. *Social Behavior: Its elementary forms.* N.Y.: Harcourt, Brace & World, 1961.

Hopwood, A. *Accounting and human behavior.* Englewood Cliffs, N.J.: Prentice-Hall, 1976.

Horngren, C. T. *Cost accounting* (4th ed.) Englewood Cliffs, N.J.: Prentice-Hall, 1977.

House, R. J. The quest for relevance in management education: Some second thoughts and undesired consequences. *Academy of Management Journal,* 1975, *18,* 323–333.

House, R. J. A path-goal theory of leadership. *Administrative Science Quarterly,* 1971, *16,* 321–338.

House, R. J. & Dessler, G. The path-goal theory of leadership: Some post hoc and a priori tests. In J. G. Hunt (Ed.) *Contingency approaches to leadership.* Carbondale, Ill.: Southern Illinois University Press, 1974.

House, R. J. & Mitchell, T. R. Path-goal theory of leadership. *Journal of Contemporary Business,* 1974, *3,* 81–98.

House, R. J. & Rizzo, J. R. Role conflict and ambiguity as critical variables in a model of organizational behavior. *Organizational Behavior and Human Performance,* 1972, *7,* 467–505.

House, R. J., Shapiro, H. J., & Wahba, M. A. Expectancy theory as a predictor of work behavior and attitude: A reevaluation of empirical evidence. *Decision Sciences,* 1974, *5,* 481–506.

House, R. J. & Wigdor, L.A. Herzberg's dual factor theory of job satisfaction and motivation. *Personnel Psychology,* 1967, *20,* 369–390.

Huberman, J. Discipline without punishment. *Harvard Business Review,* 1964, *42* (4), 62–68.

Hull, C. L. *Principles of behavior.* New York: Appleton-Century-Crofts, 1943.

Hunt, J. McV. Intrinsic motivation and its role in psychological development. *Nebraska Symposium on Motivation,* 1965, *13,* 189–282.

Ilgen, D. R. Satisfaction with performance as a function of the initial level of expected performance and the deviation from expectations. *Organizational Behavior and Human Performance,* 1971, *6,* 345–361.

Ilgen, D. R. & Hollenback, J. H. The role of job satisfaction in absence behavior. *Organizational Behavior and Human Performance,* 1977, *19,* 148–161.

Ilgen, D., Fisher, C., & Taylor, M. Consequences of individual feedback on behavior in organizations. *Journal of Applied Psychology,* 1979, *64,* 349–371.

Ilgen, D. R. & Seely, W. Realistic expectations as an aid in reducing voluntary resignations. *Journal of Applied Psychology,* 1974, *59,* 452–455.

Ivancevich, J. M. & McMahon, J. T. The effects of goal setting, external feedback, and self-generated feedback on outcome variables: A field experiment. *Academy of Management Journal,* 1982, *25,* 359–372.

Ivancevich, M. J. & Donnelly, J. H. Jr. A study of role clarity and need for clarity for three occupational groups. *Academy of Management Journal,* 1974, *17,* 28–36.

Jablonsky, S. F. & DeVries, D. L. Operant conditioning principles extrapolated to the theory of management. *Organizational Behavior and Human Performance,* 1972, *7,* 340–358.

Jaccard, J., King, G. W. & Pomazal, R. Attitudes and behavior: An analysis of specificity of attitudinal predictors. *Human Relations,* 1977, *9,* 817–824.

Jacques, E. *Equitable payment.* New York: Wiley, 1961.

Jamal, M. & Mitchell, V. F. Work, nonwork, and mental health: A model and a test. *Industrial Relations,* 1980, *19,* 88–93.

James, L. R. & Jones, A. P. Organizational structure: A review of structural dimensions and their conceptual relationships with individual attitudes and behavior. *Organizational Behavior and Human Performance,* 1976, *16,* 74–113.

333

Jamieson, D. Behavioral problems with management by objectives. *Academy of Management Journal,* 1973, *16,* 496–505.

Janz, T. Manipulating subjective expectancy through feedback: A laboratory study of the expectancy-performance relationship. *Journal of Applied Psychology,* 1982, *64,* 480–485.

Jenkins, D. Beyond job enrichment. *Working Papers for a New Society,* 1975, *2,* 51–57.

Joad, C. E. M. *Guide to philosophy.* New York: Dover Publications, 1957.

Johns, G. Difference score measures of organizational behavior variables: A critique. *Organizational Behavior and Human Performance,* 1981, *27,* 443–463.

Jones, M. R. (Ed.) *Nebraska Symposium on Motivation.* Lincoln: University of Nebraska Press, 1955.

Kahn, R. F., Wolfe, D. M., Quinn, R. P., Snoek, J. D. & Rosenthal, R. A. *Organizational stress.* New York: Wiley, 1964.

Kanfer, F. H. Self management methods. In F. H. Kanfer and A. P. Goldstein (Eds.) *Helping people change.* (2nd ed.). New York: Pergamon Press, 1980.

Karmel, B. (Ed.) *Point & counterpoint in organizational behavior.* Hillsdale, Illinois: The Dryden Press, 1980.

Karp, H. B. & Nickson, J. W. Motivator-hygiene deprivation as a predictor of job turnover. *Personal Psychology,* 1973, *26,* 377–384.

Katerberg, R. & Blau, G. J. An examination of level and direction of effort and job performance. *Academy of Management Journal,* 1983, *26,* 249–257.

Katz, D. & Kahn, R. L. *The social psychology of organizations* (2nd ed.). New York: Wiley, 1978.

Katz, R. Job Enrichment: Some Career Considerations. In J. Van Maanen (Ed.) *Organizational careers.* Chichester: Wiley, 1977.

Katz, R. Job longevity as situational factor in job satisfaction. *Administrative Science Quarterly,* 1978, *28,* 204–223.

Katz, D. The motivational basis of organizational behavior. *Behavioral Science,* 1964, *9,* 131–146.

Katz, R. Time and work: Toward an integrative perspective. In B. M. Staw and L. L. Cummings (Eds.) *Research in Organizational Behavior,* Vol.2, Greenwich, Conn.: JAI Press, 1980.

Kavanagh, M. J., Hurst, M. W. & Rose, R. The relationship between job satisfaction and psychiatric health symptoms for air traffic controllers. *Personnel Psychology,* 1981, *34,* 691–707.

Kazdin, A. E. *Behavior modification in applied settings.* Homewood, Ill.: Dorsey, 1975.

Kazdin, A. E. *History of behavior modification.* Baltimore: University Park Press, 1978.

Kelly, J. E. A reappraisal of sociotechnical systems theory. *Human Relations,* 1978, *31,* 1069–1099.

Kempen, R. W. & Hall, R. V. Reduction of industrial absenteeism: Results of a behavioral approach. *Journal of Organizational Behavior Management,* 1977, *1,* 1–21.

Kerr, S. On the folly of rewarding A, while hoping for B. *Academy of Management Journal,* 1975, *18,* 769–783.

Kerr, S. Some characteristics and consequences of organizational reward systems. University of Southern California working paper, 1982.

Kerr, S. & Jermier, J. M. Substitutes for leadership: Their meaning and measurement. *Organizational Behavior and Human Performance,* 1978, *22,* 375–403.

Khandwalla, P. N. *The design of organizations.* New York: Harcourt Brace Jovanovich, 1977.

Kidder, L. H., Bellettirie, G. & Cohn, E. S. Secret ambitions and public performances: The effects of anonymity on reward allocation made by men and women. *Journal of Experimental Social Psychology,* 1977, *13,* 70–80.

Kim, J. S. & Hamner, W. C. Effect of performance feedback and goal setting on productivity and satisfaction in an organizational setting. *Journal of Applied Psychology,* 1976, *61,* 48–57.

King, N. Clarification and evaluation of the two-factor theory of job satisfaction. *Psychological Bulletin,* 1970, *74,* 18–31.

Kinkead, G. Socko productivity. *Fortune,* September 8, 1980, 72–74.

Knowles, H. P. & Saxberg, B. O. Human relations and the nature of man. *Harvard Business Review,* 1967, *45,* 22–24, 28, 30, 32, 34, 36, 38, 40, 172, 174, 176, 178.

Kochan, T. A. *Collective bargaining and industrial relations.* Homewood, Ill.: Irwin, 1980.

Kolb, D. A. & Plovnick, M. S. The experiential learning theory of career development. In J. Van Maanen (Ed.) *Organizational careers.* Chichester: Wiley, 1977.

Komaki, J., Barwick, K. D. & Scott, L. R. A behavioral approach to occupational safety: Pinpointing and reinforcing safe performance in a food processing plant. *Journal of Applied Psychology,* 1978, *63,* 434–445.

Komaki, J., Heinzmann, A. T. & Lawson, L. Effect of training and feedback: Component analysis of a behavioral safety program. *Journal of Applied Psychology,* 1980, *65,* 261–270.

Komaki, J., Waddell, W. M. & Pearce, M. G. The applied behavior analysis approach and individual employees: Improving performance in two small businesses. *Organizational Behavior and Human Performance,* 1977, *19,* 337–352.

Kondrasuk, J. N. Studies in MBO effectiveness. *Academy of Management Review,* 1981, *6,* 419–430.

Kopelman, R. E. Across-individual, within-individual and return on effort versions of expectancy theory. *Decision Sciences,* 1977, *8,* 651–662.

Kopelman, R. E. A causal-correlational test of the Porter and Lawler framework. *Human Relations,* 1979, *32,* 545–556.

Kopelman, R. E. & Schneller, G. O. A mixed-consequence system for reducing overtime and unscheduled absences. *Journal of Organizational Behavior Management,* 1981, *3,* 17–28.

Kopelman, R. E. & Thompson, P. H. Boundary conditions for expectancy theory predictions of work motivation and job performance. *Academy of Management Journal,* 1976, *19,* 237–258.

Korman, A. K. Toward a hypothesis of work behavior. *Journal of Applied Psychology,* 1970, *54,* 31–41.

Korman, A. K. *Industrial and organizational psychology.* Englewood Cliffs, N. J.: Prentice-Hall, 1971.

Korman, A. K. *The psychology of motivation.* Englewood Cliffs, New Jersey: Prentice-Hall, 1974.

Korman, A. K. Hypothesis of work behavior revisited and an extension. *Academy of Management Review,* 1976, *1,* 50–63.

Kornhauser, A. *Mental health of the industrial worker.* New York: Wiley, 1965.

Kraut, A. I. Predicting turnover of employees from measured job attitudes. *Organizational Behavior and Human Performance,* 1975, *13,* 233–243.

Larwood, L. & Wood, M. M. *Women in management.* Lexington, Mass.: Lexington Books, 1977.

Latham, G. P. & Baldes, J. J. The 'practical significance' of Locke's theory of goal setting. *Journal of Applied Psychology,* 1975, *60,* 122–124.

Latham, G. P. & Dossett, D. L. Designing incentive plans for unionized employees: A comparison of continuous and variable ratio reinforcement schedules. *Personnel Psychology,* 1978, *31,* 47–61.

Latham, G. P. & Sarri, L. M. The effects of holding goal difficulty constant on assigned and participatively set goals. *Academy of Management Journal,* 1979a, *22,* 163–168.

Latham, G. P. & Kinne, S. B. III. Improving job performance through training in goal setting. *Journal of Applied Psychology,* 1974, *59,* 187–191.

Latham, G. P. & Locke, E. A. Increasing productivity with decreasing time limits: A field replication of Parkinson's Law. *Journal of Applied Psychology,* 1975, *60,* 524–526.

Latham, G. P., Mitchell, T. R. & Dossett, D. L. Importance of participative goal setting and anticipated rewards on goal difficulty and job performance. *Journal of Applied Psychology,* 1978, *63,* 163–171.

Latham, G. P. & Saari, L. M. Importance of supportive relationships in goal setting. *Journal of Applied Psychology,* 1979b, *64,* 151–156.

Latham, G. P. & Steele, T. P. The motivational effects of participation versus goal setting on performance. *Academy of Management Journal,* 1983, *26,* 406–417.

Latham, G. P., Steele, T. P. & Saari, L. M. The effects of participation and goal difficulty on performance. *Personnel Psychology,* 1982, *35,* 677–686.

Latham, G. P. & Wexley, K. N. *Increasing productivity through performance appraisal.* Reading, Mass.: Addison-Wesley, 1981.

Latham, G. P. & Yukl, G. A review of research on the application of goal setting in organizations. *Academy of Management Journal,* 1975, *18,* 824–845.

Lawler, E. E. Managers' perception of their subordinates' pay and of their superiors' pay. *Personnel Psychology,* 1965, *18,* 413–422.

Lawler, E. E. The mythology of management compensation. *California Management Review,* 1966, *9,* 11–22.

Lawler, E. E. Secrecy about management compensation: Are there hidden costs? *Organizational Behavior and Human Performance,* 1967a, *2,* 182–189.

Lawler, E. E. Attitude surveys and job performance. *Personnel Administration,* 1967b, *30* (5), 3–5, 22–24.

Lawler, E. E. Equity theory as a predictor of productivity and work quality. *Psychological Bulletin,* 1968, *70,* 596–610.

Lawler, E. E. Job design and employee motivation. *Personnel Psychology,* 1969, *22,* 426–435.

Lawler, E. E. *Pay and organization effectiveness: A psychological view.* New York: McGraw-Hill, 1971.

Lawler, E. E. Secrecy and the Need to Know. In H. Tosi, R. J. House, and M. D. Dunnette (Eds.) *Managerial motivation and compensation.* East Lansing, Mich.: MSU Business Studies, 1972.

Lawler, E. E. *Motivation in work organizations.* Monterey, California: Brooks/Cole, 1973.

Lawler, E. E. Individualizing Organizations: A Needed Emphasis in Organizational Psychology. In H. Meltzer and F. R. Wickert (Eds.) *Humanizing organizational behavior.* Springfield, Ill.: Charles C. Thomas, 1976.

Lawler, E. E. & Hall, D. T. Relationship of job characteristics to job involvement, satis-faction, and intrinsic motivation. *Journal of Applied Psychology,* 1970, *54,* 305–312.

Lawler, E. E. & O'Gara, P. W. Effects of inequity produced by underpayment on work output, work quality, and attitudes toward the work. *Journal of Applied Psychol-ogy,* 1967, *51,* 403–410.

Lawler, E. E. & Porter, L. W. The effect of performance on job satisfaction. *Industrial Relations,* 1967, *7,* 20–28.

Lawler, E. E. & Suttle, J. L. A causal correlational test of the need hierarchy concept. *Organizational Behavior and Human Performance,* 1972, *7,* 265–287.

Lawler, E. E. & Suttle, J. L. Expectancy theory and job behavior. *Organizational Be-havior and Human Performance,* 1973, *9,* 482–503.

Lawrence, P. R. & Lorsch, J. *Organization and environment.* Homewood, Ill.: Irwin, 1969.

Lazer, R. I. The "Discrimination" Danger in Performance Appraisal. In W. F. Glueck (Ed.), *Personnel: A book of readings.* Dallas: Business Publications Inc., 1979.

Leon, F. R. Number of outcomes and accuracy of prediction in expectancy research. *Organizational Behavior and Human Performance,* 1979, *23,* 251–267.

Lepper, M. R. & Greene, D. (Eds.) *The hidden costs of reward.* Hillsdale, New Jersey: Lawrence Erlbaum Associates, 1978.

Leventhal, G. S. Reward allocation by males and females. Paper presented at the meeting of the American Psychological Association, Montreal, August 1973.

Levine, F. M. (Ed.) *Theoretical readings in motivation.* Chicago: Rand McNally, 1975.

Levinson, H. Management by whose objectives? *Harvard Business Review,* 1970, *48* (4), 125–134.

Levy, L. H. *Conceptions of personality.* New York: Random House, 1970.

Lewin, K. The conceptual representation and the measurement of psychological forces. *Contributions to Psychological Theory,* Durham, N.C.: Duke University Press, 1938, 1, No.4.

Locke, E. A. Interaction of ability and motivation in performance. *Perceptual and Mo-tor Skills,* 1965, *21,* 719–725.

Locke, E. A. Toward a theory of task motives and incentives. *Organizational Behavior and Human Performance,* 1968, *3,* 157–189.

Locke, E. A. What is job satisfaction? *Organizational Behavior and Human Perfor-mance,* 1969, *4,* 309–336.

Locke, E. A. The Nature and Causes of Job Satisfaction. In M. D. Dunnette (Ed.) *Handbook of industrial and organizational psychology.* Chicago, Rand McNally, 1976.

Locke, E. A. The ubiquity of the technique of goal setting in theories of and ap-proaches to employee motivation. *Academy of Management Review,* 1978, *3,* 594–601.

Locke, E. A. The ideas of Frederick W. Taylor: An Evaluation. *Academy of Manage-ment Review,* 1982, *7,* 14–24.

Locke, E. A. & Latham, G. P. *Goal setting: A motivational technique that works.* Engle-wood Cliffs, N.J.: Prentice-Hall, 1984.

Locke, E. A. Personnel attitudes and motivation. *Annual Review of Psychology,* 1975, *26,* 457–480.

Locke, E. A. The myths of behavior mod in organizations. *Academy of Management Review,* 1977, *2,* 543–553.

Locke, E. A. Myths in the myths of the myths about behavior mod in organizations. *Academy of Management Review,* 1979, *4,* 131–136.

Locke, E. A. Latham versus Komaki: A tale of two paradigms. *Journal of Applied Psychology,* 1980, *65,* 16–23.

Locke, E. A., Cartledge, N. & Knerr, C. S. Studies of the relationship between satisfaction, goal setting, and performance. *Organizational Behavior and Human Performance,* 1970, *5,* 135–158.

Locke, E. A., Shaw, K. N., Saari, L. M. & Latham, G. P. Goal setting and task performance: 1969–1980. *Psychological Bulletin,* 1981, *90,* 125–152.

Lodahl, T. & Kejner, M. The definition and measurement of job involvement. *Journal of Applied Psychology,* 1965, *49,* 24–33.

Lofquist, L. H. & Dawis, R. V. *Adjustment to work.* New York: Appleton-Century-Crofts, 1969.

Longenecker, J. G. & Pringle, C. D. *Management.* (5th ed.). Columbus, Ohio: Charles E. Merrill, 1981.

Louis, M. R. Surprise and sense making: What newcomers experience in entering unfamiliar organizational settings. *Administrative Science Quarterly,* 1980, *25,* 226–251.

Luthans, F. & Ottemann, R. Motivation vs. Learning Approaches to Organizational Behavior. In F. Luthans (Ed.) *Contemporary readings in organizational behavior* (2nd ed.). New York: McGraw-Hill, 1977.

Luthans, F. & Reif, W. E. Job enrichment: Long on theory, short on practice. *Organizational Dynamics,* 1974, *2* (3), 30–37, 43.

Luthans, F. & Kreitner, R. *Organizational behavior modification.* Glenview, Ill.: Scott, Foresman and Company, 1975.

Luthans, F. & Kreitner, R. The management of behavioral contingencies. *Personnel,* 1974, *51,* 7–16.

Lyons, T. F. Role clarity, need for clarity, satisfaction, tension, and withdrawal. *Organizational Behavior and Human Performance,* 1971, *6,* 99–110.

McCaskey, M. B. A contingency approach to planning: Planning with goals and planning without goals. *Academy of Management Journal,* 1974, *17,* 281–291.

McClelland, D. C. *The achieving society.* Princeton, N.J.: Van Nostrand, 1961.

McClelland, D. C. Business drive and national achievement. *Harvard Business Review,* 1962, *40,* 99–112.

McClelland, D. C. Achievement motivation can be developed. *Harvard Business Review,* 1965, *43,* 6–24, 178.

McClelland, D. C. & Winter, D. G. *Motivating economic achievement.* New York: The Free Press, 1969.

McConkie, M. L. A clarification of the goal setting and appraisal processes in MBO. *Academy of Management Review,* 1979, *4,* 29–40.

MacCorquodale, K. & Meehl, P. E. On a distinction between hypothetical constructs and intervening variables. *Psychological Review,* 1948, *55,* 95–107.

McDonald, L. Wages of Work. In M. Stephenson (Ed.) *Women in Canada* (Rev. ed.) Don Mills, Ontario: General Publishing Co., 1977.

McDougall, W. *Outline of psychology.* New York: Scribner, 1923.

McFetridge, D. G. Research and Development Expenditures. In G. B. Doern (Ed.), *How Ottawa spends your tax dollars.* Toronto: James Lorimer & Co., 1981.

McGregor, D. M. An uneasy look at performance appraisal. *Harvard Business Review,* 1957, *35* (3), 89–94.

McGregor, D. M. The human side of enterprise. *Management Review,* 1957, *46* (11), 22–28, 88–92.

McGregor, D. M. *The human side of enterprise.* New York: McGraw-Hill, 1960.

McKelvey, W. W. *Organizational systematics.* Berkeley, Calif.: University of California Press, 1982.

Machlowitz, M. *Workaholics: Living with them, working with them.* Reading, Mass.: Addison-Wesley, 1980.

Maddi, S. R. *Personality theories: A comparative analysis* (3rd ed.). Homewood, Ill.: The Dorsey Press, 1976.

Maddi, S. R. *Personality theories: A comparative analysis* (4th ed.). Homewood, Illinois: The Dorsey Press, 1980.

Magnusson, D. & Endler, N. S. Interactional Psychology: Present Status and Future Prospects. In D. Magnusson and N. S. Endler (Eds.) *Personality at the crossroads.* Hillsdale, N.J.: Erlbaum, 1977(a).

Magnusson, D. & Endler, N. S. (Eds.) *Personality at the crossroads.* Hillsdale, N.J.: Erlbaum, 1977(b).

Mahoney, M. J. *Cognition and behavior modification.* Cambridge, Mass.: Ballinger, 1974.

Mahoney, T. A. Compensation preferences of managers. *Industrial Relations,* 1964, *3,* 135–144.

Mahoney, T. A. & Weitzel, W. Secrecy and managerial compensation. *Industrial Relations,* 1978, *17,* 245–251.

Mahoney, T. A. Another Look at Job Satisfaction and Performance. In T. A. Mahoney (Ed.) *Compensation and reward perspectives.* Homewood, Ill.: Irwin, 1979.

Mahoney, T. A. & Blake, R. H. Judgements of appropriate pay as influenced by occupational characteristics and sex stereotypes. Unpublished manuscript, University of Minnesota, 1982.

Mahoney, T. A. Approaches to the definition of comparable worth. *Academy of Management Review,* 1983, *8,* 14–22.

Maier, N. R. F. *Psychology in industrial organizations* (4th ed.). Boston: Houghton Mifflin, 1973.

Main, J. Why government works dumb. *Fortune,* August 10, 1981, 146–148, 152, 155, 156, 158.

Malkiel, B. G. Productivity—the problem behind the headlines. *Harvard Business Review,* 1979, 57 (3), 81–90.

Mann, F. C. & Williams, L. K. Organizational Impact of White Collar Automation. In L. E. Davis & J. C. Taylor (Eds.) *Design of jobs.* Hammondsworth: Middlesex, England: Penguin, 1972, pp. 83–90.

March, J. G. & Simon, H. A. *Organizations.* N.Y.: Wiley, 1958.

Maslow, A. H. A theory of human motivation. *Psychological Review,* 1943, *50,* 370–396.

Maslow, A. H. *Motivation and personality.* New York: Harper & Row, 1954.

Maslow, A. H. Deficiency motivation and growth motivation. In M. R. Jones (Ed.) *Nebraska Symposium on Motivation.* Lincoln, Nebraska: University of Nebraska Press, 1955.

Maslow, A. H. *Toward a psychology of being.* New York: Van Nostrand Reinhold, 1962.

Maslow, A. H. *Toward a psychology of being* (2nd ed.). New York: Van Nostrand Reinhold, 1968.

Massie, J. L. Management Theory. In J. G. March (Ed.) *Handbook of organizations.* Chicago: Rand McNally, 1965.

Matsui, T., Kagawa, M., Nagamatsu, J. & Ohtsuka, Y. Validity of expectancy theory as a within-personal behavioral choice model for sales activities. *Journal of Applied Psychology,* 1977, *62,* 764–767.

Matsui, T. and Ohtsuka, Y. Within-person expectancy theory predictions of supervisory consideration and structure behavior. *Journal of Applied Psychology,* 1978, *63,* 128–131.

Mawhinney, T. C. Operant terms and concepts in the description of individual work behavior: Some problems of interpretation, application, and evaluation. *Journal of Applied Psychology,* 1975, *60,* 704–712.

Mawhinney, T. C. Intrinsic and extrinsic work motivation: Perspectives from behaviorism. *Organizational Behavior and Human Performance,* 1979, *24,* 411–440.

Mayes, B. T. Incorporating time-lag effects into the expectancy model of motivation: A reformulation of the model. *Academy of Management Review,* 1978a, *3,* 374–379.

Mayes, B. T. Some boundary conditions in the application of motivation models. *Academy of Management Review,* 1978b, *3,* 51–58.

Mayhew, G. L. Approaches to employee management: Policies and preferences. *Journal of Organizational Behavior Management,* 1979, *2,* 103–111.

Mento, A. J., Cartledge, N. D. and Locke, E. A. Maryland vs. Michigan vs. Minnesota: Another look at the relationship of expectancy and goal difficulty to task performance. *Organizational Behavior and Human Performance,* 1980, *25,* 419–440.

Merton, R. K. *Social theory and social structure.* New York: The Free Press, 1968.

Michaels, C. E. & Spector, P. E. Causes of employee turnover: A test of the Mobley, Griffeth, Hand and Meglino model. *Journal of Applied Psychology,* 1982, *67,* 53–59.

Middlemist, R. D. & Peterson, R. B. Test of equity theory by controlling for comparison co-workers' efforts. *Organizational Behavior and Human Performance,* 1976, *15,* 335–354.

Migliore, R. H. *MBO: Blue collar to top executive.* Washington, D.C.: Bureau of National Affairs, 1977.

Miles, R. H. A comparison of the relative impacts of role perceptions of ambiguity and conflict by role. *Academy of Management Journal,* 1976, *19,* 25–35.

Miles, R. H. & Perreault, W. D. Jr. Organizational role conflict: Its antecedents and consequences. *Organizational Behavior and Human Performance,* 1976, *17,* 19–44.

Miles, R. H. & Petty, M. M. Relationships between role clarity, need for clarity, and job tension and satisfaction for supervisory and non-supervisory roles. *Academy of Management Journal,* 1975, *18,* 877–883.

Milkovich, G. T. & Anderson, P. H. Management compensation and secrecy policies. *Personnel Psychology,* 1972, *25,* 293–302.

Milkovich, G. T. Pay inequalities and comparable worth. In B. D. Dennis (Ed.) *Proceedings of the Thirty-Third Annual Meeting.* Madison, Wisc.: Industrial Relations Research Association, 1980.

Miller, L. M. Improving roles and forecast accuracy in a nationwide sales organization. *Journal of Organizational Behavior Management,* 1977, *1,* 39–51.

Miller, L. M. *Behavior management: The new science of managing people at work.* New York: Wiley, 1978.

Mills, P. K. Self-management: Its control and relationship to other organizational properties. *Academy of Management Review,* 1983, *3,* 445–453.

Miner, M. G. Pay policies: Secret or open? And why? *Personnel Journal,* 1974, *53* (2), 110–115.

Mintzberg, H. *The nature of managerial work.* New York: Harper & Row, 1973.

Mirvis, P. & Lawler, E. E. Measuring the financial impact of employee attitudes. *Journal of Applied Psychology,* 1977, *62,* 1–8.

Mischel, W. *Personality and assessment.* New York: Wiley, 1968.

Mitchel, J. O. The effect of intentions, tenure, personal, and organizational variables on managerial turnover. *Academy of Management Journal,* 1981, *24,* 742–751.

Mitchell, J. J. (Ed.) *Human nature: Theories, conjectures, and descriptions.* Metuchen, N.J.: The Scarecrow Press, 1972.

Mitchell, T. R. Motivation and participation: An integration. *Academy of Management Journal,* 1973, *16,* 670–679.

Mitchell, T. R. Expectancy models of satisfaction, occupational preference and effort: A theoretical, methodological and empirical appraisal. *Psychological Bulletin,* 1974, *81,* 1053–1077.

Mitchell, T. R. Motivation: New directions for theory, research and practice. *Academy of Management Review,* 1982, *7,* 80–88.

Mitchell, T. R. & Biglan, A. Instrumentality theories: Current uses in psychology. *Psychological Bulletin,* 1971, *76,* 432–454.

Mitchell, T. R., Green, S. G., & Wood, R. E. An Attributional Model of Leadership and the Poor Performing Subordinate. In B. M. Staw and L. L. Cummings (Eds.) *Research in Organizational Behavior,* Vol.3, Greenwich, Conn.: JAI Press, 1981.

Mitchell, T. R. & Kalb, L. S. Effects of outcome knowledge and outcome valence on supervisors' evaluations. *Journal of Applied Psychology,* 1981, *66,* 604–612.

Mitchell, T. R. & Nebeker, D. M. Expectancy theory predictions of academic effort and performance. *Journal of Applied Psychology,* 1973, *57,* 61–67.

Mitchell, V. F. & Moudgill, P. Measurement of Maslow's need hierarchy. *Organizational Behavior and Human Performance,* 1976, *16,* 334–349.

Mobley, W. H., Griffeth, R. W., Hand, H. H. & Meglino, B. M. Review and conceptual analysis of the employee turnover process. *Psychological Bulletin,* 1979, *86,* 493–522.

Mobley, W. H. *Employee turnover: Causes, consequences, and control.* Reading, Mass.: Addison-Wesley, 1982.

Moch, M. & Seashore, S. E. How Norms Affect Behaviors in and of Corporations. In P. C. Nystrom and W. H. Starbuck (Eds.) *Handbook of organizational design.* Vol.1. New York: Oxford University Press, 1981.

Moore, L. F., Johns, G. & Pinder, C. C. Toward Middle Range Theory: An Overview and Perspective. In C. C. Pinder and L. F. Moore (Eds.) *Middle range theory and the study of organizations.* Boston: Martinus Nijhoff, 1980.

Morris, J. H. & Sherman, J. D. Generalizability of an organizational commitment model. *Academy of Management Journal,* 1981, *24,* 512–526.

Muczyk, J. P. A controlled field experiment measuring the impact of MBO on performance data. *Journal of Management Studies,* 1978, *15* (3), 318–329.

Murphy, G. C. & Remnyi, A. G. Behavioral analysis and organizational reality: The need for a technology of program implementation. *Journal of Organizational Behavior Management,* 1979, *2,* 121–131.

Murray, H. *Explorations in personality.* New York: Oxford University Press, 1938.

Murray, H. A. & Kluckhohn, C. Outline of a Conception of Personality. In C. Kluckhohn, H. A. Murray and D. Schneider (Eds.) *Personality and nature, society, and culture* (2nd ed.). New York: Knopf, 1953.

Nadler, D. A. *Feedback and organization development: Using data-based methods.* Reading, Mass.: Addison-Wesley, 1977.

Naylor, J. D., Pritchard, R. D., & Ilgen, D. R. *A theory of behavior in organizations.* New York: Academic Press, 1980.

Nealey, S. M. Pay and benefit preference. *Industrial Relations,* 1963, *3,* 17–28.

Nebeker, D. M. & Mitchell, T. R. Leader behavior: An expectancy theory approach. *Organizational Behavior and Human Performance,* 1974, *11,* 355–367.

341

Newman, W. H. & Wallender, H. W. Managing not-for-profit enterprises. *Academy of Management Review,* 1978, *3,* 24–31.

Nicholson, N., Wall, T. & Lischeron, J. The predictability of absence and propensity to leave from employees' job satisfaction and attitudes toward influence in decision making. *Human Relations,* 1977, *30,* 499–514.

Nord, W. R. Beyond the teaching machine: The neglected area of operant conditioning in the theory and practice of management. *Organizational Behavior and Human Performance,* 1969, *4,* 375–401.

Nord, W. R. Improving attendance through rewards. *Personnel Administration,* 1970, *33,* (6), 37–41.

Nord, W. R. Job satisfaction reconsidered. *American Psychologist,* 1977, *32,* 1026–1035.

Nord, W. R. & Durand, D. E. Beyond resistance to change: Behavioral science on the firing line. *Organizational Dynamics,* 1975, *4* (2), 2–19.

Nord, W. R. & Durand, D. E. What's wrong with the Human Resources approach to management? *Organizational Dynamics,* 1978, *6* (3), 13–25.

Norman, R. G. & Bahari, S. *Productivity measurement and incentives.* London: Butterworths, 1972.

Notz, W. W. Work motivation and the negative effects of extrinsic rewards. *American Psychologist,* 1975, *30,* 884–891.

Nunnally, J. C. W. *Psychometric theory.* New York: McGraw-Hill, 1967.

Oates, W. *Confessions of a workaholic.* New York: World Publishing Co., 1971.

Odiorne, G. S. *MBO II.* Belmont, California: Fearon Pitman Publishers, 1979.

Oldham, G. R. & Hackman, J. R. Work Design in the Organizational Context. In B. M. Staw and L. L. Cummings (Eds.) *Research in Organizational Behavior,* Vol.2, Greenwich, Connecticut: JAI Press, 1980.

O'Kelly, C. O. The 'impact' of equal employment legislation on women's earnings. *American Journal of Economics and Sociology,* 1979, *38,* 419–429.

Ondrack, D. A. Defense mechanisms and the Herzberg Theory: An alternate test. *Academy of Management Journal,* 1974, *17,* 79–89.

Oppenheimer, V. K. The sex-labeling of jobs. *Industrial Relations,* 1968, *7,* 219–234.

Organ, D. W. Inferences about trends in labor force satisfaction: A causal-correlation analysis. *Academy of Management Journal,* 1977, *20,* 510–519.

Orpen, C. Effects of bonuses for attendance on the absenteeism of industrial workers. *Journal of Organizational Behavior Management,* 1978, *1,* 118–124.

Orpen, C. The effects of job enrichment on employee satisfaction, motivation, involvement, and performance: A field experiment. *Human Relations,* 1979, *32,* 189–217.

O'Toole, J. *Making America work.* New York: Continuum, 1981.

Ouchi, W. G. *Theory Z.* New York: Avon Books, 1981.

Owens, W. A. Toward one discipline of scientific psychology. *American Psychologist,* 1968, *23,* 782–785.

Owens, W. A. Background Data. In M. D. Dunnette (Ed.) *Handbook of industrial and organizational psychology.* Chicago: Rand McNally, 1976.

Oxford English Dictionary. Oxford: The Clarendon Press, 1961.

Painter, B., Sutton, A. & Burton, S. *Provincial Worklife Survey: A Pilot Project.* Vancouver, B.C. Socio-Technical Systems Group, B.C. Research, 1982.

Parker, D. F. & Dyer, L. Expectancy theory as a within person behavioral choice model: An empirical test of some conceptual and methodological refinements. *Organizational Behavior and Human Performance,* 1976, *17,* 97–117.

Parkinson, C. N. *Parkinson's law and other studies in administration.* Boston: Houghton Mifflin, 1957.

Parmerlee, M. & Schwenk, C. Radical behaviorism in organizations: Misconceptions in the Locke-Gray debate. *Academy of Management Review,* 1979, *4,* 601–607.

Patchen, M. *The choice of wage comparisons.* Englewood Cliffs, N.J.: Prentice-Hall, 1961.

Paul, W. J., Robertson, K. B. & Herzberg, F. Job enrichment pays off. *Harvard Business Review,* 1969, *47* (2) 61–78.

Peak, H. Attitude and motivation. In M. R. Jones (Ed.) *Nebraska Symposium on Motivation.* Lincoln: University of Nebraska Press, 1955.

Pedalino, E. & Gamboa, V. U. Behavior modification and absenteeism: Intervention in one industrial setting. *Journal of Applied Psychology,* 1974, *54,* 694–698.

Perrow, C. A framework for the comparative analysis of organizations. *American Sociological Review,* 1967, *32* (3), 194–208.

Perry, J. L. & Porter, L. W. Factors affecting the context for motivation in public organizations. *Academy of Management Review,* 1982, 7, 89–98.

Pervin, L. A. Performance and satisfaction as a function of individual-environment fit. *Psychological Bulletin,* 1968, *69,* 56–68.

Peter, L. J. & Hull, R. *The Peter Principle.* New York: Bantam, 1969.

Peter, L. H. & O'Connor, E. J. Situational constraints and work outcomes: The influences of a frequently overlooked construct. *Academy of Management Review,* 1980, *3,* 391–397.

Petrock, F. Analyzing the balance of consequences for performance improvement. *Journal of Organizational Behavior Management,* 1978, *1,* 196–205.

Petrock, F. & Gamboa, V. Expectancy Theory and Operant Conditioning: A Conceptual Comparison. In W. Nord: *Concepts and controversies in organizational behavior* (2nd ed.). Pacific Palisades, Cal.: Goodyear Publishing Co., 1976.

Pfeffer, J. & Salancik, G. R. Organizational decision making as a political process: The case of the university budget. *Administrative Science Quarterly,* 1974, *19,* 135–151.

Pierce, J. L. & Dunham, R. B. Task design: A literature review. *Academy of Management Review,* 1976, *1* (4), 83–97.

Pinder, C. C. Additivity versus nonadditivity of intrinsic and extrinsic incentives: Implications for work motivation, performance, and attitudes. *Journal of Applied Psychology,* 1976, *61,* 693–700.

Pinder, C. C. Concerning the application of human motivation theories in organizational settings. *Academy of Management Review,* 1977, *2,* 384–397.

Pinder, C. C. The marginal utility of the marginal utility criterion: A reply to Bobko. *Academy of Management Review,* 1978, *3,* 910–913.

Pinder, C. C. & Das, H. Hidden costs and benefits of employee transfers. *Human Resource Planning,* 1979, *2,* 135–145.

Pinder, C. C. & Moore, L. F. The resurrection of taxonomy to aid the development of middle range theories of organizational behavior. *Administrative Science Quarterly,* 1979, *24,* 99–118.

Pinder, C. C. & Moore, L. F. (Eds.) *Middle range theory and the study of organizations.* Boston: Martinus Nijhoff, 1980.

Pinder, C. C. Mutualism Between Management and Behavioral Science: The Case of Motivation Theory. In J. Kelly and V. V. Baba (Eds.), *The new management scene: Readings on how managers manage.* Englewood Cliffs, N.J.: Prentice Hall, 1982.

343

Pinder, C. C., Nord, W. R. & Ramirez, C. An experimental test of Deci's cognitive evaluation theory. University of British Columbia unpublished working paper (no.708), 1984.

Pinder, C. C. & Walter, G. A. Personnel transfer and employee development, in K. M. Rowland and G. R. Ferris (Eds.) *Research in Personnel and Human Resource Management,* Vol. 2. Greenwich, Conn.: JAI Press, 1984.

Pinto, P. R. Your trainers and the law: Are they breaking it in and out of the classroom? *Training,* October, 1978.

Pondy, L. R., Frost, P. J., Morgan, G. & Dandridge, T. C. (Eds.) *Organizational symbolism.* Greenwich, Conn.: JAI Press, 1983.

Popper, K. R. *The logic of scientific discovery* (2nd ed). New York: Harper, Torchbooks, 1968.

Porac, J. F. & Salancik, G. R. Generic overjustification: The interaction of extrinsic rewards. *Organizational Behavior and Human Performance,* 1981, *27,* 197–212.

Porter, L. W. Job attitudes in management: I. Perceived deficiencies in need fulfillment as a function of job level. *Journal of Applied Psychology,* 1962, *46,* 375–384.

Porter, L. W. Job attitudes in management: II. Perceived importance of needs as a function of job level. *Journal of Applied Psychology,* 1963, *47,* 144–148.

Porter, L. W. & Lawler, E. E. *Managerial Attitudes and Performance.* Homewood, Illinois: Dorsey Press, 1968.

Porter, L. W. & Steers, R. M. Organizational, work, and personal factors in employee turnover and absenteeism. *Psychological Bulletin,* 1973, *80,* 151–176.

Porter, L. W., Steers, R. M., Mowday, R. T. & Boulian, P. V. Organizational commitment, job satisfaction, and turnover among psychiatric technicians. *Journal of Applied Psychology,* 1974, *59,* 603–609.

Porter, L. W., Crampon, W. J. & Smith, F. J. Organizational commitment and managerial turnover: A longitudinal study. *Organizational Behavior and Human Performance,* 1976, *15,* 87–98.

Porter, L. W. Turning Work into Nonwork: The Rewarding Environment. In M. D. Dunnette (Ed.) *Work and nonwork in the year 2001.* Monterey, California: Brooks/Cole, 1973.

Porter, L. W. & Lawler, E. E. Properties of organizational structure in relation to job attitudes and job behavior, *Psychological Bulletin,* 1965, *64,* 23–51.

Porter, L. W., Crampon, W. J. & Smith, F. J. Organizational commitment and managerial turnover: A longitudinal study. (Tech.Rep. 13, Individual-Organization Linkages Research Project). Irvine, Calif.: University of California, 1972.

Porter, L. W., Lawler, E. E. & Hackman, J. R. *Behavior in organizations.* New York: McGraw-Hill, 1975.

Premack, D. Catching Up With Common Sense or Two Sides of a Generalization: Reinforcement and Punishment. In R. Glaser (Ed.), *The nature of reinforcement.* New York: Academic Press, 1971.

Price, J. L. *The study of turnover.* Ames: Iowa State University Press, 1977.

Pringle, C. D. and Longenecker, J. G. The ethics of MBO. *Academy of Management Review,* 1982, *7,* 305–312.

Pritchard, R. D. Equity theory: A review and critique. *Organizational Behavior and Human Performance,* 1969, *4,* 176–211.

Pritchard, R. D., Campbell, K. M. & Campbell, D. J. Effects of extrinsic financial rewards on intrinsic motivation. *Journal of Applied Psychology,* 1977, *62,* 9–15.

Pritchard, R. D., Dunnette, M. D. & Jorgenson, D. O. Effects of perceptions of equity and inequity on worker performance and satisfaction. *Journal of Applied Psychology,* 1972, *56,* 75–94.

Prue, D. M. & Fairbank, J. A. Performance feedback in organizational behavior management: A review. *Journal of Organizational Behavior Management,* 1980, *3,* 1–16.

Raia, A. *Managing by objectives.* Glenview, Ill.: Scott, Foresman and Company. 1974.

Rabinowitz, S. & Hall, D. T. Organizational research on job involvement. *Psychological Bulletin,* 1977, *84,* 265–288.

Rauschenberger, J., Schmitt, N. & Hunter, J. E. A test of the need hierarchy concept by a Markov model of change in need strength. *Administrative Science Quarterly,* 1980, *25,* 654–670.

Reddin, W. J. *Effective management by objectives.* New York: McGraw-Hill, 1971.

Rees, Albert. On Interpreting Productivity Change. In S. Maital and N. M. Meltz (Eds.), *Lagging productivity growth.* Cambridge, Mass.: Ballinger, 1980.

Reif, W. E. & Luthans, F. Does job enrichment really pay off? *California Management Review,* 1972, *15* (1), 30–37.

Reilly, B. J. & Fuhr, J. P. Productivity: An economic and management analysis with a direction towards a new synthesis. *Academy of Management Review,* 1983, *8,* 108–117.

Reinharth, L. & Wahba, M. A. A test of alternative models of expectancy theory. *Human Relations,* 1976, *29,* 257–272.

Repucci, N. D. & Saunders, J. T. Social psychology of behavior modification: Problems of implementation in natural settings. *American Psychologist,* 1974, *29,* 649–660.

Reynolds, G. S. *A primer of operant conditioning.* Glenview, Ill.: Scott, Foresman and Co., 1975.

Ritti, R. R. & Funkhouser, G. R. *The ropes to skip and the ropes to know.* Columbus, Ohio: Grid, 1977.

Rizzo, J. R., House, R. J., & Lirtzman, S. E. Role conflict and ambiguity in complex organizations. *Administrative Science Quarterly,* 1970, *15,* 150–163.

Roberts, K. H. & Glick, W. The job characteristics approach to task design: A critical review. *Journal of Applied Psychology,* 1981, *66,* 193–217.

Roethlisberger, F. J. The foreman: Master and victim of double-talk. *Harvard Business Review,* 1945, *23,* 283–298.

Roethlisberger, F. J. & Dickson, W. J. *Management and the worker.* Cambridge, Mass.: Harvard University Press, 1939.

Rogers, C. R. A Theory of Therapy, Personality, and Interpersonal Relationships, as Developed in the Client-Centered Framework. In S. Koch (Ed.) *Psychology: A study of a science (Vol.3),* New York: McGraw-Hill, 1959.

Rogers, C. R. & Skinner, B. F. Some issues concerning the control of human behavior: A symposium. *Science,* 1956, *124,* 1057–1066.

Rose, S. More bang for the buck: The magic of electronic banking. *Fortune,* May 1977, 202–205, 208, 212, 216, 218, 221, 223, 226.

Rosen, B. & Jerdee, T. H. Effects of applicant's sex and difficulty of job on evaluations of candidates for managerial positions. *Journal of Applied Psychology,* 1974a; *59,* 511–512.

Rosen, B. & Jerdee, T. H. Influence of sex role stereotypes on personnel decisions. *Journal of Applied Psychology,* 1974b, *59,* 9–14.

Rosen, B. & Jerdee, T. H. Factors influencing disciplinary judgements. *Journal of Applied Psychology,* 1974c, *59,* 327–331.

Rosen, B. & Jerdee, T. H. The influence of age stereotypes on managerial decisions. *Journal of Applied Psychology,* 1976, *61,* 428–432.

Ross, A. *Trade union wage policy.* Berkeley: University of California Press, 1948.

Ross, M. Salience of reward and intrinsic motivation. *Journal of Personality and Social Psychology,* 1975, *32,* 245–254.

Rotondi, T. Organizational identification: Issues and implications. *Organizational Behavior and Human Performance,* 1975, *13,* 95–109.

Rotter, J. B. The Role of the Psychological Situation in Determining the Direction of Human Behavior. In M. R. Jones (Ed.) *Nebraska Symposium on Motivation,* Lincoln: University of Nebraska Press, 1955.

Rousseau, D. M. Technological differences in job characteristics, employee satisfaction, and motivation: A synthesis of job design research and sociotechnical systems theory. *Organizational Behavior and Human Performance,* 1977, *19,* 18–42.

Rowan, R. Rekindling corporate loyalty. *Fortune,* 1981, *103* (3), 54–58.

Roy, D. Quota restriction and gold bricking in a machine shop. *American Journal of Sociology,* 1952, *57,* 427–442.

Runkel, P. J. & McGrath, J. E. *Research on human behavior.* N.Y.: Holt, Rinehart and Winston, 1972.

Runnion, A., Johnson, T. & McWhorter, J. The effects of feedback and reinforcement on truck turnaround time in materials transportation. *Journal of Organizational Behavior Modification,* 1978, *1,* 110–117.

Runnion, A., Watson, J. O. & McWhorter, J. Energy savings in interstate transportation through feedback and reinforcement. *Journal of Organizational Behavior Management,* 1978, *1,* 180–191.

Russell, J. W. and Ward, L. M. Environmental psychology. *Annual Review of Psychology,* 1982, *33,* 651–688.

Ryan, T. A. *Intentional behavior.* New York: The Ronald Press, 1970.

Saari, L. M. & Latham, G. P. Employee reactions to continuous and variable ratio reinforcement schedules involving a monetary incentive. *Journal of Applied Psychology,* 1982, *67,* 506–508.

Salancik, G. R. & Pfeffer, J. An examination of need satisfaction models of job attitudes. *Administrative Science Quarterly,* 1977, *22,* 427–456.

Salancik, G. R. & Pfeffer, J. A social information processing approach to job attitudes and task design. *Administrative Science Quarterly,* 1978, *23,* 224–253.

Saleh, S. D. & Hosek, J. Job involvement: concepts and measures. *Academy of Management Journal,* 1976, 213–224.

Sandler, B. E. Eclecticism at work: Approaches to job design. *American Psychologist,* 1974, *29,* 767–773.

Sarason, I. G. The Growth of Interactional Psychology. In D. Magnusson and N. S. Endler (Eds.) *Personality at the crossroads.* Hillsdale, N.J.: Erlbaum, 1977.

Sayles, L. & Strauss, G. *Managing human resources.* Englewood Cliffs, N.J.: Prentice-Hall, 1977.

Schein, E. H. *Organizational psychology.* (2nd ed.) Englewood Cliffs, N.J.: Prentice-Hall, 1970.

Schein, E. H. *Career dynamics,* Reading, Mass.: Addison-Wesley, 1978.

Schein, V. The relationship between sex role stereotypes and requisite management characteristics. *Journal of Applied Psychology,* 1973, *57,* 95–100.

Schein, V. Relationships between sex role stereotypes and requisite management characteristics among female managers. *Journal of Applied Psychology,* 1975, *60,* 340–344.

Schlesinger, L. A. & Walton, R. E. Work Restructuring in Unionized Organizations: Risks, Opportunities, and Impact on Collective Bargaining. In J. L. Stern and B. D. Dennis (Eds.) *Proceedings of the Twenty-Ninth Annual Winter Meeting:* Madison, Wisc.: Industrial Relations Research Association, 1976.

Schoderbek, P. P. & Plambeck, D. L. The missing link in Management by Objectives-continuing responsibilities. *Public Personnel Management,* 1978, *7,* 19–25.

Schmitt, N. & McCune, J. T. The relationship between job attitudes and the decision to retire. *Academy of Management Journal,* 1981, *24,* 795–802.

Schmitz, L. M. & Heneman, H. G. Do positive reinforcement programs reduce employee absenteeism? *Personnel Administrator,* 1980, *25,* 87–93.

Schneider, B. *Staffing organizations.* Pacific Palisades, Calif.: Goodyear, 1976.

Schneier, C. E. Behavior modification in management: A review and critique. *Academy of Management Journal,* 1974, *17,* 528–548.

Schriesheim, C. A. Job satisfaction, attitudes toward unions, and voting in a union representation election. *Journal of Applied Psychology,* 1978, *63,* 548–552.

Schriesheim, C. A. & DeNisi, A. S. Task dimensions as moderators of the effects of instrumental leadership: A two-sample replicated test of path-goal leadership theory. *Journal of Applied Psychology,* 1981, *66,* 589–597.

Schriesheim, C. & Von Glinow, M. A. The path-goal theory of leadership: A theoretical and empirical analysis. *Academy of Management Journal,* 1977, 398–405.

Schriesheim, J. F., & Schriesheim, C. A. A test of the path-goal theory of leadership and some suggested directions for future research. *Personnel Psychology,* 1980, *33,* 349–370.

Schuler, R. S. Role perceptions, satisfaction, and performance. *Journal of Applied Psychology,* 1975, *60,* 683–687.

Schuster, F. E. & Kindall, A. S. Management by Objectives, Where we stand—A survey of the Fortune 500. *Human Resource Management,* 1974, Vol.13 (1), 8–11.

Schuster, J. R. Another look at compensation preferences. *Industrial Management Review,* 1969, *10,* 1–18.

Schwab, D. P. Construct Validity in Organizational Behavior. In B. M. Staw and L. L. Cummings (Eds.) *Research in Organizational Behavior,* Vol.2, Greenwich, Conn.: JAI Press, 1980.

Schwab, D. P. & Cummings, L. L. Theories of performance and satisfaction: A review. *Industrial Relations,* 1970, *9* (4), 408–430.

Schwab, D. P. & Cummings, L. L. A theoretical analysis of task scope on employee performance. *Academy of Management Review,* 1976, *1* (2), 23–35.

Schwartz, H. & Davis, S. M. Matching corporate culture and business strategy, *Organizational Dynamics,* 1981 (Summer), 30–48.

Schwartz, H. S. Job involvement as obsession-compulsion. *Academy of Management Review,* 1982, *7,* 429–432.

Schwarz, H. W. Budgeting and the Managerial Process. In H. W. A. Sweeny and R. Rachlin (Eds.) *Handbook of budgeting.* New York: Wiley, 1981.

Schwyhart, W. R. & Smith, P. C. Factors in the job involvement of middle managers. *Journal of Applied Psychology,* 1972, *56,* 227–233.

Scott, W. E., Jr. Activation theory and task design. *Organizational Behavior and Human Performance,* 1966, *1,* 3–30.

347

Scott, W. E., Jr. The effects of extrinsic rewards on intrinsic motivation: A critique. *Organizational Behavior and Human Performance,* 1976, *156,* 117–129.

Scott, W. E., Jr. & Podsakoff, P. M. *Behavioral principles in the practice of management.* New York: Wiley, 1983.

Seashore, S. E. *Group cohesiveness in the industrial work group.* Ann Arbor: University of Michigan, Institute for Social Research, Social Research Center, 1954.

Seybolt, J. W. Work satisfaction as a function of the person-environment interaction. *Organizational Behavior and Human Performance,* 1976, *17,* 66–75.

Shepard, H. A. Nine dilemmas in industrial research. *Administrative Science Quarterly,* 1956, *1,* 295–309.

Shepard, J. M. & Houghland, J. G. Contingency theory: "Complex man" or "complex organization?" *Academy of Management Review,* 1978, *3,* 413–427.

Shull, F. A. & Cummings, L. L. Enforcing the rules: How do managers differ? *Personnel,* 1966, *43* (2), 33–39.

Sibson, R. E. The high cost of hiring. *Nation's Business,* February, 1975, 85–88.

Siegel, A. & Ruh, R. A. Job involvement, participation in decision making, personal background, and job behavior. *Organizational Behavior and Human Performance,* 1973, *9,* 318–327.

Simon, H. A. *Administrative behavior.* (2nd ed.) New York: Macmillan, 1957.

Sims, H. P. & Szilagyi, A. D. Job characteristic relationships: Individual and structural moderators. *Organizational Behavior and Human Performance,* 1976, *17,* 211–230.

Sirota, D. & Wolfson, A. Job enrichment: What are the obstacles? *Personnel,* 1972, *49* (3), 8–17.

Skinner, B. F. *Science and human behavior.* New York: Macmillan, 1953.

Skinner, B. F. *Contingencies of reinforcement: A theoretical analysis.* New York: Appleton-Century-Crofts, 1969.

Skinner, B. F. *Beyond freedom and dignity.* New York: Knopf, 1971.

Skinner, B. F. *About behaviorism.* New York: Knopf, 1974.

Slichter, S. J., Healy, J. J., & Livernash, E. R. *The impact of collective bargaining on management.* Washington, D.C.: Brookings Institution, 1960.

Smith, F. J. Work attitudes as predictors of attendance on a specific day. *Journal of Applied Psychology,* 1977, *62,* 16–19.

Smith, F., Roberts, K. H., & Hulin, C. L. Ten year job satisfaction trends in a stable organization. *Academy of Management Journal,* 1976, *19,* 462–469.

Smith, F. J., Scott, K. D., & Hulin, C. L. Trends in job-related attitudes of managerial and professional employees. *Academy of Management Journal,* 1977, *20,* 454–460.

Smith, P. C., Kendall, L. M. & Hulin, C. L. *The measurement of satisfaction in work and retirement.* Chicago: Rand McNally, 1969.

Spector, P. E. Organizational frustration: A model and review of the literature. *Personnel Psychology,* 1978, *31,* 815–829.

Spencer, H. *The principles of psychology.* Vol. 1 (2nd ed.) New York: Appleton, 1870.

Stagner, R. *Psychology of industrial conflict.* New York: Wiley, 1956.

Standing, T. E. Satisfaction with the work itself as a function of cognitive complexity. *Proceedings,* 81st Annual Convention, American Psychological Association, 1973, 603–604.

Staw, B. M. *Intrinsic and extrinsic motivation.* Morristown, N.J.: General Learning Press, 1976.

Staw, B. M. Motivation in Organizations: Toward Synthesis and Redirection. In B. M. Staw and G. R. Salancik (Eds.) *New directions in organizational behavior.* Chicago: St. Clair Press, 1977.

348

Steers, R. M. Antecedents and outcomes of organizational commitment. *Administrative Science Quarterly,* 1977, *22,* 46–56.

Steers, R. M. & Mowday, R. T. The motivational properties of tasks. *Academy of Management Review,* 1977, *2,* 645–658.

Steers, R. M. & Porter, L. W. (Eds.) *Motivation and work behavior.* New York: McGraw-Hill, 1975.

Steers, R. M. & Porter, L. W. (Eds.) *Motivation and work behavior.* (2nd ed.). New York: McGraw-Hill, 1979.

Steers, R. M. & Rhodes, S. Major influences on employee attendance: A process model. *Journal of Applied Psychology,* 1978, *63,* 391–407.

Stein, A. H. & Bailey, M. M. The socialization of achievement motivation in females. *Psychological Bulletin,* 1973, *80,* 345–366.

Stein, C. I. Objectives management systems: Two to five years after implementation. *Personnel Journal,* 1975, *54,* (10), 525–528, 548.

Stevens, J. M., Beyer, J. M., & Trice, H. M. Assessing personal, role, and organizational predictors of managerial commitment. *Academy of Management Journal,* 1978, *21,* 380–396.

Stewart, A. J. (Ed.) *Motivation and society.* San Francisco: Jossey-Bass, 1982.

Strauss, G. Workers Participation in Management: An International Perspective. In B. M. Staw and L. L. Cummings (Eds.) *Research in Organizational Behavior,* Vol.4, Greenwich, Conn.: JAI Press, 1982.

Stumpf, S. A. & Dawley, P. K. Predicting voluntary and involuntary turnover using absenteeism and performance indices. *Academy of Management Journal,* 1981, *24,* 148–163.

Swan, K. P. Union Impact on Management of the Organization: A Legal Perspective. In J. Anderson and M. Gunderson (Eds.) *Union-management relations in Canada.* Don Mills, Ontario: Addison-Wesley, 1982.

Taylor, E. K. & Griess, T. The missing middle in validation research. *Personnel Psychology,* 1976, *29,* 5–11.

Taylor, F. W. *The principles of scientific management.* New York: Norton, 1967. (Originally published, 1911.)

Tead, O. *Instincts in industry.* New York: Arno and The New York Times, 1918.

Tead, O. *Human nature and management.* N.Y.: McGraw-Hill, 1929.

Telly, C. S., French, W. L. & Scott, W. G. The relationship of inequity to turnover among hourly workers. *Administrative Science Quarterly,* 1971, *16,* 164–171.

Terborg, J. R. Validation and extension of an individual differences model of work performance. *Organizational Behavior and Human Performance,* 1977, *18,* 188–216.

Terborg, J. R. & Ilgen, D. R. A theoretical approach to sex discrimination in traditionally masculine occupations. *Organizational Behavior and Human Performance,* 1975, *13,* 352–376.

Thompson, J. D. *Organizations in action,* New York: McGraw-Hill, 1967.

Thomsen, D. Compensation and benefits. *Personnel Journal,* 1981, *60* (4), 258–259.

Thoresen, E. & Mahoney, M. *Behavioral self control.* New York: Holt, Rinehart & Winston, 1974.

Thorndike, E. L. *Animal intelligence.* New York: Macmillan, 1911.

Thurow, L. C. *The zero-sum society.* New York: Penguin Books, 1980.

Tolman, E. C. *Purposive behavior in animals and men.* New York: Century Co., 1932.

Tolman, E. C. Principles of Purposive Behavior. In S. Koch (Ed.) *Psychology: A Study of a Science.* Vol.2. New York: McGraw-Hill, 1959.

Törnblom, K. Y. Distributive justice: Typology and propositions. *Human Relations,* 1977, *30,* 1–25.

Tosi, H. L. The Human Effects of Budgeting Systems on Management. In F. Luthans (Ed.) *Contemporary readings in organizational behavior.* New York: McGraw-Hill, 1977.

Tuckman, B. W. Personality and satisfaction with occupational choice: Role of environment as a mediator. *Psychological Reports,* 1968, *23,* 543–550.

Turner, A. N. & Miclette, A. L. Sources of satisfaction in repetitive work. *Occupational Psychology,* 1962, *36,* 215–231.

Turner, A. N. & Lawrence, P. R. *Industrial jobs and the worker.* Boston: Harvard University, School of Business Administration, 1965.

Tyler, L. E. *The Psychology of Human Differences.* N.Y.: Appleton-Century-Crofts, 1965.

Urwick, L. F. Organization and theories about the nature of man. *Academy of Management Journal,* 1967, *10,* 9–15.

U.S. Department of Labor. *Seniority in promotion and transfer provisions.* Bureau of Labor Statistics Bulletin 1425-11. Washington, D.C., 1970.

Van Der Merwe, S. What personal attributes it takes to make it in management. *The Business Quarterly,* 1978, *43* (4), 28–35.

Van Maanen, J. Experiencing Organization: Notes on the Meaning of Careers and Socialization. In J. Van Maanen (Ed.) *Organizational careers: Some new perspectives.* New York: Wiley, 1977.

Vannoy, J. S. Generality of cognitive complexity-simplicity as a personality construct. *Journal of Personality and Social Psychology,* 1965, *2,* 385–396.

Vroom, V. H. *Work and motivation.* New York: Wiley, 1964.

Wahba, M. A. & Bridwell, L. G. Maslow reconsidered: A review of research on the need hierarchy theory. *Organizational Behavior and Human Performance,* 1976, *15,* 212–240.

Wall, T. D. & Lischeron, J. A. *Worker participation.* London: McGraw-Hill, 1977.

Wallace, M. J. Methodology, research practice, and progress in personnel and industrial relations. *Academy of Management Review,* 1983, *8,* 6–13.

Walter, G. A. & Pinder, C. C. Ethical ascendance or backsliding? *American Psychologist,* 1980, *35,* 936–937.

Walter, G. A. & Marks, S. E. *Experiential learning and change.* New York: Wiley, 1981.

Walton, R. E. The diffusion of new work structures: Why success didn't take. *Organizational Dynamics,* 1975, *3* (3), 2–22.

Wanous, J. P. Individual differences and reactions to job characteristics. *Journal of Applied Psychology,* 1974, *59,* 616–622.

Wanous, J. P. *Organizational entry.* Reading, Mass.: Addison-Wesley, 1980.

Wanous, J. P. & Lawler, E. E. Measurement and meaning of job satisfaction. *Journal of Applied Psychology,* 1972, *56,* 95–105.

Ward, L. M. Multidimensional scaling of the molar physical environment. *Multivariate Behavioral Research,* 1977, *12,* 23–42.

Ward, L. M. & Porter, C. A. Age-group differences in cognition of the molar physical environment: A multidimensional scaling approach. *Canadian Journal of Behavioral Science,* 1980, *12,* 329–346.

Ward, L. M. & Russell, J. A. The psychological representation of molar physical environments. *Journal of Experimental Psychology,* 1981, *110,* 121–152.

Webb, E. J., Campbell, D. T., Schwartz, R. D. & Sechrest, L. *Unobstrusive measures: Nonreactive research in the social sciences.* Chicago: Rand McNally, 1966.

Weick, K. E. Dissonance and task enhancement: A problem for compensation theory? *Organizational Behavior and Human Performance,* 1967, *2,* 189–207.

Weick, K. E. & Nesset, B. Preferences among forms of equity. *Organizational Behavior and Human Performance,* 1968, *3,* 400–416.

Weick, K. E., Bougon, M. G., & Maruyama, G. The equity context. *Organizational Behavior and Human Performance,* 1976, *15,* 32–65.

Weil, F. A. Management's drag on productivity. *Business Week,* No.2614 (Dec.3, 1979), 14.

Weiner, Y. Commitment in organizations: A normative view. *Academy of Management Review,* 1982, *7,* 418–428.

Weiner, Y. & Vardi, Y. Relationships between job, organization, and career commitments and work outcomes—an integrative approach. *Organizational Behavior and Human Performance,* 1980, 81–96.

Wexley, K. N. & Yukl, G. A. *Organizational behavior and personnel psychology.* Homewood, Ill.: Irwin, 1977.

Wexley, K. N. & Latham, G. P. *Developing and training human resources in organizations.* Glenview, Ill.: Scott, Foresman and Company, 1981.

Wheeler, H. Punishment theory and industrial discipline. *Industrial Relations,* 1976, *15,* 235–243.

White, J. K. Individual differences and the job quality-worker response relationship: Review, integration, and comments. *Academy of Management Review,* 1978a, *3,* 267–280.

White, J. K. Generalizability of individual difference moderators of the participation in decision-making-employee response relationship. *Academy of Management Journal,* 1978b, 21, 36–43.

White, R. Motivation reconsidered: The concept of competence. *Psychological Review,* 1959, *66,* 297–333.

Whitsett, D. A. & Winslow, E. K. An analysis of studies critical of the Motivation-Hygiene Theory. *Personnel Psychology,* 1967, *20,* 121–132.

Whyte, W. F. Pigeons, persons, and piece rates. *Psychology Today,* 1972, *5* (11), 66–68, 96, 98, 100.

Wilcoxon, H. C. Historical Introduction to the Problem of Reinforcement. In J. T. Tapp (Ed.) *Reinforcement and behavior.* N.Y.: Academic Press, 1969.

Williams, L. K., Seybolt, J. W., & Pinder, C. C. On administering questionnaires in organizational settings. *Personnel Psychology,* 1975, *28,* 93–103.

Wohlwill, J. F. & Kohn, I. Dimensionalizing the Environmental Manifold. In S. Wapner, S. B. Cohen, and B. Kaplan (Eds.) *Experiencing the environment.* New York: Plenum, 1976.

Wong, P. T. P. Frustration, exploration, and learning. *Canadian Psychological Review,* 1979, *20,* 133–144.

Woodworth, R. S. *Dynamic psychology,* New York: Columbia University Press, 1918.

Yankelovich, D. The work ethic is underemployed. *Psychology Today,* 1982, *16* (5), 5, 6, 8.

Yerkes, R. M. & Dodson, J. D. The relation of strength of stimulus to rapidity of habit-formation. *Journal of Comparative and Neurological Psychology,* 1908, *18,* 459–482.

Yolles, S. F., Carone, P. A. & Krinsky, L. W. *Absenteeism in industry.* Springfield, Ill.: Charles C. Thomas, 1975.

Yorks, L. *Job enrichment revisited.* New York: AMACOM, 1979.

Yukl, G. A., Wexley, K. N. & Seymore, J. Effects of pay incentives under variable ratio and continuous reinforcement schedules. *Journal of Applied Psychology,* 1972, *56,* 19–23.

Yukl, G. A. & Latham, G. P. Consequences of reinforcement schedules and incentive magnitudes for employee performance: Problems encountered in an industrial setting. *Journal of Applied Psychology,* 1975, *60* (3), 294–298.

Yukl, G. A., Latham, G. P. & Pursell, E. D. The effectiveness of performance incentives under continuous and variable ratio schedules of reinforcement. *Personnel Psychology,* 1976, *29,* 221–231.

Zajonc, R. B. The concepts of balance, congruity, and dissonance. *Public Opinion Quarterly,* 1960, *24,* 280–296.

Zalkind, S. S. & Costello, T. W. Perception: Some recent research and implications for administration. *Administrative Science Quarterly,* 1962, *7,* 218–235.

Zaltman, G. & Duncan, R. *Strategies for planned change.* New York: Wiley, 1977.

Zedeck, S. An information processing model and approach to the study of motivation. *Organizational,Behavior and Human Performance,* 1977, *18,* 47–77.

NAME INDEX

SUBJECT INDEX